Can NGOs Make a Difference?

Can NGOs Make a Difference?

The Challenge of Development Alternatives

edited by Anthony Bebbington,
Samuel Hickey and Diana Mitlin

ZED BOOKS
London & New York

Can NGOs Make a Difference? The Challenge of Development Alternatives was first published in 2007 by Zed Books Ltd, 7 Cynthia Street, London N1 9JF, UK and Room 400, 175 Fifth Avenue, New York, NY 10010, USA

www.zedbooks.co.uk

Designed and typeset in Monotype Bembo
by illuminati, Grosmont, www.illuminatibooks.co.uk
Cover designed by Andrew Corbett
Printed and bound in United States

Distributed in the USA exclusively by Palgrave Macmillan,
175 Fifth Avenue, New York, 10010, USA

A catalogue record for this book is available from the British Library
Library of Congress Cataloguing in Publication Data available

ISBN 978 1 84277 892 0 hb
ISBN 978 1 84277 893 7 pb

Contents

List of Figures and Tables   viii

Acknowledgements   ix

PART I Critical Challenges

1   Introduction: Can NGOs Make a Difference? The Challenge of
Development Alternatives   3
Anthony Bebbington, Samuel Hickey and Diana Mitlin

2   Have NGOs 'Made a Difference?' From Manchester to
Birmingham with an Elephant in the Room   38
Michael Edwards

PART II NGO Alternatives under Pressure

3   Challenges to Participation, Citizenship and Democracy:
Perverse Confluence and Displacement of Meanings   55
Evelina Dagnino

4   Learning from Latin America: Recent Trends in European NGO
Policy-making   71
Kees Biekart

5 Whatever Happened to Reciprocity? Implications of Donor Emphasis on 'Voice' and 'Impact' as Rationales for Working with NGOs in Development   90
Alan Thomas

6 Development and the New Security Agenda: W(h)ither(ing) NGO Alternatives?   111
Alan Fowler

PART III   Pursuing Alternatives: NGO Strategies in Practice

7 How Civil Society Organizations Use Evidence to Influence Policy Processes   133
Amy Pollard and Julius Court

8 Civil Society Participation as the Focus of Northern NGO Support: The Case of Dutch Co-financing Agencies   153
Irene Guijt

9 Producing Knowledge, Generating Alternatives? Challenges to Research-oriented NGOs in Central America and Mexico   175
Cynthia Bazán, Nelson Cuellar, Ileana Gómez, Cati Illsley, Adrian López, Iliana Monterroso, Joaliné Pardo, Jose Luis Rocha, Pedro Torres and Anthony Bebbington

10 Anxieties and Affirmations: NGO–Donor Partnerships for Social Transformation   196
Mary Racelis

PART IV   Being Alternative

11 Reinventing International NGOs: A View from the Dutch Co-financing System   221
Harry Derksen and Pim Verhallen

12 Transforming or Conforming? NGOs Training Health Promoters and the Dominant Paradigm of the Development Industry in Bolivia   240
Katie S. Bristow

13 Political Entrepreneurs or Development Agents: An NGO's
Tale of Resistance and Acquiescence in Madhya Pradesh, India 261
Vasudha Chhotray

14 Is This Really the End of the Road for Gender Mainstreaming?
Getting to Grips with Gender and Institutional Change 279
Nicholas Piálek

15 The Ambivalent Cosmopolitanism of International NGOs 298
Helen Yanacopulos and Matt Baillie Smith

16 Development as Reform and Counter-reform: Paths Travelled
by Slum/Shack Dwellers International 316
Joel Bolnick

PART V   **Taking Stock and Thinking Forward**

17 Reflections on NGOs and Development: The Elephant,
the Dinosaur, Several Tigers but No Owl 337
David Hulme

Contributors 346

Index 351

Figures and Tables

Table 2.1   The Manchester conferences: a summary   40

Table 2.2   NGO imperatives   48

Figure 2.1   Trajectories of NGO impact   51

Table 4.1   European NGOs involved in the mapping exercise,
             by size of combined Latin America programme   73

Table 5.1   NGO and official aid to developing countries   94

Figure 6.1   Overview of potential NGDO limitations due to aid
             in a security strategy   113

Figure 7.1   The policy cycle   135

Table 7.1   What matters for influencing the key components
             of policy processes?   148

Figure 8.1   The power cube   156

Table 8.1   Overview of countries involved in the CSP programme
             evaluation   161

Figure 12.1 Diagrammatic representation of relationships
             between fields   255

Box 16.1   SDI influence in city and national policies
             to address urban poverty   321

Acknowledgements

This book is based on papers presented at the fourth 'Manchester' NGO conference, held in late June 2005 and entitled 'Reclaiming Development: Assessing the Contribution of NGOs to Development Alternatives'. Financial support from the Economic and Social Research Council funded Global Poverty Research Group, Ford Foundation and the Canadian International Development Agency helped defray costs associated with the conference and the preparation and circulation of this volume. We would like to take this opportunity to express our gratitude for this generous support.

Our collective debts – intellectual and logistical – are too great for us to acknowledge everyone who helped make the conference a success and the book a reality. However, we do want to record a few specific and heartfelt thanks. As has been the case since the first Manchester NGO conferences in the early 1990s, Debra Whitehead provided excellent administrative support to ensure that all ran smoothly. David Hulme, a force behind the three prior NGO conferences, has been a source of inspiration and guidance. Leonith Hinojosa, researcher at the University of Manchester's Institute for Development Policy and Management, was an expert and remarkably efficient editor as the manuscript was being prepared. Thanks also to our publishers for their support and encouragement throughout the project, and particularly to our commissioning editor Susannah Trefgarne and her predecessor Anna Hardman, who was closely involved in the early stages. Anthony Bebbington also thanks the Centro Peruano de Estudios Sociales (CEPES) for providing such a supportive home during the preparation of this book. Finally, inspiration has come from often close and long-standing ties with particular NGOs and NGO networks as well as more academic sources. In particular, the editorial thinking underlying the book benefited immensely from the contributions of and our discussions with conference participants.

This book is dedicated to our children – Anna, Carmen, Michael, Rachel and Matthew – in the hope that the development that accompanies them through the remainder of their lives will be different from that which accompanies us today.

Anthony Bebbington, Samuel Hickey and Diana Mitlin

PART I

Critical Challenges

Introduction: Can NGOs Make a Difference?
The Challenge of Development Alternatives

Anthony Bebbington, Samuel Hickey
and Diana Mitlin

'Not another Manchester book on NGOs!' some bookstore browsers will comment on spotting this text. The short response, of course, is 'Yes, another one.' The longer response is this introductory chapter. In it we argue why this is once again a good moment to take the pulse of the NGO world. This time, though, we take the pulse not merely as a health check, which was the spirit of the three Manchester conferences: in 1992 to check their fitness to go to scale (Edwards and Hulme, 1992); in 1994 to check their fitness in the face of increased societal scrutiny (Edwards and Hulme, 1995; Hulme and Edwards, 1997); and in 1999 to check their fitness in the face of globalization (e.g. Eade and Ligteringen, 2001; Edwards and Gaventa, 2001; Lewis and Wallace, 2000. Instead, participants in a conference in 2005 took the pulse of NGOs to see whether the patient was still alive. The conviction underlying the book is that NGOs are only NGOs in any politically meaningful sense of the term if they are offering alternatives to dominant models, practices and ideas about development. The question that the book addresses is whether − in the face of neoliberalism, the poverty agenda in aid, the new security agenda, institutional maturation (if not senescence), and the simple imperatives of organizational survival − NGOs continue to constitute alternatives.

As the reader will see, the authors are far from certain about the health of the patient, though none of them is yet ready to write the certificate declaring the death of alternatives and the irrelevance of NGOs (an irrelevance that would somewhat invert the scales of Edwards's polemic in 1989 that declared development studies irrelevant to NGOs, the place where real development was being done: Edwards, 1989). There are serious doubts regarding how far NGOs in the North are able to do anything that is especially alternative to their host countries' bilateral aid programmes. There is a sense that their room for manoeuvre has been seriously constrained by the security agenda, increasing political disenchantment with NGOs, the constraints of a poverty impact agenda that will only fund activities with measurable impacts on some material dimension of poverty, and also a sense in which 'alternatives' have been swallowed whole within the newly 'inclusive' mainstream. And there are just as serious questions about NGOs in the South, who, in addition to facing these constraints, transmitted to them through funding decisions and the ever more constraining conditionalities linked to them, have to operate in political economic environments defined by both the ravages and the domesticating hands of neoliberalism as well as the never-ending struggle to secure the financial bases of organizational survival.

That said, these doubts do not lead the majority of the authors to conclude that 'there is no alternative' and that therefore there is no reason for NGOs to exist. Indeed, the strength of all the chapters – and, we hope, the primary contribution of this collection – is that they each take a hard-headed and theoretically informed look at the constraints on NGOs ability to exist, speak and act as development alternatives, but then also explore the ways in which NGOs have either found points where the stitching of these straitjackets is coming unpicked, or found ways simply to reframe the debate, to say that the game they were previously playing is no longer interesting, and it is time to design a new one.

In this chapter we flesh out some of the themes that the book elaborates. We begin by elaborating the idea of 'alternatives' that runs through the book, and the ways in which it might relate to NGOs. We then use this framework to give a brief, historical discussion of NGOs and the differing ways in which they have sought to be alternative (both sections rely heavily on Mitlin, Hickey and Bebbington 2007). The third section introduces the middle three sections of the book: a section focusing on the different ways in which NGO-led alternatives have come under increasing pressure in the last decade; a section exploring ways in which NGOs have continued to seek ways of fostering alternative forms of development; and a section that explores how far NGOs have sought ways to simply *be* alternative, and, in so *being*, to suggest that there are different ways in which the broader development enterprise might be thought about and engaged in. The closing section of this chapter then charts implications for the future both of NGOs and of the struggle to carve out development alternatives.

Conceptualizing Alternatives

D(d)evelopment/A(a)lternative(s)

In their history of 'doctrines of development', Cowen and Shenton (1996, 1998) distinguish between two meanings of the term 'development' that have been consistently confused: 'development as an immanent and unintentional process as in, for example, the "development of capitalism" and development as an intentional activity' (1998: 50). Hart (2001: 650) amends this distinction slightly to talk of 'little d' and 'big D' d/Development, whereby the former involves the 'geographically uneven, profoundly contradictory' set of processes underlying capitalist developments, while the latter refers to the 'project of intervention in the "third world" that emerged in a context of decolonization and the cold war'. This insistence on distinguishing between notions of intervention and of deeper forms of political, economic, structural change should not lead us to lose sight of the clear, if non-deterministic, relationships between these two dimensions of development. Rather, it offers a means of clarifying the relationship between development policy and practice and the underlying processes of uneven development that create exclusion and inequality for many just as they lead to enhanced opportunities for others.

The role of NGOs in promoting development alternatives can be thought of in relation to this distinction. Much discussion of alternatives has been in relation to 'big D' Development — NGOs have been seen as sources of alternative ways of arranging microfinance, project planning, service delivery and so on: that is, alternative ways of intervening. These are reformist notions of alternatives and, as Bolnick (this volume) argues, NGOs' location within the aid industry has influenced how such alternatives come to be constituted. However, alternatives can also be conceived in relation to the underlying processes of capitalist development, or 'little d' development. Here the emphasis is on alternative ways of organizing the economy, politics and social relationships in a society. The distinction, then, is between partial, reformist, intervention-specific alternatives, and more radical, systemic alternatives. Importantly, some of our contributors warn against drawing too sharp a distinction between these types of alternative. Both Chhotray and Guijt (this volume), for instance, draw attention to the links that NGOs can forge between apparently technocratic interventions such as service delivery and broader transformations in political development and social relations. Nonetheless, we argue here that one of the disappointments of NGOs has been their tendency to identify more readily with alternative forms of interventions than with more systemic changes, and that there are strong grounds for reversing this trend.

Civil society as an alternative to the state and market

The second element of our framework links these distinctions to a reflection on state, market and civil society. The tripartite division between these spheres is often used to understand and locate NGOs as civil society actors (Bebbington, 1997; Fowler, 2000b). Yet many of these renderings are problematic. First, the treatment of civil society is often excessively normative rather than analytical: it is seen as a source of 'good', distinct from a 'bad' imputed to the state and market. Such approaches understate the potential role of the state in fostering progressive change while also downplaying the extent to which civil society is also a realm of activity for racist organizations, business-sponsored research NGOs or other organizations that most of these authors would not consider benign (e.g. Stone, 2000).

Second, even if the need to understand the three spheres in relation to each other is often recognized, the relative fluidity of boundaries between the spheres, and the growing tendency for people to move back and forth between NGOs, government and occasionally business, have received less attention (see Racelis, this volume, for a discussion of some of these relationships in the Philippine context). Such movements have further problematized the understanding of NGOs as being an integral part of civil society, something already called into question by those who argue that NGOs can be more accurately seen as corporate entities acting according to the logic of the marketplace, albeit a marketplace in service provision (Stewart, 1997; Uphoff, 1995). Perhaps more important, though, is that NGOs are a relatively recent organizational form, particularly when compared to more deep-seated social arrangements such as religious institutions, political movements, government and transnational networks of various kinds. Why NGOs exist, what they do, what they say, who they relate to, can only be understood in terms of their relationship to more constitutive actors in society, as well as in terms of the relationships among these constitutive actors, and between them, state and market.

Civil society – and the place of NGOs within it – must therefore be treated carefully, historically, conceptually and relationally. Within development studies, civil society has been predominantly understood in two main ways, at each of two main levels (Bebbington and Hickey, 2006). At the level of ideology and theory, the notion of civil society has flourished most fruitfully within either the neoliberal school of thought that advocates a reduced role for the state or a post-Marxist/post-structural approach that emphasizes the transformative potential of social movements within civil society. At the conceptual level, civil society is usually treated in terms of associations (so-called civil society organizations), or as an arena within which ideas about the ordering of social life are debated and contested. Proponents of both approaches often present civil society as offering a critical path towards what Aristotle described as 'the good society' (Edwards, 2004).

We work from a broadly Gramscian understanding of civil society as constituting an arena in which hegemonic ideas concerning the organization of economic and social life are both established and contested. Gramsci (1971) perceived state and civil society to be mutually constitutive rather than separate, autonomous entities, with both formed in relation to historical and structural forces akin to our processes of 'little d' development. He was centrally concerned with explaining the failures of both liberalism and socialism, and of the role that counter-hegemonic movements within civil society might play in promoting social and also revolutionary change. The resulting contestations, and the hegemonies which emerge and the roles (if any) that distinct NGOs play in this, must in turn be understood in terms of the relationships and struggles for power among the constitutive actors of society. Importantly, this also means that agents from within the state may join forces with civil society actors in forging counter-hegemonic alternatives as well as dominant hegemonies (see Chhotray, this volume).

These contestations over hegemony are thus closely related to our framing of 'alternatives'. One can imagine certain alternatives in the domain of 'big D' Development that challenge ideas that are dominant, but not foundational. For instance, dominant ideas about how health care ought to be organized might be contested and challenged by NGOs proposing distinct models of provision. Such alternatives, important though they may be in welfare terms, do not challenge the more basic arrangements that order society (as Bristow suggests in her chapter). Conversely, one can also imagine hegemonic ideas that are far more foundational – for instance, in the present moment, neoliberal ideas regarding how society and market ought to be governed; or ideas about property rights. These ideas thus require contestation in relation to alternatives that relate to the domain of little 'd' development – akin to what Escobar (1995) frames as 'alternatives to development' rather than 'development alternatives'.

Glocal NGOs

While concepts of global civil society may have their difficulties, there can be little doubt that, as the most potent force within late modernity, globalization has (re)shaped NGOs and ideas about NGOs. One effect has been that (at least some) NGOs have increasingly become a transnational community, itself overlapping with other transnational networks and institutions (Townsend, 1999). These linkages and networks disperse new forms of development discourse and modes of governance as well as resources throughout the global South; and some Southern NGOs have (albeit to a lesser extent) begun to gain their own footholds in the North with their outposts in Brussels, Washington and elsewhere (see, for example, the Grameen Foundation, BRAC, Breadline Africa or the Asociación Latinoamericana de Organizaciones de Promoción, ALOP). Yet these transnationalizing tendencies, especially in the form of global advocacy networks and campaigns, may have also excluded certain actors and groups for whom engagement in such processes is harder (Chiriboga, 2001). Thus these moves to scale have simultaneously increased the distance between constituent parts of the sector and led to the emergence of international civil society elites who come to dominate the discourses and flows that are channelled through this transnational community. This raises serious questions as to *whose alternatives* gain greater visibility in these processes.

The transnationalizing of 'big D' interventions (e.g. structural adjustment and the subsequent phenomenon of poverty-reduction strategy papers, or PRSPs) reflects structural transformations in the workings of national and international capitalisms and the nature of organizations in capitalist society (Craig and Porter, 2006). These changes make it important for any alternative project (in a Gramscian sense) to work simultaneously at different points within these chains of intervention. The specific forms of intervention have also involved the increased channelling of (national and multilateral) state-controlled resources through NGOs – a channelling in which resources become bundled with particular rules and ideas regarding how they must be governed and contribute to the governing of others. This bundling has meant NGOs become increasingly faced with opportunities related to the dominant ideas and rules that travel with development finance – in particular in the current context, ideas related to neoliberalism and security. Acceptance of such opportunities has made life difficult for many northern NGOs, who in turn pass on these difficulties to their partners.

It is a short step to move from such observations to suggest that NGOs are becoming vehicles of neoliberal governmentality (e.g. Manji and O'Coill 2002; Townsend et al., 2002), disciplining local organizations and populations in much the same way as Development has done in the past (Escobar, 1995; also Duffield, 2001). Such a reading clearly has a significant degree of purchase and cannot be wished away. However, it also understates the extent to which such pressures are being resisted by some NGOs (Edwards and Gaventa, 2001; Townsend et al., 2004), and to which some NGOs might actively seek to advance progressive forms of globalization through promoting 'cosmopolitan' forms of politics (Yanacopulos and Smith, this volume). An NGO's ability to sustain a broader funding base can be a tool that helps it negotiate and rework some of these pressures, while the potential ability of NGOs to mobilize the broader networks and institutions within which they are embedded can also be a means of muting such disciplining effects. These networks, whose contribution to NGO activities is exemplified by the studies of the International Campaign to Ban Landmines and Jubiliee 2000 (Edwards and Gaventa, 2001), can provide other resources and relationships of power on which the organization can draw – be these based in the Jesuit community, transnational corporate actors (who appear on a number of NGO boards), or underlying networks of power within the movements for social democracy, to name but a few.

Transnational NGO networks are not necessarily characterized by uneven North–South relations. As the more horizontal experience of Shack/Slum Dwellers International shows, the spatial reworking of development has increased opportunities for socially excluded groups themselves to speak, and some NGOs are working with such groups to increase the representation of these voices (Patel and Mitlin, 2002; Bolnick, this volume). Equally the reconstruction of ActionAid, from a Northern NGO with a UK headquarters to one based in Johannesburg with all country programmes being equally involved in determining the direction of the organization, reveals the lengths to which a Northern NGO can go in seeking to realize a progressive mission in the face of growing geopolitical inequalities.

Nonetheless, it remains essential to understand NGOs – as well as states, markets and civil societies – in the context of these transnational relations and flows. NGOs are *part of* while trying to be *apart from* the political economy – and the workings of this political economy are transnational in nature and global in reach. As such, we reiterate the point that, for NGOs to regain a sense of being and offering alternatives, it is critical that they (re)consider themselves in relation to struggles over 'little d' development as a foundational, underlying and increasingly globalized form of social change – and not simply in relation to the state or market, or to doing 'big D' development differently.

NGOs as 'Alternatives': A Brief History

Integral to reflections on NGOs for two decades, thinking about NGOs as alternatives has gone somewhat missing of late. The NGO literature has been voluminous since the 1980s, termed by some the 'NGO decade', with these new actors frequently lauded as the institutional alternative to existing development approaches (Hirschman, 1984; Korten, 1990). Critical voices at this point were largely muted, confined to expressing concern that NGOs might be an externally imposed phenomenon that, far from being alternative heralded a new wave of imperialism (Tandon, 1991). Apparently inclined to offer the benefit of the doubt, much of the literature focused on locating the importance of NGOs as a key plank within the emerging 'New Policy Agenda', including a new role at the vanguard of donor agendas on 'civil society' and 'democratization' (Robinson, 1995). However, as the 1980s and 1990s proceeded, NGOs came under closer and more critical scrutiny, from both supporters and sceptics alike. 'Internal' debates looked both ways. On the one hand were discussions of how to scale-up NGO activities (Edwards and Hulme, 1992), how to run NGOs more successfully and ensure their sustainability as organizations (e.g. Fowler, 2000a; Lewis, and Wallace, 2000), and how NGOs might better manage their relationships (Robinson et al., 2000). On the other hand, commentators feared that closeness to the 'mainstream' undermined their 'comparative advantage' as agents of alternative development, with particular attention falling on problems of standardization and upwards accountability (Edwards and Hulme, 1996; Wallace et al., 1997), on the effectiveness of NGOs in reaching the poorest (Riddell and Robinson, 1995; Vivian, 1994), and on an apparent increased tendency to employ 'radical' methods of empowerment as technical means rather than as political ends in themselves. The apparently limited success of NGOs as agents of democratization came under critique from within (e.g. Fowler, 1993) and without (e.g. Marcussen, 1996; Mercer, 2002; Harvey, 2004), while the simmering debate re-emerged over NGOs as an externally driven phenomenon that threatened the development of 'indigenous civil society' and distracted attention from more political organizations (e.g. Hashemi, 1995; Mamdani, 1993). Such concerns culminated in a period of millennial angst within the sector, with growing calls for 'Northern' NGOs in particular to devise new roles and rationales for themselves (Lewis and Wallace, 2004) or risk becoming obsolete (van Rooy, 2000). NGOs were advised to reach beyond the aid system for alternative forms of funding (Fowler, 2000b) while also lobbying for a fundamental restructuring of the international aid system itself.

However, and while the academic output on NGOs remains more diverse than can be fully reviewed here, what has perhaps been most remarkable of late is the extent to which these critical concerns have been allowed to pass by in the academic literature with very little evidence that they have been seriously addressed. We are arguably no clearer now concerning questions of effectiveness, accountability and successful routes to scaling-up than we were when these questions were raised over a decade ago, let alone concerning the wider challenge of what being 'alternative' means at this juncture (Tandon, 2001). And while some Northern NGOs have undergone profound institutional changes (e.g. witness once more ActionAid's relocation to South Africa), a sense of complacency concerning these and other key challenges appears to have replaced the earlier sense of angst within Northern NGOs about their future role. In countries in democratic transition, such as South Africa or Chile, the NGO sector has been seeking to find a new role to enable survival, and does not appear to be concerning itself with higher order questions. It is perhaps a frustration with this as much as anything that encourages us to ask again whether and how NGOs might re-engage with their founding project of offering genuine 'alternatives'.

While the growth of NGOs has been well reviewed, Lewis (2005) argues that much of this analysis has lacked theoretical acuity. This section therefore approaches this modern history of NGOs through the lens of our reflective framework and in a way that helps speak to our overall concern for the place of NGOs in fashioning alternative forms of development. We divide this abridged history into four main phases. Although aware that this omits the deeper history to which Lewis (2005) refers, our historical starting point and our concern for alternatives (Drabek, 1987) mean that we have placed particular emphasis on the last twenty years.

An abridged history of NGO a/Alternatives

Our *first period* (up to the mid- to late 1960s) is characterized by the long history of a limited number of small agencies seeking to respond to the needs of groups of people perceived as poor and who received little external professional support. These largely issue-based organizations combined both philanthropic action and advocacy – as for instance in the case of the abolition of slavery and promotion of peace (Charnovitz, 1997, cited in Lewis, 2005). Most were Northern based, but some had a Southern presence, and they were generally embedded both in broader movements (e.g. against slavery) and in networks that mobilized voluntary contributions. They were often linked to other organizations providing them with an institutional base and funding, and frequently linked to wider religious institutions and philanthropists; see, for example, the history of the National Council of Churches of Kenya (Crouch, 1993). There were also clear interactions with the state around legal reform as well as with the market which generated most of the resources then transferred through foundations (a model that of course continues through to today, on a far more massive scale). From the North, at least some such interventions emerged from the legacy of colonialism, such as volunteer programmes sending experts to 'under-capacitated' countries or organizations that derived from missionary interventions (Cooper, 1997). While some interventions were of organizations whose mission and/or staff recognized the need for structural reform, only rarely was such work alternative in any systemic sense, or in the sense that it sought to change the balance of hegemonic ideas, be these about the organization of society or the provision of services.

Such organizations continued their work (some closed down, others were created) during the 1960s and 1970s – broadly our *second phase*, through to 1980–85. Although they remained relatively small-scale, in some countries and some sectors this period marked the early stages of the later acceleration in NGO growth. Critically this period seems to be catalysed by the consolidation of NGO 'co-financing' programmes, whose creation reflected a willingness of Northern states and societies to institutionalize NGO projects within their national aid portfolios. Reflecting the geopolitical moment, the sector became increasingly critical, engaging more fully with the notion that it was imperative that NGOs elaborate and contribute to alternative arrangements among state, market and civil society (generally on a national rather than a transnational scale), and alternatives both within, and to, capitalism. In this period development (as a project) was increasingly scrutinized, reflecting the intersection between these NGOs and political struggles around national independence and various socialisms, as well as between these political projects and intellectual debates on dependency, structuralist and broadly Marxian interpretations of the development process (Watts, 2001). The notion of 'alternative development' itself emerged most strongly in this era (e.g. Nerfin, 1977), and the publication of books such as *Small is Beautiful* (Schumacher, 1973) is illustrative of this battle of ideas.

The sector was increasingly conscious of itself and of the need to build collaborations with other non-governmental actors, particularly across North–South boundaries. Numerous influences – awareness of the need for local institutional development, reduction in the formal colonial presence, and the contradictions inherent in the Northern NGO model – resulted in a steady shift in this period from operational to funding roles for Northern NGOs and the growth of a Southern NGO sector (Smillie and Helmich, 1993).

In the South, this was a period in which a growing number of NGOs, in particular those embedded in institutions and networks of political and religious lefts, consciously sought to shift state–market–civil society arrangements through government policy. This was also a period in which very many existing and newly formed NGOs negotiated space within and alongside other political and social movements. This process was one of collaboration among actors who recognized the benefits of the joint existence of movements, supportive institutions *and* NGOs within the struggle against hegemonic and repressive structures manifested through the state (e.g. Philippines, South Africa, El Salvador). On the part of such NGOs, there was a recognized need for political change. Often, the relationships between these actors ran deep, with NGO staff being simultaneously active in political parties and movements (such as, for example, PlanAct – established in 1985 – and the ANC in South Africa).

These were also the periods when European co-financing resources were (often deliberately) given without many questions being asked, in order to channel resources to oppositional movements via NGOs without any explicit, traceable government knowledge. Meanwhile other governments and conservative forces – most notably the USA – used a not dissimilar tactic to support elements of the hegemonic forces and ideas against which these NGOs and political movements were struggling (see Hulme, this volume). Indeed, in this phase and in later arguments over neoliberalism, the role of NGOs both in strategies of contesting hegemony as well as in other strategies aimed at consolidating it, was more than apparent. The non-governmental sector was one of the more important terrains in which dominance of civil society was being contested (c.f. Howell and Pearce, 2001) and in which the alternatives at stake were systemic as much as sectoral. However, we should recognize that the bulk of this contestation revolved around political rather than economic structures.

Our *third phase* is defined by the growth in recognition for NGOs and their work and the increasing interest in funding such activities, often in relationships with the state and development agencies. This phase began in the early 1980s, reflecting the link between this changing position of NGOs and more profound systemic shifts that also date from this period. This was the period of the NGO 'boom', a boom that can only be understood in terms of its own relationship to transformations in this period in the structures of capitalisms North, South and globally. Indeed, it remains one of the central contradictions concerning NGO alternatives that the huge increase in NGO activity during the 1980s was driven to a significant extent by the unfolding neoliberal agenda and the new roles it gave to NGOs – the very agenda that development alternatives have sought to critically engage. We would draw attention to three particular shifts in the broader relationships among state, market and civil society as being important in this regard: macroeconomic instability and crisis in a significant number of countries; political democratization, from both dictatorships and 'enlightened authoritarian' regimes towards more formally liberal democracies; and a shift in dominant development discourse, with concepts and practices such as 'civil society' and participation assuming great (discursive) centrality.

The structural adjustment programmes of the 1980s led to a series of demands – across the political spectrum – for NGO intervention as programme implementers, knowledge generators and activists, depending somewhat on the political origins of those demands. The model itself was not in question and certainly this source of support for NGOs did not help them contest it, even if they wished to. Those who opposed structural adjustment looked to NGOs to document the scale of suffering caused and to demonstrate the feasibility of coherent alternatives that also took account of the previous failure of government to deliver to the poor. Arguably NGOs were far more effective at the documentation of failure than the elaboration of alternatives. Much was expected of NGOs in this period but there was little to no space to pursue large-scale or system-questioning alternative projects. Yet the 1980s were not entirely lost to systemic alternatives. Some countries witnessed a resurgence of new social movements (Alvarez et al., 1998; Ballard et al., 2005). These movements suggested other pathways through which alternatives might be built, more slowly and systematically, around concepts of citizenship, identity and organization (see Escobar, 2001, 1995; and Dagnino this volume). These alternatives, in some countries, challenged dominant thinking on the social and political order, if not the economic. In other cases, NGOs emerged to support defensive actions against the expansion of market-led development. In Asia, widespread evictions resulted in the establishment of the Asian Coalition for Housing Rights in 1988 and explicit attempts to create alliances between professionals and grassroots organization to address processes of exclusionary development.

Adjustment was also accompanied by political democratization, partly as the political correlate of neoliberalism, but also as a response to long years of organizing within civil society in which NGOs had played a role along with other actors. Ironically, this democratization brought further complications to NGOs. Once newly democratic state institutions took up alternatives for which NGOs had pushed, NGOs were left with the uncertainty of what to do next other than help the state make a success of these new orthodoxies. Indeed, many NGO staff and movement activists have moved into government precisely to try and help foster such success (Racelis, Dagnino, both this volume) – a process sometimes viewed as co-optation rather than success. If democratization marked a success in delivering a systemic alternative in which NGOs could claim some role, the alternative was incomplete and complex in two senses. First, while relationships between state and civil society were (at least partly) transformed, those between state and market were largely unaffected, and those between market and civil society appeared to further commodify social relations. Second, the growing closeness of NGOs to the 'big D' interventions moulded by national and multilateral organizations led to the concern that NGOs had become, in Edwards and Hulme's (1996) term, 'too close for comfort' to a range of other actors in a way that compromised their innovativeness, autonomy, legitimacy, accountability and ability to continue elaborating alternatives. The role of public service contractor was, if anything, stronger in the South than the North, where the move of NGO professionals into government was often accompanied by programmes (partly crafted by these same professionals) in which the NGOs became subcontracted service providers. This trend, also reinforced by donor demands and changing perceptions of the comparative advantages of the state, potentially put NGOs' more radical role at risk. For these and other reasons, authors from different regions argued that it had become increasingly difficult for NGOs to offer 'little d' development alternatives (Aldaba et al., 2000).

Not all shared the sense of pending institutional doom that was suggested by some of this literature – some NGO leaders questioned the tendency of Northern commentators to impute crises where they didn't exist. Indeed, a decade later it seems that stories of their 'coming' demise had been greatly exaggerated. Yet NGOs have hardly become more robust, and pressures over the last decade – our *fourth period* – present an additional set of health hazards, some more obvious, others less intuitive. This fourth period we date from the mid- to late 1990s with a persistent and public set of concerns about the practice, direction and focus of NGOs. It is a period in which NGOs have had to come to terms with their entry, at scale, into the reform agenda, as well as increasing diversification within the NGO sector and the apparent co-option of many 'alternatives' within the mainstream. There are three apparent trends in this period that impinge directly on NGOs and the scope for building either systemic or reformist alternatives: the continued deepening of the democratization-cum-neoliberalization agenda; the increasingly dominant poverty agenda in international aid; and the relatively more recent, hugely pernicious, security agenda, itself coupled in strange ways with the poverty agenda. We deal with these each in turn.

The current neoliberal order

With the creation of the World Trade Organization (WTO), the neoliberalization of social democracy, the end to global Communism, and the increasing tendency towards military enforcement of liberal democratic process, the joint project of liberal democracy and free trade seems to have become increasingly clear and consolidated in this latter period making it ever more difficult for NGOs or other actors to think or act outside of this neoliberal box. This is particularly so because the box has incorporated much core NGO terminology around democracy, rights, empowerment, participation, poverty and livelihoods (Craig and Porter, 2006). At the same time there are incentives to engage with – indeed, become *part of* – hegemonic forms of 'little d' development, as these begin to look more attractive, or (perhaps more often) all that is possible, as with microfinance.

The shift towards democratization and building the role of civil society has likewise brought many NGOs closer to the operations of mainstream Development. Accompanied by the scaling up of the participatory turn, this shift has offered some NGOs unprecedented levels of access to at least part of the policy process, as for instance in relation to PRSPs. But it also brings challenges, particularly concerning the capacity and legitimacy of NGOs to act as pseudo-democratic representatives of 'the poor', and the risks of being associated with processes that may in themselves undermine broader democratic norms. There are real dangers that the participatory turn can and does obscure more legitimate and effective forms of democratic representation (Brown, 2004). Some NGOs, keen to secure their seat at the new range of tables open to them within 'inclusive' policy processes, have been perhaps too keen to grasp and extend these channels, without thinking through the longer-term problems that this raises for public accountability in developing country contexts.

The poverty reduction agenda and related shifts in NGO financing

Closely related has been the new-found hegemony for 'poverty reduction' within international development. The (very considerable) resources flowing from bilateral and some multilateral agencies to NGOs are increasingly bundled with this poverty-reduction agenda, placing increasing demands on these NGOs to deliver measurable achievements in poverty reduction. While it is hard to contest the worthiness of such goals, this emphasis – especially with increased insistence on measurement and indicators – has the potential not only to rein in but also to depoliticize the range of strategies open to NGOs in promoting development (Derksen and Verhallen, this volume). There is at least some evidence to suggest that as aid becomes far more oriented to measurable poverty reduction, it has led NGOs away from relations with social movements, and towards more narrowly drawn specific targeted development improvements. These changing donor priorities are also evident in South Africa where, since 1994, international funding has been orientated to the state and state funding to charitable activities rather than to social justice organizations, with the effect that NGOs have increasingly turned to contract work and fees for service (Planact, 2006).

These trends – the deepening of both democratization and the neoliberal economic agenda in developing countries, and the onset of the poverty agenda – have thus begun to shift the political economy of development funding in ways that strengthen some roles and create new dilemmas for NGOs. Both the desire by donors to have more of international development work focused on large-scale poverty reduction, and the advance of national government funding of poverty reduction programmes in Asia, Latin America and Africa, have led to a clear shift back towards the state. Here, NGOs become framed as public-service contractors, with donor interest in funding more innovative activities – including those oriented towards systemic alternatives and challenging hegemonic ideas – concomitantly reduced. Thus, even as foreign aid flows have risen, the scope for alternatives has narrowed.

In some cases, there is competition from the private sector for these funds, although there is some awareness of mixed results (e.g. the experiences with subsidized housing and shelter improvements in Latin America). Many argue that voluntary-sector organizations in North and South have suffered from greater emphasis on cost recovery, charging for services, professionalized staff relationships, the dominance of competition and the rise of tenders (Townsend and Townsend, 2004). While this blurring between civil and market logics holds the potential to inject a stronger sense of the social within the corporate logic of the private sector and to provide greater resources for social programmes, there is perhaps greater potential for the reverse to predominate, such that the 'pro-market diversification of (NGO) relationships ... is an erosion of their potential as agents of systemic social and political change' (Fowler, 2005: 1).

A further contemporary trend in funding has been the switch to direct funding of NGOs in the South. While larger South-based NGOs and local offices of Northern NGOs have been successful in raising funds from these sources, smaller NGOs have less capacity to deal with the bureaucracy of bilateral agencies, suggesting that over time there will be more concentration in both the Northern and Southern NGO sectors. Some Southern NGOs complain that Northern NGOs are becoming more like bilateral agencies than non-governmental partners, and indeed some within these Northern NGOs feel the same. The same is also said by emerging NGOs in the South when they are funded through the capacity development programmes of big Southern NGOs. NGOs have struggled to adapt to this funding climate. Many spend considerable time chasing money that is not very useful to them. NGOs need considerable financial skills to manipulate this situation to their advantage, pursue an alternative agenda and still be seen as competent.

The 'new' security agenda

The third trend marking the most recent years has been the rise of the security agenda – not human or livelihood security but Western geopolitical security (Duffield, 2001). NGOs have long operated in the context of global conflicts, not only as humanitarian actors but also as active promoters of system change, often in ways related to the political and social justice movements onto which the NGOs mapped – think, for instance, of the conflicts in Central America. However, the issues raised by conflict have changed significantly since Edwards et al.'s (1999) comments concerning the roles that NGOs can and should play within conflict zones, not least because of the 'Global War on Terror'. The multiple challenges that this new context raises for NGO alternatives is explored in Alan Fowler's chapter, but what is most relevant for us to note here is the different positioning of Northern NGOs on this issue (Lister, 2004). While some have refused to work in countries such as Iraq and Afghanistan or to accept bilateral funding from aggressor states to work therein, others have either applied a peg to their nose and followed what they perceive to be their mission despite opposing the war on terror, or taken the view that their humanitarian aims are compatible with the new imperialism (Lister, 2004: 8). This range of positioning reveals not only the extent to which the political economy of aid, and NGO dependency on official flows, limits their room for manoeuvre, but also the immense differences among NGOs in how they understand and approach the notion of pursuing 'alternatives'. For those unable or unwilling to extract themselves from the vagaries of 'big D', the character of the latest nexus between security and development means that the result is complicity in a wider form of 'little d' that has little discernible link to a project of equity, social justice and political inclusion.

Mapping the Book's Contributions

With these conceptual and historical points of reference in mind, we have organized the chapters of the book into five main sections. The first section sets the stage, combining this chapter and one by Mike Edwards, a key player in all four of the 'Manchester' conferences. He offers a retrospective on the NGOs' conferences that began in 1991, and that have been repeated in 1994, 1999 and most recently in 2005. He argues that NGOs have taken insufficient heed of warnings to protect their integrity and that organizational self-interest has become too dominant. During the 1990s, NGOs became increasingly funded by official development assistance agencies, and the 1994 conference saw intense discussions on this theme. Whilst Edwards and Hulme (1995) suggested that NGOs faced choices, in the years that followed NGOs have failed to address real concerns about their accountability and are now vulnerable to criticism. The 1999 conference highlighted further themes with a vision to move beyond inequality and difference, and the promise of transnational organizing among NGO equals seeking systemic change – rather than NGOs having a secondary role within strategies shaped by continuing asymmetries of the foreign aid world.

Since this date, there have been some examples of NGOs using 'development as leverage' (rather than 'delivery'). Such developments, combined by the ongoing process of reflection among NGOs, suggest to Edwards that NGOs have made positive contributions to development alternatives. As a first step, it is hard to argue that the world would have been a better place without NGOs. NGOs have helped to raise important issues and lay the foundations for progress. However, the rise in aid budgets, in part due to the security agenda, has weakened the incentive to innovate within the NGO sector. NGOs have contributed to raising awareness of the downside of globalization, cementing commitments to participation and human rights, and raising critical global issues such as Africa and global warming. But

NGOs have not done well in identifying ways of changing the systems that perpetuate poverty as well as discrimination by class, race and gender. Nor have they, notwithstanding exceptions, innovated in terms of their organizational relationships and greater downward accountability, perhaps because their organizational imperatives dominate over their development vision. Underlying this situation are two contrasting visions for the future: one in which NGOs participate in a modernization process now located within the 'war on terror', and the other of an international system with international laws and in which countries and their citizens negotiate solutions within a recognition of interdependency. If NGOs fail to commit to this second vision, then they can make only incremental contributions, Edwards concludes. However, if they are prepared to accept new relationships within civic action, then they may achieve much more.

The second, third and fourth sections are organized around three principles that emerged from these two background papers and the conference itself: the sense that the scope to pursue alternatives is under particular pressure in the contemporary period; the experiments that NGOs continue to pursue with different ways of engaging in social transformation and development; and the attempts of different NGOs, North and South, simply to be different, to organize themselves differently and stand for a different way of thinking about development. We discuss these three sections below. The final section then closes the book with a provocative and forward-thinking commentary from David Hulme, another stalwart of all four Manchester conferences.

Alternatives under pressure

The second section of this book is perhaps the most depressing – at least, it is that which gives most cause to worry that the scope for pursuing development alternatives, both in general and by NGOs in particular, has become steadily more constrained. The chapters in this section – by Evelina Dagnino, Kees Biekart, Alan Thomas and Alan Fowler – explore three main sources of pressure on these alternatives: the pressures of neoliberalism in the South; the pressures deriving from the increasingly technocratic, target-oriented and also neoliberal agenda of agencies that channel resources to NGOs; and the pressures of the new security agenda, that has emerged since the later 1990s, though with far more force since 11 September 2001 and the subsequent invasions of Afghanistan and Iraq.

Taken as a whole, these pressures might be understood as the effect within the non-governmental sector of the two main geopolitical projects that have characterized the period since the first Manchester conference: the extension of neoliberal capitalism around the globe, consolidated not only in policies and institutional reforms but more importantly in taken-for-granted discourses on society and development, as well as in the practices of those very agents who are ostensibly opposed to neoliberalism (the academic world included); and the expansion, through financial flows, militarization and the practices of intelligence, of a particular way of governing this phase of neoliberal capitalism. Geopolitics has always been part of aid, of course, and so this is nothing new. However, there is some sense in these chapters that particular Western muscles are being flexed more strongly today than in the past, and that this has – among other things – reined in the possibility that NGOs or other critics of the contemporary order might experiment with and give voice to the possibility of other orders.

Importantly, though each of these chapters is sombre in its different way, they all hold out hope (and in this sense offer a bridge to the third and fourth sections). There are varying dimensions to this hope: that aid for NGOs is not necessarily under the financial pressure that many believe to be the case; that, in some areas, resources for lobbying and political work seem in fact to have increased; that even under neoliberalism it has been possible to produce democracy-deepening experiences, such as Brazil's experiments with participatory budgeting and local governance; that even within the security- and impact-oriented conditionalities of the current aid agenda, it remains possible for NGOs to carve out space for change. In the search for this space, however, perhaps the most important theme of the chapters is the importance of NGOs and other civil society actors continuing to reflect on the reality of the contexts in which they operate. As later sections of the book suggest, such honest critical reflection can – when it is willing to risk all – give rise to significant innovation.

Evelina Dagnino argues that the policy and political context of much of Latin America can be characterized by what she calls a 'perverse confluence' between the broad tendencies of neoliberalism and efforts to deepen democratic practice. Central to this confluence is a process in which core concepts within this democracy-deepening project are assumed and given new meaning by the policies and political practices of neoliberalism. In particular, she notes how under neoliberalism 'participation' comes to mean involvement in programme implementation but not in policy design, 'civil society' becomes a Third Sector of nonprofit organizations rather than a domain in which ideas about development and society are struggled over, and 'citizenship' ceases to mean the 'right to have rights' and becomes the right to receive targeted subsidies from government poverty-reduction programmes. Neoliberalism, for Dagnino, takes the core concepts of alternative development and transforms them into ideas that help sustain the neoliberal political project. In the process, many NGOs become functional to neoliberalism, doing what the state used to do, and while some of them may realize and worry about this change in their roles, the implication is that they can do little to sustain alternative societal projects and tend to become more distant from the social movements with which they were previously more organically linked. Dagnino does not paint a picture of complete pessimism and she evidently draws inspiration from some of Brazil's experiments with democracy deepening. However, her analysis suggests real pressures on the scope for alternatives and those NGOs ostensibly committed to them.

One of the most acutely felt pressures faced by many NGOs is financial – the constant search for resources to support their work. In some parts of the world, NGOs sense that this pressure has become more severe in recent years. Kees Biekart's chapter notes, for instance, how many Latin American organizations that received support from European donor NGOs fear that these agencies will gradually withdraw from the region, re-channelling funds to Africa and other (poorer) regions of the world. His chapter reports on recent research suggesting, however, that the situation is more nuanced, and not necessarily as dire as some suggest. The data show, instead, a concentration of NGO funding in a smaller set of countries, and with a more restricted group of partner organizations. This increased focus has been accompanied by a change in orientation of these resources. European agencies have moved away from areas such as rural development, agriculture and the environment, and have instead increased their attention for rights-based approaches combined with more integrated joint lobbying and advocacy work. This has generated a more political agenda on topics such as migration, conflict resolution, peace-building, and trade issues. These are likely to be key topics in the coming years, in which the 'creation and promotion of more synergies' among partners within the South, and between North and South, will be a central slogan in optimizing the use of available resources. Overall, then, Biekart suggests that a closer look at financial flows for NGO cooperation suggests that trends are not necessarily reducing scope for alternatives. Indeed, if anything, the shift towards more politicized approaches might even be opening new opportunities for innovative approaches to social and political change.

Even if – as Biekart suggests – NGO funding levels may be healthy, it might still be the case that the principles tied to that funding constrain NGOs' ability to be 'alternative'. This is the concern of Alan Thomas, for whom 'reciprocity' constitutes the organizing principle of NGOs and other civil society organizations (CSOs). Using UK Department for International Development (DFID) funding as an example, he then explores how far this support affects this defining principle. He suggests 'voice' and 'impact' are becoming the dominant reasons why DFID channels resources to NGOs, and in so doing they may be jeopardizing one of the important contributions of NGOs – to promote an alternative form of *relating* within a modern capitalist society with a major bureaucratic state sector. The

DFID increasingly recognizes the political role of NGOs in making the 'voice of the poor' heard so as to hold governments to account and ensure better pro-poor policies. At the same time, though, it also funds NGOs to supply services directly – seeing them simply as private actors filling gaps opened by inadequate state capacity. In these arrangements, NGOs are viewed as simply another private firm, and are expected to compete for donor contracts on the basis of efficiency and impact as measured against the Millennium Development Goals. Thomas does not naysay the importance of 'voice' and 'impact', but does suggest that to judge NGOs only by their direct results in these domains downplays other fundamental, value-based aspects of NGO work in development. These include solidarity, quality of personal relationships, partnership with local and national government agencies, the contributions of participatory service provision to broader processes of empowerment, and advocacy for forms of 'public action' in which NGOs contest the very definition of what is a public need while at the same time supplying that need. These values – which he subsumes into the principle of reciprocity – are, he concludes, being marginalized and need to be upheld against these donor pressures.

In the final chapter of this section, Fowler discusses one of the most difficult challenges facing NGOs today, namely the extent to which they can maintain a sense of autonomy and commitment to social justice while operating within the new security agenda. He outlines the range of 'counter terrorism measures' that Western governments, particularly the USA, have implemented and the ways in which these inhibit the freedom of NGOs to operate. For example, NGOs face far closer scrutiny concerning the southern organizations that they partner with, a move that threatens the progressive efforts to decentralize power and resources to local organizations. The costs of compliance with these new rigours also threaten the core funding that NGOs rely on in order to retain a degree of autonomy. Moreover, as the 'development for security' agenda dictates that development finance be redirected to different regions and for different purposes, NGOs face further dilemmas. What role (if any) can they play in rebuilding the 'failed states' that apparently provide the breeding ground for terrorists? Given that the securitization agenda combines humanitarian imperatives with the 'new imperialism', can NGOs maintain an alternative, even counter-hegemonic stance while working within war zones such as Iraq? Fowler concludes that while NGOs may need to accept that their room for manoeuvre is now more limited, he suggests that if they are able to innovate in their relationships, reformulate their self-understanding and purpose, and develop a strategic awareness of the long-term game being played, then they may still be able to operate within this agenda while aligning themselves with 'a messy "transformatory-reformism"'.

Pursuing alternatives: NGO strategies in practice

If the second section of the book leaves us with a sense that, even in a context of constraint, there is still scope for pursuing alternatives, the third section explores this pursuit in more detail. The NGOs discussed in this section are committed to alternatives in a variety of senses – alternatives to underlying processes of development, to big Development agencies and to the approaches offered by states. Although such approaches remain diverse and beyond easy summary, what seems more apparent is that their relative success or failure in these ventures is shaped not only by material factors relating to the political economy of aid, but also – and perhaps more strongly – by non-material factors, including the building of relationships with other actors, and, perhaps less obviously, a strong engagement with ideas, research and knowledge.

Several chapters here emphasize the importance of evidence and research. Such activities offer legitimacy to NGOs seeking to influence policy processes, although success here may depend more on the strategic use of the evidence than on its intrinsic quality (Pollard and Court, Chhotray). Importantly, ideas and concepts also matter here. How the social world is conceptualized and the nature of the ideological positions taken by NGOs remain critical (see Guijt on power analysis, and elsewhere in this volume Piálek on feminism). More broadly, this helps emphasize the importance of NGOs engaging with the public struggle for ideas and for influence over the direction of public thinking on development or the 'good society' (Bazán et al., and the final section of this chapter).

The success of NGOs in building relationships with a wide range of popular but also potentially elitist (e.g. research-based) elements of civil society is critical, particularly where such elements form part of wider movements (as in the case of Guijt's examples of women's movements in Uganda and Sri Lanka). Relationships with the state seem to be rather more controversial. For one contributor, the state's antipathy to critical and independent NGOs can present a significant obstacle (Racelis), whereas another argues that (given the legitimacy derived from popular support and acting within state-prescribed boundaries) some NGOs can develop a dual strategy of simultaneous critique of and engagement with the state (Chhotray).

Nonetheless, the political economy of aid still matters, and different modalities and tendencies within development finance can either enable (Guijt) or constrain (Bazán et al.) the pursuit of alternatives by NGOs. This is particularly the case in relation to the degree of autonomy that they have to pursue their own strategic directions, but also regarding the paucity of funds for thinking as opposed to acting. The tendency remains for donors to fund research related to specific policy ideas within Development rather than focusing on underlying processes of uneven development.

The chapter by Amy Pollard and Julius Court reviews the literature on how civil society organizations (CSOs), and particularly NGOs, aim to reform and transform policy processes. The authors suggest that CSOs seek to influence the policy process at four distinct stages – problem identification and agenda setting; formulation and adoption; implementation; and monitoring and evaluation – and that different strategies may be required for success at each stage. In the first place, the ways in which CSOs shape and frame issues can help bring them to the attention of publics and policymakers, thus influencing agendas and processes of debate even without directly influencing policy decision-makers. Once policies are being formulated and adopted, CSOs can facilitate the engagement of excluded groups within the debate through acting as representatives and presenting research findings on the problems faced by such groups. Having a strong informational base is increasingly important for those CSOs that are well integrated in the policy process. In terms of policy implementation, the authors look at experiences in technical assistance and service provision, as well as less direct strategies involving the promotion of community activities. The importance of evidence emerges less ambiguously here. Finally monitoring and evaluation processes appear to make repeated use of evidence as NGOs seek to support self-reflection. The conclusion emphasizes that, in terms of policy influence, it is often how evidence is used rather than the nature of the evidence itself that matters most.

Echoing Mike Edwards's chapter, Irene Guijt argues that challenging power relations is central to the success of NGOs, although Guijt is rather more optimistic than Edwards in arguing that this can occur within the current system of international cooperation. Drawing on a comparative research project, she examines how far the support given by four Dutch co-financing agencies has served to advance 'civil society participation' in Colombia, Guatemala, Guinea, Sri Lanka and Uganda. As such, the initiatives engage with a key form of underlying *d*evelopment concerning long-term processes of citizenship formation, and what used to be considered the 'alternative' agenda of participation and empowerment. For Guijt, there is both a discursive and a material basis for success in this area. In discursive terms, CSOs can only fully understand their role in promoting citizenship participation among marginal groups if they focus explicitly on the power relations that they are seeking to transform (echoing Hickey and Mohan, 2004). Guijt proposes a particular conceptual tool – the power cube (Gaventa, 2006) – which NGOs can operationalize to assist them in this. In material terms, however, the type and longevity of funding (in this case from bilateral agencies through Northern NGOs and on to Southern NGOs) is also critical; and, in this discussion, she picks up themes elaborated by Racelis, who discusses new forms of relationship between Northern and Southern

NGOs. Here, the Dutch government is urged to maintain its principles of co-financing, in which funding flows are based on the partners' strategy as opposed to project-specific funding, and are maintained over the long run (see also the chapter by Derksen and Verhallen). Investing in creating a participatory culture between CFAs and CSOs and within CSOs is also significant (a sensibility also stressed by Chhotray).

The chapter by Bazán et al. is a collective contribution from members of seven NGOs who undertook a two-year reflection on the role and evolution of NGOs engaged in knowledge generation related to environment and development issues in Central America and Mexico. The chapter begins by conceptualizing the contribution of NGOs to knowledge production, and the ways in which they can contribute either to hegemonic discourses that serve to stabilize and naturalize capitalist systems of production and exchange, or to counter-hegemonic discourses that challenge and undermine dominant ideologies. The discussion highlights a tension between the counter-hegemonic intent and direction of the NGOs and their ability to represent that intent in their everyday activities. There is a felt pressure (from various sources) to engage in the production of applied knowledge rather than knowledge that analyses the structural forces that create and maintain poverty, inequality and unsustainable environmental practices. Meanwhile donor orientation towards poverty reduction has meant more money for doing and less for thinking – and the NGOs in this collective have evolved diverse strategies to address this situation. In addition to influencing policy through the development of individual relationships, the NGOs have built up networks of influence through their alliances and also through educating future generations of decision-makers. They have also sought to create spaces for dialogue, enabling greater reflection and also fostering new avenues for grassroots organizations and social movements to influence policy directly. The chapter ends with a challenge to the development assistance community: if knowledge matters, then someone has to produce and fund it.

Mary Racelis addresses the criticism of NGO ineffectiveness in the search for pro-poor social change in a context of poverty and inequality in the Philippines. Although NGOs made a significant contribution to underlying processes of political development in the Philippines – through resisting the earlier period of authoritarian rule and playing an important role in the transition to democracy – the state has since tried to resist their pressure to reform state processes and secure redistribution. However, even without a continued focus on these deeper levels of change, Racelis argues that NGOs have been effective in what they are trying to do, particularly in terms of securing change at the local level and in relation to powerful Development institutions. For example, NGOs reformed the working practices of the

Asian Development Bank in ways that ensured greater openness in their collaborations with civil society. They also helped nurture new working relationships with international NGOs in order to improve funding choices and avoid excessive Southern NGO dependence on Northern NGOs. In Naga City, urban poor communities have managed to negotiate a favourable relationship with the city and a World Bank-funded slum-upgrading programme. The residents, organized into a federation, have been effective in controlling the contractors charged with improving the area, and have developed much stronger grassroots capacity through the process. Finally, some Philippine NGOs have sought to secure their autonomy and sustainability through moving 'beyond aid' via a programme of government bond purchases, which were then used to capitalize a local foundation.

Being alternative

Within any population there are vanguards, and this subsection represents the restless edge of NGOs, documenting experiences in which organizations have pushed the boundaries of their own comfort zones. In each of these contributions, NGOs are not content just to experiment with new activities; rather, they seek to reconstruct themselves through acting out, thinking through and envisioning alternatives. In this reconstruction, the NGOs embed themselves in new kinds of social relationships, which bring with them new pressures and new opportunities. Whilst 'being different' itself catalyses change, further changes are also triggered by the interactions between these efforts, forces that resist them and the constraints that derive from existing organizational forms.

The alternatives explored and documented in this section are not abstract and theoretical; rather, these are ideas that are realized through everyday practices and negotiated with everyday agencies, the same agencies that are sources of conservatism and many of the distortions (Dersken and Verhallen) in the current world of aid. These NGOs find their alternatives through engagement and negotiations but also by avoiding complacency and being willing to challenge development conventions and outcomes. This challenge often includes seeking new orientations towards and alliances with grassroots organizations. What emerges strongly from these and overlapping experiences (e.g. Bazán et al.) is that these are not NGOs that 'go it alone'. Rather, they build relationships, particularly with people's movements, offering citizen action at scale to provide a platform for challenging existing development approaches.

But these are, in their own ways, ideas in the making and ideologies under threat. There is no sense from any of these chapters that alternatives have been fully achieved or can be sustained. Rathe,r they are being inched forward, with the organizations often having to move sideways rather than forward in attempts not to be overcome, and frequently being forced back. In this process, NGOs have to remake themselves, and become something different, constructing alternative identities. The path to being alternative has to be 'hacked out' of the present institutional landscape and, as such, these NGOs have few supportive structures within which to locate themselves. In being alternative, the challenge lies within, as well as outside, as they have to question ongoing practices, identities and perspectives, reforming themselves through the very experience of struggle. For example, the challenge of becoming alternative types of organization – as in Oxfam's efforts at gender mainstreaming that are discussed in Piálek's chapter – suggests that significant challenges remain. There is a sense both of ambition, and of often overwhelming odds against success.

In the first chapter in this section, Vasudha Chhotray offers an in-depth history of the emergence and impact of a small indigenous NGO in India, and its role in securing empowerment for people within a marginal rural environment. Her analysis challenges the notion that NGOs must choose to become *either* development agents *or* political entrepreneurs. This argument derives from a close-grained analysis of SPS, an NGO working among tribals in the central Indian state of Madhya Pradesh over a decade. The NGO has sought to combine development work regarded as legitimate by the state with practices that resist state action, 'striving to create a new type of politics in its development work with the state'. SPS's experience reveals how 'engaging with both small "d" and big "D" development is integral for the articulation of transformative politics. Here, it is precisely the synergies between state and civil society, mainstream and alternative development and dominance and resistance that matter, not their segregation as is mistakenly believed'. A series of important findings for NGO alternatives flow from this. 'First, NGOs have the power to effect concrete changes in local power relations, as SPS did by overturning wage relations, transforming common property access and challenging an exploitative anti-tribal coalition. Second, their power is often text oriented. SPS relied on a correct reading of the laws and official guidelines of the Indian state to fuel its radical initiatives.' Finally, NGO power greatly depends on its ability to construct 'a continuous interface not only with government officials, but key actors within "political society" including political representatives, activists and local courts.'

Katie Bristow's chapter explores the extent to which it is possible to 'be alternative' as an NGO working in health-care provision. Her starting point is that despite the rhetoric concerning the incorporation of alternative approaches to development, the present model of health care and development continues to be narrowly framed by neoliberalism and Western science and technology. She explains this in terms of four types of factor – what she calls ideological/philosophical, politico-economic, socio-cultural and pragmatic – and explores how these factors affect the work of two health-care NGOs in the Bolivian Andes. One of these NGOs, CODIGO, self-consciously seeks to be alternative through a systematic engagement with Andean health systems and knowledge, while the other delivers thoroughly modernized forms of health care. The emphasis of her analysis rests on the factors that undermine CODIGO's ability to sustain its alternative orientation. Two factors seem particularly important. First, while CODIGO aims to promote a culturally sensitive view of health-care knowledge and well-being in its training programmes, its promoters and clients live in a social context that emphasizes the superiority of modern medicine. CODIGO is simply unable to offset this effect. Second, CODIGO's insistence on alternative approaches makes it harder for it to gain financial support. Hence its ability to institutionalize its message, re-socialize its promoters and change the terms of public debate on health care are always limited. So too, then, is its *real* ability to be alternative itself.

If Chhotray and Bristow focus on Southern NGOs, the next two chapters in this section shift their attention to NGOs based in the North, most of which are involved – to a greater or lesser extent – in transferring financial resources from the North to the South. In the third chapter, Harry Derksen and Pim Verhallen, both from the Dutch Cofinancing Agency ICCO, give a refreshingly frank assessment of the perverse trends that have affected non-governmental aid in the North. Following a general discussion, they move quickly to consider how these trends have – coupled with certain national factors – steadily taken the heart out of the Dutch CoFinancing Programme, the programme through which tax resources are transferred to Dutch NGOs, who then transfer these to their partners in the South. Over the last decade this Programme – and NGOs more generally – have come in for increasing criticism and scrutiny in the Netherlands. One effect of this has been to break up the concentration of CFP resources in four NGOs (Cordaid, Hivos, Icco and Novib). In large measure a welcome change, this has come accompanied, however, by such a demand for impact indicators and government scrutiny that the programme has become laden with ever more bureaucracy. When programme funds were tendered in 2006, 116 separate NGOs bid for them, each submitting some 'two kilogrammes of written material detailing, among others, what the results of their work would be in 2010'. In the realization that in the face of this increasing bureaucratization and conditionality ICCO was simply transmitting the same burdens to its partners in the South, the organization has slowly come to the view that it has to change radically the way in which it operates. The final section of the chapter discusses the early stages of this attempt to change – which began only in 2006. It illustrates how ICCO is attempting to rediscover its alternative roots, through a radical devolution of power to the South in order that policy and practice will largely be defined by some twelve regional councils based in Africa, Asia and Latin America, and no longer from the Netherlands. The change process is neither easy nor complete, and the chapter notes the resistance it has elicited among ICCO staff, fearful of losing their power and jobs, and among partners, fearful of losing funding. It is also still not clear whether the Cofinancing Programme will allow ICCO to operate in this new way and still be eligible for cofinancing resources.

Through an investigation of gender mainstreaming within Oxfam–Great Britain, Nicholas Piálek reveals the challenges involved in integrating this perspective within everyday development practice. For Piálek, gender mainstreaming is an inherently political process, tied up with the desire of NGOs to frame themselves as being alternative kinds of organization. The challenge here is for NGO actors to prove their own capacity to embrace alternative agendas, most notably the 'gender and development' approach, and the feminism that underpins it. However, and despite adopting a series of progressive measures in this direction, it has been difficult for NGOs such as Oxfam to move beyond the adoption of broad organizational norms and towards a deeper institutionalization of gendered perspectives. Although part of the problem lies with the challenge of personal change at the level of individuals – echoing Robert Chambers's focus on 'the primacy of the personal' – the study also reveals the failure of development organizations to take more radical and alternative perspectives on gender analysis seriously. This stems in part from the external orientation of NGOs, more concerned with solving problems 'out there' than closer to home, but also from a refusal to accept the role that feminism and feminists must play in such processes.

The chapter by Helen Yanacopoulos and Matt Smith explores the possibility that NGOs might be agents of a particular form of alternative development, termed here 'cosmopolitanism'. By virtue of their capacity to transmit progressive ideas and practices across multiple political spaces, NGOs offer the potential for deepening projects and commitments to social justice on a transnational scale, provided they avoid the neo-imperial tendencies that threaten to dominate relations based around the transfer of resources and ideas from 'North' to 'South'. The links between NGOs and cosmopolitanism are explored both in terms of theory and in more detail through the prism of two areas of NGO practice: Development Education and Advocacy. Both reveal the ambiguity of the links between NGO praxis and cosmopolitanism. Although connected to 'cosmopolitan political formations and cosmopolitan democracy', Development Education also promotes difference to an extent that arguably undermines the universalism required to underpin assistance to 'distant strangers'. In terms of advocacy, the Make Poverty History (MPH) campaign also highlights this ambivalence. At one level, MPH was global in focus and called for solidarity rather than charity. However, MPH could also be framed 'as an uneasy mix between democratic and 'banal' cosmopolitanism', in that some supporters were unaware of the real issues underlying the campaign and 'wore the white band as a fashion statement rather than a political one'.

The experience of Slum/Shack Dwellers International (SDI), described by Joel Bolnick, explores the scope for alternative relationships between social movements and professional NGOs. SDI is an international movement that seeks to increase the provision of shelter for poor and very poor urban dwellers. Though SDI is international, its strength lies in its strong national members. In most countries these members combine federations of slum dwellers and NGOs that provide these federations with technical, advisory and other forms of support. The rationale for SDI, as explained by Bolnick, is that the normal pattern in efforts to provide shelter is that national elites – political or professional – dominate and determine the design of policies and programmes, and do so in ways that typically mis-specify the problem, generating solutions that tend to serve elite interests (through contract provision etc.) rather than the interests of the poor. In a way that resonates with Dagnino's project of participatory democracy, SDI seeks to reframe shelter provision as a citizenship issue – the right to have a right to shelter – and pushes the state and other actors to deliver on this. For this to succeed, SDI has to be led by the federations rather than by NGOs, and this is the constant struggle. The argument is clear: NGOs have a critical role to play in such a strategy – especially around financial management and capacity building – but must always be functional to the interests of the social movement as a whole. However, again echoing Dagnino (whose references to Brazil's recent past seem to call for similar types of NGO–movement relationship), this is easier said than done because of the many pressures particularly within Development that encourage NGOs to go it alone.

Thinking Forward and Acting

The book ends with a provocative intervention from David Hulme. His starting point is to question whether or not NGOs have played a significant role in the recent transition away from full-blooded neoliberalism towards a hybrid within which issues of poverty, rights and participation are increasingly central. He argues that NGOs have failed to take sufficient note of the key hegemonic actors in both the NGO world and in global power relations. Much should have been learned, he suggests, during those darker years from the ways in which neoliberal think-tanks had shaped and were shaping conservative thinking in both the UK and the USA, including US government policy towards developing countries? And surely more must be done to find ways of reshaping the way that US citizens and the US media deal with these issues today? If that were not enough, engaging with the new agenda-setting powers of China, India et al. is also essential, he says, if NGOs are to maintain relevance within the emerging geopolitical economy of development.

All the chapters in this book share the sense that to be alternative and to pursue alternatives is central to the idea of being non-governmental. To a greater or lesser extent, these are not authors who think of NGOs in terms of a 'third sector' providing services that others do not. They see them instead as part of a struggle, defined by relations of power. From Mike Edwards's chapter on, the issues of power and struggle figure prominently. Not that this is a book of hot-headed radicals. Rather, it brings together a set of thinking, reflective authors who each see development as a battleground and none of whom would accept the idea that 'we know what development is, now all we have to do is do it'. As editors we would venture that all our authors would argue that a large part of development is the battle over which ideas about development will win out and end up governing the ways societies organize themselves. It is in this battleground that they locate NGOs, and seek to understand what they do, what they are and what they have become.

We would also venture that all our authors would argue that, on this battleground, NGOs are not a very powerful actor. Therefore they must take care of, nurture carefully, and use strategically whatever sources of power they have – be these sources their ideas, their values, their relationships, their legitimacy. In this battlefield of ideas and practices, the main rules of conquest are defined by others: by discursively dominant disciplines (such as economics and public management), by particular imperial powers, by local and national actors disposed to use physical violence, and by those with preferential access to the means of communication. This constrains the scope for alternatives: in some cases alternatives cannot be pursued for lack of resources (above all money), in others by rules of public audit, in others because they are simply too high-risk for the actors involved, and in others because the actors have so internalized the dominant rules of the game that they find it difficult to think beyond them (one of the various effects of the perverse convergence that Dagnino discusses).

So can we say that the chapters leave us with a way forward for those – NGOs, academics, funders, citizens – who would want to engage in the struggle to find alternatives? Here we cannot speak for our contributors. Still, while it is impossible to synthesize the many nuanced contributions in this volume into a bullet-pointed agenda for change, it seems to us that several themes emerge with regularity, and on these we close the introduction.

The first of these themes is that while they all see scope for alternatives, there is one important sense in which 'there is no alternative'. That is, in the face of the analyses here, there can be no alternative but to change the ways in which non-governmental aid chains currently work. Dersken and Verhallen are the most blunt in this regard, but their co-contributors are not far behind. We are reminded of a paper from the 1994 Manchester conference by Zadek and Gatwood (1995) subtitled 'Transforming the Transnationals'. In their presentation, Zadek and Gatwood painted an image of large NGOs hurtling towards a wall, but refusing to recognize that it was there. With that wall in mind they cast two images of the future: one of large NGOs that had stuck to business as usual and had become completely uninteresting and irrelevant; another of NGOs that had looked deep within and changed themselves and become, if not as big, at least far more relevant as forces for social change. This volume gives the sense that the wall is now upon us.

But what changes do the contributors suggest? One is the importance of NGOs reaching out far more assertively, openmindedly, but also critically, to social movements. Indeed the imperative seems to be for NGOs to think consciously of themselves as part of a social movement in which the different constituents are equally important, and therefore in which relationships of power have to be thoroughly reworked and made more horizontal. Such relationships are necessarily complex if they are embedded within an alternative agenda, involving the sharing (and contestation) of ideas, actions and practices in pursuit of agreed social goals. Words are cheap of course – actions are far harder – and Bolnick's chapter from Slum/Shack Dwellers International (SDI) suggests just how hard it can be to build these horizontal relationships. But that same chapter – along with Dagnino's slightly poignant references back to the 1970s in Brazil – make clear that these changes are possible, and also that some funding agencies in the North will invest in them (if not yet become part of these reworked relationships themselves). Derksen and Verhallen even suggest that, in the Netherlands at least, there may be currents in government and parliament that would support such changes. The point is that we don't know, but that if we don't try we may never know.

The reference to social movements points to a second domain of change that is recurrent in the collection. One of the lessons of the social movement literature (in which Dagnino herself has been a key contributor) is that the most important role of 'social movements' is that they challenge hegemonic ideas in society about 'how things should be'. Hegemony is an important concept for this collection and for these conclusions. For while one might want to say that NGOs need to engage with 'little d' development – that development that refers to the underlying political economy and the social structures in which it is embedded – there is clearly no way in which NGOs alone are going to change the ways in which capital is accumulated and distributed in society. It is far from clear that governments can do this (even if they wanted to), so NGOs have no chance. However, the concept of hegemony reminds us that so much of the organization of society depends on citizens acquiescing to the rules that govern that society, and that much of this acquiescence comes from internalizing taken-for-granted, dominant (and in this sense hegemonic) ideas about 'how things should be'. Destabilizing these ideas thus offers the scope for change in other structures that would otherwise seem impossible to change.

If this is so, then a second important change for NGOs committed to alternatives would be to engage much more consciously in public debates about how things should be. This can be done by research and debate, and also by action. In its own way, by embarking on its process of change ICCO is challenging taken-for-granted ideas about aid in the Netherlands, and its actions may end up not only speaking louder than words, but ultimately changing the defining words used to describe Dutch aid in the future. Had Oxfam thoroughly mainstreamed gender in the way that Piálek says it has so far failed to do, then it would have been making a similar challenge to taken-for-granted ideas about the ways in which gender is treated by NGOs (and others). But debate can also be engaged in through producing knowledge, and crafting different ways of thinking about society. The chapter crafted by the collective of Central American and Mexican NGOs argues strongly for the importance of this type of engagement. Recognizing the problems with how they have generated knowledge in the past, they are calling for more strategic, embedded forms of knowledge generation.

Hard heads will respond to these sorts of reflections – indeed they have done so – by saying that none of this helps children without schools, women walking miles to collect water, communities washed away by disasters, urban dwellers without shelter, or farmers without access to markets. And of course all this is true. But governments exist for a reason, and a large part of that reason is to provide services to citizens with these sorts of needs – that is, to plan and manage resource redistribution. The fact that they fail pitifully in doing so should not mean asking NGOs to do these jobs instead, which in any case risks undermining the critical role of the state over the long run. It should mean supporting NGOs that intervene strategically in political processes perhaps to shame governments publicly so that their citizens demand better government; and/or to contribute to public debates about how government might work differently and about the ravages brought by corruption and authoritarianism. Of course, for those at the comfortable European and North American end of aid chains, or those sitting equally comfortably in their cozy embassies, this might all seem too sensitive, too difficult, and a foreign-relations nightmare. But we are talking of transformation: Dagnino talks of participatory democracy, Edwards and Guijt of power, Chhotray of minimum wages and anti-tribal coalitions, Racelis of holding construction contractors to account ... and transformation *should* be a foreign relations nightmare. It should also challenge domestic comforts – taking the bull of power by its horns will make no friends with certain powerful actors. But if one message of this book is that development is all about building relationships, this is not necessarily synonymous with building friendships. Making a difference will involve NGOs making intelligent, critical and strategic engagements with d/Development over the long-term, and particularly with processes that underpin continued problems of poverty and inequality.

References

Aldaba, F., P. Antezana, M. Valderrama and A. Fowler (2000) 'NGO Strategies beyond Aid: Perspectives from Central and South America and the Philippines', *Third World Quarterly* 21(4): 669–83.

Alvarez, S., E. Dagnino and A. Escobar (eds) (1998) *Culture of Politics/Politics of Cultures: Re-visioning Latin American Social Movements*, Westview Press, Boulder CO.

Ballard, R., A. Habib, I. Valodia and Zuern (2005) 'Globalization, Marginalization and Contemporary Social Movements in South Africa', *African Affairs* 104(417): 615–34.

Bebbington, A.J. (1997) 'New States, New NGOs? Crisis and Transition among Andean Rural Development NGOs', *World Development* 25(11): 1755–65.

Bebbington, A.J., and S. Hickey (2006) 'NGOs and Civil Society', in D.A. Clark (ed.) *The Elgar Companion to Development Studies*, Edward Elgar, Cheltenham.

Brown, D. (2004) 'Participation in Poverty Reduction Strategies: Democracy Strengthened or Democracy Undermined?', in S. Hickey and G. Mohan (eds), *From Tyranny to Transformation? Exploring New Approaches to Participation*: Zed Books, London, pp. 237–51.

Charnovitz, S. (1997) 'Two Centuries of Participation: NGOs and International Governance', *Michigan Journal of International Law* 18(2): 183–286.

Chiriboga, M. (2001) Constructing a Southern Constituency for Global Advocacy: The Experience of Latin American NGOs and the World Bank, in M. Edwards and J. Gaventa (eds) *Global Citizen Action: Perspectives and Challenges*, Lynne Rienner, Boulder CO, pp. 73–86.

Connolly, P. (2004) 'The Mexican National Popular Housing Fund', in D. Mitlin and D. Satterthwaite (eds), *Empowering Squatter Citizen*, Earthscan, London, pp. 82–111.

Cooper, F. (1997) 'Modernizing Bureaucrats, Backward Africans, and the Development Concept', in F. Cooper and R. Packard (eds), *International Development and the Social Sciences: Essays on the History and Politics of Knowledge*, University of California Press, Berkeley, pp. 64–92.

Cowen, M., and R. Shenton (1996) *Doctrines of Development*, Routledge, London.

Cowen, M., and R. Shenton (1998) 'Agrarian Doctrines of Development: Part 1', *Journal of Peasant Studies* 25: 49–76.

Craig, D., and D. Porter (2006) *Development beyond Neoliberalism? Governance, Poverty Reduction and Political Economy*, Routledge, London.

Crouch, M. (1993) *A Vision of Christian Mission: Reflections on the Great Commission in Kenya 1943–1993*, NCCK, Nairobi.

Drabek, A.G. (ed.) (1987) 'Development Alternatives: The Challenge of NGOs', *World Development* 15 (supplement).

Duffield, M. (2001) *Global Governance and the New Wars: The Merger of Development and Security*, Zed Books, London; 3rd edn 2005.

Eade, D. and E. Ligteringen (eds) (2001) *Debating Development*, Oxfam, Oxford.

Edwards, M (1989) 'The Irrelevance of Development Studies', *Third World Quarterly* 2(1).

Edwards, M. (2004) *Civil Society*, Polity, Cambridge.

Edwards, M., and J. Gaventa (eds) (2001) *Global Citizen Action: Perspectives and Challenges*, Lynne Rienner, Boulder CO.

Edwards, M., and D. Hulme (1996) 'Too Close for Comfort: NGOs, the State and Donors', *World Development* 24(6): 961–73.

Edwards, M., and D. Hulme (eds) (1992) *Making a Difference? NGOs and Development in a Changing World*, Earthscan/Save the Children, London.

Edwards, M., and D. Hulme (eds) (1995) *NGOs: Performance and Accountability: Beyond the Magic Bullet*, Earthscan, London.

Edwards, M., D. Hulme and T. Wallace (1999) 'NGOs in a Global Future', *Public Administration and Development* 19: 117–36.

Escobar, A. (1995) *Encountering Development: The Making and Unmaking of the Third World*, Princeton University Press, Princeton.

Escobar, A. (2001) 'Culture Sits in Places: Reflections on Globalization and Subaltern Strategies of Localization', *Political Geography* 20: 139–74.

Fowler, A. (1993) 'Non-governmental Organizations as Agents of Democratization: An African Perspective', *Journal of International Development* 5(3): 325–39.

Fowler, A. (2000a) *The Virtuous Spiral: A Guide to Sustainability for NGOs in International Development*, Earthscan, London.

Fowler, A. (2000b) 'NGO Futures: Beyond Aid: NGDO Values and the Fourth Position', *Third World Quarterly* 21(4): 589–603.

Fowler, A. (2005) *Aid Architecture and Counter-terrorism: Perspectives on NGO Futures*, INTRAC OPS 45, INTRAC, Oxford.

Gaventa, J. (2006) 'Finding the Spaces for Change: A Power Analysis', *IDS Bulletin* 37(6).

Gramsci, A. (1971) *Selections from the Prison Notebooks*, Lawrence & Wishart, London.

Hart, G. (2001) 'Development Critiques in the 1990s: *Culs de sac* and Promising Paths', *Progress in Human Geography* 25: 649–58.

Harvey, D. (2004) 'Neoliberalism and the Restoration of Class Power', reproduced in Harvey, D. 2006, *Spaces of Global Capitalism: Towards a Theory of Uneven Geographical Development*, Verso, London and New York.

Hashemi, S. (1995) 'NGO Accountability in Bangladesh: Beneficiaries, Donors and the State', in M. Edwards and D. Hulme (eds), *NGOs: Performance and Accountability: Beyond the Magic Bullet,* Earthscan, London, pp. 103–10.

Hickey, S., and G. Mohan (eds) (2004) *From Tyranny to Transformation? Exploring New Approaches to Participation*, Zed Books, London.

Hirschman, A. (1984) *Getting Ahead Collectively*, Pergamon Press, New York and Oxford.

Howell, J., and J. Pearce (2001) *Civil Society and Development: A Critical Exploration*, Lynne Rienner, Boulder CO.

Hulme, D. (1994) 'Social Development Research and the Third Sector: NGOS as Users and Subjects of Social Inquiry', in D. Booth (ed.), *Rethinking Social Development: Theory, Research and Practice*, Longman, Harlow, pp. 251–75.

Hulme, D. and M. Edwards (eds) (1997) *NGOs, States and Donors: Too Close for Comfort*, Macmillan, London, and St Martin's Press, New York.

Korten, D.C. (1990) *Getting to the 21st century: Voluntary Action and the Global Agenda*, Kumarian Press, West Hartford CT.

Lewis, D. (2005) 'Individuals, Organizations and Public Action: Trajectories of the "Non-governmental" in Development Studies', in U. Kothari (ed.), *A Radical History of Development*, Zed, London, pp. 200–221.

Lewis, D., and T. Wallace, (eds) (2000) *New Roles and Relevance: Development NGOs and the Challenge of Change*, Kumarian Press, West Hartford CT.

Lister, S. (2004) *The Future of International NGOs: New Challenges in a Changing World Order*, paper for BOND Futures programme, www.bond.org.uk/futures/.

Mamdani, M. (1993) 'Social Movements and Democracy in Africa', in P. Wignaraja (ed.), *New Social Movements in the South: Empowering the People*, Zed Books, London, pp. 101–18.

Manji, F., and C. O'Coill (2002) 'The Missionary Position: NGOs and Development in Africa', *International Affairs* 78(2): 567–83.

Marcussen, H.S. (1996) 'NGOs, the State and Civil Society', *Review of African Political Economy*, 69: 405–23.

Mercer, C. (2002) 'NGOs, Civil Society and Democratization: A Critical Review of the Literature', *Progress in Development Studies* 2(1): 5–22.

Mitlin, D., S. Hickey and A. Bebbington (2007) 'Reclaiming Development? NGOs and the Challenge of Alternatives', *World Development*.

Nerfin, M. (1977) (ed.) *Another Development: Approaches and Strategies*, Dag Hammarskjold Foundation, Uppsala.

Patel, S., and D. Mitlin (2002) 'Sharing Experiences and Changing Lives', *Community Development Journal* 37(2): 125–36.

Planact (2006) *NGOs as Innovators and Agents of Change: A History Interpreted by Development Practitioners*, www.planact.org.za/ (accessed 15 October 2006).

Riddell, R.C., and M. Robinson (1995) *Non-Governmental Organizations and Rural Poverty Alleviation*, ODI and Clarendon Press, London and Oxford.

Robinson, D., T. Hewitt and Harriss, J. (2000) *Managing Development: Understanding Inter-organizational Relationships*, Open University Press and Sage.

Robinson, M. (1995) 'Strengthening Civil Society in Africa: The Role of Foreign Political Aid', *IDS Bulletin* 26(2): 70–80.

Schumacher, E.F. (1973) *Small is Beautiful: A Study of Economics as if People Mattered*, Vintage Books, London.

Smillie, I., and H. Helmich (1993) *Non-Governmental Organizations and Governments: Stakeholders for Development*, Development Centre, OECD, Paris.

Stewart, S. (1997) 'Happy Ever After in the Marketplace: Non-government Organizations and Uncivil Society', *Review of African Political Economy* 71: 11–34.

Stone, D. (2000) 'Non-governmental Policy Transfer: The Strategies of Independent Policy Institutes', *Governance: An International Journal of Policy and Administration* 13(1): 45–62.

Tandon, R. (1991) 'Foreign NGOs, Uses and Abuses: An African Perspective', *IFDA Dossier* 81: 67–78.

Tandon, R. (2001) 'Riding High or Nosediving: Development NGOs in the New Millennium', in D. Eade and E. Ligteringen (eds), *Debating Development* Oxfam, Oxford, pp. 44–59.

Thomas, A. (2000) 'Development as Practice in a Liberal Capitalist World', *Journal of International Development* 12: 773–87.

Townsend, J. (1999) 'Are Non-governmental Organizations Working in Development a Transnational Community?', *Journal of International Development* 11: 613–23.

Townsend, J., G. Porter and E. Mawdesley (2002) 'The Role of the Transnational Community of Development Non-governmental Organizations: Governance or Poverty Reduction?', *Journal of International Development* 14: 829–39.

Townsend, J., G. Porter and E. Mawdesley (2004) 'Creating Spaces of Resistance: Development NGOs and their Clients in Ghana, India and Mexico', *Antipode* 36 (5): 871–89.

Townsend, J.G., and A.R. Townsend (2004) 'Accountability, Motivation and Practice: NGOs North and South', *Social and Cultural Geography* 5(2): 271–84.

Uphoff, N. (1995) 'Why NGOs Are Not a Third Sector: A Sectoral Analysis with Some Thoughts on Accountability, Sustainability and Evaluation', in M. Edwards and D. Hulme (eds), *NGOs: Performance and Accountability: Beyond the Magic Bullet*, Earthscan, London, pp. 17–30.

van Rooy, A. (2000) 'Good News! You May Be Out Of a Job: Reflections on the Past And Future 50 Years for Northern NGOs', *Development in Practice*, 10(3/4): 300–317.

Vivian, J. (1994) 'NGOs in Sustainable Development: No Magic Bullets', *Development and Change* 25: 181–299.

Wallace, T. (1997) 'New Development Agendas: Changes in UK NGO Policies and Procedures', *Review of African Political Economy* 71: 35–55.

Wallace, T., S. Crowther and A. Shepherd (1997) *Standardising Development: Influences on UK NGOs' Policies and Procedures*, World View Publishing, Oxford.

Watts, M. (2001) 'The Progress in Human Geography lecture, 1968 and all that...', *Progress in Human Geography* 25(2): 157–88.

Zadek, S., and M. Gatwood, (1995) 'Social Auditing or Bust?', in M. Edwards and D. Hulme (eds), *Beyond the Magic Bullet: NGO Performance and Accountability in the Post-Cold War World*, Earthscan, London.

2

Have NGOs 'Made a Difference?'
From Manchester to Birmingham
with an Elephant in the Room

Michael Edwards

In 1991, David Hulme and I found ourselves in a bar at the University of Hull enjoying a post-conference beer.[1] The conversation turned to a mutual interest of ours – the role and impact of NGOs in development – and after a few more pints we hit on the idea that eventually became the first 'Manchester Conference' on the theme of 'scaling-up', later to be summarized in a book titled *Making a Difference: NGOs and Development in a Changing World* (Edwards and Hulme, 1992). Fifteen years on, the NGO universe has been substantially transformed, with rates of growth in scale and profile that once would have been unthinkable. Yet still the nagging questions remain. Despite the increasing size and sophistication of the development NGO sector, have NGOs really 'made a difference' in the ways the first Manchester Conference intended, or have the reforms that animated the NGO community during the 1990s now run out of steam?

In this chapter I try to answer these questions in two ways. First, through a retrospective look at the Manchester conferences – what they taught us, what influence they had, and how NGOs have changed. And second, by picking out a couple of especially important challenges in development terms and assessing whether NGOs 'stood up to be counted', so to speak, and did their best in addressing them. These two approaches suggest somewhat different conclusions, which will bring me to the 'elephant in the room' of my title.

It is obvious that making judgements about a universe as diverse as development NGOs is replete with dangers of overgeneralization, and difficulties of attribution, measurement, context and timing. I suspect that my conclusions may be particularly relevant for international NGOs and to larger intermediary NGOs based in the South. So, with these caveats in mind, what does the last decade and a half tell us about the role and impact of NGOs in development?

The Manchester Conferences: A Short Retrospective

As Table 2.1 shows, the theme of the first Manchester Conference in 1992 was 'Scaling-up NGO impact on development: how can NGOs progress from improving local situations on a small scale to influencing the wider systems that create and reinforce poverty?' (Edwards and Hulme, 1992: 7). The conference concluded that there were different strategies suited to different circumstances, specifically: (1) working with government; (2) operational expansion; (3) lobbying and advocacy; (4) and networking and 'self-spreading' local initiatives. All of these strategies have costs and benefits, but the implicit bias of the conference organizers, and most of the participants, lay towards institutional development and advocacy as the most effective and least costly forms of scaling-up, what Alan Fowler later called the 'onion-skin' strategy for NGOs – a solid core of concrete practice (either direct project implementation or support to other organizations and their work), surrounded by successive and interrelated layers of research and evaluation, advocacy and campaigning, and public education. To varying extents, this strategy has become standard practice for development NGOs in the intervening years.

Buried away at the end of *Making a Difference* was the following statement: 'The degree to which a strategy or mix of strategies compromises the logic by which legitimacy is claimed provides a useful test of whether organizational self-interest is subordinating mission' (Edwards and Hulme, 1992: 213). For reasons that I will come back to later in my argument, that has turned out to be a prescient conclusion.

Fast-forward to the second Manchester Conference in 1994, in a context in which NGOs had begun to 'scale-up' rapidly in an environment in which they were seen as important vehicles to deliver the political and economic objectives of the 'New Policy Agenda' that was being adopted by official donor agencies at the time – deeper democratization through the growth of 'civil society', and more cost-effective delivery of development-related services such as micro-credit and community-driven development. As a result, many NGO budgets were financed increasingly by government aid, raising critical questions about performance, accountability and relations with funding sources. The key question for that conference was as follows: 'Will NGOs be co-opted into the New Policy Agenda as the favored child, or magic bullet for development?' (Edwards and Hulme, 1995: 7). And, if so, what would that do to NGO mission and relationships? Will they, as

Birmingham 1999 The changing global context poses questions about NGO roles, relationships, capacities and accountabilities. 'Adapt or die!' Three key changes:

1. globalization reshapes patterns of poverty, inequality and insecurity;
2. 'complex political emergencies' reshape humanitarian action;
3. the focus of international co-operation is moving from foreign aid to rules, standards and support for the most vulnerable.

Hence transnational organizing among equals for systemic change in North–South transfers and interventions.

This changing context gives rise to four challenges for NGOs:

1. mobilizing a genuinely inclusive civil society at all levels of the world system;
2. holding other organizations accountable for their actions and ensuring they respond to social and environmental needs;
3. ensuring that international regimes are implemented effectively and to the benefit of poor countries;
4. ensuring that gains at the global level are translated into concrete benefits at the grassroots.

NGOs must move from 'development as delivery' to 'development as leverage', or 'marry local development to worldwide leverage'. This requires more equal relationships with other civic actors, especially in the South, new capacities (e.g. bridging and mediation), and stronger accountability mechanisms.

NGOs in a Global Future: Marrying Local Delivery to Worldwide Leverage (PAD)

New Roles and Relevance: Development NGOs and the Challenge of Change

NGO Futures: Beyond Aid (TWQ)

Global Citizen Action

Manchester 2005 NGOs and Development Alternatives: have we *really* changed things?

NGOs have helped to change the debate on globalization, increase commitment to participation and human rights, and keep the spotlight on the need for reforms in the international system (trade, intervention etc.). But the foreign aid system/paradigm has changed much less than was predicted in 1999. Has this been a disincentive to deeper changes in NGO practice (the 'security blanket' effect)?

Significant changes in the external environment:

• increasing pace of global change and commonality in causes and effects (no more 'North' and 'South'?);
• geopolitical rearrangements and their impact on global governance (USA, China, India/Brazil/South Africa, Middle East);
• cultural cleavages on values and ideology (religion);
• the reality of climate change, esp. given urbanization.

But also stronger conventional international cooperation (increased ODA; continued donor influence, imposed democratization and economic reform, democratic deficits in international institutions, despite recipients' dissatisfaction and growing external criticism). Will the international system, including NGOs, change faced with new global realities?

NGOs and the Challenge of Development Alternatives

Have NGOs 'Made a Difference'?

From Manchester to Birmingham with an Elephant in the Room

Table 2.1 The Manchester conferences: a summary

Location and date	Theme(s)	Key conclusions	Published outputs
Manchester 1992	Scaling-up NGO impact on development: • 'How can NGOs progress from improving local situations on a small scale to influencing the wider systems that create and reinforce poverty?'	Different strategies suit different circumstances: (1) working with government; (2) operational expansion; (3) lobbying and advocacy; (4) networking and 'self-spreading' local initiatives. All have costs and benefits but implicit bias to institutional development and advocacy to control for dangers (the 'onion-skin' strategy): 'The degree to which a strategy or mix of strategies compromises the logic by which legitimacy is claimed provides a useful test of whether organizational self-interest is subordinating mission.'	*Making a Difference: NGOs and Development in a Changing World.* *Scaling-up NGO Impact on Development: Learning from Experience* (DIP)
Manchester 1994	NGO growth raises questions about performance, accountability and relations with funding sources: • 'Will NGOs be co-opted into the New Policy Agenda as the favored child, or magic bullet for development?' • 'If so, what does that do to NGO mission and relationships: "too close to the powerful, too far from the powerless"?'	Problems are not inevitable – they depend on the quality of relationships between actors and how 'room to maneuver' is exploited. Therefore, negotiation between stakeholders is vital, requiring innovation in performance assessment, accountability mechanisms, and relations with funders. 'The developmental impact of NGOs, their capacity to attract support, and their legitimacy as actors in development, will rest much more clearly on their ability to demonstrate that they can perform effectively and are accountable for their actions. It is none to soon for NGOs to put their house in order.'	*Beyond the Magic Bullet: NGO Performance and Accountability in the Post Cold-War World* (x 2) *NGOs, States and Donors: Too Close for Comfort?* (x 2) *Too Close For Comfort: The Impact of Official Aid on NGOs* (WD) *Policy Arena: New Roles and Challenges for NGOs* (JID)

another of the conference books put it, become 'too close to the powerful, and too far from the powerless' (Hulme and Edwards, 1997: 275)?

At the time, our conclusion was that such problems were not inevitable. Whether they arise depends on the *quality* of the relationships that develop between actors, and on how each NGO uses its 'room-to-maneuver' to control for the costs of growth and donor-dependence. Therefore, negotiation between stakeholders is vital, requiring innovation in performance assessment, accountability mechanisms, and relations with funding agencies. 'The developmental impact of NGOs,' we concluded, 'their capacity to attract support, and their legitimacy as actors in development, will rest much more clearly on their ability to demonstrate that they can perform effectively and are accountable for their actions. It is none too soon for NGOs to put their house in order' (Edwards and Hulme, 1995: 227–8).

Since 1994 there have been some important innovations in this respect, like the Humanitarian Accountability Project; the rise of self-certification and accreditation schemes, seals of approval and codes of conduct among child sponsorship agencies and other NGOs; the development of formal compacts between government and the non-profit sector in the UK, Canada and elsewhere; the Global Accountability Project in London; ActionAid's ALNAP system; and simple but powerful things like publicizing the financial accounts of an NGO on public bulletin boards that are being encouraged by MANGO and other organizations (Jordan and van Tuijl, 2007).

In retrospect, however, NGOs did not heed this call with sufficient attention, and are now suffering from it in a climate in which, unlike ten years ago, weaknesses in NGO accountability are being used as cover for an attack on political grounds against voices that certain interests wish to silence. Examples of such attacks include the NGO Watch project at the American Enterprise Institute, the Rushford Report in Washington DC, and NGO Monitor in Jerusalem. Stronger NGO accountability mechanisms won't do away with politically motivated attacks like these, but they would surely help to expose them for what they are.

In 1999, the Third NGO Conference took place in Birmingham, framed by a rapidly changing global context that posed some deeper questions about NGO roles, relationships, capacities and accountabilities. 'Adapt or die' was the subtext of that meeting, whose organizers highlighted three key sets of changes:

> First, globalization reshapes patterns of poverty, inequality and insecurity, calling for greater global integration of NGO strategies and more 'development work' of different kinds in the North;
> Second, 'complex political emergencies' reshape patterns of humanitarian action, implying more difficult choices for NGOs about intervention and the need to re-assert their independence from government interests; and,

Third, a move from foreign aid as the key driver of international cooperation to a focus on rules, standards and support for those who are most vulnerable to the negative effects of global change implies greater NGO involvement in the processes and institutions of global governance, both formal and informal. (Edwards et al., 1999: 2)

The thrust of these changes is clearly visible in the titles of the books that emerged from the Birmingham conference – *NGO Futures: Beyond Aid* (Fowler, 2000); *New Roles and Relevance* (Lewis and Wallace, 2000); and *Global Citizen Action* (Edwards and Gaventa, 2001) – holding out the promise of transnational organizing among equals for systemic change as opposed to a secondary role shaped by the continued asymmetries of the foreign aid world.

This changing context, we believed, gave rise to four key challenges resulting from the evolution of a more political role for development NGOs in emerging systems of global governance, debate and decision making:

1. how to mobilize a genuinely inclusive civil society at all levels of the world system, as opposed to a thin layer of elite NGOs operating internationally;
2. how to hold other (more powerful) organizations accountable for their actions and ensure that they respond to social and environmental needs – something that implicitly demanded reforms in NGO accountability;
3. How to ensure that international regimes are implemented effectively and to the benefit of poor people and poor countries (getting to grips with 'democratic deficits' in global institutions and protecting 'policy space' for Southern countries to embark on their own development strategies); and
4. how to ensure that gains at the global level are translated into concrete benefits at the grassroots, translating abstract commitments made in international conferences into actions that actually enforce rules and regulations on the ground (Edwards et al., 1999: 10).

NGOs, we concluded, must move from 'development as delivery to development as leverage', and this would require the development of more equal relationships with other civic actors, especially in the South, new capacities (like bridging and mediation), and stronger downward or horizontal accountability mechanisms.

Since 1999 there have certainly been some examples of innovations like these, like the 'Make Poverty History Campaign' in the UK, which has developed stronger coordination mechanisms among development and non-development NGOs, and other organizations in UK civil society, and the development of much more sophisticated advocacy campaigns on aid, debt and trade.

If one believes that there is a credible chain of logic linking these three conferences, their outputs, and those of other similar efforts that were ongoing during the same period, with the emergence of a more thoughtful and professional development NGO sector; and, going one stage further, linking the emergence of that sector with at least the possibility of a greater aggregate impact on development; then one can begin to answer the question posed by *this* volume in the affirmative, breaking down those answers by country context, type of organization, type of impact, longevity, sector, issue and so on in the ways that other chapters try to do.

I think one would have to argue an extreme version of the counterfactual to say otherwise – in other words, to claim that the world would be a better place *without* the rise of development NGOs, however patchy their impact may have been, especially given the huge and complex challenges that face all NGOs in their work today. Perhaps I am not setting the bar very high in making this point, but in critiques of NGOs it is often forgotten. There *has* been a positive change in the distribution of opportunities to participate in development debates and in democracy more broadly, and in the capacities and connections required by NGOs to play their roles effectively, even if global trends in poverty and power relations, inequality, environmental degradation and violence are not all heading in a positive direction.

In other words, some of the preconditions, or foundations, for progress are being laid, brick by brick, organization by organization, community by community, vote by vote. If one believes that democratic theory works, then, over time, more transparency, greater accountability and stronger capacities for monitoring *will* feed through into deeper changes in systems and structures. Civil society may yet fulfil Kofi Annan's prediction as the 'new superpower' – a statement that was largely rhetorical but contained at least a grain of truth. And as context for that conclusion, think back thirteen years to the first Manchester Conference when NGOs were still something of a backwater in international affairs. No one could say the same thing today.

Where We Were Wrong, and Why It Is Important

So, so far, so good. There was one major area, however, in which the analysis of previous conferences was seriously awry, and it has some significant consequences for the NGO world going forward. This was the prediction that foreign aid would be replaced by a different, healthier and more effective system of international cooperation in which the drivers of development and change would no longer be based around North–South transfers and foreign intervention.

In fact, the clear decline in real aid flows that was observed between 1992 to 1999 from US$57,950 million to US$49,062 million (German and Randel,

2004) – exactly coinciding with the first three NGO Conferences – turns out to have been an atypical period in recent history. Backed by a growing coalition of celebrities, charities, politicians, journalists and academics, we are firmly back in a period of rising real aid flows, up to around $78 billion in 2004, set to grow still further, and perhaps even reaching the promised land of $150–200 billion a year estimated to be required to meet the United Nations Millennium Development Goals. The critical literature on aid effectiveness, the importance of institutions, and the primacy of politics that emerged during the 1990s has largely been marginalized from the current discourse (Edwards, 2004b). From Jeffrey Sachs to Bob Geldof, the new orthodoxy asserts that more money *will* solve Africa's problems, and, if we add in an American twist, make the world safe from terrorism too.

Of course, in 1999 no one could have predicted some of the key reasons behind this reverse – principally the events of 9/11 and the ensuing 'war on terror', or the recent catastrophic tsunami in Asia – but previous conferences were also guilty of confusing normative and empirical arguments. Much of the discussion at the Birmingham Conference was driven by what the organizers and participants *wanted* to see happen in the future, not necessarily by a hard-nosed analysis of likely trends and opportunities.

Why is this important for the rest of my argument? The reason is that the perseverance of the traditional aid paradigm, even in its modified version of Millennium Challenge Accounts, Poverty Reduction Strategy Papers, International Finance Facilities and the rest of the current paraphernalia of aid reform, makes any kind of quantum leap in NGO impact much more difficult to achieve because it weakens the incentives for deep innovation by providing a continued 'security blanket' for current practice. Of course, one can read this as a much more positive story, particularly when calls for aid are coupled with serious action on debt relief and trade justice. And I don't mean to imply that investment in developing countries is irrelevant – simply that is difficult to detach the dysfunctional aspects of the traditional aid paradigm from the injection of ever-larger amounts of money by powerful national interests into societies with weak institutions and fragile systems of accountability. To explain what I mean, let me move to the second way in which I've chosen to answer the questions I posed at the beginning of my argument.

The 'Larry Summers Test'

I recently attended a dinner at which the keynote speaker was Larry Summers, ex-president of Harvard University. After his speech was over, one brave member of the audience – a leading Arab academic – asked him point blank whether he thought that America 'has been a force for good in the world'. His answer was unconvincing, but interesting, since he said that it would be impossible to give a sensible answer to that question in any general sense. There are too many 'ifs, buts and maybes', and too many variations of detail, context and circumstance. However, he went on to say, one *can* ask whether America 'did the right thing' at those few moments in history when a certain course of action was unquestionably important – such as intervention in World War I, World War II, and the Cold War. And in those cases, the answer was unequivocally 'yes'.

Of course, one can dispute Summers's conclusion, but I think the way in which he repositioned the question is useful in relation to the topic of development NGOs and their impact. Instead of trying to generalize across the huge diversity of the NGO universe, we can ask ourselves whether NGOs 'did the right thing' on the really big issues of our times.

On the positive side of the balance sheet, I think development NGOs have helped to do the following, albeit with limited practical results thus far:

- changed the terms of the debate about globalization, leading to the emergence of a new orthodoxy about the need to manage the downside of this process, level the playing field, and expand 'policy space' for developing countries;
- cemented an intellectual commitment to participation and human rights as basic principles of development and development assistance; and,
- kept the spotlight on the need for reforms in international institutions and global governance on issues such as unfair terms of trade and invest-ment, global warming, Africa, and the kind of warped humanitarian intervention represented by the war in Iraq.

On the other hand, there is a less positive side to this story when one looks beyond the short-term gains that have been made in the development discourse to grapple with the underlying goals that NGOs were set up to pursue. In my view development NGOs have not 'stood up to be counted' sufficiently on the following crucial questions. They have not been very in-novative in finding ways to lever deep changes in the systems and structures that perpetuate poverty and the abuse of human rights, despite the recent boom in Corporate Social Responsibility and public–private partnerships. The 'onion', to go back to Alan Fowler's phrase, is still incomplete, made up by layers of fairly conventional development projects and advocacy work. For example, development NGOs have not changed power relations on anything like the necessary scale in the crucial areas of class, gender and race. They have not faced up to the challenges of internal change – changes in personal attitudes, values and behaviour – in any significant way. They have not established strong connections with social movements that are more embedded in the political processes that are essential to sustained change. They have not come to grips with the rise of religion as one of the most powerful forces for change in the world today, increasingly expressed in fundamentalism and demanding large-scale action to build bridges between pluralists in different religious traditions.

Equally important, development NGOs have not innovated in any significant sense in the form and nature of their organizational relationships. For example, little concrete attention is paid to downward accountability or the importance of generating diverse, local sources of funds for so-called 'partners' in the South (a weakness that underpins many other problems, including legitimacy and political threats to organizations perceived as 'pawns of foreign interests'). They have internalized functions that should have been distributed across other organizations – local fundraising by international NGOs inside developing countries (or 'markets' to use a telling common phrase) provides a good example, and there are others – franchising global brands instead of supporting authentic expressions of indigenous civil society, and crowding out Southern participation in knowledge creation and advocacy in order to increase their own voice and profile, as if the only people with anything useful to say about world development were Oxfam and a handful of others.

Of course, there are exceptions to all of these generalizations. I would single out ActionAid for the changes it has made, and on a smaller scale I was struck by the Institute for Agriculture and Trade Policy's decision to transfer spaces on the NGO delegation to the Cancun trade talks from Northern NGOs to groups from the South in 2004. But these examples tend to get noticed because they are exceptions that prove the rule. The rules of the international NGO world seem to stay pretty much the same. Does anyone believe that development NGOs still aim to 'work themselves out of a job', that old NGO mantra? Maybe it was never true, but there isn't much evidence to suggest that it is taken seriously today. Let's face it: NGOs are a major growth industry, back in the 'comfort zone', and set to continue along that path. There has been little real transfer of roles or capacity in either 'delivery' or 'leverage'. It's almost as though they have taken the entire 'onion' and swallowed it whole!

NGOs may give a nod in the direction of 'levelling the playing field', diversifying NGO representation in the international arena, empowering marginalized voices, building the capacity of actors in the South for independent action, helping them to sustain themselves through indigenous resources, 'handing over the stick', becoming more accountable to beneficiaries and so on, but in practical terms the 'institutional imperatives' of growth and market share still dominate over the 'developmental imperatives' of individual, organizational and social transformation (see Table 2.2). And

Table 2.2 NGO imperatives

Developmental imperatives	Institutional imperatives
• Bottom line: empowering marginalized groups for independent action. • Downplay the role of intermediary; encourage marginalized groups to speak with their own voice. • Democratic governance; less hierarchy; more reciprocity; a focus on stakeholders. • Multiple accountability, honesty, learning from mistakes, transparency, sharing of information. • Maintain independence and flexibility; take risks. • Address the causes of poverty; defend values of service and solidarity. • Long term goals drive decision making; programme criteria lead. • Rooted in broader movements for change; alliances with others; look outwards. • Maximize resources at the 'sharp end'; cooperate to reduce overheads and transaction costs. • Maintain focus on continuity, critical mass and distinctive competence.	• Bottom line: size, income, profile, market share. • Accentuate the role of intermediary; speak on behalf of marginalized groups. • More hierarchy; less reciprocity; a focus on donors and recipients. • Accountability upwards, secrecy, repeat mistakes, exaggerate successes and disguise failures. • Increasing dependence on government funds; standardization; bureaucracy. • Deal with symptoms: internalize orthodoxies even when antithetical to mission. • Short term interests drive decision making; marketing criteria lead. • Isolated from broader movements for change; incorporate others into your own structures; look inwards. • Duplicate delivery mechanisms (e.g. separate field offices); resources consumed increasingly by fixed costs. • Opportunism – go where the funds are; increasing spread of activities and countries.

Source: Edwards 1996.

– returning to the quotation I cited from *Making a Difference* earlier in this chapter – this failure places an important, continuing question mark against the legitimacy of development NGOs and their role in the contemporary world. It is these failings, I believe, that stand in the way of increasing NGO impact in the future, and it is these failings that represent the 'elephant in the room' of my title. We don't want to recognize the beast, but we know it's there. And while it remains in the room – a hulking, largely silent presence – NGOs will never achieve the impact they say they want to achieve, because their leverage over the drivers of long-term change will continue to be weak.

One can read this story under the conventional rubric of institutional inertia, defensiveness and the difficulties of raising money for new and unfamiliar roles. But I think something more fundamental is going on. Underlying this situation is a much broader struggle between two visions of the future – one that I call 'international development', and the other 'global civil society', for want of a better phrase.

The 'international development' vision is predicated on continued North–South transfers of resources and ideas as its centrepiece, temporarily under the umbrella of US hegemony and its drive to engineer terrorism out of the world, if necessary by refashioning whole societies in the image of liberal, free-market democracy. This vision requires the expansion of traditional NGO roles in humanitarian assistance, the provision of social safety-nets, and 'civil society building' (crudely translated as support to advocacy and service-delivery NGOs; Edwards, 2004a). It privileges technical solutions over politics, and the volume of resources over their use. The role of the North is to 'help' the less-fortunate and backward South; if possible, to 'save it' from drifting ever further away from modernity, defined as liberal market democracy (God forbid there is a viable alternative, like Islam); and if that fails, then at least to 'prevent it' from wreaking havoc on Northern societies. The 'war on terror', I would argue, reinforces and exacerbates the worst elements of the traditional foreign aid paradigm.

The 'Global Civil Society' vision, and here I'm exaggerating to make a point, takes its cue from cosmopolitan articulations of an international system in which international law trumps national interests, and countries – with increasingly direct involvement by their citizens – negotiate solutions to global problems through democratic principles, the fair sharing of burdens, respect for local context and autonomy, and a recognition of the genuinely interlocking nature of causes and effects in the contemporary world. This vision, to be successful, requires action in all of the areas in which I think development NGOs have been found wanting – levelling the playing field, empowering Southern voices, building constituencies for changes in global consumption and production patterns, and injecting real accountability into the system, including personal accountability for the choices that NGOs make. The struggle for *global* civil society can't be separated from the struggle for *personal* change, since it those changes that underpin the difficult decision to hand over control, share power, and live a life that is consistent with our principles. In this vision our role is to act as 'critical friends', as I put it on the last page of *Future Positive*, sharing in 'the loving but forceful encounters *between equals* who journey together towards the land of the true and the beautiful' (Edwards, 2004b: 233).

Recent history can be read as a reversal in what the Birmingham NGO Conference predicted would be a steady, long-term transition from the 'international development' model to 'global civil society'. Led by the United States, we are seeing a retreat from the cosmopolitan vision and a return to culturally bound fundamentalisms, the hegemony of the nation-state, and the belief that the world can indeed be remade in the image of the dominant powers through foreign intervention – with Iraq as the paradigm case. That, at root, is why there are so many attacks today on the institutions, or even the idea, of global governance, the rise of non-state involvement and the threats it supposedly carries, the legitimacy of international law, and the transnational dimensions of democracy – as opposed to the domestic implantation of versions of democracy in other peoples' countries.

It is no accident that hostility to international NGOs forms a key plank of neoconservative thinking in America today. 'Post-democratic challenges to American democratic sovereignty should be clearly defined and resisted', writes John Fonte of the Hudson Institute, one of the key think-tanks of Neo-Conservatism. 'NGOs that consistently act as if they are strategic opponents of the democratic sovereignty of the American nation should be treated as such. They should not be supported or recognized at international conferences, nor permitted access to government officials' (Fonte, 2004). 'NGOs should be at the top of every Conservative's watch list', says Elaine Chao, President Bush's current secretary of labor. So, 'you have been warned'. No matter how much additional foreign aid gets pumped through the international system, NGOs are unlikely to get very far unless they recognize that there are much bigger issues at stake. This is nothing less than a battle for the soul of world politics, and NGOs need to decide which side they want to take. I was convinced in Birmingham in 1999, and I'm even more convinced today, that we need to break free from the foreign aid paradigm in order to liberate ourselves to achieve the impact that we so desperately want.

Conclusion

To sum up, my case is that the return of foreign aid to favor provides a security blanket for NGOs who might otherwise have been forced to change their ways. There may, of course be more unforeseen events in the near future that, like 9/11, provide an external shock to the system large enough to interrupt current trends and initiate new directions – or, as in this case, return us to old ways of doing business. This might happen to development NGOs, for example, if aid donors ever got serious about cutting intermediaries (national and international) out of the equation,

Figure 2.1   Trajectories of NGO impact

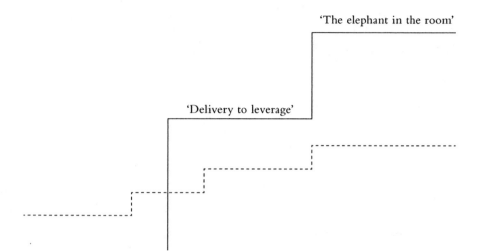

but I don't think this is very likely – the donors need a conduit on which they can rely.

Therefore I see only incremental increases in impact – shown by the hatched line in Figure 2.1 – unless NGOs can break out of the foreign aid box, as a few pioneers are already doing. As they have recognized, there is a much healthier framework for civic action available to us if we decide to choose it. In my view, the advances made by development NGOs throughout the 1990s – spurred on significantly but not exclusively by the Manchester Conferences – represented a much bigger leap in NGO strategy and potential impact, shown by the solid line in Figure 2.1. Dealing effectively with the 'elephant in the room' represents the next such quantum leap.

In conclusion, the question facing development NGOs today is the same question that faced participants in the first NGO Conference in Manchester in 1992, albeit framed in a somewhat different context. That question is less about what NGOs have achieved in the absolute sense, since they can never achieve enough, and more about how they can achieve more, however well they think they are doing. How satisfied are NGOs with their current performance? Do they wait until another 9/11 hits the system and shakes them out of their complacency, or can they 'bite the bullet' and implement their own gradual reforms now? Perhaps when the development NGO community meets again in Manchester in ten years time, there will be a different set of answers on the table.

Note

1. The views expressed in this chapter are the author's personal views and should not be taken to represent the views or policies of the Ford Foundation.

References

Edwards, M. (1996) 'International Development NGOs: Legitimacy, Accountability, Regulation and Roles', in *Meeting the Challenge of Change: The Report of the Commission on the Future of the Voluntary Sector*, Commission on the Future of the Voluntary Sector, London.

Edwards, M. (2004a) *Civil Society*, Polity Press, Cambridge.

Edwards, M. (2004b) *Future Positive: International Cooperation in the 21st Century* (rev.edn), Earthscan, London.

Edwards, M., and J. Gaventa (eds) (2001) *Global Citizen Action*, Lynne Rienner, Boulder CO, and Earthscan, London.

Edwards, M., and D. Hulme (eds) (1992) *Making a Difference: NGOs and Development in a Changing World*, Earthscan, London.

Edwards, M., and D. Hulme (eds) (1995) *Beyond the Magic Bullet: NGO Performance and Accountability in the Post Cold-War World*, Earthscan, London and Kumarian Press, West Hartford CT.

Edwards, M., D. Hulme and T. Wallace (1999) 'NGOs in a Global Future: Marrying Local Delivery to World-wide Leverage', *Public Administration and Development* 19(2): 117–36.

Fonte, J. (2004) 'Democracy's Trojan Horse', *The National Interest*, Summer: 117–27.

Fowler, A. (ed.) (2000) NGO Futures: Beyond Aid, Special Issue of *Third World Quarterly*.

German T., and J. Randel (2004) 'Global Pledges Sacrificed to National Interests', in J. Randel, T. German and D. Ewing (eds), *The Reality of Aid*, Development Initiatives, IBON Books, Manila, and Zed Books, London, pp. 181–95.

Hulme, D., and M. Edwards (eds) (1997) *Too Close for Comfort? NGOs, States and Donors*, Macmillan, London, and St Martins Press, New York.

Jordan, L., and P. van Tuijl (eds) (2007) *NGO Accountability: Politics, Principles and Innovations*, Earthscan, London.

Lewis, D., and T. Wallace (eds) (2000) *New Roles and Relevance: Development NGOs and the Challenge of Change*, Kumarian Press, West Hartford CT.

PART II

NGO Alternatives under Pressure

3

Challenges to Participation, Citizenship and Democracy: Perverse Confluence and Displacement of Meanings

Evelina Dagnino

The main purpose of this chapter is to discuss the challenges presented by recent developments in Brazil – but also elsewhere – to the participation of civil society in the building of democracy and social justice. The chapter will discuss first the existence of a *perverse confluence* between participatory and neoliberal political projects. From my point of view, this confluence characterizes the contemporary scenario of the struggle for deepening democracy in Brazil and in most of Latin America. Then it will examine the dispute over different meanings of citizenship, civil society and participation that constitute core referents for the understanding of that confluence, and the form that it takes in the Brazilian context.

The Perverse Confluence of Political Projects

The process of democratic construction in Brazil today faces an important dilemma whose roots are to be found in a perverse confluence of two different processes, linked to two different political projects. On the one hand, we have a process of enlargement of democracy, which expresses itself in the creation of public spaces and the increasing participation of civil society in discussion and decision-making processes related to public issues and policies. The formal landmark of this process was the Constitution of 1988, which consecrated the principle of the participation of civil society. The main forces behind this process grew out of a participatory project constructed since the 1980s around the extension of citizenship and the deepening of democracy. This project emerged from the struggle against the military regime, a struggle led by sectors of civil society, among which social movements played an important role.

Two elements of this struggle are particularly relevant to our argument here. First is the re-establishment of formal democracy, with free elections and party reorganization. These changes made it possible for the partici-patory project which had been configured inside civil society and which guided the political practice of several of its sectors, to be taken into the realm of state power, at the level of the municipal and state executives and of legislatures, and, more recently, of the federal executive. Indeed, the 1990s saw numerous examples of actors making this transition from civil society to the state. Second, during the 1990s the confrontation that had formerly characterized the relations between state and civil society was largely replaced by a new belief in the possibility of joint action between the two. The possibility of such joint actions itself reflected the extent to which the principle of participation had become a distinguishing feature of this project, underlying the very effort to create public spaces.

While this project traces its roots back to the late 1970s, the election of Collor in 1989 and the more general state strategy of neoliberal adjustment underlay the emergence of a quite distinct project. This project revolved around the fashioning of a reduced, minimal state that progressively exempts itself from its role as guarantor of rights by shrinking its social responsibilities and transferring them to civil society. In this context, we argue that the last decade has been marked by a perverse confluence between the participatory project and this neoliberal project. The perversity lies in the fact that, even if these projects point in opposite and even antagonistic directions, each of them not only requires an active and proactive civil society, but also uses a number of common concepts and points of reference. In particular, notions such as citizenship, participation and civil society are central elements in both projects, even if they are being used with very different meanings. This coincidence at the discursive level hides fundamental distinctions and divergences between the two projects, obscuring them through the use of a common vocabulary as well as of institutional mechanisms that at first sight seem quite similar. Through a set of symbolic operations, or discur-sive shifts, marked by a common vocabulary which obscures divergences and contradictions, a displacement of meanings becomes effective. In the process, this perverse confluence creates an image of apparent homogeneity among different interests and discourses, concealing conflict and diluting the dispute between these two projects.

This perversity is clearly perceived by some civil society activists. These would include, for example, those engaged in participatory experiences such as the Management Councils (Conselhos gestores), members of NGOs engaged in partnerships with the state, members of social movements and people who, in one way or another, participate in these experiences or have struggled for their creation, all the while believing in their democratizing potential (Dagnino, 2002). In most of the spaces that are ostensibly open to the participation of civil society in public policies, state actors are in practice unwilling to share their decision-making power with respect to the formulation of public policies. Rather, their basic intention is to have the organizations of civil society assume functions and responsibilities restricted to the implementation and execution of these policies, providing services formerly considered to be duties of the state itself.

Some civil society organizations accept this circumscription of their roles and of the meaning of 'participation', and in so doing contribute to its legitimation. Others, however, react against it and perceive this perverse confluence as posing a dilemma that expresses itself in questions regarding their own political role: 'what are we doing here?', 'what project are we strengthening?', 'wouldn't the gains be greater with some other kind of strategy which prioritizes the organization and mobilization of society instead of engaging in joint actions with the state?'

The recognition of the centrality of this perverse confluence – and the dilemma it poses – demands that we take a closer look at its mode of operation and its analytical consequences.

Perverse Confluence and the Redefinition of Meanings

The implementation of the neoliberal project, which requires the shrinking of the social responsibilities of the state and their transference to civil society, marks a significant inflection in political culture – in Brazil as well as in most countries of Latin America. Indeed, though less recognized and discussed than the restructuring of state and economy that result from this project, neoliberal transformation has also involved a redefinition of – and struggles over – a variety of cultural meanings and political concepts. What has made this transformation particularly interesting in the Brazilian case is that this implementation of neoliberalism has had to confront a consolidated participatory project that has been maturing for more than twenty years. During that period, this participatory project found significant support within the particularly complex and dense civil society that characterizes Brazil. It was because of this support that this project was able to inspire the creation of democratizing participatory experiments such as management councils, participatory budgets, sectoral chambers, and a vast array of fora, conferences and other societal public spaces and collaborations.

In other words, the neoliberal project found in Brazil a relatively consolidated contender, evidently not hegemonic but able to constitute a field of dispute. The existence of this contender and of this dispute led the forces linked to the neoliberal project to assume particular strategies and forms of action. To the extent that these strategies and actions differ from those adopted globally, their specificity derives from the extent to which the neoliberal project is forced to engage with, and establish ways of being meaningful, to this opposing field. The need for such engagement and interlocution is accentuated within those public spaces where these two projects meet face to face. Indeed, given the 1988 Constitution's recognition of the principle of participation, social movements began to participate institutionally in those formal spaces that became part of the State apparatus (councils, etc.) (Carvalho, 1997; GECD, 2000). Thus much of the articulation between the neoliberal project that occupies most of the State apparatus and the participatory project takes place precisely through those sectors of civil society that committed themselves to state–society coordination and who therefore became most active in Brazil's new participatory settings and in joint actions with the state; that is to say, those sectors of civil society that were by and large supportive of the participatory project.

It is in this context that it becomes urgent for both analysts and activists to make explicit the distinctions and divergences between these two projects in order to elucidate the dilemma posed by the perverse confluence. It is our contention that if we are to do this, one point of departure, both at a theoretical level and in defining an empirical research agenda, is the notion of 'political project'. We are using the term *political project* in a sense close to Gramsci, to designate those sets of beliefs, interests, conceptions of the world, and representations of what life in society should be that guide the political action of different subjects and play a central role in the struggle to build hegemony (Dagnino, 2002; Dagnino et al., 2006). One of the main virtues of such an approach (Dagnino, 1998, 2002, 2004) is that it insists that culture and politics are necessarily linked. Thus our view of political projects is that they cannot merely be understood as strategies of political action in the strict sense, but rather that they express, convey and produce meanings that come to integrate broader cultural matrices. It is in this sense that we referred earlier to the idea that the neoliberal project has also constituted a cultural inflection.

A careful effort to unpick the different political projects at play helps uncover and understand the ways in which the perverse confluence has blurred particular distinctions and divergences. In the following, we seek to do this by examining the displacement of meaning that occurs in such a context with respect to three deeply interconnected notions: civil society, participation and citizenship. These notions and displacements are central to the forms that have been taken by the perverse confluences between the neoliberal and participatory projects. On the one hand, they were core ideas in the origins and consolidation of the participatory project. On the other hand, they have been central ideas in mediating between the two projects. They are, in short, common references with distinct and even contradictory meanings. Furthermore, beyond their specific roles in the Brazilian scenario, these notions are also, to different degrees, constitutive of the neoliberal project at the global level.

The redefinition of the notion of civil society and of what it designates is probably the most visible (and, therefore, the most studied) displacement produced under the hegemony of the neoliberal project. For this reason, I will not explore it at length here. It should be sufficient to mention several well-known elements of this displacement: the accelerated growth and the new role played by non-governmental organizations; the emergence of the so-called 'third sector' and of entrepreneurial foundations, with their strong emphasis on a redefined philanthropy (Fernandes, 1994; Landim, 1993; Alvarez, 1999; Paoli, 2002; Salamon, 1997); and the marginalization, or what some authors refer to as 'the criminalization' (Oliveira, 1997), of social movements. This reconfiguration of civil society, in which non-governmental organizations tend increasingly to replace social movements, has resulted in a growing identification of 'civil society' with NGOs – indeed, the meaning of 'civil society' is more and more restricted to NGOs and sometimes used as a mere synonym for the 'third sector'. The emergence of the notion of a 'third sector' (the others being the state and the market) as a surrogate for civil society is particularly expressive of this attempt to implement a 'minimalist' conception of politics and to nullify the extension of public spaces for political deliberation that had been achieved by the democratizing struggles. 'Civil society' is thus reduced to those sectors whose behaviour is 'acceptable' according to dominant standards – what one analyst has called 'five-star civil society' (Silva, 2000).

The relations between state and NGOs exemplify the idea of perverse confluence. Endowed with technical competence and social insertion, 'reliable' interlocutors among the various possible interlocutors in civil society, NGOs are frequently seen as the ideal partners by sectors of the state engaged in transferring their responsibilities to the sphere of civil society. For their part it is extremely difficult for NGOs to reject such a role (Galgani and Magnólia, 2002) when these partnerships seem to present them with a real opportunity to have a positive effect – fragmented, momentary, provisory and limited, but positive – on the reduction of inequality and the improvement of living conditions of the social sectors involved. The proliferation and visibility of NGOs is, on the one hand, a reflection of a global neoliberal paradigm, in the sense that NGOs constitute a response to the demands of structural adjustment. On the other hand, with the growing abandonment of the organic links to social movements which had characterized many NGOs in former periods, the increasing political autonomy of NGOs creates a peculiar situation in which these organizations are responsible to the international agencies which finance them and to the state which contracts them as service providers, but not to civil society, whose representatives they claim to be, nor to the social sectors whose interests they bear, nor to any other organ of a truly public character. As well-intentioned as they might be, their activities ultimately express the desires of their directors.

Perhaps less explored, these reconfigurations of civil society also have important implications for the issue of representation. The question of representation assumes varied facets and/or is understood in different ways by various actors of civil society. If we take the case of the Landless Movement (MST), its capacity to pressure and to represent is, for example, evident in the protests and mass demonstrations it organizes – just as the large numbers of participants in participatory budgeting processes also reflect great capacity for mobilization. Such a capacity is here understood in the classic sense of representation. But there is also a displacement in the understanding of representation, as much by the state as on the part of actors in civil society. In the case of NGOs, for example, the capacity to represent seems to be displaced onto the kind of competence they have: the state sees them as representative interlocutors in so far as they have a specific knowledge that comes from their connection (past or present) with certain social sectors: youth, blacks, women, carriers of HIV, environmental movements, and so on (Teixeira, 2002, 2004). Bearers of this specific capacity, many NGOs also come to see themselves as 'representatives of civil society' (in a particular understanding of the notion of representation). They further consider that their capacity to represent derives from the fact that they express diffuse interests in society, to which they 'would give voice'. This representation comes, however, from a coincidence among these interests and those defended by the NGOs, rather than from any explicit articulation, or organic relationship with social actors.

This displacement of the notion of representation is obviously not innocent, neither in its intentions nor in its political consequences. The most extreme example is the composition of the Council of the Comunidade Solidária, created by the Cardoso government in 1995, where the representation of civil society took place through invitations to individuals with high 'visibility' in society – such as television performers or persons who write frequently for newspapers, and so on. This particular understanding of the notion of representation reduces it to social visibility, as made possible by various types of media. In the case of NGOs, this displacement is sustained by the organizations themselves, as well as by governments and international agencies that seek reliable partners and fear the politicization of social movements and workers' organizations, and by the media, frequently for similar motives.

Closely connected to these processes, the notion of *participation of civil society*, which has constituted the core of the democratizing project, has been appropriated and re-signified by neoliberal forces during the last decade. Such redefinition follows the same lines as those characterizing the reconfiguration of 'civil society', with the growing emphasis on 'solidary participation', 'voluntary work' and the 'social responsibility' of individuals and private enterprises. The basic principle here seems to be the adoption of a privatizing, individualistic perspective, replacing and re-signifying the collective meaning of social participation. The very idea of 'solidarity', the great banner of this redefined participation, is stripped of its original collective and political meaning and rests instead in the moral, private domain.

This principle is also very effective in an additional displacement of meaning, depoliticizing participation and dispensing with public spaces where the debate of the very objectives of participation can take place. In this process the political meaning and democratizing potential of public spaces is replaced by strictly individualized ways of dealing with issues such as social inequality and poverty.

On the other hand, in most of the spaces open to the participation of civil society in public policies, the effective sharing of the power of decision with respect to the formulation of public policies faces immense difficulties. As mentioned before, most state sectors not only resist sharing their exclusive control over decision-making but also attribute a specific role to civil society, which is the provision of public services formerly considered duties of the state itself. The role of so-called 'social organizations', through which the participation of civil society was explicitly recognized in the administrative reform of the Brazilian state (Bresser Pereira, 1996), is reduced to this function and clearly excluded from decision-making power, which is reserved to the state 'strategic nucleus'. Here again, the crucial political meaning of participation, conceived by the participatory project as an effective sharing of power between state and civil society through the exercise of deliberation within the new public spaces, is radically redefined as and reduced to management (*gestão*). In fact, managerial and entrepreneurial approaches, imported from the realm of private administration, have been increasingly adopted in joint actions by state and civil society (Tatagiba, 2006).

The notion of *citizenship* offers perhaps the most dramatic case of this process of meaning displacement − in two senses. First, because it was through the notion of citizenship that the participatory project was able to obtain its most important political and cultural gains by redefining the contents of citizenship in a way that penetrated deeply into the political and cultural scenario of Brazilian society (Dagnino, 1994, 1998). Second, because such a displacement is linked to the handling of what constitutes our most critical issue: poverty.

The extent of the displacement of meaning of citizenship can be better understood if we examine briefly the recent history of this notion and the role it played in the democratization process, not only in Brazil but in Latin America as a whole (Dagnino, 2005). Increasingly adopted since the late 1980s and 1990s by Latin American popular movements, excluded sectors, trade unions and left parties as a central element of their political strategies, the notion of citizenship has become a common reference among social movements – such as those of women, blacks and ethnic minorities, homosexuals, retired and senior citizens, consumers, environmentalists, urban and rural workers, and groups organized around urban issues such as housing, health, education, unemployment, and violence (Foweraker, 1995; Foweraker and Landman, 1997; Alvarez et al., 1998). These movements have found reference to citizenship not only to be useful as a tool for their particular struggles but also as a powerful concept for articulating links among them. The general demand for equal rights embedded in the predominant conception of citizenship has been extended by such movements and used as a vehicle for making more specific demands related to their particular concerns. In this process, the cultural dimension of citizenship has been emphasized, incorporating contemporary concerns with subjectivities, identities and the right to difference. Thus, on the one hand, the construction of a new notion of citizenship has come to be seen as reaching far beyond the acquisition of legal rights, requiring the constitution of active social subjects identifying what they consider to be their rights and struggling for their recognition. On the other hand, this emphasis on the cultural dimension of citizenship has made explicit the need for a radical transformation of those cultural practices that reproduce inequality and exclusion throughout society.

Citizenship and the concept of rights have been particularly attractive because of the dual role they play in the debate among the various conceptions of democracy that characterize contemporary political struggle in Latin America. On one hand, the struggle organized around the recognition and extension of rights has helped to make the argument for the expansion and deepening of democracy much more concrete. On the other hand, the reference to citizenship has provided common ground and an articulatory principle for an immense diversity of social movements that have adopted the language of rights as a way of expressing their demands while escaping fragmentation and isolation. Thus the building of citizenship has been seen as at once a general struggle – for the expansion of democracy – that was able to incorporate a plurality of demands, and a set of particular struggles for rights (housing, education, health, etc.) whose success would expand democracy.

As the concept of citizenship has become increasingly influential, its meaning has quickly become an object of dispute. In the past decade it has been appropriated and re-signified in various ways by dominant sectors and the state. Thus, reflecting the effects of neoliberalism, citizenship has begun to be understood and promoted as mere individual integration into the market. At the same time and as part of the same process of structural adjustment, established rights have increasingly been withdrawn from workers throughout Latin America. Related to this, philanthropic projects of the so-called third sector have been expanding in number and scope in an attempt to confront the poverty and exclusion that convey their own version of citizenship.

Citizenship has become a prominent notion because it has been recognized as a crucial weapon not only in the struggle against social and economic exclusion and inequality but also in the broadening of dominant conceptions of politics. Thus, as Latin American social movements have redefined citizenship through their concrete struggles for a deepening of democracy, they have sought to change existing definitions of the political arena – its participants, its institutions, its processes, its agenda, and its scope (Alvarez et al., 1998). Adopting as its point of departure the conception of 'a right to have rights', this redefinition has supported the emergence of new social subjects actively identifying what they consider their rights and struggling for their recognition. In contrast to previous conceptions of citizenship as a strategy of the dominant classes and the state for the gradual and limited political incorporation of excluded sectors with the aim of greater social integration, or as a legal and political condition necessary for the establishment of capitalism, this is a conception of non citizens, of the excluded – a citizenship 'from below'.

While the concern of Latin American social movements with the need to assert a right to have rights is clearly related to extreme poverty and exclusion, it is also related to the *social authoritarianism* that pervades the unequal and hierarchical organization of social relations (Dagnino, 1998). Class, race and gender differences constitute the main bases for the forms of social classification that have historically pervaded our cultures, establishing different categories of people hierarchically distributed in their respective 'places' in society. Thus, for the excluded sectors, the perception of the political relevance of cultural meanings embedded in social practices is part of daily life. As part of the authoritarian, hierarchical social ordering of Latin American societies, to be poor means not only to experience economic, material deprivation but also to be subjected to cultural rules that convey a complete lack of recognition of poor people as bearers of rights. In what Telles (1994) has called the incivility embedded in that tradition, poverty is a sign of inferiority, a way of being in which individuals become unable to exercise their rights. The cultural deprivation imposed by the absolute absence of rights, which ultimately expresses itself as a suppression of human dignity, then becomes constitutive of material deprivation and political exclusion.

The perception that this culture of social authoritarianism is a dimension of exclusion additional to economic inequality and political subordination has constituted a significant element in the struggle to redefine citizenship. It has made clear that the struggle for rights – for the right to have rights – must be a political struggle against this pervasive authoritarianism. This lays the bases for a connection between culture and politics that has become embedded in the actions of urban popular collective movements. This connection has been fundamental in establishing common ground for articulation with other social movements that are more obviously cultural, such as the ethnic, women's, gay, ecology and human rights movements, in the pursuit of more egalitarian relations at all levels, helping to demarcate a distinctive, expanded view of democracy. The reference to rights and citizenship has come to constitute the core of a common ethical-political field in which many of these movements and other sectors of society have been able to share and mutually reinforce their struggle. This was reflected, for instance, in the emergence in the early 1990s of the *sindicato cidadão* (citizen trade union) in the context of a Brazilian labour movement that had been traditionally more inclined toward strict class-based conceptions (Rodrigues, 1997).

The perception that social authoritarianism itself structures exclusion has also made possible a broadening of the scope of citizenship, whose meaning has become far from restricted to the formal-legal acquisition of a set of rights under the political–judicial system. The struggle for citizenship has thus been presented as a project for a new sociability: a more egalitarian basis for social relations at all levels, new rules for living together in society and not only for incorporation into the political system in the strict sense. This more egalitarian commitment implies the recognition that the other is also a bearer of valid interests and legitimate rights. It also implies the constitution of a public dimension to society in which rights can be consolidated as public parameters for dialogue, debate and the negotiation of conflict, making possible the reconfiguration of an ethical dimension of social life. This project has unsettled not only social authoritarianism as the basic mode of social ordering in Brazil but also more recent neo-liberal discourses in which private interest is the measure of everything, obstructing the possibilities for consolidating an ethical basis to social life (Telles, 1994).

Furthermore, the notion of rights is no longer limited to legal provisions or access to previously defined rights or the effective implementation of abstract, formal rights. It also includes the invention/creation of *new* rights, which emerge from specific struggles and their concrete practices. In this sense, the very determination of the meaning of rights and the assertion of something as a right are themselves objects of political struggle. The rights to autonomy over one's own body, to environmental protection, to housing, are examples (intentionally very different) of new rights. In addition, this redefinition comes to include not only the right to equality, but also the right to difference, which specifies, deepens and broadens the right to equality.

An additional important consequence of such a broadening in scope has been that citizenship is no longer confined to the relationship between person and state. The recognition of rights regulates the relationships not only between the state and the individual but also with society itself, as parameters defining social relations at all levels. To build citizenship as the affirmation and recognition of rights was seen as a process through which more deeply rooted social practices would be transformed. Such a political strategy implies moral and intellectual reform: a process of social learning, of building up new kinds of social relations. On the one hand, this implied the constitution of citizens as active social subjects. On the other hand, for society as a whole, it requires learning to live on different terms with these emergent citizens who refuse to remain in the places that have previously been socially and culturally defined for them.

Finally, an additional element in this redefinition transcends a central reference in the liberal concept of citizenship: the demand for access, inclusion, membership and belonging to a given political system. What is at stake in struggles for citizenship in Latin America is more than the right to be included as a full member of society; it is the right to participate in the very definition of that society and its political system. The demand for political participation certainly goes beyond the right to vote, although in some countries even the free exercise of this right is still disputed. The direct participation of civil society and social movements in state decisions is one of the most crucial aspects of the redefinition of citizenship because it contains the potential for radical transformation of the structure of power relations. Political practices inspired by the new definition of citizenship help one to visualize the possibilities opened up by this process. Clear examples of such practices would be those that emerged in the cities governed by the Partido dos Trabalhadores (Workers' Party – PT) and its allies in Brazil, who implemented participatory budgets in which the popular sectors and their organizations have opened up space for the democratic control of the state through the effective participation of citizens in the exercise of power. Initiated in Porto Alegre, in the south of Brazil, in 1989, participatory-budget experiments have been tried in approximately 200 other cities and have become models for countries such as Mexico, Uruguay, Bolivia, Argentina, Peru, Ecuador and others.

The dissemination of this conception of citizenship in Brazil was very significant and underlay not only the political practices of social movements and NGOs but also institutional changes such as those expressed in the 1988 Constitution – the so-called 'Citizen Constitution '.Thanks to this dissemination, the term 'citizenship' in Brazil – in a way that differs from the case in other countries in Latin America – assumed a clear political meaning and was far from being merely a synonym for 'population', 'inhabitants' or 'society in general'. As a consequence, this political meaning and the potential it offered for social and political transformation soon became the target of the emerging neoliberal conceptions of citizenship, within a context characterized by the sorts of struggle over meanings that characterize the perverse confluence between different political projects.

Neoliberal redefinitions of citizenship rely upon a set of basic procedures. Some of these revive the traditional liberal conception of citizenship; others are innovative and address new elements of contemporary political and social order. First, they reduce the collective meaning of the social movements' redefinition of citizenship to a strictly individualistic understanding. Second, they establish an attractive connection between citizenship and the market. Being a citizen comes to mean individual integration into the market as a consumer and as a producer. This seems to be the basic principle underlying a vast number of projects for helping people to 'acquire citizenship' – examples here would be projects helping people to initiate 'microenterprises', or to become qualified for the few jobs still being offered, etc. In a context in which the state is gradually withdrawing from its role as guarantor of rights, the market is offered as a surrogate instance of citizenship. Labor rights are being eliminated in the name of free negotiation between workers and employers, 'flexibility' of labor, etc., and social rights guaranteed by the Brazilian Constitution since the 1940s are being eliminated under the rationale that they constitute obstacles to the free operation of the market and thus restrict economic development and modernization. This rationale, in addition, transforms bearers-of-rights/citizens into the nation's new villains – enemies of the political reforms that are intended to shrink the state's responsibilities. Thus a peculiar inversion is taking place: the recognition of rights seen in the recent past as an indicator of modernity is becoming a symbol of 'backwardness,' an 'anachronism' that hinders the modernizing potential of the market (Telles, 2001). Here we find a decisive legitimation of the conception of the market as a surrogate instance of citizenship – as the market becomes the incarnation of modernizing virtues and the sole route to the Latin American dream of inclusion in the First World.

An additional step in the construction of neoliberal versions of citizenship is evident in what constitutes a privileged target of democratizing projects – the formulation of social policies with regard to poverty and inequality.

Many of the struggles organized around the demand for equal rights and the extension of citizenship have focused on the definition of such social policies. In addition, and consequently, the participation of social movements and other sectors of civil society has been a fundamental demand in struggles for citizenship in the hope that it will contribute to the formulation of social policies directed towards ensuring universal rights for all citizens. With the advance of the neoliberal project and the reduction of the role of the state, these social policies are increasingly being formulated as strictly emergency efforts directed towards certain specific sectors of society whose survival is at risk. The targets of these policies are seen not as citizens entitled to rights but as 'needy' human beings to be dealt with by public or private charity.

One of the consequences of this situation is a displacement of issues such as poverty and inequality: dealt with strictly as issues of technical or philanthropic management, poverty and inequality are being withdrawn from the public (political) arena and from their proper domain, that of justice, equality and citizenship, and reduced to a problem of ensuring the minimal conditions for survival. Moreover, the solution to this problem is presented as the moral duty of every member of society. Thus, the idea of collective solidarity that underlies the classical reference to rights and citizenship is now being replaced by an understanding of solidarity as a strictly private moral responsibility. It is through this understanding of solidarity that civil society is being urged to engage in voluntary and philanthropic activities with an appeal to a re-signified notion of citizenship now embodied in this particular understanding of solidarity. This understanding of citizenship is dominant in the action of the entrepreneurial foundations, the so-called third sector, that have proliferated in countries like Brazil over the past decade. Characterized by a constitutive ambiguity between market-oriented interests in maximizing their profits through their public image and what is referred to as 'social responsibility', these foundations have generally adopted a discourse of citizenship rooted in individual moral solidarity. As in the state sectors occupied by neoliberal forces, this discourse is marked by the absence of any reference to universal rights or to the political debate on the causes of poverty and inequality.

Such a displacement of 'citizenship' and 'solidarity' obscures their political dimension and erodes references to the public responsibility and public interest built up with such difficulty through the democratizing struggles of our recent past. As the distribution of social services and benefits comes to occupy the place formerly held by rights and citizenship, the demand for rights is obstructed because there are no institutional channels for making such demands – meanwhile distribution depends purely on the goodwill and competence of the sectors involved. Even more dramatic, the very formulation of rights – their enunciation as a public issue – becomes increasingly difficult (Telles, 2001). The symbolic efficacy of rights in the building of an egalitarian society is thus dismissed, and the consequence has been the reinforcement of an already powerful privatism as the dominant orientation of social relations.

Such a scenario cannot be considered as anything but harmful to the very subsistence of civil society, for which a culture of rights is a condition of existence. It is equally nefarious for the poor and subaltern sectors, increasingly excluded from access to equal rights and left to the arbitrariness of charity. Most importantly, such a scenario points to what may constitute a practical abandonment of the very idea of rights, particularly of social rights, so exemplarily described in the work of Marshall (1950) and incorporated into a liberal view of citizenship towards the end of the nineteenth century. This practical abandonment is evident when what counts as social rights become understood as benefits and services to be looked for in the market. In the neoliberal model, this can be seen for instance when social organizations become motivated by a moral sense of solidarity with the poor or by plain traditional charity, or in the form of governmental emergency programmes to distribute food to the needy poorest. Such a reconfiguration cannot be understood if it is not placed within the more general framework that expresses the distinctive and novel character of what has been called neoliberalism. Thus, the redefinition of citizenship is intimately connected to a new phase of capitalist accumulation and its requirements – the excessive growth of the space of the market, the restructuring of labour, the reduction of the state and its social responsibilities and the related increase in the roles of civil society. This definition also responds to the need to reduce the scope and significance of politics itself, in order to ensure the conditions for the implementation of those requirements (Dagnino, 2004). The recent adoption of the term 'third sector' as a substitute for civil society is indicative of this, if we recall that the expression 'civil society' emerged in the political vocabulary of Brazil in the mid-1970s as part of the struggle for democracy, claiming and affirming both a space for politics and the existence of a set of political subjects that had previously been denied and repressed by the military regime.

Conclusion

The interconnected displacements of meaning discussed in this chapter seem to be articulated by a single aim: the depoliticization of concepts which have been central references in the democratizing struggle for the extension of citizenship and democracy. This depoliticization represents a counteroffensive to the gains made in redefining the political arena that have derived from that struggle. In this sense, these displacements point towards a broader redefinition, that of the very notions of politics and democracy. Thus, along with a conception of a minimal or reduced state, the neoliberal project also works with a minimalist conception of both politics and democracy. Under an apparent homogeneity of discourse, the perverse confluence active in the public spaces of participation of civil society produces a minefield, where, in fact, what is at stake is the success or failure of very different political projects.

References

Almeida, Carla (2006) 'O marco discursivo da "participação solidária" e a nova agenda de formulação e implementação das ações sociais no Brasil', in E. Dagnino, A. Olvera and A. Panfichi (eds), *A Disputa pela Construção democrática na América Latina*, Paz e Terra, São Paulo.

Alvarez, S.E. (1999) 'Advocating Feminism: The Latin American Feminist NGO "Boom"', *International Feminist Journal of Politics* 1(2): 181–209.

Alvarez, S.E., E. Dagnino and A. Escobar (eds) (1998) *Cultures of Politics/Politics of Cultures: Revisioning Latin American Social Movements*, Westview Press, Boulder CO.

Bresser Pereira, L. C. (1996) 'Da administração pública burocrática à gerencial'. *Revista do Serviço Público*, 120(1).

Carvalho, M. do C. (1997) '"*Eppur si muove...*" Os movimentos sociais e a construção da democracia no Brasil', M.A. thesis, University of Campinas,Campinas, Sao Paulo.

Dagnino, E. (1994) 'Os Movimentos Sociais e a Emergência de uma Nova Noção de Cidadania', in E. Dagnino (ed.), *Os Anos 90: Política e Sociedade no Brasil*, Editora Brasiliense, São Paulo.

Dagnino, E. (1998) 'Culture, Citizenship and Democracy: Changing Discourses and Practices of the Latin American Left', in S. Alvarez, E. Dagnino and A. Escobar (eds), *Cultures of Politics/Politics of Cultures: Revisioning Latin American Social Movements*, Westview Press, Boulder CO.

Dagnino, E. (2002) 'Sociedade Civil, Espaços Públicos e a Construção democrática no Brasil: Limites e possibilidades', in E. Dagnino (ed.), *Sociedade Civil e Espaços Públicos no Brasil,* Paz e Terra, São Paulo.

Dagnino, E. (2004) 'Sociedade civil, participação e cidadania: de que estamos falando?', in D. Mato (ed.), *Políticas de ciudadanía y sociedad civil en tiempos de globalización*, FACES-Universidad Central de Venezuela, Caracas.

Dagnino, E. (2005) 'Meanings of Citizenship in Latin America', *IDS Working Papers* 258, University of Sussex, Brighton.

Dagnino, E. (ed.) (2002) *Sociedade Civil e Espaços Públicos no Brasil*, Paz e Terra, São Paulo.

Dagnino, E., A. Olvera and A. Panfichi (2006) *A Disputa pela Construção democrática na América Latina*, Paz e Terra, São Paulo.

Doimo, A.M. (1995) *A Vez e a Voz do Popular*, Relume-Dumará, Rio de Janeiro.

Fernandes, R.C. (1994) *Privado, porém público*, Relume-Dumará, Rio de Janeiro.

Foweraker, J. (1995) *Theorizing Social Movements*, Pluto Press, London.

Foweraker, J., and T. Landman (1997) *Citizenship Rights and Social Movements: A Comparative and Statistical Analysis*, Oxford University Press, Oxford.

Galgani, G., and S. Magnólia (2002) 'O Conselho Cearense dos Direitos da Mulher (CCDM) – Espaço de interlocução entre as demandas dos Movimentos de Mulheres e o Estado', in E. Dagnino (ed.), *Sociedade Civil e Espaços Públicos no Brasil*, Paz e Terra, São Paulo.

GECD (Grupo de Estudos sobre a Construção Democrática) (2000) 'Os Movimentos sociais e a construção democrática: Sociedade Civil, Espaços Públicos e Gestão Participativa', *Idéias* 5/6 IFCH–UNICAMP, Campinas, São Paulo.

Landim, L. (1993) 'A invenção das ONGs – do serviço invisível à profissão sem nome', Ph.D. dissertation, Universidade Federal do Rio de Janeiro, Rio de Janeiro.

Marshall, T.H. (1950) *Citizenship, Social Class and Other Essays*, Cambridge University Press, Cambridge.

Oliveira, F. (1999) 'Privatização do público, destituição da fala e anulação da política: o totalitarismo neoliberal', in F. Oliveira and M.C. Paoli (eds), *Os Sentidos da Democracia. Políticas do Dissenso e Hegemonia Global*, Vozes/NEDIC/FAPESP, São Paulo.

Paoli, Maria Célia (2002) 'Empresas e responsabilidade social: os enredamentos da cidadania no Brasil', in B. de Souza Santos (ed.), *Democratizar a Democracia – Os caminhos da democracia participativa*, Civilização Brasileira, Rio de Janeiro.

Rodrigues, I.J. (1997) *Sindicalismo e Política: A Trajetória da CUT*, Scritta/FAPESP, Sao Paulo.

Salamon, L. (1997) 'Estratégias para o Fortalecimento do Terceiro Setor', in E.B. Ioschpe (ed.), *Terceiro Setor: Desenvolvimento Social Sustentado*, Paz e Terra, Rio de Janeiro.

Silva, C.A. (2001) 'Oral comment in a debate transcribed in 'Os Movimentos Sociais, a Sociedade Civil e o "Terceiro Setor" na América Latina: Reflexões Teóricas e Novas Perspectivas', in E. Dagnino and S. E. Alvarez (eds), *Primeira Versão* 98, IFCH, UNICAMP, Campinas.

Tatagiba, L. (2002) 'Os conselhos gestores e a democratização das políticas públicas no Brasil', in E. Dagnino (ed.) *Sociedade Civil e Espaços Públicos no Brasil*, Paz e Terra, São Paulo.

Tatagiba, L. (2006) 'Los desafíos de la articulación entre sociedad civil y sociedad política en el marco de la democracia gerencial. El caso del Projeto Rede Criança (Proyecto Red para la Niñez), en Vitória/ES', in E. Dagnino, A. Olvera and A. Panfichi (eds), *La Disputa por la Construcción Democrática en América Latina*, Fondo de Cultura Económica, México.

Teixeira, A.C. (2002) 'A atuação das Organizações Não-Governamentais: Entre o Estado e o conjunto da Sociedade', in E. Dagnino (ed.), *Sociedade Civil e Espaços Públicos no Brasil*, Paz e Terra, São Paulo.

Teixeira, A.C. (2004) *Identidades em Construção: Organizações Não-Governamentais no Processo Brasileiro de Democratização*, Annablume/Fapesp, São Paulo.

Telles, V. da S. (2001) *Pobreza e Cidadania*, Editora 34, São Paulo.

4

Learning from Latin America: Recent Trends in European NGO Policy-making

Kees Biekart

It is often assumed that Latin America has been a crucial region for innovation in social struggles and policies as well as a pilot area for new forms of aid delivery (Pearce, 1997; Fowler, 2000). There is indeed a long tradition of Northern NGO involvement in Latin America with an impressive record of promoting new approaches to rights, participation, gender, the informal sector, and civil society strengthening, just to name a few areas (Carroll, 1992; Biekart, 1999; Howell and Pearce, 2001; Bebbington, 2005). However, key changes have taken place in Latin America which have gradually affected aid policies and priorities of the international donor community. The impact of globalization, the crisis of the neoliberal orthodoxy (such as the peso crisis in Argentina), and the popular response to privatization and rising inequality have triggered an entirely new agenda. Migration and remittances, decentralization and local resource generation, rising criminal violence by youth gangs, just to name a few trends, have each changed the previous context in which democracy, human rights and inequality were the key issues. In this changing context, many in Latin America believe that European private aid agencies are gradually withdrawing from the region. After almost three decades of constantly growing aid disbursements to Latin American partner organizations, a general diversion of aid from Latin America to poorer regions such as Africa is seen as an inevitable trend. In particular, partner organizations in the relatively more prosperous countries such as Brazil, Peru, Colombia and El Salvador fear that they will be affected by these reductions of foreign aid.

This chapter analyses these changing policies and agendas of the twenty most important European private aid agencies and networks active in Latin America over the past decade (see Table 4.1). The analysis is based on a 'mapping exercise, initiated by ALOP, a Latin American network of NGOs. This network feared a gradual withdrawal of this more committed non-governmental aid. This, it argued, could undermine many important capacity-building and civil society strengthening initiatives currently undertaken in the region' (Ballón and Valderrama, 2004). Moreover, the Latin American NGOs felt that important lessons beneficial for other regions in the world could be learned from Latin America. The study was also intended to contribute to the search for a new type of partnership between European and Latin American NGOs. The chapter will assess trends in priority countries and regions, followed by an analysis of changing policy priorities, funding allocations by European NGOs, trends in selecting partner organizations, and perspectives for co-ordination and joint lobbying work. The chapter also reviews some of the central issues that have been discussed in the dialogue between European donor agencies and their Latin American partners, and the lessons that can be learned from their interventions.

Trends and Perspectives in Priority Countries

European NGOs have supported partner organizations in virtually all (independent) countries of Latin America and the Caribbean over the past decade, with the exception of a few (more prosperous) island states in the Caribbean. The actual number of countries where partner organizations have been supported has remained pretty much constant at around twenty (eight in Central America and twelve in South America). However, it is also clear that several policy shifts have occurred in the country priorities of the European private aid agencies.

First, twelve countries stand out as preferred countries by European private aid agencies: four in Central America (El Salvador, Guatemala, Nicaragua and Honduras), six in South America (Peru, Bolivia, Colombia, Brazil, Chile and Ecuador) and two in the Caribbean (Haiti and Cuba). Other countries, such as Paraguay and Mexico, were supported only by 44 per cent of the selected agencies. This suggests that European NGOs have been rather constant in their preferred priority countries, and that this priority choice has been relatively small. The vast majority had already reduced their programme countries in the early 1990s, generally due to efficiency pressures, and leading to an even more explicit concentration, with five of the priority countries still supported by at least 80 per cent of the European agencies involved in the survey. Peru clearly leads the list, followed by Guatemala, Bolivia, Nicaragua, El Salvador and Honduras. Colombia, Haiti and Brazil are still supported by more than two-thirds of

Table 4.1 European NGOs involved in the mapping exercise,
by size of combined Latin America programme (2004)

Agency	Country	Overseas budget (€m)	LA budget (€m)	LA budget as % of total	No. of LA country progs	No. of LA partner orgs
Misereor	Germany	151.6	43.5	28.6	22	944
Oxfam–GB	UK	142.3*	23.0*	16.2	20	–
Novib	Netherlands	123.3	22.0	17.8	11	200*
ICCO	Netherlands	130.0	21.0	16.2	11	180
Hivos	Netherlands	66.0	18.5	28.0	11	269
Cordaid	Netherlands	150.0	17.4	11.6	11	300
EED	Germany	105.6	15.8	15.0	17	145
SNV	Netherlands	59.3	12.8	21.6	5	285
Bread/World	Germany	46.2	12.0	26.0	21	190
Intermon	Spain	25.0	11.6	46.4	12	209
Diakonia	Sweden	28.1	10.0*	35.7	9	129*
Trocaire	Ireland	37.2*	9.0	24.2	12	188*
Christian Aid	UK	118.4*	7.8*	6.6	11	132
IBIS	Denmark	20.6	7.3	35.4	5	70
CCFD	France	30.0	3.0	10.0	14	100
Oxfam–B	Belgium	10.3*	2.9*	28.1	10	25
Danchurchaid	Denmark	38.0	2.7*	7.1	3	40
11.11.11	Belgium	4.1	1.1	25.6	5	16

Note: Total overseas budget of agency: all project expenses, generally excluding agency overheads. Some agencies also include their 'global programmes' and/or their advocacy activities in the North. * figures for 2003 or 2003/04.

Source: data collected from each individual private aid agency (not included here are data from the networks Eurostep and CIDSE as these are donor networks, rather than individual donors)

the agencies, while Ecuador and Cuba still are preferred by slightly more than half of the agencies.

A second visible trend is that concentration of priority countries was generally combined with a reduction of agencies per country. This holds in particular for South America, where a number of countries are clearly on the 'phasing out list'. Clear examples are Chile, in which half of the European agencies still maintaining programmes in 1995 had left by 2004. The same (if less dramatically) is true for Uruguay, Argentina, Venezuela,

Costa Rica, Panama, Jamaica and the Dominican Republic. Due to their higher GDP per capita these countries no longer fit the criteria of many European government co-financing schemes. That said, neither Mexico nor Brazil experienced this rapid decrease. This is due to the high levels of inequality in these countries, with substantial numbers of inhabitants living in 'poor' and 'extreme poor' conditions, justifying a continuation of European NGO interventions. This is confirmed by the focus on the poorest regions in these countries, such as Chiapas in Mexico and the north-eastern region of Brazil, and on some key social movements (such as the landless movement MST in Brazil).

The only country that seems to escape the trend of concentration and reduced agency presence, and where agency activity has substantially increased over the past decade, is Cuba. The improved diplomatic relationships between the European Union and the Castro government have provided favourable conditions for European NGO support to Cuban partner organizations, particularly in the area of human rights promotion. To a lesser extent, Honduras also seems to have become a 'more favoured country' for European NGOs, reflected in the recent establishment of several regional offices of European agencies in Tegucigalpa during the reconstruction operations to deal with the devastation caused by hurricane Mitch in 1998.

We asked the agencies which country budget had been the highest in the period 1995–2004. Agency budgets are, of course, not an entirely accurate indicator of prioritization, as the larger countries with more inhabitants (Brazil and Peru) tend to lead these tables. Still, the past five years suggest some new priorities. For example, Peru apparently is losing its priority status which we had identified in previous paragraphs, whereas three countries have risen in priority lists of the European NGOs: Bolivia, Colombia and Haiti. Chile, Uruguay and Argentina have clearly lost their preferred position – a result of their return to democratic governments after the end of military rule and of lower (average) poverty levels.

In Central America, Guatemala has become more central in agency priorities, whereas El Salvador is being gradually phased out by many agencies that used to have large programmes in this country's post-war period (such as Diakonia, IBIS and Hivos). The two poorest countries in Central America (Nicaragua and Honduras) have maintained their priority position, albeit often with lower funding allocations. The 'return' of Mexico to the higher ranks of funding priorities is also remarkable, which can be explained by increased support to partner organizations in Chiapas but also by active support to advocacy efforts of Mexican networks against the new American Free Trade Agreement.

To summarize, the most important geographical trend over the past decade has been that European NGOs have reduced the total number of countries in which they support programmes. A concentration has evolved towards a group of around a dozen countries, of which Brazil still receives the largest amount of European NGO allocations. Old favourites (Peru, Nicaragua, El Salvador) have been replaced by new ones (such as Bolivia, Colombia and Guatemala). However, the feared 'withdrawal' from South America turns out to be valid only for the 'richer' countries such as Chile, Uruguay and Argentina.

Some predictions can be made about future preferences for priority countries in Latin America. The impression is that after concentrating geographical priorities over the past few years, it is not likely that major changes will occur in priority countries in the near future. Some European agencies, such as Trocaire, indicated that they will opt for a more regional approach in the coming years, linking up partners in countries such Peru and Bolivia or Nicaragua and Honduras that are working on PRSPs. This search for (regional) synergies is also voiced by other agencies, basically in order to increase the impact of individual interventions.

Some countries with higher GDP per capita will continue to lose donor support. This will particularly affect El Salvador and Guatemala. El Salvador has already been phased out by several European governments, such as the Danish government, which perceives El Salvador as being 'too rich'. This will have consequences for Danish NGOs that depend on government funding, such as IBIS and Danchurchaid. The overall tendency, however, is that the agencies will not further reduce the countries where they are currently operating, but rather that efforts and funding will be more focused. If countries still have to be erased from priority lists, these are likely to be the more prosperous countries in South America and in the Caribbean. The process of concentrating geographical priorities by the European NGOs, however, is apparently over in Latin America.

Trends and Perspectives in Thematic Priorities

We requested the European agencies to list their thematic priorities over the past decade and asked them whether any explicit shifts had occurred in these priorities. We tried not to influence their answers by giving prefixed options, but rather opted to collect open answers. This resulted in an impressive list of themes and policy priorities, from which the frequency of the top five priorities was calculated. Seven main trends became visible in this ranking exercise.

First, *political participation*, and everything related to this theme, is the most frequently mentioned priority of European NGOs. Human rights promotion, especially in a more political sense of promoting political participation by excluded groups, has been a key target of the European private aid agencies over the past decade. Some agencies stressed the area of civil society building (Hivos, Bread for the World, Trocaire), whereas others focused more on increasing citizen's participation (Danchurchaid, ICCO, Misereor). Rather than emphasizing human rights abuses, or guaranteeing rights for refugees and displaced people, agencies have started to focus more on civil and political rights and on the development of active citizenship.

This emphasis on practising citizenship is closely related to the focus on local governance, which also has been prioritized by the European agencies. The aim here is to increase citizen's participation, stimulate collaboration between civil society groups and municipalities, and provide 'local spaces' for political participation in countries in which national governments are inaccessible for citizens. Democratization has generally shown better advances at this local level, which was targeted in particular by Diakonia, Novib, IBIS and SNV. Interest has grown in processes of decentralization and also in new forms of local governance, such as 'participatory budgeting'. In terms of excluded groups for which participation had to be enhanced, particular attention was given (by Intermon, IBIS, Hivos and Oxfam–Belgium) to organizations of indigenous people in the Andean countries and in Guatemala and Honduras.

A second explicit trend of the last decade is a strong emphasis on *socio-economic rights and economic development*. From the mid-1990s onwards the emphasis had been on 'productive projects', the provision of micro-credits and efforts to make partner organizations more financially self-sufficient. In the late 1990s new elements were added, such as attention to 'fair trade', new free-trade agreements and negotiations related to the World Trade Organization (WTO), which was one of the Oxfam International priority advocacy topics in recent years.

More attention for socio-economic rights is also reflected in the Oxfam–wide focus on the 'Right to Sustainable Livelihoods', in which communities and excluded groups are supported to gain better access to markets and land, and where indigenous groups are encouraged in efforts to claim their historical rights. Attention to this second generation of human rights has increased since the early 1990s, and it is interesting to see how explicit these are in the agendas of many European agencies a decade later. This focus on socio-economic rights has two other angles in which relationships with the private sector and the market are emphasized. One is the area of micro-credit provision, which has expanded especially in South America (Brazil, Bolivia, Peru, Colombia), often as part of programmes to contribute to the self-sufficiency of partner organizations. It has become an area of major innovation since it incorporated participatory approaches, environmental concerns and gender criteria. 'Corporate social responsibility' has so far received less attention, though trade unions and local NGOs have been working on this topic in Brazil, Peru, Chile and Colombia, and local organizations working on trade issues (including fair trade) have incorporated these efforts to promote socially responsible behaviour by market actors. By connecting it to network development and improving production and consumer chains (and, more generally, by linking this up with civil society building) a new set of linkages between state, market and civil society has emerged.

A third general trend in agency priorities is that *rural development* and in particular *agricultural production* have become less prominent, though still important, especially in Central America. Several agencies indicated that they had reduced their support to traditional rural development projects and that they had shifted their attention from production to creating better market conditions for agricultural products. The 'sustainability' aspect has also lost its dynamic: after the environmental focus of the early 1990s, attention to explicit environmental criteria seems to have vanished. Only 22 per cent of the European agencies under review were still paying explicit attention to the environment or 'natural resource management' as part of their programme priorities.

The fourth visible trend in agency priorities over the past decade has been the continued interest in *conflict resolution, peace building and reconciliation*. In Peru and in Central America of the mid-1990s this was of course a key issue. After the peace processes in Nicaragua, El Salvador and Guatemala, attention to conflict resolution continued in countries such as Colombia and Mexico (Chiapas). Guatemala was still receiving considerable attention in the decade after the 1995 peace accords, also because of the high crime rates (especially affecting women) that are apparently linked to unresolved post-war problems. It was this wave of so-called 'new violence' in Latin America – visible in particular in large cities – that spurred many European agencies to support initiatives aimed at conflict prevention and resolution, reintegration of (former) youth gang members, arms control measures, and, in general, initiatives trying to tackle the destabilizing effects of violence and impunity.

Fifth, *gender* and *gender mainstreaming* have been constant and important focal issues for most agencies. Explicitly mentioned is security for women, but also the access of women to decision-making spaces, markets and organizations, plus attention to reproductive rights and its consequences. Throughout the 1990s it was often argued by (generally male) representatives of Latin American partners that a 'focus on women' was fashionable and that this would very soon vanish. Our findings suggest the opposite trend: attention to gender issues has remained a priority for 39 per cent of all the agencies reviewed.

A sixth trend over the past decade has been attention to *humanitarian relief and disaster preparedness*. This topic gained prominence after the devastations following hurricane Mitch in Central America in 1998, which struck Honduras, Nicaragua and El Salvador. European NGO support was aimed at preparing the population better for disasters such as earthquakes, flooding and mud waves. Special attention was given to environmental degradation in urban areas, as a result of which the number of victims had been rising. An indirect consequence of increased emergency assistance after Mitch was the renewed interest of many agencies in supporting activities in Honduras.

Finally, a seventh trend that has been valid also for other regions is that many agencies have adjusted their policies towards *output-related criteria*, in particular the 'rights-based approach' which was incorporated by the Oxfam agencies in 2000 and later by many others. The major difference with the earlier 'needs-based approach' is the particular attention paid to partner performance and the introduction of results-based management tools. With the gradual reduction of priority countries in Latin America, the search for new sources of finance is nowadays also included under the umbrella of 'partner development'.

Apart from these trends, it is also important to note that many priorities that were already identified in the mid-1990s have kept their importance throughout the past ten years. One of these ongoing priorities is primary health care (with special attention to people affected by HIV–AIDS), and of course education. These basic social services still account for a substantial amount of total European agency support, though less than in 1995. Novib, for example, decided in the mid-1990s not to stick any longer to the 'Copenhagen target' of channelling at least a quarter of its total overseas resources to basic social services. Instead, it decided, as part of the newly introduced rights-based approach, to put more pressure on national governments to comply with their duties to deliver these public services. Other agencies, such as Trocaire, made similar decisions to cut down drastically on health programmes and to refocus on civil society and community building, human rights and participation.

These shifts in thematic priorities suggest increasing attention to political processes, socio-economic and cultural rights, rural livelihoods and food security issues. Agencies indicated that these trends are likely to be central to European NGO policies over the next couple of years. However, in the interviews we also spotted some slight changes, which require closer analysis. The overall policy trend is away from the delivery of basic social services and towards national advocacy campaigns to commit the state to take responsibility for these social services. This is not to suggest that social service delivery is no longer important, but it seems that it becomes more integrated with macro-developments and with national policymaking. For example, European agencies are going to assess their results more in terms of the Millennium Development Goals (MDGs), in particular because this is being promoted by the bilateral and multilateral agencies. But central to the MDGs is the idea, or at least the intention, to show more clearly the results of external interventions. This visibility of results continues to be a cross-cutting theme.

The range of new progressive governments in Latin America will likely facilitate the implementation of a more politicized social service programme aimed at poverty reduction and social justice. Key words used by the European agencies are 'synergies' between various actors, regions and countries, and 'joint advocacy initiatives' in order to get this agenda implemented. However, agencies approach this in different ways and do not emphasize the same issues. Misereor, for example, will focus more on health issues and on youth groups, whereas Trocaire foresees more attention to migration issues, violence and security, rural poverty reduction and trade issues. The Oxfam agencies indicated that they would probably pay more attention to human security in all its aspects. Diakonia and 11.11.11 also perceive that trade and debt issues will continue to be central in agency priorities over the coming years, whereas IBIS expects more attention to education as its core theme.

A more political approach with a central role for 'lobbying and advocacy' is therefore dominant, whilst at the same time agencies keep searching for their own 'niche' in order to become even better in what they are already doing well. The need for a clear profile has become accepted and is no longer seen as a source of competition or as an obstacle for joint action. To the contrary, it is likely that agencies will work more closely together over the coming years on issues such as migration, peace-building and trade issues. These are likely going to be some of the key topics for the next few years, in which the 'creation and promotion of more synergies' is a central slogan by which to maximize the use of scarce resources.

Patterns in Funding Allocations

One of the main concerns of the Latin American partner organizations is that funding levels from European NGOs have gone down in recent years, or will decline in the years to come. Even though we did expect a reduction of funds for Latin America in relative as well as absolute terms, the pattern turned out to be more complex. First, there *has* been a gradual reduction of the *relative budget allocations* to Latin America, especially after 2000. But since agency budgets also have grown substantially over the last few years, the funding volume for Latin America in absolute terms did not seem to have decreased significantly. In fact, one can actually detect a slight increase between 1995 and 2000. Even if this can be largely explained by additional relief aid for the victims of hurricane Mitch, it is still an increase and not a gradual reduction of aid disbursements to Latin America, as many partner organizations feared.

Another remarkable tendency is that the vast majority of European agencies have actually experienced no budget cuts to Latin America over the past decade. Only two agencies (IBIS and 11.11.11) were faced with nominal reductions of their total overseas budget, basically due to new priorities of their governments. In the case of IBIS this effectively led to a reduction of their Latin America budget, but for 11.11.11 this actually remained the same. For most of the other agencies where the Latin America budgets were reduced (one-third of the agencies interviewed), it was generally a slight reduction – in the cases of Danchurchaid and Hivos – or a relative reduction barely affecting the total expenditures for Latin America (ICCO, Oxfam–GB and Christian Aid). Danchurchaid, for example, never had a high budget for Latin America, and the reductions in the new century were relatively small. Hivos had experienced a constant reduction of its Latin America budget – which had been as high as 65 per cent of the total overseas expenditures in 1987 – and a gradual reduction was therefore inevitable. In the meantime, Hivos's overall budget went up quite sharply, which basically compensated the relative decrease in spending for Latin America.

Only three European agencies reduced their Latin America budgets more or less substantially over the past decade: Bread for the World, Novib and Cordaid. Bread for the World reduced its Latin America budget over the past three years by 25 per cent. The main reason was its decision to focus more on Africa, especially to deal with the enormous challenges faced by the HIV–AIDS crisis in that region. Novib had already started to reduce its budget for Latin America in late 1999, but this was initially compensated by overall income growth and additional credit funding. Within a three year period the Latin America budget was reduced in absolute terms by 30 per cent. The justification was threefold: (i) Latin America had become 'too rich' and had received disproportionately more resources than Africa; (ii) Novib had become the second largest partner in a coalition (Oxfam International) that primarily focused on direct poverty reduction strategies with massive funding for service delivery (largely in Africa); and (iii) Latin America policies emphasized less costly lobbying and campaigning activities. However, with a Latin America budget of €22 million in 2004 Novib is still among the largest European non-governmental donors in Latin America.

Another Dutch donor agency, Cordaid, reduced its Latin America budget by a radical 50 per cent between 2000 and 2004, despite a growth of overall funds. While a quarter of Cordaid's total overseas funding went to Latin

America in 2000, four years later this had dropped to 11 per cent. This drastic move had to do with a refocusing of Dutch development aid in general towards Africa, due to poverty figures and ongoing crises. Some observers also commented that for many years Cordaid's Latin America budget had been rather high compared to its Africa budget, although other reasons also seem to have played a role. Cordaid grew out of a merger of several Catholic agencies, including the former Cebemo, whose Latin America department had always been an influential player – too influential, according to insiders, which might explain why it was decided internally to dismantle the large Latin America programme following a number of staff changes.

The survey indicates that it is simply not true that European NGOs on average have reduced their Latin America budgets over the past decade. This applies only to one-third of the agencies involved. In particular those agencies that used to have high disbursements for Latin America (higher than 25 per cent of total overseas expenditures) seem to have lowered this level in favour of poorer countries in other regions. After a previous period of growth in the late 1990s, it is likely that budgets will remain stable at this level, providing that no new emergencies occur. What is going to change over the next few years are the sources of income for European NGOs. In Germany, for example, a significant reduction of income from churches will affect the level of co-funding that church-based organizations can secure. Many agencies, among them Oxfam–Belgium, Hivos and Diakonia, will have to search for additional funding opportunities from other major donors, in particular from the European Union, but also from the embassies of other countries. This search for new funding is also stimulated by European governments, as in the Netherlands, where pressure is put on the co-financing agencies to find additional funding up to a quarter of their total income. In addition, voices in bilateral circles have become stronger that Latin America needs to be phased out as a target for development cooperation as it has become 'too rich'. However, others have argued that Latin America's problem is about 'inequality' rather than 'poverty', and that various related issues (migration, violence, etc.) stem from the complications caused by an unequal income distribution. This more politically oriented approach might help keep funding levels for Latin America unchanged in the short term.

Trends and Perspectives in Partner Selection and Partner Relationships

We also mapped trends and perspectives related to the choice of partner organizations and new types of relationships with these partners. It was expected that a concentration of funding would lead to a reduction in the total number of partner organizations, whilst the funding allocation for each individual partner would increase slightly. This tendency was indeed confirmed in our survey, with 64 per cent of the European agencies having more partner organizations in 1995 than in 2004.

Part of the reduction of the total number of partners can be explained by decreasing budgets. But strategies also changed: agencies such as Hivos that had invested considerable funding in a large group of smaller partners concluded that it was too expensive to maintain this network. To put it bluntly, as one interviewee did, 'agencies are punished by their *back donors* for supporting small partner organizations. The system encourages a trend towards supporting larger programmes with even larger organizations, as these minimise the overhead per donor euro spent. Overall, the tendency is for longer term and 'strategic' partners (as emphasized by Christian Aid, Cordaid, and Trocaire), rather than for shorter term project-oriented partnerships.

Apart from the numbers, it was also important to assess whether the *type* of partner organization also had changed over the past ten years. One of the contradictory trends is that support to membership organizations and community-based organizations was gradually replaced in favour of (often specialized) NGOs, giving less priority to 'those NGOs that are (or have been) capable of everything' (as Novib puts it). This trend was clearly visible with Intermon, Diakonia, IBIS and Hivos. Conversely, agencies such as Trocaire, 11.11.11 and CCFD went in a different direction by providing more direct support to grassroots organizations. Another (and probably related) contradictory trend is that some agencies decided to move their focus from a rural orientation to more urban-based partner organizations (Cordaid, Diakonia, Oxfam–Belgium), often with what Diakonia calls a more 'political advocacy-oriented focus'. Other agencies seem to direct their attention more to rural areas, either to work more directly with smaller organizations (Trocaire) or to target indigenous groups and their networks better (IBIS).

Most of the larger ecumenical NGOs traditionally supported by the Protestant agencies have been gradually phased out. The main reason for terminating these long-term partnerships was that these NGOs had become huge multipurpose agencies which simply did not deliver well enough according to the new performance criteria. The ecumenical edge that had been important for so many years in determining partner relationships thus had been replaced by output quality criteria.

The survey suggests that the European NGOs tend to have given more support to partner organizations working directly with (local) governments. Oxfam–GB indicated that the time was over when non-governmental was synonymous with anti-governmental. Political lobbying and advocacy work has become more central to agency preferences, and some argue therefore that a renewed politicization of European NGO aid is becoming visible. However, when reference is made to the 1980s, the political angle is of course very different from the period in which liberation movements and their support organizations were supported. Political work nowadays aims at maximizing the political impact of campaigns and the results of development projects, and involving membership organizations more directly in national and global campaigns. This increased attention on political work is also reflected by a general concern to reinforce micro-macro linkages and to encourage synergy between partner organizations in similar regions. Lobbying is no longer an activity of specialized NGOs: European agencies want Southern NGOs to be effectively accountable to their constituencies. Moreover, they have to demonstrate that these multiple micro–macro linkages are actually beneficial to organizations working at the grassroots level.

New Priorities and Issues for the Near Future

Lobbying and advocacy campaigns with Latin American partners have increased substantially. This trend will even become stronger and is part of what some consider a 're-politicization' of their programme. Several agencies decided – also due to governmental incentives – to dedicate up to a quarter of their total overseas budget to advocacy activities in the North. In the case of ICCO this also implies collaboration with a number of strategic partners in the Netherlands and Europe to increase synergies, and to keep Latin American issues on the agenda. European agencies will focus their campaigns on pressing national developments (Colombia, Bolivia, Guatemala), on PRSP, trade (in particular with the EU), migration issues (especially in Central America), external debt, and socio-economic rights. It is also expected that more joint lobbying campaigns with partner organizations will be initiated and that European platforms such as CIFCA and PICA (of the Protestant agencies) and the ecumenical Process of Articulation and Dialogue (PAD) in Brazil will play a more prominent role in these campaigns.

Oxfam GB expects campaigning to grow further, although it depends on the extent to which institutionally it is possible to develop a global campaigning force. This is likely not to happen in the UK (or in Europe), but rather in the Latin American countries themselves, where organizations have become more strategic and autonomous in their campaigning agenda. This is important, according to Oxfam–GB, because national campaign work can better address cultural specificities and languages, as local activists better understand their own political culture, public opinion and local media. Agencies such as Oxfam–Belgium are therefore aiming to strengthen local campaigning capacities.

European agency representatives predicted that the trend towards more programmatic and process approaches, and away from traditional project approaches, will sustain itself in the years to come. Trocaire expects to provide more multi-annual funding, rather than year-by-year allocations. Many agencies also foresee that the number of partner organizations will be reduced further, but that the quality of these relations will be increased. ICCO, for example, expects that more South–South cooperation between partners (generally on advocacy) also implies higher qualification criteria for these partners. Hivos indicates that it will invest in more knowledge-sharing with and between partner organizations.

Several burning global issues may impact on Latin America in the coming years, and thus on partner organizations. *Security* is the obvious one, and the growing European (official) donor trend to shift money away from development to pay for their interventions in Iraq, Afghanistan and several African countries (such as Sudan) are indirectly related to the withdrawal of donors from Latin America. The role and influence of the United States government in this development, in particular related to donor withdrawal from Central America, is critical.

Aid effectiveness continues to be another big issue; the performance of both official aid and NGO funding in Latin America has been questioned, also given the growing levels of socio-economic inequality. This develop-ment has contributed to 'donor fatigue' and requires appropriate attention from European NGOs. After all, donors are dropping countries that are considered to be 'ineffective', and this will impact on NGO funding from co-financing sources. Many European official donors now only focus on just a few countries in Latin America and some want to ensure their co-financing via NGOs is also concentrated in these countries. On the other hand, this might also offer new opportunities for European NGOs if they are going to compensate for reductions in bilateral funding.

New social and political actors are emerging in the region. The reduced influence of some key civil society actors from the past (notably the trade-union movement and peasants' associations) is an illustration of important shifts that have taken place in Latin American societies. It implies that the European agencies will need to find new ways of working to promote the defence of rights of vulnerable groups. In Central America there is a feeling that civil society groups are losing their edge due to many internal divisions and difficulties in influencing public policies. There is little new thinking and capacity to articulate a vision of what 'sustainable human development' means in the new century. On the other hand, the important role of social movements in bringing about progressive political change in many South

American countries is promising (see Biekart, 2005). It also highlights an increased linkage of grassroots movements to transnational networks, which was previously not very developed.

Governance issues have become critical. There is a widespread public dissatisfaction with political processes, parties and politicians. Fewer people seem to believe in the benefits of democracy and the current political system. Given the history of authoritarianism in the region this is a motive for serious concern. In addition, the World Bank and the IMF continue to exert huge leverage over development policies and development actors (especially on Latin American governments and bilateral donors), even though they are not known for promoting serious empowerment of excluded groups. Related to that, *transparency and (anti-)corruption* have become important themes in Latin America; corruption is growing and is not only limited to the state and the private sector. The process of liberalization and privatization of state industries and services has generated immense corruption with politicians benefiting, and the culture of impunity has corroded values in society regarding corruption. Local NGOs are certainly not immune from these trends.

Lessons Learned

Over the past few decades European NGOs have built up an impressive record of experiences and interventions aiming at poverty reduction and social change. What has been learned from all these experiences and interventions, and which keys lessons have been incorporated into new European NGO policies?

It turns out that one of the most frequently mentioned lessons is the importance of establishing *strategic alliances*. More specifically, agencies seem to agree that initiatives towards setting up networks (locally, nationally or globally) as key instruments to facilitate lobbying and campaigning at all levels have triggered a breakthrough over the past decade. These more systematic and collaborative lobbying efforts illustrate what some agencies call 'strategic alliances', which in several cases have demonstrated a capacity to achieve tangible results and influence global agendas. Examples are the debt campaign, the WTO summit in Cancún (where a coalition of Southern countries, led by Brazil, took a position against the powerful Northern members of the WTO), the PRSP processes and the World Social Forum (WSF). These more global interactions also benefited the influence and thus the legitimacy of the European agencies in their home countries. A key element in this lobbying work is that coalitions of social movements and NGOs no longer strictly maintain 'anti-governmental' positions, but that these strategic alliances are being formed together with Northern and/or Southern governments, international financial institutions (such as the World Bank) or UN agencies such as UNDP. The Oxfam agencies in particular stress that they have learned to cooperate with global institutions over the past decade and that they managed to play a stimulating role in the 'globalization for social justice movement' that has become so dynamic since the WTO summit in Seattle in 1999.

A second major lesson comes from the faith-based European agencies, from both Catholic and Protestant backgrounds. They seem to have learned that *Church-related organizations are not by definition the best implementers of development-oriented programmes.* The Churches are still considered important actors in, for example, contributing to peace and reconciliation, but no longer as key development agents. This has also had consequences for the European agencies themselves. The Swedish Protestant agency Diakonia explained that it had watched the downward development of the ecumenical development movement (especially in Central America) with some regret, but it had learned that a more autonomous position from the Swedish churches was in fact a better option. Trocaire, the Irish Catholic agency, maintains however that the Church continues to be an important instrument for community organizing and civil-society building, especially in those areas where it is the only institutional structure.

A third lesson mentioned by several agencies is that *longer-term support to partner organizations has eventually paid off.* Latin America shows many examples where prolonged support to partners has contributed to a lobby-ing and advocacy capacity that, compared to other regions of the world, is superior in terms of quality and impact. Christian Aid, for example, points at the flexible role of European agencies and their position as a *partner* in these processes, giving advice and some resources, rather than determining the processes from the outside. It does recognize the problems of how this can be combined with increased demands for accountability, and thus with more formal relationships (see Jordan and Van Tuijl, 2006). Other agencies also pointed to this tension, but all agree that relationships with Latin American partners are often more mature than anywhere else. Those partnerships with a higher degree of 'trust' and 'confidence' are generally favoured by the agencies, as they generate more benefits in terms of policy formulation, allow more transparency, more mutual learning and are therefore often part of arrangements with 'institutional support'. Dutch, German and Nordic agencies emphasized the importance of these 'strategic partnerships' that also proved to be crucial for the North–South lobbying campaigns mentioned earlier.

A fourth lesson commonly drawn by the European agencies is that the emergency aid following hurricane Mitch in 1998 has re-emphasized the need to improve *agency coordination*. Many lessons were drawn from the post-Mitch relief operation, which was probably the biggest ever in the region, but central was the lesson that working closely together as agencies in such a crisis situation helps to prevent many of the post-disaster problems that can accompany external aid. Several key partner organizations in the Central American region had been overstretched and overfunded due to Mitch, which in some cases had contributed to their demise.

Conclusion

Many Latin American organizations that received support from European donor NGOs now fear that these agencies will gradually withdraw from the region, re-channelling funds to Africa and other (poorer) regions of the world. This chapter has suggested that most of these fears are not based on evidence. The data show, instead, a concentration of NGO funding in a smaller set of countries, involving fewer partner organizations. European agencies have paid increased attention to rights-based approaches, with more integrated joint lobbying and advocacy components. This has generated a more political agenda on topics such as migration, conflict resolution, peace-building and trade issues (Fernández, 2006). These are likely to be key topics in the coming years, in which the 'creation and promotion of more synergies' is the central slogan in order to maximize the use of more scarcely available resources.

Regarding the medium and longer term, however, our interviews with donor staff do suggest that many of the traditionally strong Latin American partner organizations will inevitably experience a gradual reduction of European NGO funding allocations. Assuming that this trend continues over the coming years, the question arises as to how these partners will survive as key organizations in promoting alternative development approaches. Do the reorientation, concentration and overall reduction of European NGO funding indirectly imply the end of alternative development agendas in Latin America? This crucial question can be addressed by exploring three possible scenarios. The first is that the more flexible funding resources from European NGOs will be (partly) replaced by funds from bilateral and multilateral organizations, or even from the corporate sector. New and tighter conditions will be attached to this type of financing, which are likely going to force Latin American NGOs to commit themselves to the broader directions of the mainstream development agenda. This is in fact already happening, if one considers how many Latin American organizations are implementing in a rather uncritical way World Bank discourses or UN millennium agendas.

In a second scenario, alternative approaches are undermined in a different way: due to reduced funding from abroad, the autonomous and politically consistent partner organizations involved in strategic alliances and pursuing a political agenda oriented at empowering civil society groups will find themselves without any financial allies or alternative sources of income. This will be either because official funding has withdrawn from the country, or because the organization is unable or unwilling to pursue this new type of income. Temporarily such a former European NGO partner organization will derive some of its income from market-based consultancy contracts or state-related service delivery operations. However, this will compromise its manoeuvring space considerably: committed staff will voluntarily leave the organization, its credibility will be damaged, strategic allies will turn away, and the demise of the organization will be merely a matter of time. This is a scenario that has come about in slightly different ways for many partner organizations in several of the former priority countries such as Chile, Costa Rica and El Salvador.

A scenario in which the organization does not disappear, nor is compromised by new donor agendas – and in which alternative development agendas are maintained – will therefore have to take into account a number of key lessons learned over the past decade. One such lesson is that sustained capacity-building can contribute to a strong and transparent organization which is horizontally well-connected (strategic alliances) and downwardly accountable to its clients and constituents when this is explicitly aimed for. Another lesson is that an organization is able to diversify its income base, acquiring sufficient resource mobilization power to pursue its political agenda without having to make major compromises. The Latin American experience shows that a prolonged period of committed external support does not by definition lead to a loss of autonomy and increased external dependency. In fact, the current political swing in the region towards progressive policymaking on poverty reduction and empowerment is likely offering favourable conditions for many former partner organizations of European agencies to reduce further these external vulnerabilities. However, given that each of these three scenarios is an equally realistic possibility, they have to be monitored closely in order to judge which scenario is to set the tone in the coming years.

References

Ballón, E., and M. Valderrama (2004) 'Las relaciones de las ONGD de América Latina y las agencies privadas de cooperación internacional europeas en el contexto de la globalización', in F. Negrón et al. (eds), *Mito y realidad de la ayuda externa: América Latina al 2004*, ALOP, Lima.

Bebbington, A. (2005) 'Donor–NGO Relations and Representations of Livelihood in Non-governmental Aid Chains', *World Development* 33(6): 937–50.

Biekart, K. (1994) *La cooperación no gubernamental europea hacia Centroamérica: La experiencia de los ochenta y las tendencies en los noventa*, PRISMA, San Salvador.

Biekart, K. (1999) *The Politics of Civil Society Building: European Private Aid Agencies and Democratic Transitions in Central America*, International Books, Amsterdam, and Transnational Institute, Utrecht.

Biekart, K. (2005) 'Seven Theses on Latin American Social Movements', *European Review of Latin American and Caribbean Studies* 68, October.

Biekart, K. (2006) 'Políticas de las ONGs Europeas para América Latina: Tendencias y perspectivas', in F. Negrón et al. (eds), *Mito y realidad de la ayuda externa: América Latina al 2006*, ALOP, Lima.

Carroll, T. (1992) *Intermediary NGOs: The Supporting Link in Grassroots Development*, Kumarian Press, West Hartford CT.

Fernández, R. (2006) 'Realidad de la ayuda 2006: Conflicto, seguridad y desarrollo, una mirada política general', in F. Negrón et al. (eds), *Mito y realidad de la ayuda externa: América Latina al 2006*, ALOP, Lima.

Fowler, A. (2000) 'NGO Futures: Beyond Aid: NGDO Values and the Fourth Position', *Third World Quarterly* 21(4), 589–603.

Howell, J., and J. Pearce (2001) *Civil Society and Development: A Critical Exploration*, Lynne Rienner, Boulder CO.

Jordan, L., and P. Van Tuijl (2006) *NGO Accountability: Politics, Principles and Innovations*, Earthscan, London.

PAD (2003) *International Solidarity in the New Millennium: Facing Old and New Challenges*, PAD, Rio de Janeiro.

Pearce, J. (1997) 'Between Cooption and Irrelevance? Latin American NGOs in the 1990s', in D. Hulme and M. Edwards (eds), *Too Close for Comfort? NGOs, States and Donors*, St. Martins Press, London, pp. 257–74.

Valderrama, M. (2004) 'Empoderamiento y participación de la sociedad civil en la cooperación internacional: el caso peruano', in F. Negrón et al. (eds), *Mito y realidad de la ayuda externa: América Latina al 2004*, ALOP, Lima.

5

Whatever Happened to Reciprocity? Implications of Donor Emphasis on 'Voice' and 'Impact' as Rationales for Working with NGOs in Development

Alan Thomas

Eliminating world poverty is a job for everyone, not just governments. In 2005, people around the world raised their voices to demand change. ...NGOs will help deliver services, especially in fragile states. ... civil society groups will hold the Government to account in the UK, and encourage their counterparts in developing countries to do the same. (UK White Paper on *Eliminating World Poverty*, DFID, 2006: 81).

This chapter concerns non-governmental organizations (NGOs) and the rationale for their involvement in development. It analyses how donors view NGOs, looking particularly at the example of DFID, arguing that NGOs are expected to conform to one of two prescribed models of what they do, which tends to ignore or downplay the value basis of what NGOs *are* and the variety of ways they relate to development.

The chapter suggests *reciprocity* (Polanyi, 1957) as an organizing principle that incorporates the variety of values underlying NGOs and differentiates them from both private firms, based on a rationale of self-interest and exchange through the market, and government agencies, based on a rationale of legitimate authority and coercive redistribution. At the same time, it seeks to place NGOs within 'civil society', which in political rather than economic discourse has also been used to describe the space between the state and the market. However, usage differs as to whether 'NGO' is a synonym for 'civil society organization' (CSO) or refers to one particular type of CSO – for example, one that delivers humanitarian relief or promotes 'development' for others.

Both the private and state sectors are modern sectors contrasting with a 'traditional', 'community' sector, based on a rationale of mutuality, reciprocal relations and ascribed roles. NGOs can be regarded as belonging to a third modern sector, based on some of the positive values of community but with more openness and universality. Arguably this third sector also corresponds to the organizational dimension of civil society.

Invoking the idea of 'civil society' is one way of investing the third (modern) sector with some positive attributes. Many authors agree that it should not be defined as just a residual category (*non*-profit and *non*-governmental) but consists of 'value-based' or 'value-led' organizations (Paton, 1991; Hudson, 1995), though which values are to the fore is subject to much debate. Suggestions include voluntary association (Streeck and Schmitter, 1985), charity (Butler and Wilson, 1990), membership (Stryjan, 1989), trust and solidarity (Gherardi and Masiero, 1990), enthusiasm (Bishop and Hoggett, 1986), among others. The values underlying development NGOs in particular are if anything even more varied, although many relate to participation or empowerment. Some derive specifically from movements based in developing countries, for example Freire's (1972) conscientization, or Gandhian concepts such as *gram swaraj* (village self-rule) or *sarvodaya* (the welfare of all). Other value-based ideas taken up by many NGOs, while of Northern derivation, are specific to attempts to deal with problems of development, such as Schumacher's (1973) 'small is beautiful', Korten's (e.g. 1990) 'people-centred development' and Chambers's (e.g. 1997) ideas of participative rural appraisal and power reversals.

It might appear that the values involved are too diverse to generalize about the underlying principles. Some are the values of groups set up for the mutual benefit of their members while others relate to organizations set up for the benefit of others or for general public benefit. However, over time successful voluntary organizations tend to combine elements of all three categories of benefit (Handy, 1988). Indeed, all organized voluntary action can be seen as combining the human impulse to act directly in response to a perceived need with the need to pool resources by acting in groups. I suggest that the best attempt at defining this impulse in terms of a single principle is Polanyi's (1957) idea of reciprocity, where goods, services or effort are given freely not for immediate exchange but in the expectation of reciprocal assistance being available when required (a similar notion underlies Titmuss's (1970) 'gift relationship'). However, a general understanding of voluntary, non-profit or 'civil society' organizations must also recognize that they are often small and specific in their area of operation. Thus the third sector — or 'civil society organizations', including NGOs — comprises organizations which may all be value-based and rely on reciprocity but are based on a variety of specific values and focus on the needs and interests of particular groups.

NGOs have become increasingly important in development since the 1980s, as the neoliberal combination of market economics and liberal democratic politics became dominant. As Edwards and Hulme explain,

NGOs fitted into the 'New Policy Agenda' promoted by donors, appearing simultaneously 'as market-based actors' and 'as components of "civil society"' (1995: 849). Thus, on the one hand, the increase in provision of services or 'gap-filling' (Vivian, 1994) by NGOs was seen as part and parcel of the privatization of state services, despite NGOs' non-profit basis. On the other hand, NGOs were seen as prime agents of democratization (Clark, 1991), or even as intrinsically democratic simply by virtue of being part of civil society (ROAPE, 1992).

In practice the contribution of NGOs to development is enormously varied and multidimensional, reflecting their sheer numbers and diversity. There is a huge difference between international NGOs, mostly based in the developed world, and indigenous local or national NGOs in the developing world. Often started as charitable relief or missionary welfare organizations, the former generally work in developing countries through their own branches or with local partner organizations, often NGOs themselves. The majority of the latter are small, but they include organizations such as the Bangladesh Rural Advancement Committee (BRAC), the largest national NGO in the developing world, with over 97,000 employees in 2005.[2] BRAC and other large NGOs (especially in South-Asia) often function as para-governmental or quasi-governmental organizations, operating in parallel with the state and complementing it in the provision of social services.

However, for some time, many working in NGOs have wished to go beyond simply providing relief or other services within the neoliberal model of market-led development. A symposium on 'Development Alternatives: the Challenge for NGOs' held in London in March 1987 explored the suggestion of a distinctive 'NGO approach' to development based on empowerment and the idea that poor people could be supported to become the agents of their own development (World Development, 1987; see also Poulton and Harris, 1988; Thomas, 1992). However, despite a number of well-reported success stories at the local level, it was unclear whether this 'NGO approach' could have a broader impact. In one of the papers from that London conference, Sheldon Annis (1987) asked, 'Can Small-scale Development be a Large-scale Policy?', and this question of how to 'scale up' from local experience became perhaps the most important of a number of distinct challenges to development NGOs which remain relevant today.

A number of writers have seen these challenges in terms of a sequence of strategies. At the same conference, David Korten distinguished between three 'generations' of NGO strategies: the first committed to relief and welfare activities, the second promoting small-scale local development that empowered local communities and broke their dependency on humanitarian assistance, and the third involved in a range of activities designed to achieve institutional and policy change. Later, he suggested the need for a 'fourth generation' strategy, committed to increasingly complex networks and to advocacy at international as well as national level (Korten, 1990: 123–4). Individual NGOs could be involved in various mixes of the strategies. In a similar vein, Alan Fowler (1997: 220–21) characterized NGO activities as a mixture of three types of effort: 'welfare and delivery (the global soup kitchen)', 'strengthening people's organizations and movements', and 'learning for leverage'. He suggested NGOs should shift away from the first by either 'concentrating on building people's capacities to look after and demand for themselves' or 'gaining leverage on structural changes to governments and markets which benefit the poor' (Fowler, 1997: 220–21).

The rest of this chapter concentrates not on the NGO perspective but on how donors justify working with NGOs. The next section charts the changes in donor funding and expectations of NGOs from the 1970s to date. The following two sections analyse more closely how 'voice' and 'impact' are currently the dominant rationales put forward by donors for working with NGOs, looking in particular at policy and other statements by DFID. The final section considers how these two rationales may 'squeeze out' fundamental aspects of NGO work in development, many of which can be summed up in terms of the concept of 'reciprocity', and concludes with some implications.

Changes in Donor Funding of NGOs and its Rationale

Throughout the period of the above-mentioned discussions on how to move from small-scale successes to making a bigger difference, resources for development through NGOs have increased consistently. From 1970 to 1999, NGO aid went up from US$3.6 billion to US$12.4 billion annually, equivalent to 21.6 per cent of total development assistance from members of the OECD (see Table 5.1).

For most of that time official donor grants to NGOs also increased. Although the proportion of official aid going through NGOs has reduced since the mid-1990s, private funding of NGOs continues to increase and more than offsets this decline. In fact, the proportion of NGOs' resources coming from private sources has never fallen below 65 per cent and by 1999 it was above 85 per cent and rising. Nevertheless, access to official aid funds has become extremely important to NGOs generally, and particularly for some NGOs. Thus, although NGOs have their own agendas and cannot be regarded simply as vehicles for implementing official aid policies and programmes, donors' expectations of what NGOs should do has a considerable influence on them.

Table 5.1   NGO and official aid to developing countries
(constant 1990 $bn)

	1970	1980	1988	1999
Total NGO aid to developing countries	3.6	5.2	6.9	12.4
private donations	3.5	3.6	4.5	10.7
official grants	0.1	1.6	2.4	1.7
OECD official aid	29.5	42.1	51.4	46.6
NGO aid as % of OECD aid	11.0	11.4	12.3	21.6

Source: Clark, 2003: 130.

Within the general upward trend, official funding has been affected by contradictory factors at different times, stemming from changing donor views on how to achieve aid effectiveness and the best role for NGOs. Thus there was a dramatic increase in official aid channelled through NGOs from the mid-1970s, consolidated through the 1980s and early 1990s, influenced by the rise of governments in the West committed to neoliberal economics and the disenchantment of many Western donors with the performance of government in the developing world. However, from the early 1990s most leading donors reduced aid relative to their GNP until, by 1997, OECD donors gave the smallest share of their GNPs in aid since comparable statistics began in the 1950s – less than 0.25 per cent (World Bank, 1998: 2). Aid channelled through NGOs also fell dramatically. Since 1997, with increasing commitment to the International Development Targets (IDTs) and now the Millennium Development Goals, aid/GNP ratios are increasing again. However, donors seem to be continuing to reduce aid flows through Northern NGOs, in relative if not in absolute terms, perhaps because they are revising their view of the state as an obstacle to pro-poor change and are now working to strengthen state capacity. Nevertheless, as already noted, the resources of Northern NGOs have remained buoyant due to growth in private donations (Table 5.1).

The figures in Table 5.1 are heavily influenced by trends in the United States, which by virtue of its size accounts for almost half of official and private funding channelled by Northern NGOs to developing countries. However, the various members of the OECD vary considerably in how much official aid goes through NGOs and how much the latter depend on these funds compared to private donations. In Britain, for example, official support to NGOs is relatively low, although it has fluctuated over the years, increasing from 1.3 per cent between 1983 and 1986 to 7.6 per cent of DFID expenditure in 1999, and falling back to 5.5 per cent of an increased DFID budget by 2003. By comparison, the US percentage has been close to 10 per cent throughout.

It is US development NGOs that are largely responsible for the statistic that Northern NGOs derive a large and increasing proportion of their funding from non-government sources, since they are even more heavily privately funded than those based in other Northern countries. Nevertheless, official aid accounts for much less than half the funds of British NGOs. According to one estimate, NGOs with an international development remit receive 20 per cent of all donations to UK charities (Randell and German, 1999a: 236), equivalent to £1.5 billion in 2001/02.

These changes in aid funding have each been accompanied by changes in donor expectations of NGOs. Thus in the 1980s, with donors favouring structural adjustment lending including deregulation, liberalization and privatization, the increase in official aid funds going through NGOs corresponded with the view that they could deliver humanitarian relief and local development effectively, reaching the poorest communities at relatively low cost. However, many Northern NGOs continued with building long-term relations of trust with Southern partner organizations and working politically towards social transformation and alternative models of development based on empowerment and reciprocity. The tension between these approaches was exacerbated with the adoption of the IDTs in the 1990s and then the MDGs. Bebbington (2005) examines the case of Dutch aid and changes in the 'co-financing programme' with Dutch NGOs up to early 2002. He shows how the need to demonstrate impact in terms of poverty reduction and other specific targets has undermined trust and partnership relationships. Dutch NGOs have shifted to working with different types of local CSO and reduced those programmes which had less immediately measurable impact, such as research or broader political empowerment through social movement organizations.

More recently, along with rediscovering the importance of the state (World Bank, 1997), donors have discovered 'civil society'. There is a new rationale for working with NGOs which is applied to working with civil society organizations (CSOs) more broadly. It is argued that they can facilitate a certain type of empowerment process involving making the voice of the poor heard, thus helping to hold government agencies to account, and these 'voice and accountability' roles can help ensure that pro-poor policies are designed and implemented. Hence a partnership with CSOs that play these roles can complement a shift to the promotion of poverty reduction strategy programmes (PRSPs) together with direct budget support or sector-wide approaches (SWAps) on the part of donors.

Donors still put considerable amounts of finance into NGO provision of relief and services, despite the growing presumption that state provision is the best long-term solution (and NGOs should shift to the above 'voice and accountability' role). However, there are many states without the capacity to undertake poverty reduction programmes, or lacking the political commitment or willingness to do so within the PRSP framework preferred by donors. Within the past two years a specific secondary role for NGOs has developed in donor thinking, namely to deliver humanitarian relief and other services in these 'fragile' or 'failed' states, in the hope of achieving direct impact on the MDGs.

The next two sections discuss 'voice' and 'impact', respectively, as the main current donor rationales for working with NGOs.

'Voice' as the New Donor Rationale for Working with NGOs

Interpreting the political role of NGOs in terms of 'voice' can be traced back to an influential paper by Samuel Paul (1992), which applies the seminal work of Hirschman (1970) on 'exit, voice and loyalty' to the question of accountability in public services. Paul suggests it is important to have available both the option of 'exit' – via a market-based alternative to state services – and that of 'voice' – promoting responsiveness and opportunities for public participation:

> Public service accountability will be sustained only when the 'hierarchical control' (HC) over service providers is reinforced by the public's willingness and ability to exit [i.e. marketization] or to use voice [i.e. direct participation]. (Paul, 1992: 1047–8)

By 1999, at the Third International NGO Conference in Birmingham, on 'NGOs in a Global Future', Harry Blair (2000) could claim that 'much and probably most of the international donor community' embraced a 'democratic development paradigm' involving a linear model in which participation for marginalized groups leads to representation and hence empowerment, which in turn allows these groups to influence policy to benefit their constituencies, leading over time to poverty reduction and finally to sustainable human development. This model is not directly about NGOs, and Blair himself expressed doubts about its effectiveness. However, he characterized the paradigm, and NGOs' role in it, as follows:

> [N]ewly *empowered* groups become part of *civil society* and within a political environment of *democratic pluralism* they advocate policy changes that lead to *poverty reduction*. Northern and Southern NGOs, along with developing country

governments and international donors, are the principal outside actors motivating, supporting, and in many way shepherding the process along. (Blair, 2000: 109)

Thus, as with the older rationale of NGOs providing effective relief and development services, the newer idea of donor support for NGOs as part of civil society is a means to an end rather than an end in itself. Currently, the *ends* (or aims) of donor policy are very publicly focused on the MDGs, none of which concerns support to NGOs or CSOs or to civil society per se.

In the UK case, DFID has a biannual Public Service Agreement with the British Treasury, which commits it to a programme of activities and a number of specific targets relating to strategic objectives in support of the MDGs. However, there is no mention of working with NGOs and other CSOs in DFID's PSA 2003–06 (the 2005–08 PSA mentions NGOs, but only as sources of monitoring information on conflict situations), and only brief mention of NGOs and civil society in DFID's latest self-evaluation, the 2006 Autumn Performance Report, which reports against the objectives of the PSAs. The impression is not of any systematic working with NGOs and civil society but rather that this happens to be useful in particular cases, reinforcing the view that working with NGOs is a means rather than an end. This is stated explicitly in the recent National Audit Office report on DFID's engagement with civil society (NAO, 2006).

By 2005, DFID had produced several Institutional Strategy Papers, some identifying specific roles that NGOs and civil society may play with respect to achieving particular MDGs. However, DFID has no strategy paper or other single authoritative benchmark statement of policy on engagement with NGOs and other CSOs. Hence its rationale for working with NGOs has to be inferred from a range of sources, including ministerial speeches, the 1997, 2000 and 2006 White Papers on International Development, the internal DFID guide on *How to Work with Civil Society*, target strategy papers, country assistance plans and programme partnership agreements.

Clare Short, Secretary of State for International Development, made a speech to the 1999 Birmingham NGO conference suggesting a model very similar to that put forward by Harry Blair at that same conference. For Clare Short, government provision is the best way to provide core public services such as basic health and education. Civil society can push for the major reforms required if governments are to meet poverty reduction and other development goals. In this model, aid to governments is more effective than 'isolated development projects', but only if there is 'local leadership committed to poverty reduction which is backed by access to expertise'. Civil society is the source of the political will that ensures that commitment:

> What we need in order to ensure that we meet the 2015 targets is for [civil society] groups throughout both the developed and developing world to know that a major

advance in poverty reduction is possible, and to demand of their governments
that the international system is put to work to ensure that it is done.

Within this general model, Southern NGOs are seen as having 'a crucial role
in helping local people to realize their human rights and demand improvements in the provision of core government services', while Northern NGOs
are 'building a popular base for development' in the north, 'lobbying governments and international institutions", and 'helping to empower the poor'.

In her speech, Clare Short says that 'it is important that southern NGOs
do not confine themselves to service delivery or advocacy on behalf of the
poor' (they should move beyond that to 'enable the poor to make their
own demands'). This perhaps implies that service delivery and advocacy
work continue alongside the new emphasis on 'development-as-leverage'.
However, service delivery otherwise has no specific place in this basic model
of the role of civil society.

With no DFID strategy paper specifically on civil society or the role of
NGOs, the 2006 White Paper on International Development (*Eliminating
World Poverty: Making Governance Work for the Poor*) is possibly the most
authoritative statement of government and DFID policy on engagement
with CSOs. The ideas have partly become embedded and partly changed
from the previous White Paper in 2000 (*Eliminating World Poverty: Making
Globalisation Work for Poor People*), produced very shortly after Clare Short's
Birmingham speech.

The 2000 White Paper made it clear how DFID was impressed by the
Jubilee 2000 debt campaign and saw support for this type of international
campaigning and networking as potentially more cost-effective than funding NGOs to run small-scale development projects. It signalled a move
away from working specifically with NGOs to engagement with a broader
range of civil society organizations, with more emphasis on working with
Southern CSOs and with faith groups in particular. Thus,

> It is particularly important to strengthen the voices of civil society in developing
> countries and of a range of organizations including faith groups, human rights
> and women's organizations, trade unions, NGOs and cooperatives, each of
> which can play a stronger role in giving poor people a greater voice. (HMG,
> 2000: para. 361)

The DFID document and online resource *How to Work with Civil Society*[3]
works out the implications of this 'voice' model within developing countries.
It explores a variety of ways in which DFID can work with Southern CSOs
to achieve 'a means for poor people to claim their rights', quoting the idea
that 'effective and accountable states need effective and accountable civil
society'. Importantly, it states that strategy for working with CSOs must
depend on an analysis of civil society in each particular country.

In fact, several DFID country offices have worked out somewhat different versions of a similar rationale. Some now have funds specifically for local civil society, usually managed by locally created consortia or boards drawn from a range of local CSOs, with their own criteria for the projects and organizations that will be supported. Thus in Orissa: 'DFID aims to develop partnerships with CSOs in order to help strengthen the capacity of poor people to articulate their needs, and to improve the policies that affect them.' From this basis, the Orissa civil society fund is oriented specifically towards strengthening 'voice', 'knowledge' and 'identity', in order to promote accountability, transparency and responsiveness in government.

The Southern Africa Trust was set up in 2005 with support from DFID and the Swiss Agency for Development and Cooperation, following a consultative process including a commissioned study by CPS (2002). It is very clear about the importance of recognizing power relations and the contested nature of poverty reduction policies:

> Effective policies that have strong popular support are a political outcome of negotiation and bargaining amongst many different interests and constituencies in society. These processes are crucial to building democratic participation and to creating accountable, responsive governance....
>
> The Southern Africa Trust was therefore established in 2005 to support civil society organizations in southern Africa to participate effectively and with credibility in policy dialogue so that the voices of the poor can have a better impact in the development of public policies.[4]

It is also noted that most Southern African states are at best 'emerging' democracies, while civil society is generally weak and fragmented. The Southern Africa Trust explicitly adopts a 'rights-based approach', and it puts forward a rather different emphasis from the Orissa fund, on the promotion of regional dialogue, learning and joint action.

The largest civil society fund is the Poorest Areas Civil Society (PACS) programme, with £27 million allocated over seven years and covering the poorest districts of six states of India. Others include Manusher Jonno in Bangladesh, the background paper for which explicitly links good governance and human rights, stressing that 'the rights-based approach demands a paradigm shift from welfare/charity ... to entitlement' and looking for practical approaches to development which operationalize this link. (Beall et al., n.d.). By 2004, Tanzania and Nigeria also had similar funds, with others planned for Ghana, the Caribbean (region-wide), Iraq and Indonesia (CDS, 2004). Some DFID country offices have a specific Civil Society Strategy – for example, Nigeria, Cameroon, South Africa – although no new ones appear to have been developed in the last two years. In all cases the rationale is a variation on the theme of promoting accountability through making the 'voice of the poor' heard.

The 2006 White Paper further acknowledges the important role of civil society in international campaigning, with very positive mention of the Make Poverty History campaign, which like Jubilee 2000 before it prominently included faith groups. In his Preface, Hilary Benn, now Secretary of State, states that 'Governments did change their policies and made new promises' (HMG, 2006: 5) in response to the global campaign. However, the White Paper implies that there will be no need to change policy again; apparently we now know how to achieve the MDGs, and the challenge is to implement agreed policies and 'to make good on these commitments' (6). The main way this is to be done is through 'good governance', both globally and in individual developing countries. This means that 'the capacity and accountability of public institutions needs to be strengthened' (9).

The focus on governance includes a clear importance given to civil society, though this is stated in a rather general way. Thus, '[b]uilding effective states and better governance' means that 'we need to work not just with governments, but also with citizens and civil society' (HMG, 2006: 21). However, a large part of the rationale is exactly as in the 'voice' model described by Blair: helping to articulate needs, especially those of the poor, participating in policy formulation and particularly holding governments to account. This includes monitoring international donors' performance, but is particularly important in helping build the capacity and accountability of developing states:

> Accountability is at the heart of how change happens ... beyond the formal structures of the state, civil society organizations give citizens power, help poor people get their voices heard, and demand more from politicians and government. (HMG, 2006: 23)

NGOs are mentioned in the White Paper mainly as service providers and particularly in the context of 'fragile states' – which lack entirely the capacity or political will to implement poverty-reducing policies. This is a new and major concern of the 2006 White Paper. NGOs are hardly mentioned in the discussion of how to achieve good governance, as though they are quite distinct from civil society. Nevertheless, DFID's funding of CSOs still goes overwhelmingly to international development NGOs, particularly British ones. However, as announced in the White Paper, a new £100 million Governance and Transparency Fund was launched in 2006, which is 'designed to help citizens hold their governments to account through strengthening the wide range of groups that can empower and support them'[5]. It will be interesting to see whether this new fund in practice broadens the range of types of civil society group supported directly or indirectly by DFID.

'Impact'

Alongside 'voice' is a quite different rationale, of service provision having a direct impact on achieving the MDGs. As noted above, where democratic accountability is not the logic, then funding services by NGOs and other CSOs may still occur if this is seen as the best way to achieve 'aid effectiveness' in a particular context. Note that there is no specific theoretical view about civil society or NGOs underlying this rationale.

DFID defines the concept of aid effectiveness in terms of achieving the MDGs not only through increasing aid but also by ensuring 'better' aid, which among other things means aid that is 'delivered through effective institutions' and 'focuses on results not inputs'.[6] The clear preference is for state provision of basic services, but NGOs may continue to supply services directly if they happen to provide the most effective means of achieving results in terms of impact on the MDGs. This may be the case where they have a strong historical presence and government agencies lack capacity, or particularly in what are increasingly referred to as 'fragile states'. Also, within a neoliberal logic, private service providers can be awarded contracts on a competitive basis, and some of these may be NGOs or other CSOs. They may simply offer the best deal in commercial terms. In other words, NGOs may be regarded as just another private firm, expected to compete for donor contracts on the basis of meeting criteria of efficiency and impact.

In its 2006 White Paper, the UK government lists four public services – education, health, water and sanitation, and 'social protection' – as essential for achieving the MDGs (HMG, 2006: 52). In cases where a government is committed to the MDGs but lacks the capacity to provide these services to the mass of poor people at a sufficient quality to make an impact, they might be contracted out to NGOs (53). The danger of undermining the development of state services is noted: 'in fragile states ... giving aid only through non-governmental organizations (NGOs) or private contractors can actually hold back the process of building the capability of the state' (25).

In practice, in many countries, despite the dominance of 'voice' as the rationale for working with NGOs and other CSOs, these organizations continue to be contracted to provide all kinds of services aimed directly at development goals. Thus, on 2 March 2005, in a written parliamentary answer about support to CSOs in Bangladesh, Secretary of State Hilary Benn pointed out that the Bangladesh Country Assistance Plan 'emphasizes access for the poor to resources and services, and the realization of their rights'. He said that approximately 40 per cent of DFID's Bangladesh programme is channelled through CSOs, but this includes funding for NGO programmes on education, livelihoods improvement and HIV/AIDS (including some very large amounts to certain NGOs – BRAC, CARE

Bangladesh, Samata), as well as considerable but smaller amounts for 'voice' and 'accountability' activities and strengthening civil society – for example, through the Manusher Jonno fund, mentioned above, which provides grants to smaller CSOs 'demanding better human rights and governance'. In other words, the main publicly stated rationale only accounts for a minority of the funds channelled through CSOs.

Bangladesh may be a special case in having several large, well-established NGOs providing services to huge numbers of poor people in parallel with state services. When DFID's 2006 Autumn Performance Report gives examples of how DFID intends 'to address underperformance on those PSA targets that are off track', Bangladesh accounts for three of only six mentions of working with NGOs. Nevertheless, there is no sign of any general model of mixed provision of basic services in donor thinking, as represented by DFID, despite the fact that voluntary organizations form an important part of such mixed provision on a sustainable basis in the UK itself.

As well as countries suffering extreme civil conflict or attempting post-conflict reconstruction, the concept of 'fragile states' also covers cases like Zimbabwe and Burma where the government currently is hostile to donor-promoted models of 'good governance' and refuses to take part in, for example, the PRSP process. The point is made that it is precisely in those countries where the model of good governance breaks down entirely that there is the greatest need for basic services to try to reach the MDG targets. With other donors, the UK is prepared in such cases to bypass government and use CSOs and other agencies to deliver aid:

> Where the government is not committed to helping its citizens, we will still use our aid to help poor people and to promote long-term improvements in governance. But we will do this by working outside government, and with international agencies like the UN and civil society organizations. (HMG, 2006: 24)

Finally, NGOs and other CSOs may be included in sectoral programmes at a global level – for example, on health or education – within which there is a considerable amount of co-funding between donors. In these cases there may be no systematic attempt to keep track of the involvement of NGOs and other CSOs as such. For example, one of DFID's major programmes is the Global Health Initiatives and Global Health Fund, which has a commitment to funding through Public–Private Partnerships (PPPs). While the majority of private partners are commercial firms, NGOs also figure strongly, but would not be treated differently from any private-sector entity. An example in Tanzania is SMARTNET, a joint project between DFID and the Royal Netherlands Embassy for social marketing of insecticide-treated bednets, regarded as a 'trailblazer' for the global 'Roll-Back Malaria' partnership,[7] and implemented by Population Services International, a non-profit organization based in Washington DC, which prides itself on being 'an amalgam of the worlds of commerce and charity'.[8]

'Squeezing Out' Fundamental Aspects of NGO Work in Development

Both these rationales have importance, but judging NGOs only by their direct results in terms of either 'voice' or 'impact' downplays several fundamental aspects of NGO work in development.

First, the discourse on 'voice' fails to acknowledge sufficiently the organizational aspect of facilitating democratic participation. One example is a recent report for DFID on general budget support (sometimes called Direct Budget Support – DBS) (Lawson and Booth, 2004). DBS can replace project-based finance, and potentially cut NGOs out of aid finance entirely. Lawson and Booth state the chain of causality and the key assumptions behind the DBS approach in some detail, explaining the role of policy dialogue, democratic accountability, participatory budget processes, human rights and empowerment, but do not specify a role for CSOs or NGOs. The 2006 White Paper identifies civil society as a source of democratic accountability, but separates this from NGOs – seen as a type of private service provider useful where state capacity is lacking.

However, NGOs also epitomize the organizational element of civil society and play a range of specific roles in democratization (Clark, 1991; Fisher, 1998) and in what we may call 'development governance' (Clarke and Thomas, 2005). These have several dimensions, which do not all conform neatly to one model. For example, Clark (2003) takes the World Bank's (1992) four 'pillars of good governance' (transparency, accountability, rule of law, citizen's voice) and suggests that NGOs should work to hold multilateral institutions and transnational corporations as well as governments to these principles. Tandon (2003: 70–72) suggests a number of roles for civil society in governance in addition to the 'watchdog' role of ensuring the accountability of market institutions and of government at all levels, as well as monitoring elections and compliance with international obligations. These include a demonstration role in how NGOs and other CSOs govern themselves, contesting the dominant development paradigm, and acting to 'influence public negotiations for public good'. They all seem valid, but go well beyond what is implied by the simple 'voice' model.

Second, there is a contradiction between fitting NGOs' political activities into a prescribed 'voice' model and their advocating and contesting policy issues from an independent position. The CPS (2002) report on the

Southern African case, and the related quote above, show how conflictual are the issues.

Development governance involves both cooperative arrangements and conflict. An emphasis solely on cooperative arrangements may neglect the ingrained ideological assumptions of governance and overlook the contested nature of development. For example, in South Africa Wooldridge and Cranko (1995: 344) argue that although governance is about mediation between various social interests, the process is not impartial and involves the state as a 'biased broker'. Donors such as DFID generally adopt a model of 'good' governance similar to that of the World Bank, which reflects neoliberal values by requiring marketization (Leftwich, 1996). In this model NGOs are expected to help promote development in the sense of poverty reduction or other actions aimed at 'ameliorating the disordered faults of progress' (Cowen and Shenton, 1996), while accepting the inevitability of the form 'progress' is taking through the combination of globalized capitalist industrialization with liberal democracy.

Some NGOs, however, may challenge the assumptions and values that underlie particular models of governance and development, while others (or even the same NGOs in different contexts) accept them. Howell and Pearce (2001) consider this a basic distinction, contrasting NGOs which participate in donor-supported 'good governance' within the 'mainstream' neoliberal project with the 'alternative', where CSOs mobilize and act as a focus for 'strong publics' that contest this project with its associated vision of development. Thus, NGOs' advocacy and facilitation is not always aimed at holding government to account to ensure that pro–poor policies are carried out within the existing economic framework, but may in some cases oppose the whole basis of government and donor policies. An obvious example is opposition to privatization where that is a condition for development assistance that includes backing for a civil society 'voice and accountability' role.

A third aspect relates to how NGOs provide humanitarian relief and other services. These activities can fit into the 'mainstream' discourse of development, not questioning the neoliberal basis of globalization, but there are possible 'alternative' roles which challenge this discourse. This occurs when services are provided on a non-market basis. Just as the facilitation of opposition to neoliberal marketization and globalization may be 'squeezed out' by the dominance of the linear model of 'voice and accountability', so 'alternative' forms of service provision may be 'squeezed out' by the dominance of the logics of 'efficiency' and 'impact'.

In fact NGOs often provide quality services for their own sake, not to achieve specific targets. Many working in co-operatives, mutual or charitable organizations would argue that some quality comes specifically from the value basis of such organizations – which can often be summarized as aspects of 'reciprocity'. For example, a local CSO may promote community- and family-based support to AIDS orphans by building up reciprocal relationships which are valuable in their own right, beyond the impact on poverty measures. It is perhaps surprising that this type of rationale seems to have been lost completely – there are sound arguments why mutual or non-profit provision has advantages in particular circumstances.

Using outcomes like impact or efficiency to compare services provided by NGOs and other agencies has several serious deficiencies. Wallace and Chapman (2003) point out that two important issues tend to be glossed over in outcome-based evaluations: the quality of relationships (between donor and NGO, between Northern NGO and local partner organization, between all these and 'beneficiaries'), and the process or methods through which NGOs and CSOs work (e.g. trying to empower women or address the needs of the most excluded at the same time as meeting specific output targets). Both are aspects of reciprocity. The 2006 UK White Paper does mention empowerment of women and girls through NGO activities, but does not consider how NGOs come to be good at this type of work as a result of their value basis.

Concentrating on impact implies measuring the short-term performance of interventions or organizations, and may disregard sustainability (see e.g. LaFond, 1995). Some authors go further, arguing that pressure for measurable accountability actually acts *against* sustainable development. For example:

> the demands of sustainability contradict the requirements for an unambiguous demonstration of [NGO] achievements. To be sustainable, benefits of external inputs must be generated from changes in economic, social, political, environmental and other processes – which continue once external assistance withdraws. To achieve this, the outcomes of an [NGO's] activities must merge into ongoing processes rather than clearly stand apart from them.... If they do their work properly, [NGO] effects cannot be kept separate in order to be measured. (Fowler, 1997: 162–3)

A fourth point is about the relationship of NGOs and other CSOs with government agencies. The dominant donor rationale sees NGOs either playing a part in holding governments to account or else filling in gaps in services where governments cannot or will not provide them. But there is also the possibility of working in partnership with government, either through 'co-production' of services by governmental and non-governmental actors (Tendler, 1997) or 'co-governance' in the political and policy arena (Ackerman, 2004). However, although the 2006 UK White Paper repeatedly calls for government and civil society (and indeed the private sector) to 'work together', this remains rather vague. Neither 'co-production' nor 'co-governance' ideas seem to figure in current donor thinking.

Fifth, NGOs' service delivery and promoting 'voice' or rights work are not necessarily separate but may reinforce each other. Thus, for example, developing a new and innovative approach to a particular service will provide that NGO with experience and data to inform lobbying for a change in approach by state agencies. Similarly, a participative style of service provision can lead to empowerment as well as staff satisfaction and hence underpin advocacy or demands for rights.

To illustrate this point, consider the following case study, taken from research by Johnson and Thomas (2003, 2004). A Ugandan NGO shifted its aims from providing services for children with disability (CWDs) to promoting their rights. The idea was to achieve an institutional set-up with an expectation that provision for CWDs should be included in state services, so that the resources of other agencies (schools, ministries) would be leveraged in and accountability demanded if services did not become available. Rather than abandoning the NGO's own work with disabled children in favour of a combination of state provision and a lobbying role for the NGO, its director insisted that the NGO should continue providing services which embodied the notion of rights for such children by treating them with full respect, as a means of promoting these rights more generally. This was undertaken at the same time as participation in the national poverty strategy forum and lobbying nationally and internationally for the rights of disabled children.

This combination seems crucial (rather than concentrating either only on service delivery or only on lobbying). Grassroots involvement motivates staff and helps to maintain the organization's values internally, while at the same time providing credibility as well as the evidence of detailed examples to assist the lobbying effort. Conversely the policy involvement and networking strengthens the NGO's commitment to children's rights and participation, and reinforces its resolve to carry these particular values through into its everyday practices.

Finally, NGOs and other CSOs have a strong role at a global level which is underplayed by concentrating on the role of 'voice' in holding individual governments to account and the 'impact' of services provided in particular countries. The 2006 UK White Paper has a chapter on promoting good governance internationally, which has just a couple of mentions of CSOs with respect to particular examples, but no systematic role for global civil society, and another chapter on reforming the international development system which does not mention civil society and only discusses NGOs with respect to improving the international response to humanitarian crises. Similarly, in the chapters on promoting peace and security and managing climate change there is virtually no mention of NGOs or civil society and certainly not of their potential global lobbying role. This is a remarkable omission from DFID's rationale for working with NGOs, particularly since apparently it was admiration for global civil society campaigns like Jubilee 2000 and Make Poverty History that led DFID to incorporate such a strong 'voice and accountability' role for civil society in their model of good governance.

In conclusion, it appears that the value basis of NGOs and other CSOs is in danger of being devalued. At the beginning of this chapter we noted the diversity of values and interests underpinning NGOs and other CSOs. I argued that many of these values can be brought together under the rubric of reciprocity (Polanyi, 1957), as an organizing principle that differentiates NGOs from both private-sector and government agencies. NGOs' work can be divided into their political role in civil society and their practical role in providing services. Donors such as DFID conceptualize their work with NGOs mainly in terms of these two roles, but in each case they are expected to perform in a very limited way, conforming to a prescribed model based on the rationales of 'voice' and 'impact'. This tends to ignore or downplay the importance of reciprocity as an organizing principle, and the variety of values underpinning the way NGOs relate to development within this principle.

What are the implications? We should not throw out the baby with the bathwater. The 'voice and accountability' agenda is a great advance on what went before. Where there is recognition of the contested and conflictual nature of the issues, as in the Southern African example, there seems to be a very good basis to build on. But it also seems essential not to lose what is specific and uniquely valuable about NGOs by making them fit into simple linear models.

In DFID's case, the recent paper *Civil Society and Development* also mentions civil society's roles in conflict resolution, global advocacy and innovation in service delivery approaches, plus an 'elusive' role in 'global fellowship and solidarity'.[9] These ideas are found very little elsewhere in recent DFID documents. They probably represent a description of the variety of roles played by CSOs in different parts of the world, where they have various histories of action and relate to donors such as DFID in many different ways. It is not clear if the simpler dual rationale of 'voice' and 'impact', found for example in the 2006 White Paper, is likely to be imposed more strongly in the future, with the concomitant danger of 'squeezing out' other valuable aspects of NGOs in respect of development. The alternative is that the variety of civil society roles in *Civil Society and Development* shows the potential for DFID policy, and hence that of other donors, to evolve in a way that brings back a recognition of the importance of the variety of values motivating NGOs and other CSOs, particularly the underlying principle of reciprocity.

Notes

1. Part of the introductory section is based on material published in the *Handbook of International Development Governance* (Clarke and Thomas, 2005). Some of the data were collected for use in a study of DFID's Engagement with Civil Society commissioned by the National Audit Office. Thanks to Gerard Clarke for his collaboration. Thanks too to Diana Mitlin and participants at the Manchester Conference for their critical comments. The overall argument, and its weaknesses, are mine.

2. www.brac.net/about (accessed 5 March 2007).

3. www.dfid.gov.uk/aboutdfid/DFIDwork/workwithcs/cs-how-to-work-intro.asp (accessed 6 March 2007).

4. www.southernafricatrust.org/background.html (accessed 5 March 2007)

5. Governance and Transparency Fund Criteria and Guidelines, www.dfid.gov. uk/funding/gtf-guidelines07.asp (accessed 6 March 2007).

6. See note on Aid Effectiveness on DFID website: www.dfid.gov.uk/mdg/aid-effectiveness/what-is.asp (accessed 6 March 2007).

7. www.dfid.gov.uk/casestudies/files/africa/tanzania-malaria.asp (accessed 26 February 2005); for an update see www.dfid.gov.uk/pubs/files/tb-malaria-control.pdf (accessed 6 March 2007).

8. www.psi.org/about_us/explained.html (accessed 6 March 2007).

9. www.dfid.gov.uk/pubs/files/civil-society-dev.pdf (accessed 6 March 2007).

References

Ackerman, J. (2004) 'Co-Governance for Accountability: Beyond "Exit" and "Voice"', *World Development* 32(3), 447–63.

Annis, S. (1987) 'Can Small-scale Development Be a Large-scale Policy? The Case of Latin America', *World Development* 15 (supplement): 129–34.

Beall, J., D. Lewis and C. Sutherland (n.d.) 'Supporting Human Rights and Governance: A Background Paper on Conceptual and Operational Approaches', draft background paper to Manusher Jonno Civil Society Fund for Bangladesh, www.manusher. org/draft.pdf (accessed 27 March 2005 and 05 March 2007)

Bebbington, A. (2005) 'Donor-NGO Relations and Representations of Livelihood in Nongovernmental Aid Chains', *World Development* 33(6): 937–50.

Bishop, J., and P. Hoggett (1986) *Organising around Enthusiasms*, Comedia, London.

Blair, H. (2000) 'Civil Society, Empowerment, Democratic Pluralism and Poverty Reduction: Delivering the Goods at National and Local Levels', in D. Lewis and T. Wallace (eds), *New Roles and Relevance: Development NGOs and the Challenge of Change,* Kumarian Press, West Hartford CT, pp. 109–119.

Butler, R., and D. Wilson (1990) *Managing Voluntary and Non-profit Organizations*, Routledge, London.

CDS (2004) 'A Leap of Faith? DFID Engagement with Faith-Based Organizations and the Role of Faith Groups in Poverty Reduction', report to DFID, Centre for Development Studies, University of Wales, Swansea, December.

Chambers, R. (1997) *Whose Reality Counts? Putting the First Last*, Intermediate Technology Publications, London.

Clark, J. (1991) *Democratizing Development: The Role of Voluntary Organizations*, Kumarian Press, West Hartford, CT.

Clark, J. (2003) *Worlds Apart: Civil Society and the Battle for Ethical Globalization*, Earthscan, London.

Clarke, G., and Thomas, A. (2005) 'Non-governmental Organizations, Civil Society and Development Governance', in H. Zafarullah and A. Huque (eds), *Handbook of International Development Governance*, Marcel Decker.

Cowen, M., and R. Shenton (1996) *Doctrines of Development*, Routledge, London.

CPS (Centre for Policy Studies) (2002) 'Civil Society and Poverty Reduction in Southern Africa: Analytical Overview of the Political Economy of the Civil Society Sector in Southern Africa with regard to the Poverty Reduction Agenda', research report prepared for DFID, July.

Edwards, M., and D. Hulme (1995) 'NGO Performance and Accountability in the Post-Cold War World', *Journal of International Development* 7(6): 849–56.

Fisher, J. (1998) *Nongovernments: NGOs and the Political Development of the Third World*, Kumarian Press, West Hartford CT.

Fowler, A. (1997) *Striking a Balance: A Guide to Enhancing the Effectiveness of Non-Governmental Organizations in International Development*, Earthscan, London.

Freire, P. (1972) *The Pedagogy of the Oppressed*, Penguin, Harmondsworth.

Gherardi, S., and A. Masiero (1990) 'Solidarity as a Networking Skill and a Trust Relation: Its Implications for Cooperative Development', *Economic and Industrial Democracy* 11(4): 553–574.

Handy, C. (1988) *Understanding Voluntary Organizations*, Penguin, Harmondsworth.

Hirschman, A. (1970) *Exit, Voice and Loyalty: Responses to Decline in Firms, Organizations and States*, Harvard University Press, Cambridge MA.

HMG (2000) *Eliminating World Poverty: Making Globalisation Work for the Poor*, White Paper on International Development, Her Majesty's Government.

HMG (2006) *Eliminating World Poverty: Making Governance Work for the Poor*, White Paper on International Development, Her Majesty's Government.

Howell, J., and J. Pearce (2001) *Civil Society and Development: A Critical Introduction*, Lynne Rienner, Boulder CO.

Hudson, M. (1995) *Managing without Profit: The Art of Managing Third-sector Organizations*, Penguin, Harmondsworth.

Johnson, H., and A. Thomas (2003) 'Education for Development Policy and Management: Impacts on Individual and Organizational Capacity-Building – A Study of Four Postgraduate Programmes Based in UK and Southern Africa', Report to DFID, unpublished.

Johnson, H., and A. Thomas (2004) 'Professional Capacity and Organizational Change as Measures of Educational Effectiveness: Assessing the Impact of Postgraduate Education in Development Policy and Management', *Compare* 34(3): 301–14.

Korten, D. (1990) *Getting to the Twenty-First Century: Voluntary Action and the Global Agenda*, West Hartford CT, Kumarian Press.

LaFond, A. (1995) *Sustaining Primary Health Care*, London, Earthscan.

Lawson, A. and D. Booth (2004) 'Evaluation Framework for General Budget Support', Report to Management Group for the Joint Evaluation of General Budget Support, Overseas Development Institute, London, February.

Leftwich, A. (1996) 'On the Primacy of Politics in Development', in A. Leftwich (ed.), *Democracy and Development*, Polity Press, Cambridge, pp. 3–24.

NAO (2006) 'Department for International Development: Working with Non-Governmental and Other Civil Society Organizations to Promote Development', Report by the Comptroller and Auditor General, HC1311 Session 2005–2006, National Audit Office, London.

Paton, R. (1991) 'The Social Economy: Value-based Organizations in the Wider Society', in J. Batsleer, C. Cornforth and R. Paton (eds), *Issues in Voluntary and Non-profit Management,* Addison-Wesley, Reading, pp. 3–12.

Paul, S. (1992) 'Accountability in Public Services: Exit, Voice and Control', *World Development* 20(7): 1047–60.

Polanyi, K. (1957) *The Great Transformation* (1944), Beacon Press, Boston.

Poulton, R. and M. Harris (1988) *Putting People First: The NGO Approach to Development,* Macmillan, London.

Randell, J., and T. German (1999) 'United Kingdom', in I. Smillie and H. Helmich (eds), *Stakeholders: Government–NGO Partnerships for International Development,* Earthscan, London.

ROAPE (1992) 'Democracy, Civil Society and NGOs', Special Issue of *Review of African Political Economy* 20(55): 3–8.

Schumacher, E.F. (1973) *Small is Beautiful,* Abacus, London.

Streeck, W., and P. Schmitter (eds) (1985) 'Community, Market, State and Associations? The Prospective Contribution of Interest Governance to Social Order', in W. Streeck and P. Schmitter (eds), *Private Interest Government: Beyond Market and State,* Sage, London.

Stryjan, Y. (1989) *Impossible Organizations – Self Management and Organizational Reproduction,* Greenwood Press, Westport CT.

Tandon, R. (2003) 'The Civil Society–Governance Interface: An Indian Perspective', in R. Tandon and R. Mohanty (eds), *Does Civil Society Matter? Governance in Contemporary India,* Thousand Oaks, New Delhi, and Sage, London, pp. 59–76.

Tendler, J. (1997) *Good Governance in the Tropics,* Johns Hopkins University Press, Baltimore.

Thomas, A. (1992) 'Non-governmental Organizations and the Limits to Empowerment', in M. Wuyts, M. Mackintosh and T. Hewitt (eds), *Development Policy and Public Action,* Oxford University Press, Oxford, pp. 117–146.

Titmuss, R. (1970) *The Gift Relationship: From Human Blood to Social Policy,* Penguin, Harmondsworth.

Vivian, J. (1994) 'NGOs and Sustainable Development in Zimbabwe: No Magic Bullets', *Development and Change* 25(1): 167–193.

Wallace, T., and J. Chapman (2003) 'Some Realities behind the Rhetoric of Downward Accountability', paper to INTRAC 5th Evaluation Conference, Netherlands, 1 April.

Wooldridge, D., and P. Cranko (1995) 'Transforming Public Sector Institutions', in P. Fitzgerald, A. McLennan and B. Munslow (eds), *Managing Sustainable Development in South Africa,* Oxford University Press, Cape Town, pp. 328–49.

World Bank (1991) *World Development Report 1991: The Challenge of Development,* World Bank and Oxford University Press, New York.

World Bank (1998) *Assessing Aid: What Works, What Doesn't and Why,* World Bank and Oxford University Press, New York.

World Development (1987) *Development Alternatives: The Challenge for NGOs,* World Development 15 (supplement).

6

Development and the New Security Agenda: W(h)ither(ing) NGO Alternatives?

Alan Fowler

In the space of some twenty years, non-governmental development organizations (NGDOs) have established a distinct, influential position within the international arena. While improvement is always possible, there are many areas and scales where NGDOs have brought positive change in people's lives, in societies and in the workings of national and international institutions (e.g. Fowler, 2000; Edwards, this volume; Batliwala and Brown, 2006). However, as other chapters argue, success has been accompanied by shadow sides.

The evolution of NGDO-ism has itself worked against the achievement of 'alternative development' in the sense expressed in the mid-1980s: a distinct philosophy and theory of change allied to effective, people-centred development practices (Drabek, 1987: x). Examples of NGDO shadows are: compromise in self-determination, growing dependency on official finance, semi-detachment from the mass of civil society formations, and adopting apolitical state-centric development agendas while claiming to operate according to a distinctive, autonomous logic. In the 1980s, some of these challenges were already anticipated. Others emerged in response to the major discontinuity in the world order caused by the collapse of the Soviet Union.

This chapter does not dwell on the many – both just and unjust – critiques of NGO-ism in terms of these and other shortcomings as self-generated constraints on being 'alternative' (e.g. Lewis and Wallace, 2000; Katsui and Wamai, 2006). Rather, the task is to approach the issue of limitations on NGDOs as development alternatives from the direction of a significant reframing of the aid system, broadly labelled 'securitization' (e.g. Duffield, 2002; Fowler, 2005; Howell, 2006).

Within the competitive geopolitics of the Cold War and a modernization perspective, development and security have always been intertwined as a mutually reinforcing reciprocity in a particular sense. Security creates the predictable conditions required for investment to translate into economic growth, which, in its turn, feeds the expansion of human well-being that reinforces the value of stability and hence of security. Until the Soviet collapse, the notion of NGOs as development alternatives was premised on their application of distinct competencies and comparative advantages to serve this virtuous circularity.

Post-Cold War, the supposedly reluctant but necessary American hegemonic pursuit of a particular type of world order argued for by Mallaby (2002), with its monotheistic undertones lamented by Lal (2004), have invited increasingly violent reactions and the emergence of international insecurity with a new, complex configuration. While perhaps elevated to global consciousness by the terror of al-Quaeda, contemporary insecurity is not simply arising from a supposed clash of cultures, beliefs or civilizations. Insecurity also stems from deeper and wider responses against the dysfunctions – in change-driven anxiety, in environmental unsustainability, in inequality, in injustice – of an enforced globalization of free-market capitalism to which there is, apparently, no alternative either possible or to be tolerated. At a world level at least, the relationship between growth in wealth and national and human security appears not virtuous but inherently destabilizing (Hardt and Negri, 2000). The quest for economic equilibrium on an increasing scale contains forces for disequilibrium (Harvey, 2003). The global system requires active control and management through global governance that may not be up to the task but in any event stubbornly favours the interests of those already empowered.

In this contrary context, NGDOs – within the contending concepts and concomitant agency of civil society – face substantive questions about what 'alternative' means and entails in theory, strategy and practice. In light of the ever deepening reliance of NGDOs on official forms of aid, serious questions arise from the growing integration of overseas development assistance (ODA) into a comprehensive security strategy for the West. Such a strategy is not uniformly employed by each donor country within the Organization for Economic Cooperation and Development (OECD). Nevertheless, the contours of an emerging development for security agenda (DfS) seem likely to shape the possibility of NGDOs either offering or becoming alternatives.

The following section establishes an analytical framework for understanding this problematic. It does so by sketching the major domains of policy and action that donors can deploy to operationalize their foreign relations in an era where domestic security is seen as dependent on the (preventive) development of countries overseas (Beall et al., 2006). Subsequent analysis concentrates on a security-premissed official aid system. The anticipated roles of NGDOs are investigated in terms of conditions that militate for or against behaviours or as 'alternatives' in this security for development triad. The concluding section draws the optics together in a discussion of what alternatives might mean and the extent to which the imperatives of NGDO-ism predispose towards particular choices and possibilities.

Figure 6.1   Overview of potential NGDO limitations due to aid in a security strategy

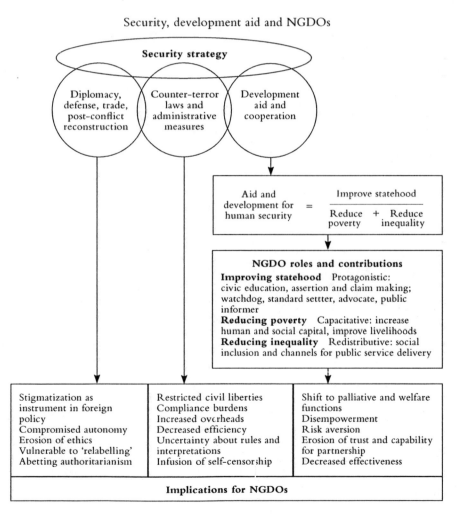

International Security: A Strategic Framework

Figure 6.1 sets out one perspective on the overall strategy towards international security being deployed by 'traditional' donor countries of the industrialized West. It contains three overlapping domains with components that are applied in different combinations depending on the geopolitics in play for any particular donor. The first focuses on dilemmas that can act as constraints on (humanitarian) NGDOs involved in security-related reconstruction. Second are limitations faced by NGDOs arising from the introduction of and compliance with counter-terrorism and related legislation and administrative measures (CTMs). The third lens places NGDOs within a development-for-security imperative to stabilize, strengthen or prevent the falling apart of states considered to be failed, weak or simply unable to govern effectively. Here, the major tasks of aid are substantively to reduce poverty and inequality while simultaneously redressing inadequate statehood, understood as conditions of poor governance. Each domain brings implications for NGDOs either directly through a financing relationship or indirectly by the ways in which operating environments are shaped through security-premissed interactions within and between countries.

The aim is to analyse the implications for NGDO alternatives that emerge from the growing emphasis on each of the three domains of action outlined above, namely: post-conflict reconstruction; counter-terrorism measures; and the securitization of the development agenda. Given the recent nature of the shifts we are discussing, and the contested character of the implications, such an analysis is necessarily contingent and to some extent speculative. Nonetheless, there are initial signs that the evolving security agenda has started to make life even more difficult for NGDOs seeking to forge meaningful alternatives in this new geopolitical context.

Taking Sides in the War on Terror: Sharpening the Dilemmas of Complicity in Managing Imperialism

The Global War on Terror (GWOT) was sold as a pledge to eventually ensure stability and security for all the world's citizens. Thus, perversely justified military force, lacking in UN legitimacy, was applied to protect the interests and extend the influence of the existing political and economic power holders in today's imperial hierarchy. The premiss underlying the pledge is a long-standing belief in the universalism of Western values and political-economy that informed colonialism and orientalism (Wallerstein, 2006). Today, this conviction is pursued through the peaceful assertion of diplomacy, trade and negotiation in international institutions. But, when (violently) challenged, it is imposed and managed using force and favour.

However, hard military power has limits. In the aftermath of violence the 'soft power' of mobilizing public support is necessary to create the conditions required for stabilization of a new order. A key soft power element of the security agenda is provision of aid for post-conflict reconstruction, particularly as witnessed in Afghanistan and Iraq.

One outflow is a role for the military in 'armed social work' to win hearts and minds through reconstruction while maintaining order by force of arms (Kukis, 2006). For example, through the US Army Peacekeeping and Stability Operations Institute (PKSOI) and Department of Defence Directive 3000.05, of 28 November 2005, America has probably gone furthest in its policy and practice of integrating military functions with aid efforts.

> Stability operations are conducted to help establish order that advances U.S. interests and values. The immediate goal often is to provide the local populace with security, restore essential services, and meet humanitarian needs. The long-term goal is to help develop indigenous capacity for securing essential services, a viable market economy, rule of law, democratic institutions, and *a robust civil society*. (USDoD, 2005: 2, emphasis added)

The blurring of military and humanitarian efforts in post-conflict settings is already well explored in terms of moral issues (Schweizer, 2004). For example, while NGDOs may be non-uniformed 'alternatives' to the military, they can be locally perceived as indistinct from their home country's interests. Associated pitfalls include: stigmatization as an instrument of foreign policy; compromised autonomy; eroded ethics; vulnerability to political relabelling of states or groups within them as 'terrorist'; and exposure to charges of abetting authoritarian regimes that are of geopolitical interest to a donor government (FIFC, 2004).

However, the contemporary security situation sharpens existing dilemmas for NGDOs in that it more clearly exposes the extent to which, in providing humanitarian relief and post-conflict reconstruction services, they are complicit in serving a geopolitical agenda of dubious moral and legal grounding. So, can NGDOs fulfil humanitarianism in 'alternative' ways that do not make them politically complicit? To do so,

> NGOs would require a radical change in their relationships to western governments, UN agencies, and the marginalized communities they work in. The political analysis of humanitarian crises and humanitarian action is deeply challenging to humanitarians, particularly NGOs. Its central message is that, in a global economy with global communications, no one sits outside the power structures that shape people's lives, least of all NGOs with a western genesis largely funded by western governments and a western public. These are not easy issues for NGOs to face, not least because they are premised on political-economy models which owe as much to one's political beliefs as they do to empirical evidence. As a result, opting for these models requires agencies to make political judgments. (Feinstein Centre, 2004: 82)

Some NGDOs reach political judgement by refusing to work in post-conflict settings such as Iraq and Afghanistan or do so without finance from assailant states. Others assume that it is possible to finesse, deny or ignore ethical ambiguities which implies a compatibility between a unilaterally pursued hegemonic world order, respect for human rights and politically neutral humanitarianism that may be more fiction than fact. Pragmatism rules. Yet others assume that, through on-the-ground experience, their advocacy can 'humanitarianise politics without politicizing humanitarianism', a position of business as usual (Janz, 2006).

The second dilemma of alternative lurks in the quotation from the US military. This is the role of NGDOs in building a robust post-conflict civil society. In whose image? With what methods when shielded by an occupying military force? With what approach to political autonomy given the overbearing presence of external power? These and other difficult questions also apply to the development lens detailed later. But here, after the trauma of war and destruction, neither NGDOs or anyone else seem capable of building civil society in the conflict-ridden hinterlands of the latest imperial encounter.

A third dilemma flows from the second and can be applied to other types of complex political conflicts, such as Darfur and the Ivory Coast. This is the enduring question of an appropriate division of roles between local and foreign NGDOs. Are alternative policies and strategies required that may or may not be served by the developmental notion of 'partnership? And, given the political-economy of Northern NGDOs alluded to on the Feinstein quotation, are empowering relational alternatives feasible?

Constraints on NGDOs Associated with Counter-terrorism Measures

Enhanced counter terrorism measures (CTMs) were prompted by the al-Quaeda-instigated attack in America, with United Nations Resolution 1371 of 2001 calling on all members to apply themselves to combat terror within their areas of jurisdiction. Satisfying this entreaty has typically relied on counter-terrorism measures that apply to all citizens and organizations, with what most observers agree are negative implications for the exercise of basic civic rights (Sidel, 2004). Our reading of CTMs suggests that they are likely to have a series of negative implications for NGDOs, in terms of:

• restriction on the basic civil liberties under which they are created and operate;
• additional burdens for compliance;
• increase in overhead costs;
• uncertainty about rules and their application;

- infusion of self-censorship;
- heightened risk aversion.

We outline each concern in greater depth before exploring the evidence to date.

Legal and administrative demands

A primary structural response to prevent violent terrorism has been the passing of new legislation in countries of the North and South, alongside the employment of existing administrative procedures to achieve similar ends. The breadth and scope of these laws has rendered their effects pervasive within the aid system – from back donor to the local office of an International NGDO to Southern NGDOs, communities and residents. They are critical tools in a central approach to combating terrorism: starvation of funding, allied to tracing terrorists through the resources they mobilize. The sums involved in terrorist attacks are not necessarily large and could easily be hidden within transfers between NGDOs. For example, the Madrid train bombing is thought to have cost around €15,000.

To a significant extent, CTMs introduce and rely on government-specified lists of proscribed individuals and organizations. Such lists are shared between governments and posted on the Internet. Because lists come from security services and the prospect of terrorist acts makes governments more mistrustful, secretive and risk averse, they cannot be effectively challenged.

Know yourself and beyond

Legislation and 'voluntary best practices' require an NGDO to ensure that none of their staff or those known to be providing funding is on a proscribed list. 'Know yourself' also implies adopting and continually monitoring procedures and systems to ensure compliance with what CTM requires. A natural tension arises from the 'know yourself' maxim when NGDO employees find themselves subject to employer scrutiny. Demonstrating and confirming in writing that an applicant for public finance is able to comply with CTM are now part and parcel of USAID's procedures and a formal requirement for Australian Aid.

Know (beyond) your partner

Counter-terrorism legislation is creating a direct obligation on Northern NGDOs, foundations and similar funders to vouch for the probity of the recipients of their support in terms of eligibility and ultimate use of assistance. Approaches to the interpretation of CTM laws also appear to require a funder to vouch for a partner's partner or, even further, for the bona fides of the final recipient of benefits that funds create. Some US government agencies also now require a Northern NGDO or Foundation to certify in writing that it has not only checked lists of terrorist organizations but also investigated the data available publicly about its grantees.

Follow the money to and from your organization

To ensure that financial resources are not directly or indirectly deployed to support terrorists or their causes, new laws on international financial transfers are now being applied to NGDOs, as well as remittances. In addition, previously existing laws or regulations defined and propagated by the Financial Action Task Force (FATF) in the US are being more vigorously enforced. Originally established to counter money laundering, in 2002 FATF's mandate was extended to combat terrorism financing.

Two other constraints arise in the 'follow the money' issue. First, the US Laws apply to not only the transfer of money but also prohibit 'material support' to terrorists or foreign terrorist organizations. These and related laws define support to include 'lodging, training, expert advice or assistance, safe houses ... communications equipment or other physical assets except medicine or religious materials' (InterAction, 2004). Second, U.S. and many other laws prohibit making illegal money legal. This means that the NGDO must not only follow where it sends money, but also know where it came from to ensure that the organization is not being used as a 'laundry' (US Government, 2002; OECD, 2002).

Administrative measures

Alongside these public and overt measures are preliminary indications of subtler ways in which counter-terrorism strategies are pursued. In the case of aid, governments are seldom legally challenged about the way public funds are allocated to NGDOs. Consequently, a choice can easily be made to tighten procedures and requirements – for example, by demanding more information and to apply more stringent risk assessments. Moreover, one of the reasons why decisions about fund reallocation may not be challenged is because Northern NGDOs seldom want to 'rock the boat' or seem to be too difficult or too demanding – the dilemma of being 'too close for comfort' (Edwards and Hulme, 1995). NGDOs that do take issue with such moves are often financed from other (private) sources, which can deepen schisms and the strength of a united front among NGDOs. Thus, self-censorship can result in grudging compliance, although the political realities of a country determine the degree to which this covert scenario plays out.

Organizational implications: burdens and risks

It is clear that laws and procedural changes require much greater NGDO diligence. Examples are: staff educational programmes on the laws, background checks on employees, internal notification systems and confidential procedures for reporting suspicious transactions, manual or electronic review of lists of 'blocked' organizations, use of 'red flag' checklists to identify potentially dangerous grantees, more complex grant agreements and procedures, reduction or elimination of cash transfers in favour of international correspondent banks, and certification by the recipient NGDO confirming proper fund use.

The costs involved in compliance are likely to be added to organizational overheads. This places additional strain on an already contested (comparative) measure of NGDO efficiency. And, it is far from clear that donors will allow their funds to be used to satisfy CTM requirements. Unlike others, the USA has accepted high overhead levels due to auditing compliance requirements. The danger for non-U.S. NGDOs is that their respective countries adopt CTM but are not willing to accept the extra costs of conforming to what the law requires. At the same time, violation of the laws has serious consequences. In the USA, organizations and individuals associated with the organizations that make improper financial transfers are subject to both criminal and civil penalties. Additionally, charities run the risk of losing their charitable and tax-exempt status.

A normal organizational response to increased threats and uncertainties is to reduce risk, and NGDOs have several options here. Selection of partners and programmes is one of the most obvious. But making significant effort and investment in order to comply fully with legal and administrative requirements can also reduce risk. Another possibility is for a governing body to redefine their risk tolerance levels and risk management strategies and communicate them publicly to show both awareness and openness that improve public image and funders' confidence.

Although the cases of diversion of non-profit funds to terrorism may be few and far between, the precautionary and preventive intensions of counter-terrorism measures mean that, like all other CSOs, NGDOs have to conform.

Implications and experiences

Evidence that CTMs are tightening the space for civil society is increasingly available via the journals and periodic publications of specialist NGDOs, like the Civicus civil society watch programme (CIVICUS, n.d.), which monitor and report on the refinement of legislation and rules justified by terrorism. A common move – under way for example in India – is to (further) increase government oversight and discretionary control on the flow of foreign funds to local CSOs. Enhancing a state's legal ability to restrict the freedom of (religious) association is also becoming more common. However, and although it is not easy to establish effects in practice, some insights are possible.

For example, in order to create awareness and stimulate well-considered, collective responses, during 2006 and 2007, the International NGO Training and Research Centre (Intrac) organized a series of exploratory workshops on CTMs. These events, each with about twenty-five participants mainly from the region concerned, took place in Europe, South Asia, Central Asia, the Middle East, the USA and with the Somali diaspora in the United Kingdom. These forums provided an opportunity to gather and share information about NGO experiences of these measures in action. The difficulties involved in doing so became readily apparent.

For example, after the first event in the Netherlands, the term 'counter-terrorism' was seldom used to title subsequent workshops. Participants envisaged significant problems with security and immigration services if this term was used in correspondence or invitations, and so urged caution for reasons of obtaining visas and reducing visibility of the initiative. Instead, workshops were often labelled as reviews of relations between state and civil society.

To provide confidence in a space for open discussion, workshop results were not widely published and were only accessible on the Intrac website for those with passwords. Further, workshop notes or reports did not attribute comments to any specific person or organization. Even then, exchanges were often guarded. Self-censorship is in play, particularly with Southern NGDOs. Talking about the constraints imposed by CTMs can too readily be treated as an attempt to discredit the government, inviting punitive responses with little expectation of legal redress.

There are the signs of other effects. Some are well-publicized cases of NGOs, such as Interpal. This British charity was designated a terrorist organization by the US government for its alleged role in channelling funds to Hamas. Despite the Charity Commission finding the charity 'well run and committed', the British government would not intercede to have the designation removed. A Danish NGO found itself in a similar situation and, when cleared of any wrongdoing, was advised to change its name because the government was unable to get the organization take off of the US listing. Examples are also emerging of the 'war on terror' being used as a cover for government harassment of NGDOs and popular forces raising critical voices on issues such as the environment in Peru and land rights in Pakistan (Intrac, 2007).

In refusing to sign CTM certification clauses, some NGDOs are reducing their resource base. Others are having to deal with government requests to accompany staff to the field as well as having to explain their partners to government agents. Paradoxically, this effect may induce Northern NGOs to remain or re-become development implementers so that they can avoid the hassle and risks of this role being taken up by their local counterparts, which many have been striving for. This would mark a step backwards in the wider project of Northern NGDOs 'handing over the power' to Southern NGDOs, particularly vis-à-vis the 'authentic partnership' mode of building inter-organizational relationships (Fowler, 1998). Further, for some American Foundations the administrative burdens of CTM compliance are being accommodated by reducing the number (and increasing the amounts) of grants. A result may be less small seed finance for innovation and for experimenting with alternative forms of social development.

Overall, evidence of the impact of CTMs on NGDOs and development processes is still scanty. One reading suggests that a situation of unclear effects may continue as a form of resistance often adopted by a weaker party (Scott, 1990). Faced by a shifting burden of proof of innocence onto their shoulders, NGDOs are adopting a position of limited disclosure of CTM impact. They are doing so to protect their relationships and to avoid an insinuation that CTMs are making a notable difference, which would suggest their house was not in order.

A natural collective response of NGDOs would be to argue against the blanket effects of CTMs by advocating for risk assessments of individual organizations. But this approach involves complicity in making easier the government's job of implementing unreasonable regulations. Instead, the body representing UK NGDOs involved in international development recommended compliance with requirements of the Charity Commission – the oversight body – which would thus be burdened with working through thousands of pages of reports to gauge regulatory observance (Pers. Comm., BOND).

There are very few legally challenged, let alone proven, cases of NGDOs as supporters of terrorism, making it difficult to assess actual outcomes. One possible reason for the lack of hard evidence could be of a Machiavellian character. For example, one could imagine governments everywhere not only enhancing CTMs for the formal restraint they impose on civil society, but also because the power of (ambiguous) CTMs lies less in their actual application – which would open up challenges showing their limitations – than in their potential to create an atmosphere of fear and uncertainty. Without much additional state effort at monitoring compliance, CTMs provide an opportunity to induce a self-shrinking of space for NGDOs to be 'alternative' in practice as well as in thinking.

Constraints Associated with Development Aid for Security

Counter-terrorism measures were an immediate response to violent at-tack. Later analysis of terrors causes and remedies has given rise to a comprehensive security strategy, outlined in Figure 6.1, where ODA is allocated an important role. The recalibration of overseas development assistance places it more firmly alongside diplomacy, trade and defence as a key instrument of the security agenda (Duffield, 2001; OECD/DAC, 2003; Natios, 2006). Whether or not the use of ODA as a preventative investment can reduce the causes of insecurity (e.g. DFID, 2005) remains subject to ongoing debate. This section describes what this means in terms of possible constraints for NGDOs as alternatives.

Security and ODA

Terrorism provided an urgent impulse to reconsider the link between aid and security. This process has updated development thinking, goals and policy, particularly in relation to the obligations and capabilities of na-tion-states to ensure order. The official development community (UNDP, 2005; UN, 2005a, 2005b; DFID, 2005; HSC, 2005: 152) has signalled three expected contributions from official aid to the DfS agenda: enhancing the quality of statehood in terms of both effectiveness and accountability, while simultaneously eliminating systemic sources of instability stemming from both poverty and inequality.

In terms of statehood, all societies contain forces with a potential to undo or block progress in human well-being, destabilize the polity, perpetuate instability and lead to violence. A government's ability to contain disruption is ultimately premised on monopoly possession and application of physical coercion, but also on its capacity to secure popular legitimacy in a broader sense. For donors, this involves a significant shift in relation to their agendas of 'good governance' and 'democratization', in the direction of addressing more fundamental questions of overcoming 'state failure'. While remain-ing problematic in terms of its pejorative colonial overtones, and largely self-interested in character, this agenda may signal an overdue engagement with the project of promoting 'state formation'.

Importantly, 'state failure' is also conceptualized in socio-economic terms where even if there is peace, a substantial proportion of the population are stuck in poverty (Chauvet and Collier, 2005): a state has failed its people. The relationship between absolute poverty and insecurity as understood by aid agencies is expressed in the following quotation:

> Poor countries are most at risk of violent conflict. Research on civil war shows that lower levels of GDP per capita are associated with a higher risk of violent and more prolonged conflict. All other things being equal, a country at $250 GDP per capita has an average 15% risk of experiencing a civil war in the next five years. At a GDP per capita of $5,000, the risk of civil war is less than 1%. (DFID, 2005: 8; also OECD/DAC, 2003)

Such a causative link underlies the standards employed by the World Bank to define a country as fragile, with development assistance dedicated to poverty reduction thus seen to have a critical, preventive security dimension.

While absolute poverty matters, Lia and Hansen (2000: 13) argue that relative deprivation is also a driver of disaffection and terrorism. In other words, inequality is a source of insecurity. This causal association is restated in an analysis of the global social situation (UN, 2005b) and finds echoes in the World Development Report 2006 (World Bank, 2005). The general position is that

> Violence is often rooted in inequality. It is dangerous for both national and international peace and security to allow economic and political inequality to deepen. Such inequalities, especially struggles over political power, land and other assets can create social disintegration and exclusion and lead to conflict and violence. (UN, 2005a)

In sum, there is a donor conviction that ODA can decrease the potential for (inter)national security by enhancing the quality of statehood while reducing poverty and inequality respectively. What are the possible implications for NGDOs?

NGDO roles and contributions to development for security

Each dimension of development for security – reducing inequality and poverty while improving statehood – offer potential sites for NGDOs both to be and to produce 'alternatives'. However, it is equally the case – and perhaps to a greater extent – that each site also creates significant difficulties for such projects. Here we explore constraints further, first through each dimension separately and then taken together.

In terms of challenging inequality, NGDOs face considerable obstacles and not just because other constraints combine to steer them towards apolitical functions. They have neither the assets required to promote equality nor the means to redistribute them even if they did. Moreover, they lack the political capacity and uniformity of view or of theory (see Hulme, this volume) to challenge significantly the ways in which socio-economic inequalities have become institutionalized within political norms and structures. Nonetheless, NGDOs can focus on exacting government compliance regarding their obligations to ensure equitable access to public goods, pursuing popular mobilization to this end (World Bank, 2005: 222). Further support can be offered to popular struggles against discrimination. As of old, 'alternatives' lie in operating in niches populated by the most excluded. Given their enduring resource limitations, the security perspective of combining niche with outreach invites exploration of alternative ways of scaling up NGDO ways of working rather than in the identification and demonstration of innovation solely or per se (Uvin et al., 2000). Another way of looking at alternatives is, therefore, for NGDOs to reorient towards systemic collaboration with civic actors and grassroots energies to be found in social movements and other member-based formations. An alternative lies in being non-dominant, or exploitive parties in new configurations of rights- and demand-driven civic relationships.

Establishing a clearer or bigger role for NGDOs in tackling poverty reduction is no less a challenge. The sheer scale of the global problem demands forms of public action that only developmental states have historically been able to offer, while NGOs have not unambiguously demonstrated an ability to reach the poorest groups in society (Riddell and Robinson 1995; Fowler, 2000). An alternative approach to NGDOs in poverty reduction is, therefore, to rethink the task as one of redistributing the risk and uncertainty of globally connected, locally articulated change away from those most vulnerable and least able to cope. This would be an alternative to technocratic approaches to poverty reduction that are dominated by assets, capital and capabilities, as bringing into focus the substantial 'churning' of populations into and out of poverty that make an emphasis on beneficiary targeting a questionable strategy (Krishna, 2006). The fear and the (frustrated) hope associated with dropping into and of (not) escaping from poverty feeds social anxiety and hence instability. Risk-based thinking invites an alternative discussion when engaging, for example, with poverty-reduction strategies and processes (PRSP). States are sensitive to discontent and the potential for civic disobedience and insurrection. In responding to such sensitivity, development for security offers NGDOs opportunities for creative thinking about and strategizing towards the relationship between poverty, injustice and instability in ways that open up space for civic agency in order to reduce the potential for instability.

States are weak or fragile for many reasons. Donors are only beginning to understand how they might go about addressing this problem, let alone think through the proper role of NGDOs in such context-specific processes. And there is a strong sense that NGDOs may be less important here than other more political actors. For official aid, the DfS agenda is hampered by the Westphalian principle of non-interference in a country's internal affairs, perhaps rendering apolitical and technocratic approaches inevitable. An NGDO alternative is to not self-impose this principle. Instead, in civic solidarity, an option is to work on the foundations of legislative self-determination. This alternative has theoretical, process and substance dimensions worthy of elaboration.

A development-for-security agenda that foresees a robust and democratic developmental state as a condition for enduring stability both highlights and sharpens a perceived contradiction and tension between NGDO roles as civic protagonists, on the one hand, and compliant service providers, on the other. Put another way, it opens up the necessity for a conversation about NGDOs in relation to good governance in the sense of the distribution of power between state and citizen that is inherent to all conceptualizations and theories of civil society. It points, on the one hand, towards alternatives in the direction of building and deepening the capacities of civil society to redistribute different types of power-selecting processes and time frames that are most likely to succeed under different country conditions and historical trajectories. On the other hand, it implies relational capabilities and strategies to engage with, rather than circumvent, political society in a mutual strengthening that brings the state under the influence of society instead of the other way around (see Guijt, this volume). For Gaventa (2006: 21–30), both reflecting and extending the above, it involves processes of CSO capacity development that are driven by political analysis directed at rediscovering what attaining a robust democracy – now atrophying in 'mature' democracies – means by, inter alia,

1. Recognizing the need for context-resonating democracies, rather than the implied one-size-fits-all democracy modelled on the West.
2. Appreciating the multiple identities and the sources of civic energy that political society should reflect.
3. Under constraints of increasing inequality, directing greater attention to the material/financial resource base required for autonomous civic action.
4. Rethinking the grounding of representative legitimacy.

This direction of alternatives towards more politically informed, civic-driven change is highly problematic for many NGDOs. It calls for a quality of partnership that is rooted more in a solidarity perspective and purpose than in efficient redistribution. It calls for creative use of technological innovations that enable horizontal and vertical connections between levels of civic action and governance engagement (Bard and Söderqvist, 2002). Such facilities enable the real-time dialogues required to hold the tensions between the pace, pressures and interests of different environments and constituency expectations. But it also calls for a quality of resources – long-term, process-oriented, flexible and enabling – that are hard to create or to access (although see Guijt, and also Verhallen, this volume). Shifting the rules of the aid game in the direction of this type of quality over greater quantity remains a serious problem. Nevertheless, a paradigm that positions civil society and citizens as central agents in establishing the quality of statehood required for robust security is, arguably, an alternative particularly worthy of the name.

Conclusions

The preceding analysis suggests that challenges coming from the new security agenda call for the notion of NGDO alternatives to be rethought and reconstructed. Two reasons for this stand out. First, there are signs that power holders already regard (some) NGDOs to be sufficiently 'alternative' to require constraint. Put another way, governments are waking up to the fact that, at different socio-political scales, civil society contains and exhibits compliant, indifferent and counter-hegemonic formations and agency. While this mix has always been the case, the concern for security shifts the benefit of the doubt about NGDO presence, behaviour and intentions from benign to suspicious. As Mark Sidel observes, development for security now places NGDOs in an ambivalent position of being treated as both an abettor of insecurity and a collaborator in its prevention.

> A number of governments and political actors seem to regard the third sector as a source of insecurity, not as a civil society but as encouraging uncivil society, not as strengthening peace and human security but as willing conduit for, or an ineffective, porous and ambivalent barrier against insecurity in its most prominent modern forms, terrorism and violence. (Sidel, 2006: 201)

This apparent contradiction can be traced to selective, disputed understandings of civil society and its role in mediating power between citizen and state. The forces involved are played out between different segments, values and interests within the civic arena, dynamics which can be misused by regimes to extend control over citizens' lives. In other words, inter-civic disputes between classes, ethnicities, religions, genders, ages, nationalities and so on allow states to reinforce their mechanisms of constraint on and beyond NGDOs. This self-inflicted limitation invites a different approach to what 'alternative' might mean.

A second reason for rethinking the idea of NGDOs as 'alternatives' stems from a sharper 'for us or against us' pressure to work within and perhaps reform a particular type of globalization or adopt a counter-position that is unlikely to be funded by mainstream official aid. As one activist observed, the revolution will not be funded (Del Moral, 2005). Through this lens, political neo-conservative ideologists, to be found for example in the American Enterprise Institute, argue that NGDOs lack the accountability, legitimacy or right to act as an 'alternative' voice to legally constituted governments (see Hulme, this volume). In contrast, the political far left argues that, far from being an 'alternative', NGDOs are complicit in perpetuating a US-led hegemonic, globalizing capitalist economic system that is the root of the social injustice, instability and the very causes they raise money to fight (Bond, 2006). In this framing, the real meaning of 'alternative' and the ultimate source of security is structural transformation of the world order (Sen et al., 2007).

There is little to be gained by trying to adjudicate between these perspectives on alternatives as reformation or transformation, or possibilities reflecting other ideological streams and traditions (Chambers and Kymlicka,

2002; Hodgkinson and Foley, 2003). For they all rely on definitions and uses of the concept of civil society that are self-referential to the theory in which they are embedded. As a result, identifying NGDOs as civic actors makes discourse about 'alternatives' depend on the theoretical frame being applied: as much an issue of ideological predisposition as of empirical validity of theoretical predictions over disparate time scales.

More pertinent is to look behind contending theories to their common challenge: this is the task of coherently describing and explaining the evolution, constitution and distribution of power between state and citizens over time (Haugaard, 1997; Lukes, 2005). Such a perspective is intrinsically about politics. And, while the distribution of roles and authority across a society's institutions remains contested across the secular political-ideological spectrum, common cause is that political dispensations should ultimately derive from power founded on and exercised from an adequately informed, capable and self-aware citizenry.

Achieving this condition requires initiatives based on a thorough reading of power in its overt and covert forms, identification of the spaces where they are played out and the dynamics of inclusion and exclusion they contain (Guijt in this volume; Gaventa, 2006). Such a capability also calls for what Foucault (1987) terms self-care. That is an honest, critical NGDO self-awareness of power deeply embedded and locked within language and discourse – like 'alternatives' – which determine the very thoughts and hence knowledge through which meaning and power relationships are themselves understood, communicated and manipulated.

Adopting this perspective on alternatives could imply an (unlikely) bifurcation of NGDOs towards the ends of a spectrum of compliance or resistance. This would alter today's 'bell curve' NGDO ecology of mainly middle-of-the-road, more or less critical fellow travellers – with a few more autonomous outliers that eschew public funding – that work for stability within a unipolar, enforced world economic and political order. Realistically, much militates against this future direction for NGDO alternativism, particularly as governments possess a growing array of instruments to impede NGDOs adopting this type of alternative. Nevertheless, relational innovation between civic actors, reformulation of self-understanding and purpose, and strategic awareness of the long game being played, could all be aligned towards a messy 'transformatory-reformism'. For this condition is likely to be the lived reality in rediscovering and reinvigorating the notion of 'alternative' such that this dimension of NGDO-ism does not wither away on the security vine.

References

ActionAid/Care (2006) *Where To Now? Implications of Changing Relations between DFID, Recipient Governments and NGOs in Malawi, Tanzania and Uganda: Implications of Direct Budget Support for Civil Society Funding and Policy Space*, ActionAid/Care UK, London.

Bard, A., and J. Söderqvist (2002) *Netocracy: The New Power Elite and Life after Capitalism*, Pearson Educational, Harlow.

Batliwala, S., and D. Brown (eds) (2006) *Transnational Civil Society: An Introduction*, Kumarian Press, Bloomfield.

Beall, J., T. Goodfellow and J. Putzel (2006) 'Introductory Article: On the Discourse of Terrorism, Security and Development', *Journal of International Development* 18: 51–67.

Bond, P. (2006) 'Civil Society in Global Governance: Facing Up to Divergent Analysis, Strategy, and Tactics', *Voluntas* 17(4): 359–71.

Burrell, S., and S. Maxwell (2006) 'Reforming the International Aid Architecture: Options and Ways Forward', *Working Paper* 278, Overseas Development Institute, London.

Chambers, S., and W. Kymlicka (eds) (2002) *Alternative Conceptions of Civil Society*, Princeton University Press, Princeton NJ.

Chauvet, L., and P. Collier (2005) 'Policy Turnarounds in Fragile States', Centre for the Study of African Economies, Oxford.

CIVICUS (n.d.) 'Civil Society Watch programme', www.civicus.org/csw.

Del Moral, A. (2005) 'The Revolution Will Not Be Funded', *LiP Magazine*, 4 April, www.LiPmagazine.org.

DFID (2005) *Fighting Poverty to Achieve a Safer World: A Strategy for Security and Development*, Department for International Development, London, March.

Drabek, A. (ed.) (1987) 'Development Alternatives: The Challenge for NGOs', *World Development* 15 (supplement 1): ix–xv.

Duffield, M. (2001) 'Governing the Borderlands: Decoding the Power of Aid', *Disasters* 25(4): 308–20.

Duffield, M. (2002) *Global Governance and the New Wars: The Merging of Development and Security*, Zed Books, London.

Feinstein Center (2004) *Ambiguity and Change: Humanitarian NGOs Prepare for the Future*, Feinstein International Famine Center, Tufts University, Medford MA.

FIFC (2004) 'The Future of Humanitarian Action: Implications of Iraq and Other Recent Crises', Report of an International Mapping Exercise, www.famine.tufts.edu.

Foucault, M. (1987) 'The Ethics of Care for Self as Practice of Freedom', in J. Bernauer and D. Rasmussen (eds), *The Final Foucault*, Cambridge University Press, Cambridge.

Fowler, A. (1998) 'Authentic Partnerships in the New Policy Agenda for International Aid: Dead End or Light Ahead?' *Development and Change* 29(1): 137–59.

Fowler, A. (2000) 'NGOs, Civil Society and Social Development: Changing the Rules of the Game', *Geneva 2000 Occasional Paper* No. 1, United Nations Research Institute for Social Development, Geneva.

Fowler, A. (2005) 'Aid Architecture: Reflections on NGO Futures and the Emergence of Counter Terrorism', *Occasional Paper* No. 45, International NGO Training and Research Centre, Oxford.

Gaventa, J. (2006) 'Finding the Spaces for Change: A Power Analysis', *IDS Bulletin*, 37(6), Institute of Development Studies, University of Sussex.

Hardt, M., and A. Negri (2000) *Empire*, Harvard University Press, Cambridge MA.

Harvey, D. (2003) *The New Imperialism*, Oxford University Press, Oxford.

Haugaard, M. (1997) *The Constitution of Power: A Theoretical Analysis of Power, Knowledge and Structure*, Manchester University Press, Manchester.

Hodgkinson, V., and M. Foley (eds) (2003) *The Civil Society Reader*, Tufts, University Press of New England, Hanover.

Howell, J. (2006) 'The Global War on Terror, Development and Civil Society, *Journal of International Development* 18: 121–35.

HSC (2005) *Human Security Report: War and Peace in the 21st Century*, Human Security Center, University of British Colombia, Oxford University Press, Oxford.

InterAction (2004) *Handbook on Counter-Terrorism Measures: What U.S. Nonprofits and Grantmakers Need to Know*, Interaction, Washington DC.

Intrac (2007) *Intrac 35*, International NGO Training and Research Centre, Oxford.

Janz, M. (2006) 'Ambiguity and Change: Humanitarian NGOs Prepare for the Future', in *Global Future*, World Vision, Monrovia, November, pp. 22–3.

Katsui, H., and R. Wamai (eds) (2006) *Civil Society Reconsidered: A Critical Look at NGOs in Development Practice*, Institute of Development Studies, University of Helsinki, Helsinki.

Krishna, A. (2006) 'For Reducing Poverty Faster: Target Reasons Before People', *World Development*.

Kukis, K. (2006) 'Looking the Other Way', *Time Magazine*, December, p. 2.

Lal, D. (2004) *In Praise of Empires: Globalization and Order*, Palgrave, New York.

Lewis, D., and T. Wallace, T. (eds) (2000) *New Roles and Relevance: Development NGOs and the Challenge of Change*, Kumarian Press, Bloomfield.

Lia, B. and A. Hansen (2000) 'Globalisation and the Future of Terrorism: Patterns and Predictions', FFI Report 2000/01704, Norwegian Defence Research Establishment, Kjeller.

Lukes, S. (2005) *Power: A Radical View*, 2nd edn, Palgrave, London.

Mallaby, S. (2002) 'The Reluctant Imperialist: Terrorism, Failed States, and the Case for American Empire', *Foreign Affairs*, March/April.

Natios, A., 2006, 'Five Debates on International Development: The US Perspective', *Development Policy Review* 24(2): 131–9.

OECD (2002) *Combating the Abuse of Non-profit Organizations*, Financial Action Task Force, Organization for Economic Cooperaton and Development, Paris, December.

OECD/DAC (2003) *Development Co-operation Lens on Terrorism Prevention: Key Entry Points of Action*, www.oecd.org/dataoecd/17/4/16085708.pdf.

Riddell, R. and M. Robinson (1995) *Non-Governmental Organizations and Rural Poverty Alleviation*, Clarendon Press, London.

Schweizer, B. (2004) 'Moral Dilemmas for Humanitarianism in the Era of "Humanitarian" Military Interventions', *IRRC* 86(855): 547–64.

Scott, J. (1990) *Domination and the Arts of Resistance: Hidden Transcripts*, Yale University Press, New Haven CT.

Scott, T. (2006) 'Decentralization and Human Development Reports', *NHDR Occasional Paper* 6, National Human Development Report Series, Human Development Report Office, United Nations Development Programme, New York.

Sen, J., A. Escobar and P. Waterman (eds) (2007) *World Social Forum: Challenging Empires*, Viveka, New Delhi.

Sidel, M. (2004) *More Secure Less Free? Antiterrorism Policy and Civil Liberties after September 11*, University of Michigan Press, Ann Arbor.

Sidel, M. (2006) 'The Third Sector, Human Security, and Anti-Terrorism: The United States and Beyond', *Voluntas* 17(3): 199–210.

UN (2004) 'A More Secure World: Our Shared Responsibility', Report of the High Level Panel on Threats, Challenges and Change, A/59/565, United Nations, New York, December.

UN (2005a) 'General Assembly Summit Outcome 2005', A/60/L.1, United Nations, New York, in http://i-Newswire.com/pr43973.html (accessed on 26th August).

UN (2005b) *Report on the World Social Situation 2005: The Inequality Predicament*, United Nations, New York.

UNDP (2005) *International Cooperation at a Crossroads: Aid, trade and security in an unequal world*, Human Development Report, 2005, United Nations Development Program, New York.

US Government (2002) *Money Laundering: A Banker's Guide to Avoiding Problems*, Office of the Controller of the Currency, Washington DC, December.

USDoD (US Government Department of Defence) (2005) 'Department of Defence Directive 3000.05, of 28 November', Department of Defence, Washington DC.

Uvin, P., P. Jain and L. Brown (2000) 'Think Large and Act Small: Toward a New Paradigm for NGO Scaling Up', *World Development* 28(8): 1409–19.

Wallace, T., L. Bornstein and J. Chapman, J. (2006) *The Aid Chain: Coercion and Commitment in Development NGOs*, Intermediate Technology Development Group, Rugby.

Wallerstein, I. (2006) *European Universalism: The Rhetoric of Power*, New Press, New York.

World Bank (2005) *Equity and Development: World Development Report 2006*, World Bank, Washington DC.

PART III

Pursuing Alternatives:
NGO Strategies in Practice

How Civil Society Organizations Use Evidence to Influence Policy Processes

Amy Pollard and Julius Court

The concept of civil society is not new; it has been contested within political philosophy, sociology and social theory for hundreds of years.[1] What is new is the increasing emphasis on the concept over the last decade – 'civil society' has become a buzzword within international development. All manner of claims have been made about the potential of 'civil society', and specifically 'civil society organizations' (CSOs), to act as a force to reduce poverty, promote democracy and achieve sustainable development. But how exactly do they do this? Are CSOs always a force for good? What is the proper role of CSOs in international development? How do they influence policy? A number of studies have responded to these questions, identifying a number of issues around the accountability, legitimacy and effectiveness of the sector (Howell and Pearce, 2001; Lewis, 2001; Edwards, 2004; Van Rooy, 1999; Anheier et al., 2004).

Meanwhile, literature on bridging research and policy in international development has started to explore these very same issues from a different perspective. So far, these streams of thinking have existed in relative isolation. There is remarkably little systematic work on the role of evidence as CSOs attempt to influence policy processes. Does evidence matter to CSO work? If so, how, when and why? Can evidence improve the legitimacy and effectiveness of CSOs? This review will attempt to respond to these questions by bringing together literature on the use of evidence in policymaking with literature on civil society organizations in international development.

We hope that bridging these streams of thinking may help to answer some of the questions that have emerged from the civil society literature as it has grown in prominence. Whilst some consider that the claims made for civil society have reduced the notion to an 'analytic hatstand' (Van Rooy, 1999) on which any number of ideas about politics, organization and citizenship can be hung, others consider that the diversity of thinking around this single subject invigorates civil society itself, as an 'intellectual space for critical thought and action' (Howell and Pearce, 2001). Debates around the role of CSOs in international development have often focused on the nature of those organizations themselves. This approach has often made it difficult to pinpoint the influence CSOs have in policy processes, developing into a tautology – a definition of CSOs as organizations which work towards democracy and development makes it difficult to identify *how* exactly they achieve these ends. This chapter will examine how CSOs influence policy processes from the opposite end of this puzzle – taking policy processes as the starting point for analysis.

The Policy Cycle

Following Lasswell (1977), the most common approach to the study of public policy disaggregates the process into a number of functional components. These can be mapped onto an idealized model of the policy cycle (see Figure 7.1).

Whilst policymaking may not work logically through these stages in real life, this model does provide a useful entry point for thinking about how CSOs may influence different parts of the process. If policy processes tend to have similar functional elements, it is likely that CSOs will impact upon its various aspects in different ways. It may well be that success in influencing an agenda, for example, often requires a different kind of approach than influencing the implementation of policy.

For the purposes of this chapter, the functions of the policy processes will be simplified into four categories:

- Problem identification and agenda setting
- Formulation and adoption
- Implementation
- Monitoring and evaluation (and reformulation)

These four functions will be used to organize the literature in this section. In each part we will map the specific issues which arise as CSOs use evidence to influence different parts of the policy process, hoping to identify how CSOs may maximize their chances of policy impact.

Figure 7.1   The policy cycle

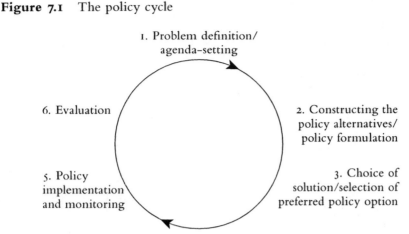

1. Problem definition/
agenda-setting

6. Evaluation

2. Constructing the
policy alternatives/
policy formulation

5. Policy
implementation
and monitoring

3. Choice of
solution/selection of
preferred policy option

4. Policy design

Source: Young and Quinn, 2002.

Identifying Problems and Setting the Agenda

In order to introduce a problem to the policy agenda – or 'turn the problem into an issue' (Young and Quinn, 2002: 13) – it is necessary to convince the relevant policy actors that the problem is indeed important and solvable. For many CSOs, being part of setting the policy agenda is a task which plays to their strengths. Those CSOs with practical experience are often in an excellent position to crystallize and articulate the problems facing ordinary people with whom they work. The key issues are often around how the understanding that CSOs have of development problems can be 'packaged' up and communicated effectively so that they gather momentum.

Building awareness

CSOs have played a critical role in fostering individual awareness and and knowledge – which can eventually lead to incremental policy changes or which can create policy windows. Whether they instigate opportunities directly, respond to them, or simply lay their foundations, to create policy windows CSOs must be adept at understanding and negotiating the contexts in which they work. In the long term, the role that many CSOs play in education may develop a well-informed community with the capacity to pinpoint and articulate development problems in the future (Arko-Cobbah, 2004). For example, Arko-Cobbah argued that libraries in South Africa have been important repositories for information on good governance, which maintain the possibility for policy shift as enthusiasm on the subject waxes and wanes.

CSOs can also be much more proactive in creating policy opportunities. Court (2005) documents various examples where CSOs highlight the urgent need to address the disease. To be successful in identifying the problem to both policymakers and the general public, CSOs need to combine personal testimonies with macro-level analysis – emphasizing both the gravity of the situation and the opportunity for action.

Combining personal and wider social analysis was also effective for the Addis Ababa Muslim Womens' Council, working to raise awareness of women's rights in Ethiopia. Mohammed (2003) notes that their meticulous community-based research was matched by detailed engagement with the text of the Qu'ran on the rights of women. Equipping women with this knowledge at community workshops helped them to raise the issues with both their families, communities and sharia courts. Here, it seems that established issues, knowledge and understanding can be an important lever to bring new issues to the fore. Ideology, religious beliefs and mainstream views can work in tandem with more challenging ideas – 'piggybacking' on the respectability of the former.

Framing the terms and mobilizing opinion

CSOs can be key agents in coining or popularizing a particular vocabulary within policy debates. Shaping terminology is often more than just wordplay, but is critical to which ideas and interests are noted, and which are not. Roe (1991), among others, has emphasized the importance of 'policy narratives' from a theoretical perspective. Thompson and Dart (2004) use the case of welfare reform in Canada to argue also that, through the discourses that they use, CSOs have framed the 'subjects' which social policy is intended to benefit, thereby framing the ultimate trajectory of this policy.

Many religious CSOs take this further, using language derived from spiritual sources to emphasize a moral dimension in policy agendas. They can create ideas that carry a sense of morality in policy debates without alienating those who don't share their religious derivation (Omar, 2004). Hutanuwatr and Rasbach (2004) suggest that Buddhist values provide an alternative to modernizing development agendas, providing a conceptual basis on which self-reliant, non-violent communities can form.

The concepts which underlie CSOs can be critical in inspiring and energizing their members. It seems here that the communication of evidence, rather than its empirical basis, is the critical factor for policy influence. Whether sparking a trend or creating a vantage point within a long-running discussion, the key is to coin ideas which have resonance within a particular social context.

Crystallizing the agenda

Some policy processes are tied to specific institutional arrangements through which agendas must formally be set. When it comes to interfacing with complex bureaucracies, donors and governments, the importance of evidence in the work of CSOs comes quickly to the fore. Many writers are particularly pessimistic about the ability of CSOs to influence 'high' policy agendas. Brock and McGee (2004), for example, suggest that trade policy processes are so dominated by the liberalization ideology of donors that CSOs lose any legitimacy in discussions around the agenda as soon as they begin to question it. The technical nature of the languages through which these discussions take place can also exclude those who might critique them. The value placed on donor 'coordination and convergence' is used to sideline CSOs from agenda setting unless they bolster the consensus view. Cornwall and Gaventa (2001) note that knowledge derived from more academic sources is privileged against that from CSOs involved in the practical provision of services. There is a dilemma here as to whether CSOs should respond to this by using more academic evidence in their work to bolster its credibility or find other ways to capture their practical expertise as evidence in a more credible way.

Pettifor (2004) has argued that this dilemma places a particular impetus on the importance of analysing evidence well. She explained the success of the Jubilee 2000 campaign in raising the issue of debt relief through its ability to 'cut the diamond' of evidence – amassing a substantial volume of data and being able to present it in a way which makes the policy implications clear. It may be that the amount of evidence needed to change an agenda is directly proportional to how radical this change may be.

When CSOs are specifically mandated to influence agenda setting, they may find more success. Many poverty-reduction-strategy processes have made explicit attempts to fold CSOs into how problems are framed and which issues are to be addressed. Participative poverty assessments (PPAs) have been reasonably successful in working towards this (Driscoll et al., 2004; Pollard and Driscoll, 2005). In both Rwanda and Kyrgyzstan, PPAs were undertaken by CSOs, commissioned by the government. Both documents were very successful in setting the agenda for poverty reduction in an evidence-based way. In Rwanda, a CSO facilitated the 'Ubdbeme' initiative as an action research tool. This was based on traditional Rwandan practice of community self-help, and became a central feature of the PRS. In Kyrgyzstan, CSOs gained access to communities usually sceptical of government officials, gathering rich data on poverty in the country (Cornwall and Gaventa, 2001). Here, the question of whether CSO research is influential or not may be a question of whether they are included in policy processes in the first place.

There seems to be a difference between the tactics which are effective where CSOs are deliberately incorporated in the *process* of agenda setting, and where they are not. Where the contribution of CSOs is already written into the policy process, their work seems most effective when it is demonstrably rigorous; with an explicit method to synthesize public interests and views (see also Keck and Sikkink, 1998). Where CSOs must compete to influence agendas, this empirical quality is perhaps less effective than how they package their work. Those aiming to make more radical changes to mainstream agendas may need to make special efforts to be explicitly systematic and empirically rigorous, whereas those closely aligned with dominant views may have need to position their work against a network of overlapping interests.

Influencing the Formulation and Adoption of Policy

For many CSOs, involvement in the formulation and adoption of policy is central to a mandate of 'representing' the interests and view of poor people. CSOs are often key in both outlining the different policy options and deciding between them. This role gives them status as 'democratic' actors. But why should the views of CSOs be taken into account? The major issue is how CSOs can hold a legitimate place in the eyes of policymakers, and also in the eyes of the communities they 'represent'. Another important set of issues concerns the political context within which CSOs operate. There is increasing democratization in many countries at the macro-level and many governments see CSOs as a legitimate and helpful partner. However, the context is less favourable in other countries and CSO activity may be actively discouraged. CSOs will need to respond differently depending on the macro-context as well as regarding each specific policy issue.

Working from 'outside the tent'

Some CSOs work as mediators, influencing the formulation of policy by influencing the process in which it is formed. Van der Linde and Naylor (1999) use the example of Kenya's Nairobi Peace Initiative to demonstrate the value of having an independent agent who can facilitate dialogue between two warring factions. This informal network of NGOs was able to act as a go-between, using their tacit knowledge of the area to disseminate sensitively examples of inter-community cooperation to build a process for rebuilding peace. In other circumstances, the political nature of evidence was critical in making it influential. An Indonesian CSO, lobbying to reformulate the government's birth control programme into a family welfare programme, deliberately integrated their findings on the effectiveness of this approach with passages from the Qu'ran and Hadith. This inflected the proposal with a call to respect the interests of the Muslim majority, who had recently been under pressure from Christian, Confucian, Hindu and Buddhist groups. Drawing out the political aspect of this evidence made it more attractive for the government to act upon – because they could do so as a statement of support for Muslims.

Some moves towards 'participative' policymaking – involving local communities in decisions which will affect them – have had more influence 'outside the tent' than inside, where they were originally directed. Brinkerhoff and Goldsmith (2002) note that the efforts to engage civil society participation in macroeconomic policy have often had more success as an education process (for both civil society and policymakers) than as a means for civil society to contribute ideas which directly shape policy. The influence of civil society is 'softer', raising issues in the minds of policymakers, but leaving it to them to interpret how these confer specific policy options. This kind of influence is difficult to gauge, which has made the monitoring of participative practices problematic, and their accountability challenging (Driscoll et al., 2004). Accountability problems are underscored by the difficulties of getting the full range of community members to take part in participative formulation processes. Reflecting wider experience, a project in Argentina found that the most marginalized groups were loath to participate unless they could see the tangible and immediate benefits of doing so (Schusterman et al., 2002). The process of attempting to elicit their participation, however, did improve their awareness of the issues and was useful as a kind of education exercise. It seems that initiatives to include civil society in the formulation of policy have unintended benefits, even where they have less direct influence.

To influence formulation from 'outside the tent' CSOs must often be simultaneously persuasive to policymakers and local people. Where there is a specific need to act and appear independent, tacit knowledge can be a valuable tool to negotiate complex situations. Sometimes CSOs may influence the course of events in ways they did not originally intend. Here knowledge is not exactly used as evidence (in a deliberate and persuasive way) by CSOs, but it does create opportunities for individuals to apply this knowledge as they choose.

Working from 'inside the tent'

When CSOs have become formal participants in the formulation and adoption of policy, a number of questions have been raised over whether they are 'too close for comfort' with government and donors, who often control the terms of that engagement. Hulme and Edwards (1997) suggest that when bilateral and multilateral donors provide funding for CSOs, and place these same CSOs at the centre of their 'good governance' work, CSOs quickly start to justify their position in terms of ideology, rather than any empirical verification of their legitimacy or performance.

Many have argued that those CSOs that are selected to take part in formulation processes tend to be those whose political sympathies and approaches are already well-aligned with donors, limiting the extent to which they influence policy in any meaningful way (Bazaara, 2000; Ottaway and Carothers, 2000). A related issue may be the funding structures of CSOs. Ottaway and Carothers point out that donor efforts to 'strengthen' the capacity of CSOs to participate in formulating their assistance programmes often risks undermining the legitimacy on which their inclusion is premissed. Lewis (1999a) concurs that the pressures of maintaining good relations with donors when part of formulation processes can divert NGOs from their primary task of demonstrating accountability to those whose interests they are supposed to advance.

Evidence may be a useful tool to deal with these issues. For example, the WTO exhibited a bias towards CSOs that conformed with the institution, neglecting its reformist and radical critics to maintain an artificially positive view of its policies (Scholte et al., 1998). There were, however, some CSOs which, despite their radical stances, backed up their views with systematic, rigorous and accessible evidence. These organizations were an influential minority, whom the WTO would seek out as representatives of dissenting views. It may be that CSOs can adjust their use of evidence to carve out a specific role within the formulation process.

Malena (2000) suggests that NGOs working with the World Bank fall into four categories: 'beneficiaries', 'mercenaries', 'missionaries' and 'revolutionaries', each of whom are involved for different reasons, and can use evidence to elicit influence in different ways. Those that take very adversarial positions (the 'revolutionaries') may do well if they make their views accessible with thorough and indisputable evidence. Whilst their views may not be directly represented in policy, they form a 'reference point' in the debate which sets the parameters within which policy will form. Those whose interests are closely aligned with the Bank (the 'beneficiaries') may seek to highlight the political aspects of evidence – acknowledging their stake in it and the potential for it to be disputed, to avoid being accused of exploiting their opportunities.

Some policy processes, notably PRSPs, explicitly require civil society to be involved in the formulation process. CSOs have often been critical agents in facilitating this. To take just one example from the PRSP literature, during the first Bolivian PRS, the Catholic Church organized a large consultation exercise, 'Jubilee 2000', which was highly successful in engaging the public with formulation issues (Booth, pers. comms; Driscoll et al., 2004).

Among Bolivia's diverse and fractious civil society, the Church was one of the few organizations that held widespread credibility and respect. Strong links to local communities and to the government allowed it to generate high-quality, well-evidenced contributions to debates on PRS formulation that were successful in feeding into the strategy.

Scale and rigour may not, however, always be enough to allow consultations to influence formulation processes. Maglio and Keppke (2004) describe how almost 360 activities involving 10,000 participants failed to influence the planning of Strategic Regional Plans in São Paulo. Whilst these events were extremely effective in galvanizing the energies of the CSO community, they did not capture the imagination of the elite economic and business communities. These elite groups acted through their traditional lobby in the City Council, where policies were officially approved and enacted. The absence of elites from the CSO activities undermined the credibility of these consultations – which had staked their claim to legitimacy on gathering comprehensive public opinion from all groups. Instead, the consultations became simply political representations of the interests of CSO groups, which eroded their legitimacy as part of the *process* of policy formulation.

These examples demonstrate that even where some kind of evidence is used to try to generate CSO policy influence, it does not follow that this will happen – or if policy does change that it will be pro-poor. It may not even strengthen the accountability of CSOs to the poor. Evidence can be a critical means to create 'reference points' for arguments within a debate, but, overall, the important factor in whether CSOs can use evidence to influence policy here is how well they are integrated within a policy process. A CSO which uses evidence in a rigorous and robust way may increase its chances of being included, but it may need to provide evidence of its political position as much as its competence.

If political use of evidence matters, as much as technical use, CSOs are bound to face dilemmas when there is a trade-off between promoting positions that are based strictly on the evidence and those that are may not be as supported or at all supported by evidence but which fit with political reality. In sum, there may be trade-offs between influence and evidence-based influence. The nature of the political context is crucial to CSO strategy.

Influencing the Implementation of Policy

Many CSOs directly influence the implementation of policy as the primary agents responsible for instituting policy shift and making it a reality 'on the ground'. They may be commissioned as 'service providers' by governments or donors, or they may work independently. CSOs can also provide valuable expertise to other agencies responsible for implementing policies. In all of these cases, evidence may be a valuable tool to make the implementation of policy more effective.

Providing services

Providing services is one of the most widespread, and also one of the most controversial, parts of the sector's work. CSOs are often well placed to provide key services like health and education – particularly where states are weak and/or where CSOs have embedded relationships at community level. There is huge diversity in the sector, of course, and many CSOs will not have the resources or connections to provide services effectively. Simielli and Alves (2004) have argued that the key to effective service provision can essentially be reduced to social capital. This may be manifested differently in different parts of the world, but at its root successful CSO services are those which create strong, two-way connections with a wide range of community members.

The idea that providing services brings CSOs closer to local communities has been widely criticized. A host of authors argue that when CSOs enter into contractual agreements to provide services with governments or donors, they cater their activities to these interests rather than to those of local communities (see Lewis 1999b for an overview). Foweraker (1995) has argued that even if CSOs have been successful in providing services to small areas, they may face problems in scaling these up or implementing services outside any immediate community in which they have roots.

Both Foweraker (1995) and Robinson and White (2000) argue that governments should improve efforts to capitalize on the experience of CSOs in policy; creating an 'enabling environment' where their expertise in implementation is translated into shifts in the agenda, formulation and evaluation of policy. Mismatch between the implementation of services and the other parts of the policy process is a major source of frustration for many CSOs. Whilst CSOs have a great direct influence on policy as a course of action, this work is often disconnected from any influence over policy as a plan of action. CSOs often find problems in translating their practical knowledge and experience into evidence which can inform the shape and direction of future policy.

Technical assistance

Many CSOs do not play a practical part in implementing policy themselves, but do offer technical advice and expertise on how it might be implemented better. Think-tanks have become a growing part of this sector, often acting as a bridge between those with practical experience of implementation and those with responsibility for policymaking. Booth suggests that in Bolivia the key to the success of the think-tank sector has been bridging these two communities (Booth, pers. comms). During the PRS process, several think-tanks there mediated a rather antagonistic relationship between grassroots CSOs and government agencies. They have provided clear and independent explanations of the process for both groups, taking much of the heat from their discussions to isolate the key issues for debate. Lewer (1999) warns that groups with access to 'technical' evidence must be careful not to create hierarchies that exclude other kinds of evidence, such as the views and experiences of local communities.

Issues of hierarchy often seem to arise around 'capacity building' efforts. These are another key way that CSOs with technical expertise contribute to the implementation of policy, by facilitating the development of those CSOs that are responsible for implementation. Many capacity-building CSOs might shy away from aiming to 'influence policy' themselves – in this role they work to facilitate the influence of others, not to steer what that influence might be. To take another example from Bolivia, INGOs came under great pressure to avoid 'interfering' with local politics whilst ensuring that local community monitoring systems were not dominated by patronage (Driscoll et al., 2004). Here, it was difficult for INGOs to use their understanding of 'what works' in monitoring systems directly as evidence, as they were not seen as having a right to do this. Instead, this understanding had to be used in a tacit form, to underpin the process through which they worked and ensure that the appropriate parties had all full information and opportunities to make decisions. This demonstrates the need for a 'people-centred' approach to capacity building, focusing on the personal and cultural challenges involved, and that technical 'experts' need to be more adept at *asking* questions than *knowing* the answers (James, 2002).

Those contributing to implementation through technical assistance must be as adept in using their knowledge in an appropriate way. To ensure that technical understanding does not dominate the knowledge of others, they must foster a 'learning approach', and be able to translate their expertise into tacit, implicit as well as explicit, forms. These skills may help CSOs involved with technical assistance to negotiate delicate relationships in their work.

Independent action

Some CSOs have sidestepped all these problems by simply getting on with the job of changing their communities, and paying no attention to whether this is acknowledged in 'official' policy spheres. Bayat (1997) notes that the most effective means for CSOs in the Middle East to change the course of events on the ground has been through direct action – as he puts it, 'the quiet encroachment of the ordinary'. This has been far more successful than demand-led social movements, which have been dogged by clientelism and hierarchy. Here, direct action has created realities on the ground which authorities will 'sooner or later' have to adjust their policies to suit.

A similar case demonstrates how evidence may be important in improving the effectiveness of independent action. Young (et al., 2003) found that independent veterinarians working to provide illegal, but highly effective, animal care in Kenya relied heavily on sharing evidence to do their work. Workshops bringing together qualified vets with those with basic training were critical forums to share and solve problems, monitor the success of the scheme and allow it to grow. Whilst sharing evidence was key in allowing the scheme to be effective, it did little to help it become legitimate, and policymakers were roundly dismissive of the initiative. Here, evidence was highly influential on policy as a course of action, but dislocated from policy as legislation, largely due to the contextual factors at play.

This section brings out three broader points regarding evidence and policy implementation. First, expertise can help improve service delivery. Second, the sharing of experience on the ground – promoting 'seeing is believing' – can be very convincing for policy change. Third, there seem to be needs for more effective ways to link implementation experiences with other parts of the policy process.

Monitoring and Evaluating Policy

Evidence is an intrinsic element of monitoring and evaluation, which must invariably synthesize and analyse information to substantiate judgements on the successes and failures of policies. The effectiveness of CSOs in influencing evaluation processes depends on two factors: whether they can gather and use evidence to make a sound assessment of policy; and whether they can use evidence to demonstrate their legitimacy in doing this.

Promoting information availability and transparency

CSOs have a key role in making information on policy publicly available and in an accessible format. Where they retain independence from the state, media organizations have often led the CSO community in this task. The advance of the Internet has enabled groups such as One World and IPS to become global hubs for the civil society media, publishing stories on a wide range of development issues, and creating opportunities for both large and small groups to publish informative reports, commentary and opinion pieces. Placing policy within the public domain has historically been the main contribution of the media to democracy, and is fiercely protected by groups such as AMARC, the association for community radio broadcasters.

They have successfully used media campaigns to hold the Brazilian government to account over their closure of the Porto Alegre independent radio station. While the role of the media in monitoring is frequently asserted, there is a lack of research assessing its impact on policy in any systematic manner.

Those CSOs more oriented around research have often played a part in synthesizing information so that it can be used as evidence. Tracing the success of Mexican activists in critiquing the World Bank, Fox (2001) argues that the lack of good-quality information on institutional performance has allowed independent advocacy groups to gain great leverage through their own monitoring work. In other contexts, the independence of CSOs, combined reputable expertise, has been critical to the success in monitoring. There are numerous other agencies, often based in the North, which provide centres for monitoring information. One of the most successful has been the International Budget Project (IBP), which helps to facilitate CSOs in developing countries to analyse and influence budgets (e.g. Mwenda and Gachocho, 2003).

Promoting transparency depends on a CSO's ability to use clear, conclusive and easily accessible evidence which explicitly proves a point to a wide audience. Policy impact depends on how far the evidence is communicated – when an issue is highly 'exposed' in itself this creates pressure for change. High exposure is likely to come from an agency which is well-networked, reputable and high status. These agencies can act as conduits for less-well-resourced CSOs.

Participative monitoring

Whilst promoting transparency is perhaps most effectively performed by large 'elite' CSOs – the best networked media organizations and the most reputable research groups – a much wider variety of groups can be successful in 'participative monitoring'. Participation in monitoring and evaluation has been a relatively recent addition to the 'participation paradigm', which has gained momentum in development in recent years (Driscoll et al., 2004). Some have argued that when CSOs are involved in evaluation they will find greater parity with those who contract them to provide services (Cornwall and Gaventa, 2001). The major difference between participative monitoring and conventional evaluation techniques is that local people collaborate with development agencies and policymakers to decide what constitutes successful policy, and what indicators might demonstrate this success (Guijt et al., 1998). It requires a greater emphasis on negotiation, learning and flexibility between these agents – which has translated into a focus on the processes that must be undertaken to incorporate the views of different parties.

The key issues for whether CSOs are successful in influencing participative monitoring seem to be process and timing. Krafchik (2003) notes that whilst civil-society organizations are making effective contributions to the formulation of budgets in developing countries, the timing of auditing processes gives them little incentive to scrutinize these budgets once they are spent. Audit reports are usually presented two years after the close of the financial year, at a time when other budgeting issues compete for CSO attention. By this time, in the fluid structures of many CSOs, the relevant individual and institutional knowledge of this spending may have been lost.

If process is the key to participative monitoring, the way to maximize CSOs' chances of influence may be to build good learning processes internally. Developing better institutional memory can be an effective means to ensure that past events are analysed, referred to and followed up. This allows CSOs to draw on their full range of available knowledge, allowing it to be capitalized on as evidence.

Reflective practice

Another major theme in CSO influence on monitoring and evaluation is how these tools can be turned on CSOs themselves. As we have touched on earlier, the CSO sector, and particularly the NGOs within it, has come under increasing pressure to raise the standard of its own monitoring procedures. This is a key element to improving CSO work in service provision, but also in ensuring that work in advocacy and mediation is done on a sound basis. Many argue that the measurement and improvement of accountability goes hand in hand with the measurement and improvement of CSO influence. In order to enhance their influence on policy, CSOs need to demonstrate more clearly their sources of legitimacy. Macdonald (2004) proposes that the sector develops 'fluid mechanisms for institutional authorization', which may involve monitoring NGO representatives and holding them accountable.

Providing evidence of legitimacy seems to be critical to policy influence for many CSOs, often those working on advocacy – which need to demonstrate that their arguments are reflections of the interest groups they represent. It may also be critical for the effectiveness of CSOs working to provide services, which must be sure that they have the confidence of the communities they serve, and to substantiate the position of those that offer technical assistance, like think-tanks, to show their advice is given on the basis of real expertise (Pettifor, 2004). In other circumstances, CSO influence is not necessarily contingent on providing any evidence that influence is deserved. In fact, some CSOs seem to manage rather well without it.

So, reflective practice may not necessarily determine whether CSOs will have influence, although it may help others determine how desirable they judge any influence to be. The key question, then, is who is doing the judging? It may be that different kinds of evidence are required to legitimate CSO practice to different audiences, and for some audiences evidence is not necessarily important in the short term.

Conclusion

This chapter has focused on the role of evidence as CSOs attempt to influence policy processes. The aim has been to try to synthesize the patchy literature, draw lessons and identify areas for future work. Overall, it seems clear that using evidence effectively can be critical to the success of CSOs in influencing policy, but it is often *how* evidence is used, rather than the nature of evidence itself, which is the critical factor.

Evidence does not always work in a way that is straightforward, obvious or 'rational'. For many CSOs, making evidence rigorous and accessible is the first step for maximizing their chances of policy influence. Clearly, though, the context in which CSOs operate and the relationships between different actors in a policy arena is often at least as important as whether evidence is robust.

If CSOs are to use evidence to bring about pro-poor policy they need to do three main things, which will of course differ according to the social and political context:

- *Inspire*: to generate support for an issue or action; to raise new ideas or question old ones; to create new ways of framing an issue or 'policy narratives'.
- *Inform*: to represent the views of others; to share expertise and experience; to put forward new approaches.
- *Improve*: to add, correct or change policy issues; to hold policymakers accountable; to evaluate and improve their own activities, particularly regarding service provision; to learn from each other.

This is much more easily said than done, and reality is of course much more complex. Rather than focus on the nature of those organizations themselves or take CSOs as the starting point, we have taken the key elements of policy processes (agenda setting; formulation; implementation; monitoring and evaluation) as the starting point for analysis. We focus on how CSOs contribute to different components of the policy process and how they use evidence in their efforts.

To influence *agenda setting*, it seems that the key factor is the way evidence is communicated by CSOs. They may need to generate or crystallize a body of evidence as a policy narrative around a problem or issue. This can help

Table 7.1   What matters for influencing the key components of policy processes?

Component of the policy process/ aspects of evidence	Agenda setting	Formulation	Implementation	Monitoring and evaluation
Availability		•		•
Credibility		•		
Generalizability			•	
Rootedness	•	•	•	•
Relevance		•	•	•
Accessibility (communication)	•			•

create a window for policy change. However, CSOs often use evidence to build momentum behind an idea, until it reaches a 'tipping point' and becomes widely accepted. They will need to use credible evidence if they are to establish themselves as legitimate actors.

To influence the *formulation* of policy, evidence can be an important way to establish the credibility of CSOs. Here, the quantity and quality credibility of the evidence which CSOs use seems to be important for their policy influence. CSOs need to be adept at adapting the way they use evidence to maintain credibility with local communities and with policymakers, combining their tacit and explicit knowledge of a policy context. CSOs may need to present evidence of their political position, as much as their competence, in order to be included within formulation discussion.

To influence the *implementation* of policy, evidence is critical to improving the effectiveness of development initiatives. For many CSOs involved in providing services and implementing policy directly, a key issue has been translating their practical knowledge and expertise into evidence which can be shared with others. Capitalizing on the practical knowledge and experience of many CSOs can require careful analytic work to understand how technical skills, expert knowledge and practical experience can inform one another. The key to influencing the implementation of policy is to demonstrate the operational relevance of evidence and in making such evidence relevant across different contexts.

To influence the *monitoring and evaluation* of policy, the key factors seem to be to generate relevant information and communicating evidence in a clear, conclusive and accessible way (whether internally within CSOs or to external policymakers). Many CSOs have pioneered participative processes which transform the views of ordinary people into indicators and measures which can make policy processes accountable. Others focus much more on empirical approaches to address issues of relevance. Direct communication with policymakers regarding the impact of their policies is often the key to influence in this arena of the policy process. However, may CSOs have often been influential by gaining high media 'exposure' for their policy critiques.

Stripped down, then, the issues emerging in each part of the policy process can be mapped against the five different aspects of evidence which matter for policy influence (see Table 7.1):

Recommendations

Taken as a whole, our review suggests seven main ways that CSOs could use evidence to improve their chances of policy influence:

1. *Legitimacy* Legitimacy matters for policy influence. Evidence can especially be used to enhance the technical sources of legitimacy of CSOs, but also their representative, moral or legal legitimacy. Making their legitimacy explicit can help others make decisions about whether they wish to endorse CSO work. Linked to this is a more general point that CSOs are more likely to have an impact if they work together.
2. *Effectiveness* Evidence can be used to make CSO work more effective. Gathering evidence can be a tool for CSOs to evaluate and improve the impact of their work, share lessons with others, and capture the institutional memory and knowledge held within organizations.
3. *Integration* There is often disconnect between CSO work on implementation or service delivery and the rest of the policy process. CSOs can have greater influence if they find better ways to turn their practical knowledge and expertise into evidence which can be used to inform other parts of the policy process (agenda setting, formulation and evaluation). This could also help improve the learning which occurs across CSOs.
4. *Translation* Expert evidence should not be used to 'trump' the perspectives and experience of ordinary people. CSOs should find ways to turn peoples' understanding into legitimate evidence and to combine community wisdom with expert evidence.
5. *Access* Access to policymaking processes is vital for CSOs to use evidence to influence policy. Examples in the paper indicate that the question of whether CSO research is influential or not is often a question of whether they are included in policy processes and can respond accordingly. Evidence can help CSOs gain better access to policy arenas. Using high quality and uncontested evidence can allow even politically radical CSOs be fully included in policy debate.

6. *Credibility*   Evidence must be valid, reliable and convincing to its audience. CSOs may need to adapt the kind of evidence they use to different groups – the same evidence may be credible to some but not to others. Using high-quality and uncontested evidence can allow even politically radical CSOs to be fully included in policy debate. Credibility can depend on factors such as the reputation of the source and whether there is other accepted evidence which substantiates it.

7. *Communication*   Evidence must be presented in an accessible and meaningful way. The most effective communication is often two-way, interactive and ongoing.

Note

1. This paper is an edited version of our ODI Working Paper 249, July 2005, reproduced with kind permission of the Overseas Development Institute.

References

Anheier, H., M. Glasius and M. Kaldor (eds) (2004) *Global Civil Society 2004/5*, Sage, London.

Arko-Cobbah, A. (2004) 'The Role of Libraries in Student-centered Learning: The Case of Students from the Disadvantaged Communities in South Africa', *International Information and Library Review* 36: 263–71.

Bayat, A. (1997) 'The Quiet Encroachment of the Ordinary: The Politics of the 'Informal People', *Third World Quarterly* 18(1): 53–72.

Bazaara, N (2000) 'Legal and Policy Framework for Citizen Participation in East Africa: A Comparative Analysis', LogoLink Report, Centre for Basic Research, University of Sussex.

Booth, D. pers. comm. to A. Pollard, during interviews for Pollard and Driscoll, 'Strategic Communications in PRSPs: Bolivia case study', in M. Mozammel and S. Odugbemi (eds), *With the support of Multitudes: Using Strategic Communication to Fight Poverty through PRSPs*, DFID and World Bank, London and Washington DC.

Brinkerhoff, D., and A. Goldsmith (2002) 'How Citizens Participate in Macroeconomic Policy: International Experience and Implications for Poverty Reduction', *World Development* 31(4): 685–701.

Brock, K., and R. McGee (2004) 'Mapping Trade Policy: Understanding the Challenges of Civil Society Participation', *IDS Working Paper*, IDS, Brighton.

Cornwall, A. and J. Gaventa (2001) 'From Users and Choosers to Makers and Shapers: Repositioning Participation in Social Policy', *Institute of Development Studies Working Paper* No. 127, IDS, Brighton.

Court, J. (2005) *Bridging Research and Policy on HIV/AIDS in Developing Countries*, Overseas Development Institute, London.

Driscoll, R., K. Christiansen and S. Jenks (2004) 'An Overview of NGO Participation in PRSPs', ODI Consultation for CARE International, unpublished.

Edwards, M. (2004) *Civil Society*, Polity Press, Cambridge.

Foweraker, J. (1995) *Theorizing Social Movements*, Pluto Press, London.

Fox, J. (2001) 'Vertically Integrated Policy Monitoring: A Tool for Civil Society', *Policy Advocacy Nonprofit and Voluntary Sector Quarterly* 30: 616–27.

Guijt, I., J. Gaventa and G. Barnard (ed.) (1998) 'Participative Monitoring and Evaluation: Learning from Change', *IDS Policy Briefing* 12, November, IDS, Brighton.

Howell, J. and J. Pearce (2001) *Civil Society and Development: A Critical Exploration*, Lynne Rienner, Boulder CO.

Hulme, D. and M. Edwards (1997) *NGOs, States and Donors: Too Close for Comfort*, Macmillan, London.

Hutanuwatr, P. and J. Rasbach (2004) *Engaged Buddhism in Siam and South-East Asia*, case study for WFDD, Birmingham.

James, R. (2002) *People and Change: Exploring Capacity Building in NGOs*, INTRAC, Oxford.

Keck, M., and K. Sikkink (1998) *Activists beyond Borders*, Cornell University Press, Cornell.

Krafchik, W. (2003) *Can Civil Society Add Value to Budget Decision-making? A Description of Civil Society Budget Work*, International Budget Project, Washington DC.

Lasswell, H. (1977) 'The Politics of Prevention', in *Psychopathology and Politics*, University of Chicago Press, Chicago.

Lewer, N. (1999) 'International Non-government Organizations and Peacebuilding – Perspectives from Peace Studies and Conflict Resolution', *Working Paper* No. 3, Centre for Conflict Resolution, Department of Peace Studies, University of Bradford.

Lewis, D. (ed.) (1999a) *International Perspectives in Voluntary Action: Reshaping the Third Sector*, Earthscan, London.

Lewis, D. (1999b) 'Development NGOs and the Challenge of Partnership' in C. Jones-Finer (ed.), *Issues in Transnational Social Policy*, Blackwell, Oxford.

Lewis, D. (2001) 'Civil Society in a non-Western Context: Reflections on the 'Usefulness' of a Concept', *Civil Society Working Paper* 13, LSE, London.

Macdonald, T. (2004) 'We the Peoples': The Democratic Authorization and Accountability of NGOs in Global Governance', ISTR Sixth International Conference, Toronto, 11–14 July.

Maglio, I., and R. Keppke (2004) 'The City of Sao Paulo Strategic Master Plan – the Making of: From Pressure Groups to NGO's', *ISTR Sixth International Conference*, Toronto, 11–14 July.

Malena, C. (2000) 'Beneficiaries, Mercenaries, Missionaries and Revolutionaries: 'Unpacking' NGO Involvement in World Bank-financed Projects', *IDS Bulletin* 31(3).

Mohammed, B. (2003). 'Addis Ababa Muslim Women's Council', online case study for World Faith Development Dialogue, October.

Mwenda, A., and M. Gachocho (2003) 'Budget Transparency: A Kenyan Perspective', *IEA Research Paper Series* 4, Institute of Economic Affairs, Nairobi.

Omar, R. (2004) *Does Public Policy Need Religion? The Importance of the Inter-Religious Movement*, Claremont Main Road Mosque, Cape Town.

Ottaway, M. and T. Carothers (2000) *Funding Virtue: Civil Society Aid and Democracy Promotion*, Carnegie Endownment for International Peace, Washington DC.

Pettifor, A. (2004) 'Some Lessons from Jubilee 2000', *Research and Policy in Development: Does Evidence Matter?* Meeting Series, Overseas Development Institute, London.

Pollard, A., and R. Driscoll (2005) 'Strategic Communications in PRSPs: Bolivia case study', in M. Mozammel and S. Odugbemi (eds), *With the support of Multitudes:*

Using Strategic Communication to Fight Poverty through PRSPs, DFID and World Bank, London and Washington DC.

Robinson, M., and G. White (2000) 'The Role of Civic Organizations in the Provision of Social Services: Towards Synergy', in G. Mwabu, C. Ugaz and G. White (eds), *New Patterns of Social Provision in Low Income Countries*, Oxford University Press, Oxford.

Roe, E. (1991) 'Development Narratives, or Making the Best of Blueprint Development', *World Development* 19(4): 287–300.

Scholte, J., R. O'Brien, and M. Williams (1998) 'The WTO and Civil Society', *CSGR Working Paper*, 14, Centre for the Study of Globalisation and Regionalisation, University of Warwick.

Schusterman, R., F. Almansi, A. Hardoy, C. Monti and G. Urquiza (2002) *Poverty Reduction in Action: Participatory Planning in San Fernando, Buenos Aires, Argentina*, IIED, London.

Simielli, L., and M. Alves (2004) 'Nonprofit Sector, Civil Society and Public Policies: A Comparative Study on the Brazilian and Canadian Experiences', ISTR Sixth International Conference, Toronto, Canada July 11–14.

Thompson, S. and R. Dart (2004) 'Third Sector Discourse(s) on Welfare Recipients: How Framing Affects the Social Policy Landscape', ISTR Sixth International Conference, Toronto, Canada July 11–14.

Van der Linde, A., and R. Naylor (1999) 'Building Sustainable Peace: Conflict, Conciliation, and Civil Society in Northern Ghana', *Oxfam Working Papers*, Oxfam–GB.

Van Rooy, A. (ed.) (1999) *Civil Society and the Aid Industry*, Earthscan and the North–South Institute, London.

Young, E., and Quinn, L. (2002) *Writing Effective Public Policy Papers: A Guide to Policy Advisers in Central and Eastern Europe*, Open Society Institute, Budapest.

Young, J., J. Kajume and J. Wanyama (2003) 'Animal Health Care in Kenya: The Road to Community-based Animal Health Service Delivery', *ODI Working Paper* 214, ODI, London.

8

Civil Society Participation as the Focus of Northern NGO Support: The Case of Dutch Co-financing Agencies

Irene Guijt

Of the Dutch development cooperation budget, between 11 and 14 per cent is allocated to Dutch non-government organizations that are known as 'co-financing agencies' for supporting partner organizations in the global South. The co-financing agencies (CFAs) claim to further civil society participation in diverse ways: by supporting basic rights education, capacity building on democratization issues, advocacy efforts to address myriad injustices, and strategic networking. In this they take up a long-standing challenge for civil society actors committed to promoting alternative development and social justice: the promotion of citizenship status and rights for marginal people and groups (Nerfin, 1987; Friedmann, 1992). However, and although talk of participation and rights-based approaches is central in their organizational discourse, few use coherent frames of analysis to shape their programmatic strategy or a lens through which to understand the results of the work they fund.

This chapter draws on a recent evaluation that examined how the support given between 1999 and 2004 was used by four of the CFAs – CORDAID, HIVOS, Oxfam NOVIB and Plan Netherlands – to further 'civil society participation' in Colombia, Guatemala, Guinea, Sri Lanka and Uganda (Guijt, 2005). The evaluation teams considered over 330 civil society organizations and over 760 contracts from Cordaid, Hivos and Novib, plus three country programmes for Plan. In exploring the efforts of these CFAs to increase and strengthen the participation of citizens and civil society organizations in decision-making processes, within diverse, violent and conflict-ridden contexts, two issues stand out as having a wider relevance for the theme of NGO alternatives. The first relates to the integration of new forms of analysis within the strategic and operational work of development agencies, and thus concerns the research/action interface that has been identified as critical with regards to the role of NGOs in promoting development alternatives (Hulme, 1994: Introduction). The second concerns the possibility that NGOs can help build progressive linkages between 'big D' interventions and 'little d' processes of development – in this case processes of citizenship building – through recognized funding modalities *within* the international aid system, rather than departing from it altogether (see Edwards, this volume).

In this chapter, I proceed by providing a contextual discussion of how Dutch NGOs have tended to conceptualize and fund work on civil society participation (CSP) in developing countries, before outlining the contextual features affecting CSP in the five countries involved in the evaluation. I then describe some of the CSP work that was observed, in terms of approaches and outcomes, before proceeding to outline the key ways forward for NGOs seeking to support civil society participation.

Understanding and Promoting Civil Society: Perspectives and Approaches from the Netherlands

Conceptually, understandings of civil society participation amongst the major NGOs or CFAs in the Netherlands originated around concerns to involve the beneficiaries or end users in designing and implementing projects that were to affect their lives, with the aim of making such projects more relevant and more sustainable. Although some aid agencies have always viewed participation through a more radical and political lens, for others it was the rise of rights-based approaches that shifted participation from an instrumental to a political meaning: the right to participate is seen as the right to claim all other rights. Thus, rather than thinking of people as beneficiaries, they are understood as citizens, not in the sense of a certain group of people with formal membership of a particular nation state, but as individuals with inalienable rights that only become effective when claimed through individual or collective action.

Yet it is the term 'civil society building' and not 'civil society participation' that is used by the CFAs to organize their work and report on results to the Dutch Ministry of Development Cooperation. Civil society building was defined by Biekart (2003: 15) in an earlier evaluation of the CFA's work as a capacity-oriented term, consisting of

- strengthening organizational capacities (of both formal and informal organizations) in civil society;
- building up and strengthening networks of, and alliances between, social organizations;

- building up and strengthening capacities for (policy) advocacy, with the aim of strengthening vertical intermediary channels between civil society and the state and/or the market;
- strengthening citizenship, social consciousness, democratic leadership, and social and political responsibility, with the aim of increasing participation of citizens in the public sphere.

Biekart's evaluation left the CFAs keen for more insights into other issues, particularly related to 'strengthening citizenship', and the concept of 'civil society participation' was proposed by the CFAs as a means to understand this. For the purposes of the follow-up evaluation, they defined it as:

> the opportunities of citizens – and more specifically of poor and/or marginalized citizens – and the organizations that represent them or can be considered their allies, to actively participate in and influence decision-making processes that affect their lives directly or indirectly. Participation includes 'agency', e.g. taking initiatives and engagement. (CORDAID et al., 2004: 6–7)

CSP is a layered concept with very diverse manifestations that links three development discourses and areas of practice: participation, civil society and citizenship. Within this, CFAs define civil society, broadly, as citizens and CSOs. As their funding is channelled through partner organizations, this was the unit of analysis of the study, and this has encouraged their adoption of an 'associational' understanding of civil society (Edwards, 2004).

Taken at face value, 'civil society participation' could be viewed as apolitical and neutral in terms of improving the lives of the poor and marginalized. As the explicit mission of these CFAs is to work towards the political empowerment of the poor and marginalized, the evaluation team qualified CSP in terms of its role in addressing societal inequalities. Thus, civil society participation is understood here as an essential contribution towards social justice, democracy and social cohesion.

To help the evaluation team operationalize this understanding, the CFAs identified the power cube framework developed by the Institute of Development Studies as the prime analytical lens for the study. The framework (see Figure 8.1) offers ways to examine participatory action in development and changes in power relations by and/or on behalf of poor and marginalized people (Gaventa, 2005). It does this by distinguishing participatory action along three dimensions:

- at three levels (or 'places): global, national and local;
- across three types of (political) 'space': closed, invited and created;
- different forms of power at place within the levels and spaces: visible (formal) power, hidden (behind the scenes) power, and invisible (internalized norms) power (see VeneKlasen and Miller, 2002).

Figure 8.1   The power cube

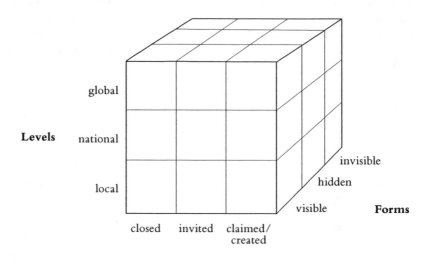

Source: Gaventa, 2005.

The framework was expected to provide more specific insights about the broad notion of 'civil society participation'. The framework understands power 'in relation to how spaces for engagement are created, the levels of power (from local to global), as well as different forms of power across them' (Gaventa, 2006: 2). Using this lens on citizen action enables strategic assessment of the possibilities of transformative action by citizens and how to make these more effective. Unpacking it to enable recognition of CSP during the fieldwork led the team to place inequitable power relations at the centre of their analysis. It meant looking for changes that represent increased, or deepened, participation in decision-making processes and/or the creation, opening or widening of spaces to this effect, either by poor and marginalized citizens or by civil society organizations.

Due to the choice of war-torn, (post-)conflict and fragile peace countries for the evaluation, this framework was supplemented by an explicit look at how violence shapes the potential for civil society participation (Pearce, 2004). The situation of spaces in such contexts adds to the cube a potential dimension of violence either as 'internalized fear/aggression' within it or 'externalized threat/force' outside it. The construction and widening of participatory spaces for the pursuit of social change agendas becomes much more problematic in such contexts, but also more urgent. Participation forces a focus on alternatives to violence as a means of achieving social change and addressing grievances. The idea of 'civil' as opposed to 'uncivil' society also encourages reflection on which elements of associational life favour 'civil' outcomes that might promote collective goals through non-violent means and which remain committed to particular interests and ends with little discrimination around means.

Using a participation focus and power analysis, the evaluation team found that the CFAs are making a significant and often unique contribution to the capacity and development of civil society – and have been doing so, in some cases, for more than two decades (Guijt, 2005). Central in the work of their partner organizations is the focus on participatory action that tackles persistent inequitable power relations. The work touches geographically isolated areas, 'forgotten' social groups and taboo topics. An important aspect of success is the intertwining of work on several levels. To achieve results of some scale, many CSOs build chains of action, from mobilizing at community level up to national advocacy. Where they do not, impact is limited. Importantly – given the apparent divide between 'technical' and 'political' approaches among NGOs – activities on 'citizenship strengthening' which made information accessible and meaningful to people is often consciously connected to efforts to improve service delivery or lobby work.

The evaluation thus raised a series of critical issues for the CFAs to consider in their support of CSP. These include how service delivery can become transformational and be foundational for other manifestations of civil society participation, the importance of basic rights education work, and the need for situated expectations about democratization. However, the use of power analysis also uncovered significant gaps in the efforts of NGOs to challenge systematically some of the most important inequalities both within the development system, including issues of power and participation in the CFAs' relationships with partners, and within developing contexts, particularly concerning gender.

Co-financing as a particular approach to development

The term 'co-financing' within the Dutch development sector refers to the stream of money that flows from the Dutch government via specific Dutch NGOs with CFA status and then onwards to partner organizations in the South. This policy is an expression of the Dutch government's recognition that much of development emerges from civil society and not the state, and makes it possible for the Netherlands to support poverty eradication in countries where the Dutch government does not want to work with the government. A total of around 25 per cent of the development cooperation budget goes to a range of different national and international civil society organizations. Six organizations currently have CFA status, namely CORDAID, ICCO, NOVIB, HIVOS, Terre des Hommes and Plan Netherlands. Other Dutch organizations are eligible to apply to this stream of funding, with conditions being that they have a broad programme of activities in various countries that does not overlap with the existing CFAs. Until recently the CFAs could count on a fixed percentage of the development budget, but this has now merged with the thematic co-financing budget into one 'co-financing' system. The co-financing system allows the CFAs to secure resources for a four-year time period, maintain autonomy over their own programmatic directions during that time period, and support a large and diverse set of initiatives. Each CFA has a different proportion of its budget that comes from the Dutch government, depending on their capacity to generate additional funds – ranging from around 30 per cent to almost 90 per cent.

In this evaluation, it became apparent that sustaining investment over long time frames was of significant importance to the success of CSP in the countries. This is particularly the case with this type of NGO work given the dynamics of democratization and the slow process of social change, as well as the need to invest in multiple 'projects' of participatory democracy simultaneously. However, as of 2007, a new system of allocating resources has led to greater uncertainty and competition among Dutch development organizations. For example, the new system demands that all CFAs must raise 25 per cent of their own funding by 2009, thus fuelling further competition among them. Although the government argues that the new system enables greater transparency and programmatic quality of Dutch development NGOs, it has been heavily criticized for its rigid formulaic approach to allocating funds, inaccuracy due to double counting of certain criteria and other errors in the allocation process, inability to recognize the strategic added value of certain organizations, and disconnection of allocation decisions from longer-term evaluations (Schulpen and Ruben, 2006). NGOs have thus invested enormous amounts of time to write highly detailed strategic plans, in an exercise that, at its worst, has become about how well an organization could present itself rather than the actual (potential) contribution to development.

Contextual Features Affecting Civil Society Participation in Conflict-affected Countries

Context is everything when it comes to the opportunities and risks for promoting civil society participation. The potential for CSP to manifest it itself is strongly influenced by political, cultural, economic and historical contexts. In all countries examined here, the history of protracted violence and/or restrictive political regimes shape what kind of participation occurs at different levels and in diverse spaces. A focused context analysis in each country provided initial insights into the challenges for and development of civil society. Although the five countries involved in this evaluation are characterized by unique histories, cultures and politics that have shaped civil society in equally unique ways (see Table 8.1), several commonalities can be noted.

All five countries deal – to varying degrees – with a state with formal institutions in which de facto power dynamics limit the effective political opportunities of those in formally elected positions. All countries struggle with relatively new constitutions that have been eroded in practice or – as in the cases of Guinea and Guatemala (Buchy and Curtis, 2005; Gish et al., 2005) – that have yet to be implemented in meaningful ways. Violence, often open conflict, and the repression of civil society efforts are characteristics of each country, with Colombia offering the starkest examples of a corrupt institutionality in which extremely powerful drug and paramilitary interests act to maintain the new status quo.

Violence has profoundly marked the psyche of civil society in these countries, both historically and today. It has contributed to a climate in which political activity is deemed subversive, and therefore subject to reprisals or condemnation, and worse. Even within this evaluation, the evaluators in Colombia were asked to stop the tape recordings when topics became too sensitive, while in Uganda it is perhaps more insidious in terms of the self-censorship of CSOs with regard to where they dare to tread. As Pearce and Vela (2005) note,

> Violence does not just imply an external effect of threat. It can be internalised and be taken into participatory spaces where it can exist in the form of silences and inner fear, or even as aggressions towards others due to years of living in violent conditions and/or lack of appropriate channels for expressing differences and conflicts.

In Guinea, Uganda and Sri Lanka, CSO activities have been focused strongly in service delivery, particularly in Guinea where many such organizations are implementing government policies and strategies. In that context, CSOs are only just discovering their potential advocacy role, while this capacity is more strongly present and strengthening in Uganda and Sri Lanka. In both Guatemala and Colombia, civil society emerged from histories of (violent) resistance against repressive regimes, with Colombia reaping some benefits from a longer history of social movements while Guatemalan CSOs are still fragile and fragmented.

Decentralization, prominent in Guatemala, Sri Lanka, Guinea and Uganda, does not appear to have lived up to the full promise of more citizen

engagement in local development. It remains captured by state procedures
and non-democratic processes, with only Uganda showing signs of potential
for citizens' direct engagement in local development – and only then when
mediated by organized groups. This is one example of the potential opening
of closed spaces and the challenges CSOs have faced to use those spaces
effectively in favour of the marginalized.

In Uganda and Guinea (although there investment is considerably less),
the influence of foreign funding agencies on CSOs appears to be strong in
terms of their financial dependency but also in terms of (active) partnership.
In Guinea, CSOs and funding agencies alike have limited political dialogue
with the state following laws that increased presidential powers, while in
Uganda funding agencies actively encourage policy advocacy initiatives by
CSOs. Guatemalan CSOs also have benefited from strong international
support prior to but in particular after the Peace Accords of 1996.

In all countries, many civil society organizations face internal challenges,
including limited human resource capacities, weak internal democratic
processes, limited strategic capacity, limited networking, and a general
related lack of confidence to engage with the demanding tasks of pro-poor
democracy-strengthening activities.

Supporting Civil Society Participation
in the South: The Role of CFAs

Approaches to CSP

Our examination of the myriad examples of 'citizen and civil society
participation' led to a framework that identified six key domains. These
domains are specifically concerned with the capacity of poor, marginalized and vulnerable people to realize their full citizenship. Each domain
describes a form of participation and achievement in which CSOs play
specific roles, and also lists a series of possible progress markers that could
be observed among those involved. Together, these six domains of CSP
can lead to structural change in societal, state and economic institutions
for the realization of citizens' rights and the enhancement of democratic
participation.

Citizenship strengthening comprises activities such as civic education about
basic rights and engaging citizens in critical reflection on and capacity
building around political processes, but also ensuring basic conditions such
as birth registration that gives people formal access to their rights. These
activities lead to better informed people who can understand their rights
and are able to engage constructively and effectively in claim making,

Table 8.1 Overview of countries involved in the CSP programme evaluation

Country	Colombia	Guatemala	Guinea	Sri Lanka	Uganda
Population (mill.) (2003)	44.2	12.0	9.0	20.4	26.9
Human Development Index rank (out of 177) (2005)	69	117	156	93	144
Inequity (% share of income or consumption of poorest 20%) (HDI)	2.7	2.6	6.4	8.0	5.9
% living below national poverty line (1990–2002) (HDI)	64	56.2	40	25	44
Official development assistance received (net disbursements per capita, US$) (HDI)	10.1	20.1	30.0	18.2	25.5
Most recent constitution	1991	1985 (reforms 1993)	1990	1978	1995
Levels of government	3: national, departments (32) plus one capital district, municipalities	3: national, provincial (departments), municipal	5: national, region, prefectures, 'rural development communities', districts	3: national, province, district	6: national, district, county council, sub-county, parish, village
History of conflict	Ongoing since 1964 (founding of the FARC guerrilla movement)	Military rule until 1985; Peace Accords signed in 1996 (everyday violence increasing)	Dictatorship until 1984; current regime authoritarian, conflicts along Sierra Leone/Liberia border	Early 1980s until now	1962–86 (regional conflicts continue)

Source: Country studies; Human Development Index.

collective action, governance and political processes. Examples of work in this domain include PREDO's work (CORDAID–Sri Lanka) that has facilitated the registration of people and helped plantation workers obtain 22,000 identity cards and 11,500 birth certificates. Plan's offices in Guinea and Uganda are working to ensure birth registration as a fundamental right of children – making these children visible citizens – and thus providing the statistical basis for good local development planning and monitoring abuse of children's rights. Local youth clubs, youth radio and village drama are enabling children to learn about and engage in the issues that affect their future as citizens. In Uganda, Plan also works to establish school health clubs that raise children's awareness about the sexual rights and responsibilities and assist them to respond effectively to inappropriate physical or sexual exploitation and abuse. CALDH (Guatemala-HIVOS) is working with young people in the Human Rights Observatory, which receives human rights complaints in fifteen municipalities and with a network of 150 representatives. The exposure of the youth to everyday rights abuses, from the family through to more public violence and abuse, via the complaints that the observers receive, gives them knowledge of the public consequences of what might otherwise remain invisible. The young people have begun to analyse and understand the negative impact on Guatemala of the everyday abuses. This understanding of the importance of 'rights' helps them to legitimize a public role as defenders of those rights. The move of a few into broader public roles, such as participation on the local councils, is a significant outcome of the work.

People's participation in CSO governance, programming, monitoring and accountability relates to the notion of 'participatory culture' within and among CSOs, looking at how CSOs themselves understand and embody what would make for good participatory development. It manifests itself as critically (self-) reflective, democratically functioning and accountable CSOs that are responsive to the rights, values, aspirations, interests and priority needs of their constituencies. Examples for this domain would have required a more thorough look at the internal mechanisms of CSOs, which was beyond the scope of this evaluation. If more time had been available to look at this in depth, it would have included examples such as that of NAFSO (Sri Lanka–HIVOS), which insists on equal representation of men and women as a democratic practice, and active participation in networks and forums.

The third domain of civil society participation relates to CSOs that facilitate *people's participation in local development and service delivery initiatives.* For pro-poor local service delivery to become a reality, CSOs are building the capacity of local people to take on new roles and responsibilities in contexts of decentralization, establishing citizen-driven planning and management structures, and working to make service deliverers more responsive to people's needs. Examples here abound, including the work of TDDA (CORDAID–Sri Lanka) to facilitate claims for service delivery under the post-conflict reconstruction programme; Oasis (HIVOS–Guatemala), which is undertaking sectoral coordination in relation to AIDS; and ACORD (NOVIB–Uganda), providing basic services to communities in northern Uganda. I comment further on the tension between service delivery and transformation in the next subsection.

Many CSOs involved in the evaluation are active in the area of *advocacy and structural change*. CSOs facilitate citizens to undertake their own advocacy work and also undertake lobbying work for certain groups. Related activities include research and consultation on 'forgotten' issues and with ignored groups, creating mechanisms for citizens to participate in public forums, putting issues on formal agendas, and mobilizing support for campaigns. Notable in many of the examples seen is the multiple levels at which activities occur, and the linkages between the levels – from community mobilization to national campaigns. Examples of work on this include:

- LABE's (Uganda–NOVIB) efforts in a national coalition focusing on adult literacy, which has been marginalized in policy making. Its advocacy and lobbying successes led to the participatory formulation of the Adult Literacy Strategic Investment Plan 2002/03, and has enabled local communities to monitor allocation of funds to literacy programmes and demand for accountability from district local councils and/or PAF funds.
- UDN (Uganda–CORDAID and HIVOS) led the campaign for debt relief, building a chain of action from community monitoring up to international advocacy, by investing in capacity-building, research and intensive use of the media for advocacy. To ensure that complaints about use of debt relief funds are acted on, UDN is facilitating communities to undertake quick-action advocacy. Nationally it remains the most reliable source of information on the effects of debt relief on poverty.
- UNIWELO (Sri Lanka–CORDAID) is a district-based CSO that has achieved official recognition of women in the Joint Plantation Development Committees, which were earlier exclusively for males.
- The National Association of Rubbish Recyclers (Colombia–NOVIB) is a grassroots social movement seeking to influence national and municipal policies towards rubbish collection and thus protect the livelihoods of some of the poorest citizens (15,000 families) of Bogotá. The Association has helped defeat President Pastrana's attempt to privatize rubbish recycling with Decree 1713.

A fifth domain in which CSOs are increasingly active is that of enhancing *citizen and CSO participation in economic life*. This work focuses on market engagement by poor, vulnerable people (and organizations working on their behalf) on their terms and for their economic needs, and aiming to make the concept of pro-poor economic growth a reality. Despite being given limited attention in the evaluation (the CFAs being involved in a separate evaluation on this issue), two types of examples were found: organizing for economic justice such as holding the business sector to account, and the insertion of a pro-poor perspective and presence in existing economic institutions. Examples of the latter include: Diocese of Fort Portal (CORDAID–Uganda), which has developed an innovative marketing model for 'high volume–low value' crops; facilitating producer groups to engage with market boards and improve their bargaining power (CORDAID–Uganda); and CONIC's (HIVOS–Guatemala) role in developing participatory methods to work out strategic approaches to agrarian reform over multiple timescales.

CSOs are also active in cultivating values of *trust, dignity, culture* and *identity* that create the bedrock for mutually respectful social relationships and engendering trust in others based on positive experiences, which is essential for joint action in other domains. CSOs active in these areas include informal support groups for minorities, cultural expressions, and working on vibrant community centres. Examples include the Butterfly Peace Garden (BPG) (Sri Lanka–HIVOS), which works to help war-affected children overcome their traumatic experiences through arts, play and counselling. Children come to the garden in mixed groups, multi-ethnic, and multi-religious, from communities that are at strife with one another, a process that is contributing towards a healing and reconciliation effect among the wider community. In Guatemala, MMK (HIVOS-supported) enables Mayan women to understand the problems they face within indigenous communities and in spaces with non-indigenous men and women. The Mayan cosmovision-oriented work has helped women, over the years, to gain confidence and discuss issues around identity and sexuality that were never discussed publicly in the past.

Transformation through service delivery

While the CFA policies are clear about how service delivery work can enhance 'civil society participation', many of the partner organizations would not necessarily consider much of their service delivery work to fall under this label. Furthermore, it was clear that while partner organizations consider issues of power, (political) space and violence in their service delivery work, it is not always guided by a clear understanding of how service delivery, empowerment and CSP are related.

Nevertheless, some examples show what is possible – but also how the context shapes what can be expected. Plan's child-centred work in Guinea, Colombia and Uganda emphasizes this. It has helped increase the number of community organizations and local capacities within these countries providing and managing development initiatives, including examples where children take overall responsibility for project management and implementation. In Guinea, this happens under very difficult circumstances where development-oriented CBOs are still a relative novelty. Initiatives such as 'Child-to-Child' and Children's Parliament increase children's participation in particular. Plan's school programmes offer models of education that encourage children to speak out, form their own opinions and engage in school decision-making. A further example comes from Uganda, where ACORD (NOVIB-supported) has evolved from a relief and infrastructure focus to an institutional and rights-based emphasis on capacity-building of local government and strengthening of civil society in the North. Local government has noticeably resisted civil society participation and CSOs have been relatively weak and contract-oriented. ACORD's encouragement and training have enabled a shift in the dynamics of civil society–local government relations, particularly in parish development committees, where CBOs are more visible and planning decisions are more transparent than at higher levels where NGOs dominate.

Since the relatively recent surge of interest in rights-based approaches (Cornwall and Nyamu-Musembi, 2005), development activities seem to be viewed by some development actors in a rather dichotomous manner as constituting either political or non-political work. Much of what is deemed to fit within a rights-based logic is considered 'political' and tackling structural causes of poverty, while the rest is considered 'old style' service delivery development that alleviates the symptoms of poverty. Again it must be noted that this is not the case for the CFAs, but has been noted among partner organizations. The CSP perspective of this evaluation challenges this simplistic dichotomy as being both unhelpful and misleading, leading to missed opportunities.

People's citizenship entitles them to basic services and provides the springboard for other developmental endeavours in terms of claiming rights. At the same time, claiming service delivery provision is itself a political act of rights realization. Therefore a critical component in service delivery is how the poor, marginalized and vulnerable (and their organizations) participate in defining needs and priorities, ensuring access to and quality of services, and collaborative service provision, including volunteer-based service provision. This is a decades-old debate that has spawned much of the participatory focus of development activities in recent times. Added to this is the renewed emphasis by many government funding agencies in the North on direct poverty alleviation goals in the form of service delivery as a technical/administrative activity, and a shift in channelling this through government channels in the interests of stimulating 'good governance'. As a result, CSOs, in general, are experiencing a squeeze on resources for this work. Simultaneously, they are also recognized by funding agencies as playing a vital role in the social change and advocacy spheres.

Thus the challenge for CSOs lies in articulating clearly the interconnectedness between their service delivery function and that of more structural change-of-power relations, or the advocacy function. And the CFAs have a role to play in enabling and encouraging this.

The never-ending challenge of gender equity

All of the CFAs fund work that addresses gender inequalities, most often in ways that reflect the more political 'gender and development' approach, as opposed to the more conservative 'women in development' approach. Many partner organizations focus on:

> creating opportunities for women to occupy claimed spaces and to gain self confidence in these claimed spaces. They prepare women to negotiate in the invited spaces with government authorities and with others with powerful positions like the police, community leaders, etc. They are equipped to challenge the power structures and to claim their rights. These women groups are further strengthened through networking and often bring information on alternative forms of development to the 'male'-streamed development processes. (Perera and Walters, 2005: 33)

In Sri Lanka, HIVOS's support focuses on violence against women and migrant workers, while in Guatemala it supports CSOs that build (indigenous) women's capacity to claim rights and access decision-making, audit government policies and work on sexual identity. Plan's work on gender issues focuses largely on capacity-building for empowerment – through training of women promoters, ensuring girls' access to schools, and awareness-raising about reproductive rights, but also facilitating equitable access services and providing legal support. CORDAID's support for gender-related work in Sri Lanka focuses on the plantation sector, including violence against women, capacity-building and representation on plantation committees. In Uganda, regional and national legal rights advocacy work is funded by CORDAID, while in Colombia the work of the CSO Conciudadania stands out for building a sense of cultural identity and belonging which could enable a civic and civil response, notably by women leaders. NOVIB's work on gender in Uganda has focused mainly on advocacy issues, such as support for women's engagement with the review of the 1995 Constitution, and advocacy on women's land rights and on the Domestic Relations Bill. In Colombia, NOVIB supports work on promoting female participation in public policymaking and generating feminist consciousness.

The results of these efforts give rise to two observations in particular. First, gender relations, violence (in all shades) and civil society participation are strongly interwoven. Intra-family violence in Colombia lays the basis for a climate of fear and social relationships mediated by conflict that affects the quality of citizen participation at other levels, such as the respect given to and felt by women in formal spaces. In Sri Lanka, the war, violence, insecurity and poverty have resulted in high levels of alcoholism, domestic violence and suicides, which adversely affect women disproportionately. Hence the importance of work such as Mujeres Maya Kaq'la (HIVOS–Guatemala) that helps Mayan women move from victimhood to public participants and that lays the foundation for more participatory society.

The second observation is the considerable variation in attitude among partner organizations to gendered aspects of CSP. The Uganda country study lauded the long-term investment by CFAs in women's organizations and the focus on gender issues, which had contributed to very significant advances for gender equality in terms of economic and political opportunities, policy analysis and change, competencies among women at all levels to have a significant voice on their issues, and strong organizations working on domestic violence, gendered dimensions of HIV/AIDS, education, and so forth. In Sri Lanka, notable advances have been made in the areas of Muslim women's rights and the lives of women tea plantation workers. By contrast, in Colombia, while women are high among the victims of sexual abuse, domestic violence and forced displacement, and have played key roles in community mobilizing and civil resistance, they still appear to be very poorly represented as political leaders and holders of power. In Guinea, while significant advances have been made in girls' schooling, which is undoubtedly foundational work, and women are now allowed to participate in (some) councils of elders and community councils, other critical opportunities for engaging with entrenched gender inequalities and abuses, such as female genital mutilation and gender issues within CSOs, have not being taken up.

Understanding the gendered dimension of power and violence is a cornerstone of effective CSO support. Separating these two perspectives risks a false separation between support for gender-related action and for civil society participation in contexts of violence. As such, three useful suggestions can be made here. First, NGOs can seek a more integrated perspective on gender policies and conflict/peace-building policies, to come to a gendered understanding of violence and conflict that can then inform their country/regional strategies. Second, support for partner organizations should go beyond strategies that simply place women in previously 'closed spaces' and invest more in strategies that seek to transform these spaces in ways that ensure that they are genuinely used to further women's interests or to address tough topics related to invisible power. Third, NGOs need to assess whether their support – in a collective sense – constitutes the type of multi-level action that is required to change patriarchal practices that exist throughout societies. Again, this will involve using the power framework to analyse where gender-equity obstacles exist, where strategic efforts are occurring and where critical gaps remain and could be addressed by the CFAs and their partner organizations.

Moving Forward: Conceptual and Practical Advances

Conceptually, two analytical tools were used within this study – the power analysis framework and the notion of CSP domains – and each emerged as having a high degree of practical relevance for how NGOs go about their work in this field. In addition, the evaluation showed that there are significant gains to be had in terms of promoting CSP where funding is sustained over significant periods; where international funder-partners encourage a participatory culture both within their local partners and between themselves; and also through the documentation and sharing of findings. I deal with each of these ways forward in turn.

The power cube framework

The 'power cube framework' that guided the study proved a valuable and flexible tool to seek answers about how power inequalities were being tackled and to stimulate discussions on strategies for and dynamics of participation with the CSOs. The workshops where partner organizations met to discuss 'civil society participation' were widely appreciated for enabling more detailed and strategic discussions on their activities. It helped the organizations locate their work alongside that of others, assess its relevance and reflect on the relative merits of different strategies being used. These discussions highlighted the changing in-country political realities, which had, for example, opened up new spaces for engagement in Uganda but in Colombia and Guatemala were threatening to close painfully conquered space. Rich-country level examples illustrated every dimension of the framework, varying greatly per context, shaped as they are by the histories and realities of violence and conflict. Clearly, there is no recipe for what constitutes effective participatory action.

The emerging issues related to 'place' and 'space' have several implications for CFAs and their partner organizations. They need to:

- continue to work at all levels (global to local) but invest more in conscious building of linkages between partners across these levels so that efforts can complement each other more strategically;
- encourage CSOs to strategise consciously about which 'space' (closed, invited, claimed) is most relevant and potentially effective for a specific

issue, but also in terms of what type of intervention is needed in each space – and then support partners to gain required capacities needed for greater effectiveness;

- be clear that 'participation' in a particular space does not necessarily mean transformation of power inequalities – there can be much action, with little political or practical change, but conversely many strategies of engagement are critical and necessary in order to affect the decision-making that affects the lives of the poor.

The dimension of 'power' has other practical potential:

- defining and recognizing the importance of different manifestations of power can ensure more consciously adopted, strategic action – and the identification of alternatives to current strategies – that can effectively transform power inequalities;
- the CFAs need to locate themselves more fully within the 'power cube framework', thus ensuring that analysis of participation and power is useful for them internally and only for the CSOs.

Notwithstanding the usefulness of the framework for critical reflection, other uses must be approached with more caution (see Gaventa, 2006). In particular, the framework should be viewed as dynamic and flexible, and not as a static checklist for categorizing organizations.

The domains of civil society participation

A second 'tool for thought' is the six-domains framework of civil society participation. It helps specify more clearly what CSP means in practice and, in more general terms, renders underlying development processes more apparent and amenable to action through development interventions. The six domains, along with the findings from the country studies, underscore the CFAs' original concern that civil society building, as it is often (but not universally) understood, does not adequately address deeper issues of participation, empowerment and voice in decision-making and political processes. In practice, CSB has often centred on strengthening civil groups and non-governmental organizations and their activities. What this study shows is the importance of questioning more critically the relationship between civil society groups and the active participation of citizens or the constituency they claim to represent in decision-making processes. The CSP concept adds a more critical perspective on the power and politics of participation in civil society action, which leads to a set of more distinct domains in which civil society can be seen to be active and where CFA support can be discerned. Significantly it untangles what funders can expect of CSOs and of citizens, as separate levels of intervention and impact.

Importantly, the domains framework can enable the CFAs to:

- assess with greater clarity the results of CSOs within each domain, thus giving them a clearer picture of their contribution towards enhanced civil society participation;
- target funding and other support more strategically; and
- be more specific about their expectations vis-à-vis specific partners and contracts.

Sustain funding through organizational and contextual transitions

Conspicuous in many of the examples is the use of multi-pronged strategies that have evolved over time. Many CSOs working on citizenship strengthening followed up with support for advocacy efforts, while citizen participation in service delivery and advocacy efforts often go hand in hand. Efforts to build dignity and relationships of trust are nested with civil rights awareness-raising. Two evolutions are evident in many of the cases. First, there is a clear shift in contexts where CSOs emerged from a history of service delivery from a welfarist to an empowerment approach. This is evident in Uganda and Sri Lanka, with early signs in Guinea. A second and related evolution is the growth of CSOs from single actions to a presence in various arenas, moving from localized, community-level activism to broader national (advocacy) efforts (Madre Selva, Guatemala–HIVOS) or from national lobby work to community capacity-building to enhance impact (UDN, Uganda–CORDAID/HIVOS). Taking on more complex issues has required more sophisticated strategizing, new competencies and the diversifying of activities.

Overall, the four CFAs collectively support a critical and diverse portfolio of relevant work in the five countries that enables the emergence and strengthening of civil society participation in diverse manifestations. This is a highly significant contribution to development at a time in which democratic and peaceful processes of social and political change are threatened in all the countries included in the evaluation. Given the vital contribution made by the CSOs funded by the CFAs to enhance civil society participation and given the urgent challenges, the CFAs must continue the nature and focus of their support to CSOs towards this effect.

The largely positive conclusion becomes even more significant when put into wider perspective, by noting how the Dutch CFAs compare to other funding agencies. All country studies except for Guinea offer views by the partner organizations of what is concluded clearly by Mukasa et al. (2005): that many other agencies funding CSP

> lack a cogent ideology and in the absence of a sustainable resource base, [so] they opportunistically shift from one issue to another due to donor dependency

and influence. ... Many of the CSOs admitted that the CFAs provide the biggest and most reliable long-term core funding to them. They in particular lauded the CFA approach to funding, which is based on the partners' strategy as opposed to project-specific funding.

Such funding support is perhaps, at times, taken for granted in the Dutch development arena. This would be a mistake – it must be valued, nurtured and reinforced.

Learn, document, share

The study revealed a relative paucity of (clear) documentation by the CFAs and CSOs on strategies that successfully promoted citizen and CSO participation. If CFAs (and partner organizations) are to make claims about 'enhancing civil society participation', then the question is on what basis such claims are made. The specific and significant methodological challenges for monitoring and evaluating social change work are increasingly recognized. Given the processual and interconnected nature of activities that enhance civil society participation, this requires due attention to qualitative approaches for capturing results and impacts. If effectiveness indicators are to be developed, then outcomes that value the processes and changes in, for example, attitudes, behaviour and knowledge become important. The CFAs should scrutinize their monitoring and evaluation of CSP work to deal better with the complexity and context-specific nature of social change processes and building capacities and processes within the CFAs and partner organizations.

Invest in participatory cultures: internally and with CSOs

Building a 'participatory culture' must receive more attention, with fieldwork revealing a need for more reflection by CSOs on their own understandings of the participation, democracy building and conflict resolution that underpin their actions. 'Participatory development' is not just about increasing the voices in decision-making but represents values, such as respectful inclusion and democracy within social movements, that qualify 'participation' and make it positive or negative. The slow, uncertain and fragile nature of progress towards enhanced 'civil society participation' is only possible with a clear vision on rights-oriented development, staying power and strategic flexibility on the part of citizens and their organizations. These qualities are also needed of the CFAs that support them. All four CFAs are viewed by CSOs as very positive funding agencies and partners. The CFAs are clearly committed to the broader endeavour of peaceful and democratic civic societies, and provide long-term core funding that sees partners and projects through difficult times and transitions. They are steadfast either in their vision of development as requiring sustained action to redress power inequalities, or in strengthening this vision where it is incipient.

This can be aided if CFAs strengthen their capacity to undertake power analysis. This can help them underpin and make more consistent their policies, strategies and procedures vis-à-vis partners, paying particular attention to assumptions about social change and what can be expected of CSOs given the challenges of their operating environment. The CFAs themselves are agents of change, which they recognize. They need to recognize their own power in-country in shaping and furthering agendas of their partner organizations and initiatives and act on this, without creating (new) dependencies and without imposing international advocacy agendas on partners. Greater clarity on this requires an internal CFA analysis of its own agency in country-focused support, reconsidering its roles vis-à-vis partners and the CSP theme.

Vis-à-vis the CSOs, all CFAs face the similar challenge – of overcoming the existing deficit of direct dialogue with partners/project staff on enhancing citizen and CSO participation based on a power analysis. This should aim to enable partners to be more (self-) critical and strategic, based on their own visions of social change and given the types of operating environment outlined here. The CFAs should also invest more in processes for enhancing participatory (organizational) culture within the CSOs they support, as a critical component for strengthening the quality of the partners' participatory action.

Overall, the experience of how NGOs seek to promote civil society participation suggests the importance of several strategic approaches by NGOs and their funders, two of which have particular relevance here. The first concerns the importance of thinking more clearly around how and where to act and of (re)conceptualizing the challenges that promoting development alternatives entails. This requires frameworks of analysis that are both critically informed and practical. Two frameworks are proposed here, both with significant potential to help NGOs close the gap between development interventions and underlying processes of development. Second, it bears repeating that historical transitions – such as those towards lived (not simply formal) citizenship – may take a long time, particularly in contexts affected by conflict and violence. In such scenarios in particular, funding flows need to be long-term, flexible and designed in ways that give local partners the time and space to continually (re)define strategies to make the most of opportunities and deal with contextual constraints. If such approaches to co-financing are diluted or disappear, then the NGOs face even tougher conditions under which to pursue social change over the long run.

NGO acronyms

ACORD	Agency for Cooperation and Research in Development
CALDH	Centro de Acción Legal en Derechos Humanos
CONIC	Coordinadora Nacional Indígena y Campesina
CORDAID	Catholic Organization for Relief and Development Aid
DENIVA	Development Network of Indigenous Voluntary Associations
HIVOS	Humanist Institute for Cooperation with Developing Countries
LABE	Literacy and Adult Basic Education
MMK	Mujeres Maya Kaq'la (Mayan Women Kaq'la)
NAFSO	National Fisheries Solidarity
NOVIB	Nederlandse Organisatie voor Internationale Ontwikkelingssamenwerking (Netherlands Organization for International Development Cooperation
PREDO	Plantation Rural Education and Development Organization)
TDDA	Trincomalee District Development Association
UDN	Uganda Debt Network
UNIWELO	United Welfare Organization

References

Biekart, K. (2003) 'Dutch Co-financing Agencies and Civil Society Building. Synthesis and Analysis of Case Studies in Mali, India and Nicaragua', Steering Committee for the Evaluation of the Dutch Co-financing Programme and DGIS/DSI, The Hague.

Buchy, M., and M.Y. Curtis (2005) 'Guinea Country Report', report on the programme evaluation 'Assessing Civil Society Participation as supported In-Country by CORDAID, HIVOS, BOVIB, and Plan Netherlands'.

CORDAID, HIVOS, NOVIB/Oxfam Netherlands, Plan Netherlands (2004) 'Preliminary Paper. Programme Evaluation Civil Society Participation 2004–2005', CORDAID, HIVOS, NOVIB/Oxfam Netherlands, Plan Netherlands, March.

Cornwall, A., and C. Nyamu-Musembi (2005) 'Why Rights, Why Now? Reflections on the Rise of Rights in International Development Discourse', IDS Bulletin 36(1): 9–18, Institute of Development Studies, Brighton.

Edwards, M. (2004) Civil Society, Polity Press, Cambridge.

Friedmann, J. (1992) Empowerment: The Politics of Alternative Development, Blackwell, Oxford.

Gaventa, J. (2005) 'Reflections on the Uses of the "Power Cube" Approach for Analyzing the Spaces, Places and Dynamics Of Civil Society Participation and Engagement. Draft', prepared for the Dutch CFA evaluation 'Assessing Civil Society Participation as supported by CORDAID, HIVOS, NOVIB and Plan Netherlands' and for the 'Power, Participation and Change' programme.

Gaventa, J. (2006) 'Finding the Spaces for Change: A Power Analysis', IDS Bulletin, 37 (6): 23–33, Institute of Development Studies, Brighton.

Gish, D., Z. Navarro, J. Pearce and J. Pettit (2005) 'Guatemala Country Report. 2005', report on the programme evaluation Assessing Civil Society Participation as supported In-Country by CORDAID, HIVOS, NOVIB, and Plan Netherlands'.

Guijt, I. (2005) 'Synthesis Report of Dutch CFA Programme Evaluation – Assessing Civil Society Participation as Support In-Country by CORDAID, HIVOS, NOVIB and Plan Netherlands 1999–2004', MFP Breed Netwerk, Netherlands. www.partos. nl/uploaded_files/1–CSP-Synthesis-English.pdf.

Hulme, D. (1994) 'Social Development Research and the Third Sector: NGOS as Users and Subjects of Social Inquiry', in D. Booth (ed.), *Rethinking Social Development: Theory, Research and Practice*, Longman, Harlow, pp. 251–75.

Mukasa, G., J. Pettit and J. Woodhill (2005) 'Uganda Country Report', Report on the Programme Evaluation 'Assessing Civil Society Participation as supported In-Country by CORDAID, HIVOS, NOVIB, and Plan Netherlands'.

Nerfin, M. (1987) 'Neither Prince nor Merchant – Citizen: An Introduction to the Third System', *Development Dialogue* 1: 170–95.

Pearce, J. (2004) 'Assessing Civil Society Participation: War and Post-War Contexts', background paper draft for the programme evaluation 'Assessing Civil Society Participation as supported In-Country by CORDAID, HIVOS, NOVIB, and Plan Netherlands'.

Pearce, J., and G. Vela (2005) 'Colombia Country Report', report on the programme evaluation 'Assessing Civil Society Participation as supported In-Country by CORDAID, HIVOS, NOVIB, and Plan Netherlands'.

Perera, S., and H. Walters (2005) 'Sri Lanka Country Report', report on the programme evaluation 'Assessing Civil Society Participation as supported In-Country by CORDAID, HIVOS, NOVIB, and Plan Netherlands'.

Schulpen, L., and R. Ruben (2006) *Een gevoelige selectie. Analyse van de beoordelingssystematiek in het nieuwe Medefinancieringsstelsel.* CIDIN, Nijmegen.

VeneKlasen, L., and V. Miller (2002) *A New Weave of People, Power and Politics: The Action Guide for Advocacy and Citizen Participation*, World Neighbors, Oklahoma City.

9

Producing Knowledge, Generating Alternatives? Challenges to Research-oriented NGOs in Central America and Mexico

Cynthia Bazán, Nelson Cuellar, Ileana Gómez, Cati Illsley, Adrian López, Iliana Monterroso, Joaliné Pardo, Jose Luis Rocha, Pedro Torres and Anthony Bebbington

What do non-profit organizations whose primary role is to produce knowledge contribute to development alternatives? The question is not an idle one. As the Millennium Development Goals and the poverty agenda impress themselves ever more firmly on the criteria used to allocate international cooperation and national development budgets, research-oriented NGOs, and research activities within multi-functional NGOs, have found it increasingly difficult to secure funding. In this context, being clear on the nature, role and purpose of such NGOs is urgent, otherwise research activities in progressive NGOs will wither away, leaving the non-profit knowledge-generation field open to business-supported, more conservative and well-funded think-tanks. This urgency is both institutional (to offset an organizational demise that occurs by default rather than because of any clear strategic reasoning) and political (to avoid the further colonization of public debate and discourse by a core set of broadly neoliberal principles encoded in different policy prescriptions and conceptual arguments).

Clarity on the nature, role and dynamics of such organizations is also of theoretical importance. A reflection on the relationship between knowledge and development alternatives forces more careful thought on the relationships between civil society and development, among knowledge, policy and the public sphere, and on the constitution of civil society itself. Thinking in a more disaggregated manner about these relationships is itself, we argue, a contribution to reflections on the nature of development alternatives, and to our conceptualization of the relationships between non-governmental organizations and alternatives.

With these opening gambits in mind, the chapter summarizes a series of collective reflections elaborated by the authors in the course of a two-year initiative addressing the role and evolution of NGOs engaged in knowledge generation related to environment and development in Central America and Mexico. The reflections are largely autobiographical in their inspiration, for the work underlying this chapter has revolved around analytical reconstructions of the authors' own organizations and the knowledge generation work done within them (Bebbington, 2007). Our analysis is, however, grounded in a broader theoretical reflection (see the following section) in order that it be relevant for research-oriented NGOs elsewhere.

The chapter proceeds as follows. First, we outline several generative concepts that underlie our reflection on research-oriented NGOs. Second, we provide a brief summary of the organizations whose experience informs the argument here. Third, we discuss the ways in which these organizations understand the relationships between knowledge, civil society and development alternatives, and in particular their approaches to the relationships between research and policy processes. Fourth, we discuss the pressures that these organizations currently face – pressures emanating from their external and internal environments. We then close discussing the types of organizational change to which these pressures have led over recent years, and the challenges that these experiences raise for thinking about the roles of knowledge-generation organizations in producing development alternatives.

Theorizing the informal University: Concepts for Thinking about Research-oriented NGOs

In his interpretation of the relationships among politics, economy and religion in post-World War II Latin America, David Lehmann emphasizes the importance of a certain type of non-governmental organization: those that combine grassroots work with various forms of research, publication and knowledge generation (Lehmann, 1990). He suggests that such organizations played an important part in processes of democratization, largely due to their roles in broadening particular types of public sphere and placing both academic and social movement knowledge within those public spheres. Lehmann referred to such organizations as the 'informal university', not only to draw attention to the intellectual nature of their work but also to suggest that their emergence was an effect of particular political and financial pressures on the formal university during that period. At the same time, this characterization (and Lehmann's analysis) suggested that the contribution of such centres was distinct from that of universities. Their private, not-for-profit nature allowed them to do and say things, to bridge the research and public spheres, to bridge direct engagement and knowledge production, and so on, in ways that universities simply could not. Being non-governmental held open the possibility of generating knowledge in quite different ways – ways that were embedded in particular social actors and social processes.

Of course, such non-profit research centres also exist in countries where political and financial pressures are not so intense (Stone, 2002; Stone and Denham, 2004; Maxwell and Stone, 2004), suggesting that their emergence is due not only to the constraints on universities. However, many such centres are linked closely to political parties, interest groups or government departments, and/or exist largely as consultancies. Such linkages serve as a source of both financial support and political legitimacy, but also raise questions such as how best to theorize about these non-profit research centres. While the tendency is to refer to them as civil society organizations, this may not be the most helpful way to conceptualize (for example) a think-tank that draws the majority of its financial support from the UK's Department for International Development, that is closely linked to the UK Labour Party or that is funded primarily by US-based energy companies. While not describing the situation of the organizations writing this chapter, these hypothetical examples suggest that it is not enough to say that we are simply civil society organizations or think-tanks. Rather, we need to think much more carefully about the sources of our legitimacy – not in order to make normative judgements about our work, but in order to be clearer about our role, and the relationships and sources of legitimacy that we must nurture carefully. Too often non-profits presume they are legitimate due to their non-profit and 'civil society' status. Yet, as the literature is clear, such claims are simply not enough (Edwards and Hulme, 1995; Hulme and Edwards, 1997).

Indeed, the special case of research-oriented NGOs is helpful for thinking about civil society – and, in turn, reflecting on these analytical approaches to civil society helps illuminate potential roles of research-oriented organizations. Here we outline two distinct approaches, one viewing civil society in associative terms, the second seeing it as 'the arena ... in which ideological hegemony is contested' (Lewis, 2002: 572). The associationalist approach views civil society as the arena of association between the household and the state, a 'third sector' which can supply services that neither state nor market can (e.g. Salamon and Anheier, 1997). In this reading, knowledge-generating NGOs might be viewed as sources of research, consulting, advice and publication, but understood in their terms of their function rather than in terms of the political project of which they are a part. This latter emphasis instead characterizes a second approach, which has roots in both Gramsci (1971) and Habermas (1984). Here, civil society is understood as the arena in which ideas and discourses become hegemonic, serving to stabilize and naturalize capitalist systems of production and exchange. Notwithstanding their hegemonic status, these ideas can be challenged and upset. Indeed, for post-Marxism and post-structuralism, this was the lens through which Latin American social movements had to be understood (Alvarez et al., 1998). It was not simply that the role of a social movement was to build counter-hegemonic ideas (around development, democracy or human rights); rather this was the very definition of a social movement. Movements were vectors of these counter-hegemonic tendencies. Given that knowledge is central to both hegemony and counter-hegemony, in this interpretation, research-oriented NGOs would have to be understood in terms of their positioning with either hegemonic (mainstream) or counter-hegemonic (alternative) tendencies.

A second, related, axis around which we have ordered our thinking derives from recent work by Evelina Dagnino and colleagues (2006). Rather than use a language of state, market and civil society to help locate the niche and roles of particular (non-governmental) actors in fostering inclusion and democracy, they suggest that it is more helpful to consider their relationship to larger political projects that cut across the spheres of state and civil society. They identify three such meta-projects in contemporary Latin America: a neoliberal (or neoliberal-deepening) project, a direct democracy (or democracy-deepening) project, and an authoritarian project. The advantage of such a framework is that it avoids the issue of whether or not an organization is an NGO or a social movement (etc.), and asks instead that an organization's essence be identified in terms of what it stands for and contributes to. This approach may also be helpful given that the ways in which other actors relate to an organization probably depend more on its relationship to distinct projects rather than on its relative purity as a civil society, market or state actor. Furthermore, for the particular case of knowledge generation, actors might deliberately interact with others whose political projects are quite distinct in order that the knowledge produced is as legitimate and evidence-based as possible.

A drawback of Dagnino et al.'s characterization, however, is that it may be too blunt to accommodate the different hybrids that exist in the region. Some of these hybrids might simply be – in Dagnino's et al.'s language – instances of 'perverse convergence' in which a neoliberal project appears to open scope for participation but in practice does so in a way that further undermines the concepts of universal rights and social justice. Others, however, may not be perverse, and may involve serious attempts to explore ways in which markets can be used (and governed) so as to allocate resources to foster greater social inclusion. Indeed, a second drawback of the framework is the tendency to associate the participatory democratic project with political practices, and the neoliberal project with market-based practices. Yet there are evidently projects – both globally and in the region – that are based on economic models that afford an important role for markets while also fostering inclusion either directly (through addressing who has access to these markets) or indirectly (through addressing the quality of growth that market development delivers). Such hybrids have different origins, often depending on the institutional context in which they have been elaborated. Some have grown out of the institutional and informational turn in economics, some from efforts to refashion socialist and social-democratic political projects so that they allow markets to play a bigger role in resource allocation and the creation of opportunities; some are based in real-world exigencies encountered by left-of-centre political projects when they assume positions of political power and need to manage resource scarcity and fiscal constraints. Whether referred to as the post-Washington Consensus (Fine, 2001, 1999), the Third Way (Giddens, 1998), or some other epithet, such efforts at hybridizing aspects of both neoliberalism's commitment to the role of markets and social democracies' commitment to the importance of governing markets so that they are less exclusive, are present in projects in contexts as diverse as Lula's Brazil, the Concertación's Chile, New Labour's Britain or even the World Bank's *World Development Report* of 2006 on Equity. Hybrids such as these offer a fourth political project to add to Dagnino et al.'s trinity. This schema can help not only to locate our organizations but also to shed light on their role and niche in the region.

A final axis for thinking about the work, nature and niche of organizations such as ours comes from understandings of the linkages between research/policy and research/social change. Diane Stone (2002) suggests three main types of explanation used to explore obstacles to research–policy linkages: supply-side explanations (which suggest that the main problem is to do with problems in the quality, usefulness and communication of research); demand-side explanations (suggesting that the main problems are to do with lack of political will or the lack of technical ability among policymakers to use research-based knowledge); and embeddedness explanations (suggesting that the main problems are related to weak links between research centres and the social actors that drive policy change). These three explanations might well be related to two broad approaches to research–policy linkages: approaches that can be characterized as the 'short route' from research to policy and the 'long route' (Bebbington and Barrientos, 2005). Supply- and demand-side explanations of the obstacles to research–policy linkages imply that once the related problems are resolved, then research should become relevant to and influential in policy formation. Therefore supply- and demand-side explanations hold open the possibility and desirability of following a *short route* from researchers to policymakers – a route in which researchers, their ideas and their publications have a direct influence on policy. Conversely, embeddedness explanations suggest that for research to influence policy, it is important that research centres embed themselves in particular social actors who will then take the knowledge that the centres produce (knowledge made more relevant through this process of becoming embedded) and use it both in their own practices and in their efforts to influence policy: a *longer route* from research to policy.

The two routes have different institutional implications for research centres. The short route suggests a more rapid, less costly and a more elitist and technocratic approach to research–policy linkages, while also implying that research-centre legitimacy would be derived primarily from the professional quality of their staff and their work, as well as from personal linkages with policymakers and policy framers. The long route suggests a slower, more expensive process and perhaps one that requires more grass-roots-oriented political commitments. In following the longer route, research centres would seek legitimacy primarily from the quality and depth of their relationships with social-change actors, and from the ways in which this embeddedness affected the research process. How a knowledge generating organization places itself with respect to the short- and long-route options will influence the types of internal capacity and external relationships it feels are most important to strengthen, the ways in which it structures itself institutionally and geographically, how it claims legitimacy for the work that it does, and quite possibly the larger political project within which it locates itself. With these conceptual axes in mind, then – namely, sources of legitimacy, positioning vis-à-vis larger political and development projects, and approaches to research–policy linkages – we discuss the organizations whose experiences drive the reflections presented in this chapter.

The Case Study Organizations

While the organizations whose experiences underlie this reflection are all non-governmental, they are non-governmental in different ways and to different degrees. Likewise the balance between research, knowledge generation and development intervention varies among them. Also, the extent to which environment and development is central to their work varies. In some cases (e.g. PRISMA and GEA) it runs through all their work; in others (e.g. Nitlapán and FLACSO) it is a programme within a wider suite of research themes, and so in these cases our collective reflection involved the parts of the organization involved in rural and environmentally related work. How might we, then, map our organizations?

At one extreme is the Group for Environmental Studies (Grupo de

Estudios Ambientales, GEA AC, Mexico), an organization that, while it takes knowledge generation seriously has done so from the basis of a strong engagement in social-change and development activities. At the other extreme are organizations whose work is very largely research-oriented. This position is most apparent in Nitlapán (Nicaragua) and PRISMA (Programa Salvadoreño sobre Desarrollo y Medio Ambiente). PRISMA is a free-standing NGO; Nitlapán functions in a similar way to PRISMA, but in formal terms is an administratively independent institute within the Universidad CentroAmericana (UCA) in Managua, a university owned by the Company of Jesús and with presence through much of Central America.

Located between these two extremes we have two other types of organization. One is much more akin to or linked to a university organization. The Latin American Faculty for Social Sciences (FLACSO–Guatemala) is an autonomous graduate school that combines research, teaching, extension and outreach. While created under the auspices of UNESCO and governed, ultimately, by its fifteen member states, it functions to a considerable degree as an NGO. It combines research, outreach and efforts to influence policy and public debate, has considerable autonomy in devising strategy, and depends in large measure on international agencies for its activities. However, it is neither as autonomous nor as purely research-oriented as is Nitlapán. The Universidad Autónoma de Yucatán is a public university one of whose roles is to contribute to development of the Yucatán. PROTROPICO, however, is a programme created within the university with the express purpose of linking research and community development processes and allowing more participatory and also policy-oriented forms of knowledge generation related to natural resource management and development. With time, however, PROTROPICO has become increasingly autonomous of the university. It too depends on external funding for its work and is not governed by formal university rules and practices.

The other intermediary grouping is of NGOs that emerged as networks or inter-organizational forums that had the explicit objective of fostering public debate with a view to influencing policy. The Network for Sustainable Development (RDS, Red de Desarrollo Sostenible) also emerged under the auspices of a UN initiative (UNDP in this case) to broaden information availability on environment and development. While it continues to emphasize information exchange and policy influence, with time it has assumed the dynamics of a free-standing NGO combining development and information exchange. The Forum for Sustainable Development (Foro Chiapas) similarly emerged to foster exchange and debate among organizations, academics and political actors in Chiapas, Mexico, but with time it has become an NGO combining development projects and research activity.

Among them, then, these case-study organizations represent different ways of trying to be a private, non-profit organization that generates knowledge with a view to influencing action, public debate and policy. These different models, while complicating simple comparisons, allow us to reflect more systematically on the prospects for knowledge generation for alternative development from the position of non-governmental organizations.

Theorizing the Relationships between Knowledge, Civil Society and Development

Each of our institutions would think of itself as a civil society organization, though in somewhat distinct ways. These visions have also taken us towards differing views on the relationships between our work, knowledge production and development. In this section we outline these views. As will be apparent, they have different implications for the ways in which our institutions need to seek legitimacy. Whatever the case, it is clear that it is not enough for us to seek legitimacy simply by claiming to be civil society groups, and in practice it is probably the case that our legitimacy derives more from the quality and effects of the knowledge we produce than from our social location. We return to this later.

In practice the concept of civil society that is most prevalent in the ways in which we understand ourselves has been the associationalist one. We have viewed ourselves as civil society organizations because we are neither government nor profit-oriented organizations. The irony here, of course, is that – at least in terms of intellectual lineage – this places us in a tradition that has tended to be more conservative than we would want to think of ourselves as being. Indeed, for most of us, our earlier years were characterized by a more Gramscian sense of our place in civil society than have been our later years. The origins of our institutions were diverse: some inhered in a determination to be alternative, and to demonstrate that it was possible to build different ways of producing knowledge with campesinos (GEA); others inhered in the effort to produce knowledge that, though not organically linked to the FMLN, certainly sought to challenge right-wing views of what El Salvador was and should be (PRISMA); others (Foro Chiapas) came from a commitment to challenge authoritarian approaches to governing Chiapas, and to build on the spaces opened up by Zapatismo in Chiapas while (as in PRISMA's case) having no organic link to this movement; and others derived from a commitment to contribute to the liberating elements of Sandinismo (Nitlapán). Common to most of our origins was a commitment to build – or to facilitate the building of – knowledge that would challenge public debate and contribute to some or other form of democracy-deepening project.

This commitment was made all the more complex by the historical moment in which many of us emerged. With the exception of FLACSO and GEA, we are all creatures and creations of the 1990s, a period of paradigmatic crisis in development and politics which was every bit as real in Mexico and Central America as it was in Northern academic and political worlds. As a result, our efforts to build alternatives were themselves challenged by a relative lack of guiding concepts – we had to build these ourselves. This is apparent in some of our work. For instance, Nitlapán's efforts to understand the dynamics of the peasant economy reflect the lack of a clear *ex ante* view on the merits of peasant production and organization (Maldidier and Marchetti, 1996); PRISMA's early (and some of its continuing) work in El Salvador reflected a conscious effort to connect discussion in El Salvador with international debates on environment and development, as a first step towards rethinking foundational concepts for an alternative Salvadoran development; by the 1980s GEA was similarly trying to elaborate with others a conceptual (and practical) base from which sustainable forest management under *campesino* control could be imagined. The more general point is that in order to challenge public debate we first had to do preliminary work in rethinking concepts for imagining development and politics.

Perhaps we and our financial supporters underestimated the challenge implied by an agenda such as this, and so with time we became part drawn, part pushed, towards more applied forms of knowledge production. Whatever the case, and while some of our knowledge production work is still oriented towards destabilizing core ideas in public debates and opening up alternative ways of thinking about development, there is also a sense in which our approach to the links between knowledge and development has become less ambitious. Albeit for some of us more than others, this change has led us to an approach that focuses more on generating knowledge for problem solving: knowledge to resolve problems in marketing chains, to generate agroecologically sound production options, to inform land-use plans and so on. In the following section we explore some of the factors that have pushed us in this direction.

Whatever the case, we believe that this role is a legitimate one, and certainly there is very great demand for us to play this role – a demand that comes from communities, peasant organizations, other NGOs, local governments. However, this change in the balance of our orientation – which is one that happened by default more than because of any conscious strategic decision – has slowly moved us towards that niche which is defined as civil society because it provides a service (in this case a knowledge service) that other organizations of the state or the market are not providing. We doubt how far this knowledge feeds into wider public and political discussions in ways that may lead people to reframe the problem of development and democracy in our societies. Moreover, the change in orientation itself takes some of the alternative edge off the very concept of civil society in our societies. That is, to the extent that we define ourselves as civil society, and what we do is increasingly to provide services, our very form of existing and operating contributes to the idea that civil society is a domain of service provision, not of contestation over hegemony. By default (again) we have steadily assumed roles that seem to project an associationalist, gap-filling understanding of civil society, not a Gramscian one.

Whether in producing knowledge that might contribute to public debate, or knowledge that solves problems of development and livelihood, what is evident is that much of our legitimacy as organizations comes from the *quality* of the knowledge we produce. While there are different metrics of quality depending on the type of knowledge, and the social relationship within which it is being produced, we cannot get away from this issue of quality. There is a clear resonance here with earlier debates on NGOs and development at the 1994 Manchester NGO conference (see Edwards's chapter in this book; Edwards and Hulme, 1995; Hulme and Edwards, 1997). One of the important messages of that conference was that the legitimacy of NGOs derived as much from their performance – the quality of what they did and delivered – as it did from the mechanisms of accountability linking them to other social actors and ensuring transparency of their actions (Edwards and Hulme, 1995).

If we look at our own knowledge-generation work, we can see efforts to build each of these sources of legitimacy. Some of us emphasize quality more than accountability, and others accountability over quality, and, while the precise meanings of these terms may vary among us, we each broadly understand accountability in terms of our relationship to social organizations, and quality in terms of the depth, nuance and internal coherence of the knowledge we produce. In the following section we reflect on the challenges we face in protecting each of these sources of legitimacy. Here we would merely comment that they are not completely substitutable one for the other (indeed, the extent to which they are at all substitutable is not great). That is, there is a relatively high baseline of quality below which we cannot fall – when oriented towards problem-solving, the knowledge we produce must indeed solve problems, whether these are *campesino* production problems or local authorities' planning problems. When oriented towards public and policy debate, this knowledge must be minimally innovative; it cannot simply recycle what is already known and that which has already been said. Achieving these levels of quality is vital, but is a great challenge for organizations with no core funding (see below). Likewise, if we turn into pure think-tanks, doing commissioned and consulting work, we lose the legitimacy that comes from being a civil society actor (with either meaning of the term). In many ways we become a pseudo-market, pseudo government, or pseudo-political party actor. That is, the knowledge we produce becomes entirely demand driven, and thus – almost by definition – loses any hope of being counter-hegemonic.

Challenges to Research-oriented NGOs

As we reflect on the challenges that our organizations face, some are similar to the generic challenges facing NGOs seeking development alternatives, others are peculiar to the case of knowledge-generating and research-oriented NGOs. We comment on each in turn, paying special attention to our specific challenges as knowledge-generating NGOs concerned with incidence.

The generic challenges

While it sounds mercenary to begin with such a statement, there is absolutely no doubt that the main challenge of our organizations is a financial and resource mobilization one. By and large the issue is not that we cannot mobilize resources in order to continue being organizations. The consulting and short-term studies option offers this means of providing jobs to our staff and development services to clients (who in this financing model tend to be become those who pay for the services more than the social organizations receiving them). In this sense, fulfilling the associationalist role of a civil society actor is not so very hard. The problem is to mobilize resources that allow us to play a civil society role in the Gramscian sense that permeates the argument of this book – the role of challenging orthodoxies and building alternatives.

In most of the agencies that historically supported the cultivation of alternatives in Central America and Mexico, a view of development as being synonymous with poverty reduction (and, note, a notion of poverty reduction that is more traditional than that even of World Bank documents such as the World Development Reports of 2000/2001 and 2006) has become increasingly hegemonic. The reasons for this are as much external (the pressure from the governments that transfer co-financing resources to them) as they are internal (the rise of a certain pragmatic institutional agenda inside these agencies). Whatever their source, they have translated into reduced funding for knowledge-generation activities in Central America and Mexico. Agencies offer several reasons for this reduction. First, if development finance is to be concentrated on poverty, then with the exceptions of Honduras and Nicaragua, Central America and Mexico are no longer priorities for most agencies, in spite of official figures establishing the existence of 50 to 72 million poor in Mexico. Second, the poverty impacts of knowledge generation are hard to discern, and it is far more appropriate therefore to fund projects that *do* things rather than people that *think and analyse* things. Implicitly, the message is that these agencies are no longer interested in alternatives, because poverty reduction is so self-evidently the right emphasis for aid that there is no alternative required. Furthermore, the assumption seems to be that the practice of poverty reduction is already understood, and can be dealt with independently of redistribution – an issue to be left to national political processes, not international cooperation.

All our organizations have experienced the effects of this. Some have been able to handle it better than others. Because of their university status or links, FLACSO and PROTROPICO have been most able to absorb this pressure – public funding and course fees for teaching offers them some financial base, and also it seems that increasingly universities have more legitimacy with certain funders than do research NGOs. After these two, PRISMA and GEA have been the next most resilient. Though two completely different organizations – the one a think-tank the other a *campesinista* group of thinking activists – the sources of their resilience are similar. Each shares a strong institutional culture regarding how they must and will operate. PRISMA insists that its work is programmatically funded or not funded at all; GEA's members' collective commitment to their political project generates massive (Chayanovian) subsidies to the organization. These commitments have helped each organization find its way through, and retain some knowledge-generating work. The remainder of our organizations – Nitlapán, Foro, RDS – have seen their work slowly but surely slip into a projectized, semi-consulting mode with serious (and negative) consequences for their ability to produce analytical or strategic knowledge oriented towards alternatives.

A second challenge – which is related to this financial pressure – has been to manage ourselves as organizations in such a way that there is coherence between what we argue to be our ideological and theoretical commitment, our ways of organizing ourselves internally, and the nature of our external relationships. Parts of this observation are distributed through different parts of this chapter – in the following paragraphs we simply bring together the parts and explain the core of the challenge.

In organizational terms, the challenge here is to find congruence between our political model, our institutional model and our financial model. In an ideal world, we would move from the first to the third of these, our financial model being functional to our political commitments (of being Gramscian civil society actors). In the real world, and in particular over the last five years, struggles with our financial model have determined everything else – our institutional model has been a retrofit to our financial reality, and to a considerable degree our political model has fallen away from this calculus, like a mission statement hovering above and largely unconnected to our everyday practices.

This problem has been more severe for some of our organizations than others, though is real in all of them. The package of financing that we are able to compose determines the time horizons of our research, the types of contract we can offer to our staff, our salary and pensions conditions, and our ability to manage human resources strategically. For instance, the more our financial model is dominated by short-term funding streams the less we can engage in strategic research – for otherwise the risk is that we will start, but never finish it. Likewise, a model dominated by shorter-term funding requires contractual conditions that make it harder to hold staff. Young staff are typically on three- to six-month contracts with relatively low pay, and other opportunities attract all but the academically purist, most stubborn and ideologically most committed. Nor can we compensate for this with staff development except in those few (valuable) cases in which we are able to develop links to international universities that allow us to send these young staff for postgraduate training. Meanwhile for the other end of our staff profile, most of our organizations make no contribution to pensions or health care. This makes us ever less attractive to those of our staff who are older – but who, for the same reason of maturity, have more knowledge of managing knowledge production, and more contacts in the political and public spheres in which we aim to intervene. These very abilities make it easier for them to find better paid positions elsewhere or close their careers doing high-end consulting work.

It is not only that our financial model makes it harder to retain and develop research staff. It is also that it leads us towards the very same sort of neoliberal human resource management model we claim to work against. This weakens both our external legitimacy – as it subjects us to criticisms of practising what we preach against – and our internal coherence – as it generates serious internal tensions among staff of different ages, on different types of contract. Those of us who have been better able to manage these tensions have done so either because of a strong institutional culture, or because of strong models of leadership. Shared institutional cultures can lead us to solutions in which the collectivity bears the costs of the financial model, and so enjoys very similar work conditions; and in other circumstances they drive an ethic of overwork that helps compensate for resource constraints (but in doing so increases staff burnout). Such cultures are not, however, immaculately and spontaneously conceived: their existence is a result of diligent, deliberate and strategic cultivation since our early years. They cannot therefore be quickly invoked from nothing in order to save an otherwise dire financial and institutional situation.

Strong leadership can help deal with these pressures through two main avenues. First, among us there are cases where the strength of a leader or leaders has given us greater negotiating power with our financing agencies, helping gain longer-term, programmatic funding streams. These leaders inspire external subsidies to the institution. Second, we can identify cases where a strong leader so embodied an institutional culture that, though perhaps not existing in all of us, forced us by example to make the same commitments to the institution as did these leaders. Such leaders inspire internal subsidies to the institution. The problem with the subsidy of leadership is that, embodied as it is in one person, it can be easily lost when that person leaves or dies. There are among us several cases of this. Particularly severe is the case (which is perhaps the norm) in which the leader inspired *both* external and internal subsidies. On leaving, they take some of our external legitimacy (and contacts) with them, and leave a heart-sized hole in the cultural fabric of the institution.

The specific challenges

Perhaps the most important challenge we face specifically as research- and knowledge-generating organizations relates to the quality of our product. While product quality is a problem for all NGOs, the market for development ideas is a far tighter one than is that for development projects. Also, we would venture, the very nature of hegemony means that the possibility of breaking into, upsetting and changing the course of public and policy debate is far more circumscribed than the possibility of innovating in a location-specific development project. In this context, the quality of the knowledge and proposals we produce is of the greatest importance: and the more counter-hegemonic the goal, the longer the time required to build both the evidence base and the relations necessary to disseminate and legitimize this evidence. Yet producing such high-quality, evidence-based, strategic knowledge requires high-quality people and resources that allow sustained research *programmes* rather than short-term research consultancies of a few months or so, or small pieces of research hidden away in what are otherwise action-oriented projects. The increasing pressure on our financial base makes each of these ever more difficult. Staff retention is a particularly serious problem. High-quality thinkers are in relatively short supply, and − particularly as they get older and need to think of retirement − many of them have moved into better-paid public-sector, international or consultancy positions. Perhaps the most significant case of this is Nitlapán, but it is not the only case. That these people make this decision is entirely understandable. However, the effect is to weaken the human capital of our organizations, and thus the quality of the strategic knowledge we produce. By the same token, it is very difficult to produce destabilizing forms of

knowledge if those who do research have constantly to complement their
income with consulting, and have research funding that reaches only several
months ahead.

Another challenge that is somewhat more specific to NGOs such as ours
also has to do with how we affect policy and public debate. For each of us,
this is an explicit part of our mission and objectives, though we pursue the
goal in different ways. The short and long routes to incidence are present
in each of our organizations, though combined in different ways. These
combinations also suggest the need to nuance this distinction and to add
to it a notion of scale, as we discuss below.

There are two main long routes to incidence in our work. One is the
link with students – which is central to PROTROPICO's and FLACSO's
way of working. PROTROPICO aims to train students who will then
become professionals working in the Yucatan. The hope is that these persons
will bring to their professional work more participatory and systems-based
understandings of the links between development and the environment.
FLACSO aims to do much the same at a wider geographical scale – indeed
FLACSO's students return to positions not only in Guatemala but throughout Mesoamerica, Ecuador, Bolivia, Peru and Chile. In each case, the
notion is that policy can be changed not only through engaging in policy
framing and formation, but also through influencing the technocracies that
manage policy. The goal is to change the human capital that makes those
technocracies function and thus influence policy through its implementation. The challenge in this case is that there is a long delay before such
incidence becomes apparent, and in neither FLACSO nor PROTROPICO
do we have a documented sense of how far the training of students has
actually influenced either bureaucratic practice or policy implementation
in the region.

The second long route is that which occurs through other social actors,
primarily social movements and social organizations. In the past, several
of us attempted to build links with national movements. Nitlapán, for
instance, engaged with the National Farmers and Livestock Producers Union
(UNAG), with a view to the movement carrying forward ideas in their
own engagement with the Nicaraguan government. In practice, however,
this has been difficult, and over time, to the extent that we support other
social actors with knowledge generation activities, we do so at a sub-national
level only. Foro has worked with coffee organizations in Chiapas, and now
works mostly with social organizations and communities that have been
displaced by environmental conflicts; GEA works with peasant organizations
in Guerrrero; PRISMA collaborates with forestry cooperatives and local
governments, and so on. These relationships with more thematically and
geographically focused organizations have proven easier to manage than ones

with more diffuse social movements. At best, however, they lead only to local and regional, or commodity-specific, influence. They rarely influence broader public debate. Indeed, the more general point here is that it has proven very difficult to sustain a social basis from which to do more basic and strategic research aimed at influencing policy and national debate. The organizations we work with have more immediate and pragmatic concerns, and our work becomes drawn towards applied activities aimed at addressing these concerns. Sometimes, along the way, more strategic issues arise and we can take these to policy debates – but by and large these are by-products of more applied work, and not the prime concerns of the organizations we interact with.

We have all tried the short route – direct to policymakers and policy working groups – to a greater or lesser extent. The advantages of this route – given our financial constraints – are that it is less resource-intensive, and does not require that we have regular or permanent presence outside the capital city. That said, it is a route that still consumes resources. Building the relationships necessary to get to the policy table takes time, and requires repeated participation in a range of events. Perhaps the most serious draw-back of this route, however – at least in the ways in which we have practised it to date – is that it tends to hinge on personal relationships built up with a small number of technocrats or political appointees inside government. These contacts are then the vehicle for allowing us to bring our knowledge to policy discussions. Yet the rate of staff turnover in our governments falls far short of the Weberian ideal (and itself reflects another limitation of this route – namely that, failing significant political change, such individuals themselves have limited room to manoeuvre within government). Thus it is that on repeated occasions we have built these relationships only to see the persons removed from their government positions for bureaucratic or political reasons. Once that happens our access has been closed and we have to start again.

Our collective experience also suggests another route to policy influence with which several of us have experimented. This has involved efforts to create what Andolina has termed new 'counter-public' (Andolina, 2003: 733) spheres in which novel debates on development and democracy might occur. Andolina was referring to debates made possible by new local assemblies created by indigenous movements. In a similar way several of us have been directly involved in attempts to create networks of organizations – mostly NGOs, but also some social organizations and occasionally public sector organizations – whose purpose is not simply to exchange information but also to create visible arenas that might allow new debates on development and environment to occur. Indeed one of us – Foro Chiapas – was created specifically for this precise purpose. For its part, RDS soon moved into this role, and has served as an arena allowing public debates on issues that the Honduran press has refused to cover (because of its ideological commitments and forms of political control). GEA has repeatedly tried to do something similar in Mexico, leading the creation of networks and platforms intended to make community forestry and themes such as bio-safety and GMOs more visible within Mexican public policy debate; and in Guatemala FLACSO uses its privileged institutional position to support (albeit more punctual) debates on issues of public importance.

The greatest challenge to this strategy has been the difficulty of sustaining such counter-public spaces over time. At an institutional level it has proven impossible to mobilize resources that would support us (Foro and RDS) to play the role of creating and nurturing these spaces. And at a practical level, pressure of work has repeatedly impinged on these spaces, and with time levels of participation fall. The tendency, repeatedly, has been for these spaces to wither away, or for organizations created in order to embody such spaces to turn into one more development NGO.

Conclusions

If 'development alternatives' are to be more than simple rallying cries, they require substance and content. This content must come from somewhere. While the everyday practice and experiential knowledge of social-movement actors might be one source of such knowledge, it cannot possibly be the only source. To become a counter-discourse with teeth, this everyday knowledge needs to be synthesized, systematized and given coherence. It also has to be linked with analytical knowledge of the contexts within which everyday practices occur – contexts which, while they impinge on people's life, are in many cases analytically inaccessible to them. Alternatives only stand a chance if they can both adapt to and change contexts, and for each of these requirements organized knowledge of those contexts is essential.

If this knowledge has to be produced, there are two implications. Somebody has to produce it, and somebody has to cover the costs associated with its production. Apart from maverick reformists here and there (Fox, 1996), government will not produce such knowledge *even if* bureaucratic pressures allowed for some space to do so. Likewise with aid agencies, non-profit and public sector alike – the bureaucratic pressures on their generally highly competent and trained staff mean that their practical capacity to think strategically about themselves, let alone about broader social processes, remains weak. So, realistically the only two bodies that might produce this knowledge are universities and non-profit organizations with research and analytical capacity.

In Central America and Mexico universities continue to be very weak. They lack budget to cover research, and more seriously still, perhaps, they lack the embeddedness in everyday social (movement) practices that might inform the production of knowledge for alternatives. Of course, there are exceptions here and there: FLACSO and PROTROPICO, in their different ways, demonstrate university efforts to become more embedded. However, the panorama is such that universities will not play this embedded knowledge-producing role, at least not alone or in the form in which they currently exist. Indeed, FLACSO and PROTROPICO each suggest that in order to become more embedded, universities need to incorporate elements of the non-governmental model into their own way of being and operating.

Non-profit research centres have different sets of strengths and weaknesses. Their greatest strength, arguably, is that their private status allows them greater flexibility in engaging with social actors in this knowledge-producing endeavour, as well as in mobilizing resources to support it. Their greatest weakness is that they have few or no core resources of their own. During the years of civil war (from Nicaragua through to Chiapas), as well as the first years after civil war began to wind down (essentially the 1980s and up to the latter 1990s), a suite of agencies, above all in Europe though also in North America, saw the importance of such non-profit production of strategic knowledge for alternative development. When development was about transformation, when it was more about redistribution than about targeted poverty reduction, agencies seemed to see an important role for these centres of knowledge production. However, since the late 1990s this has changed and international cooperation has appeared less interested in cooperating either with anything that is not a development project offering material, measurable impacts on poverty or with any actions that are deemed as occurring outside formal democratic processes. This shift in cooperation has been generally prejudicial to Latin America, and particularly so to organizations such as ours. It has meant that we have had to spend more time mobilizing resources, and engaging in activities less than consistent with the visions upon which we were founded.

The pressure to chase resources also has the effect of pulling our organizations away from social movements, with the possible exception again of GEA, whose geographical structure and strong institutional culture militate against such a trend. This is not to say that our organizations all had strong links with such movements in the first place, but with time whatever relationship there was has weakened. Several factors are at play here. First, and importantly, the weakening of movements themselves makes such links progressively more difficult and resource-consuming, precisely at a time when resources are less available. Second, and related, social organizations are far less able and willing to commit time and people to work with us in generating strategic, hegemony-challenging knowledge (as opposed to applied, problem-solving knowledge). While their leaders generally see the need for such knowledge, internal dynamics militate against any significant commitment of resources to such an endeavour. Third, the time that institute staff members have to spend chasing resources, completing consultancies and cultivating the relationships that might ensure future resource flows means – in a finite world – less time for building movement relationships. As a result, while a number of our organizations prefer the long route from knowledge to policy incidence, it is not clear that we can demonstrate that we have followed this route, or – in cases where there are elements of this – whether the route has in fact led to any such incidence. In practice we have gone the short route.

These same pressures – drawing us away from movements and other social bases, and forcing us to spend more time chasing money – have also challenged the extent to which we are accountable to society. While we all sustain relationships – some more organic than others – with social organizations, the extent to which we are able to make ourselves accountable to them has declined over time. Increasingly – again echoing Hulme and Edwards (1997) – our accountability has shifted towards those agencies that fund our increasingly short term projects and away from the social actors with whose counter-hegemonic concerns we hope to identify. *Ipso facto*, the extent to which societal accountability is a source of legitimacy for our work has also weakened.

All this has implications for how we are located vis-à-vis Dagnino et al.'s (2006) three political projects, and the fourth hybrid that we have added to them. If asked, we – as individuals and as institutions – would all identify with the direct democracy/democracy-deepening project. Yet our practices seem to contribute at least as much to a neoliberal project. We have become, to different degrees, actors operating in a funding market and – out of necessity – accepting its rules of operation. We have – to different degrees – introduced some of these market principles within the functioning of our own organizations. And, to the extent that our links with movements have become weaker, we contribute progressively less to strengthening, either directly or with the knowledge that we produce, the actors that would carry forward a democracy-deepening project in our countries. The situation is not completely depressing – we have links with progressive mayors, forest cooperatives, peasant organizations, migrant organizations and youth networks – but the challenge not to fall into what Dagnino et al. (2006) might deem the trap of perverse convergence is ever present. Indeed, it can become a source of stress within our organizations.

Looking at the trends in our countries – increasing levels of organized everyday violence and delinquency, deepening exclusion (especially of youth and indigenous campesinos), continuing inequality, environmental destruction that, especially in Central America really does threaten the bases of our countries' sustainability – it is difficult to believe that there is not a continuing need to imagine, and build analytical, careful, alternative models of development, environment and social change in our region. It would be perverse to say that poverty is not a serious problem in our region, but it is not necessarily the most serious development problem, and it is certainly not the only problem. Now, more than ever, sustainable development is far more than poverty reduction; but we are frighteningly far from having alternative models that might inch us towards that sustainability. Knowledge for those models has to be elaborated by someone. The questions for the wider community of international cooperation (in particular our traditional supporters) are therefore: if not us, then who? If not from you, then from where? These questions need to be answered with searching honesty, not with easy, policy-honed sound bites.

Note

1. We are extremely grateful to the Ford Foundation and the International Development Research Centre for their support which made possible the process that led to the preparation of this chapter. We are also grateful to the logistical and human support of the Institute of Development Policy and Management at Manchester and of PRISMA (the Salvadoran Research Programme in Development and the Environment).

References

Alvarez, S., E. Dagnino and A. Escobar (eds) (1998) *Culture of Politics/Politics of Cultures: Re-visioning Latin American Social Movements*, Westview, Boulder, CO.

Andolina, R. (2003) 'The Sovereign and its Shadow: Constituent Assembly and Indigenous Movement in Ecuador', *Journal of Latin American Studies* 35: 721–50.

Bebbington, A. (2005) 'Donor–NGO Relations and Representations of Livelihood in Non-governmental Aid Chains', *World Development* 33(6): 937–50.

Bebbington, A., and A. Barrientos (2005) 'Knowledge Generation for Poverty Reduction within Donor Organizations', *Global Poverty Research Group Working Paper* 23, GPRG, Oxford.

Bebbington, A., and S. Hickey (2006) 'NGOs and Civil Society', in D.A. Clark (ed.) *The Elgar Companion to Development Studies*, Edward Elgar, Cheltenham, pp. 417–23.

Bebbington, A. (ed.) (2007) *Investigación, sociedad civil y desarrollo en Centroamérica y México. Los pasados, presentes y posibles futuros de las ONG de investigación como proyectos alternativos*, Facultad Latinoamericana de Ciencias Sociales, Guatemala.

Dagnino, E., A. Olvera and A. Panfichi (2006) 'Para Uma Outra Leitura Da Disputa Pela Construção Democrática Na América Latina', in E. Dagnino, A. Olvera and A. Panfichi (eds), *A Disputa Pela Construção Democrática Na América Latina*, Paz e Terra, São Paulo.

Edwards, M., and D. Hulme (eds) (1995) *Beyond the Magic Bullet: NGO Performance and Accountability*, Earthscan, London.

Fine, B. (1999) 'The Developmental State is Dead – Long Live Social Capital', *Development and Change* 30(1): 1–19.

Fine, B. (2001) *Social Capital versus Social Theory: Political Economy and Social Science at the Turn of the Millennium*, Routledge, London.

Fisher, J. (1998) *Nongovernments*, Kumarian Press, West Hartford CT.

Fox, J. (1996) How Does Civil Society Thicken? The Political Construction of Social Capital in Mexico, *World Development* 24(6): 1089–103.

Giddens, A. (1998) *The Third Way: The Renewal of Social Democracy*, Polity Press, Cambridge.

Gramsci, A. (1971) *Selections from the Prison Notebooks*, Lawrence & Wishart, London.

Habermas, J. (1984) *The Theory of Communicative Action*, Polity Press, Cambridge.

Hulme, D., and M. Edwards (eds) (1997) *Too Close for Comfort: NGOs, States and Donors*, St Martin's Press, London.

Lehmann, A.D. (1990) *Democracy and Development in Latin America: Economics, Politics and Religion in the Post-war Period*, Polity Press, Cambridge.

Lewis, D. (2002) 'Civil Society in African Contexts: Reflections on the Usefulness of a Concept', *Development and Change* 33(4): 569–86.

Maldidier, C., and P. Marchetti (1996) 'El Campesino-finquero y el potencial económico del campesinado nicaragüense, Tipología y regionalización agrosocioeconómica de los sistemas de producción y los sectores sociales en el agro nicaragüense', *NITLAPÁN*, VOL. 1, Instituto de Investigación y Desarrollo, Universidad Centroamericana (UCA), Managua.

Maxwell, S., and D. Stone (eds) (2004) *Global Knowledge Networks and International Development: Bridges across Boundaries*, Routledge, London.

Salamon, L., and H. Anheier (eds) (1997) *Defining the Non-Profit Sector: A Cross-national Analysis*, Manchester University Press, Manchester.

Stone, D. (2002) 'Using Knowledge: The Dilemmas of Bridging Research and Policy', *Compare* 32(3): 285–296.

Stone, D., and A. Denham (eds) (2004) *Think-tank Traditions: Policy Research and the Politics of Ideas*, Manchester University Press, Manchester.

10

Anxieties and Affirmations:
NGO–Donor Partnerships for
Social Transformation

Mary Racelis

'We did it! We really did it!' Poor people's triumphant cries, accompanied by exuberant shouts and excited laughter, are music to the ears of seasoned community organizers. Whether the years of struggle have yielded land titles, piped water, adequately serviced health centres, a bridge to the national highway, traditional instruments for local performers, or jailed an abusive village official, the realization by once-powerless people that collective action really works is a heady experience indeed.

Years of grassroots involvement, however, have also taught NGO organizers and their community partners that the euphoria may be short-lived. Valuable as these small-scale successes are, especially when multiplied across marginalized rural and urban communities, failure to institutionalize forms of community empowerment in larger government or donor systems and make them part of social policy may only reinforce entrenched inequalities of asset and power distribution.

Further complicating the problem is globalization. Power stakes are rising as small farmers find themselves competing with commercial importers of onions, garlic or vegetables, or as urban workers in the informal manufacturing economy discover that the cheap recycled rubber-tyre footwear products are no price match for more fashionable and only slightly more expensive running shoes from China. Add to this foreign and local investors gobbling up large tracts of agricultural and coastal land for golf courses or beach resorts, or city governments evicting thousands of slum dwellers to make way for yet another shopping mall. Where national elites were once the focal points for negotiation and leverage, they may now represent only one set of links in a chain of decisions formulated a world away.

These are the kinds of threats to daily livelihood and culture that propel grassroots groups to protest openly and take action. Such pressures likewise guide NGOs facilitating community analysis and helping victims turn small-scale actions into demands for longer-term institutional and political reforms. When potential sufferers can directly link a global intervention to an imminent threat on the ground, the stage is set for tackling *both* the 'small d' of development, representative of everyday living and the effects of distorting hegemonic processes, and the 'big D' of donor agency development interventions. (Introduction, this volume).

This chapter examines ways in which Philippine NGOs and their partner People's Organizations (POs) have broadened and protected democratic spaces through mobilizing, taking action and engaging in advocacy for social reform, structural change and the redefinition of donor priorities and operational modes. After a review of development challenges faced by NGOs, the discussion features three mini-cases illustrative of both small and large d/Development processes. One account examines Naga City slum upgrading activities in the Bicol region of Southern Luzon. The two others focus on activities centred in Metro Manila but which affect NGO/PO activities nationwide

Carving Out and Protecting Democratic Space

Political scientist Joel Rocamora (2005) has commented on how miniscule civil society advocacy seems when 'measured against "need", against scandalous poverty, and the greed and incompetence of the Philippine political elite'. Yet as the Marcos dictatorship years (1972–86) have shown, the option of armed struggle brought devastatingly high costs in lives, in creating deep fissures in Philippine society, and in threatening the very survival of democracy. Rocamora concludes that the more hopeful path lies in strong and effective advocacy towards reshaping Philippine democracy for social justice and political reform (2005: 127–8).

Poverty, inequality, powerlessness and unsustainable development

The Philippine population in 2005 was estimated at 85.2 million (Racelis et al., 2005: xvii) and expected to reach 111.5 million by 2020 (Asian Development Bank 2005, quoting projections of the National Statistical Coordination Board). Some 5,000 births occur daily among women 18–45, yielding a population growth rate of 2.36 per cent. The Philippines is thus a young society with a median age of 21. Children under 18 made up 43 per cent, or 33 million, of the population in 2000 (Racelis et al., 2005: 143).

Income poverty and powerlessness affect large sections of the populace. Although poverty incidence among individuals dropped from 49.2 per cent in 1985 to 36.9 per cent in 1997, by 1998 the Asian economic crisis was taking its toll. Poverty incidence in 2000 rose again to 39.5 per cent. Moreover, although poverty rates fell by 9.7 per cent from 1985 to 2000, the absolute number of poor in the same period rose by over 4 million owing in part to high population growth rates coupled with weak poverty-reduction programmes. Subjective-poverty studies conducted by Social Weather Stations (2006) are also instructive: 62 per cent of families rated themselves as poor in 2003, while 5 per cent reported having experienced hunger, or food poverty, in the previous three months. By 2004, the hunger figure had climbed to 15.7 per cent (Asian Development Bank 2005: 18, 38), and by the fourth quarter of 2006 had reached a record-breaking 19.0 per cent, or 3.3 million affected households (Mangahas, 2006a, 2006b).

Inequality emerges in persistent and growing income disparities. In 2003, the richest 10 per cent of the population commanded twenty times the share of income than the poorest 10 per cent. The richest quintile (15.3 million people) controlled over 50 per cent of total family income, compared with the bottom quintile at only 5 per cent. Nor has this pattern changed since 1985 (Schelzig, 2005: 30). To make things worse, in real terms based on 2000 prices, the average income of the poorest 30 per cent contracted by 6 per cent between 2000 and 2003 (Schelzig, 2005: 17).

Gross disparities surface in regional comparisons, with Metro Manila/National Capital Region's poverty rating having dropped to 8.7 per cent of families in 2000, compared with 66 per cent for the Autonomous Region of Muslim Mindanao (ARMM). Metro Manila's 8.7 per cent is no cause for joy, however. Although poverty is indeed concentrated in rural areas, the low citywide average hides the glaringly high poverty incidence and hunger in densely packed urban informal settlements. Overcrowded, physically degraded neighbourhoods coupled with limited employment and basic services make poor city dwellers' anxieties all the more acute. The availability of social capital through informal neighbourhood ties alleviates somewhat their chronic insecurity and makes summary relocation extremely disruptive of existing survival strategies.

The contrasting perspectives of NGOs and government on poverty issues emerge in a perceptions study of 100 government and NGO programme staff who implement and manage poverty-reduction programmes. Over half (54 per cent) of the NGO managers felt poverty had risen somewhat or a lot over the past five years, while only one-third (34 per cent) of their government counterparts subscribed to that view. On whether poverty would worsen 'somewhat or a lot' in the coming five years, 52 per cent of NGO managers indicated agreement, compared with 38 per cent of government managers (Schelzig, 2005: 40). Clearly, government officials are more optimistic about the prospects of reducing poverty than are civil society grassroots workers.

A wide range of NGOs contest inequitable and unsustainable development by organizing community groups, or POs, around agrarian reform; upland environmental and watershed management linked to indigenous knowledge systems; participatory disaster management; savings, micro-credit and local economy investments; women's rights and gender fairness; peace, reconciliation and community rebuilding in ex-warfare zones; child rights in the context of the Millennium Development Goals; migrant families' well-being; resisting large-scale logging, mining and fishing interests in upland and coastal communities, and undertaking advocacy campaigns around these issues. On the urban scene, NGOs help build informal settlers' resistance to forced evictions and damaging resettlement while strengthening demands for secure tenure, improved livelihood and employment, food, education, health, water, sanitation, information, transport, and pro-poor policies. This usually calls for pressuring local and national officials to recognize and prioritize poor people's needs and preferences in keeping with the latter's proposals for reform and achievement of their rights.

Evidence of NGO–PO successes appear in the significant legislation enacted by the Philippine Congress in the last decade of the twentieth century. Notable examples have been agrarian reform (Comprehensive Agrarian Reform Law, 1988), urban land reform (Urban Development and Housing Act, 1992), women's rights (Anti-Rape Law, 1997), ancestral domain claims (Indigenous People's Rights Act, 1997), environmental protection (National Integrated Protected Areas System, 1992) and local government decentralization (Local Government Code, 1992). The early years of the twenty-first century have offered more limited options. Congress in 2001–03 passed only three bills of national importance that had been championed by civil society, and even then, as in the case of the party list and overseas voting bills, 'they get mangled beyond recognition' (Rocamora, 2005: 128). This pattern of reduced social legislation may, however, be a product of the most pressing reforms having already been addressed. The declining number of NGOs in legislative advocacy may also have contributed to the trend.

NGOs have dealt with the realities of legislative activism over the years by developing networks for intense and effective lobbying. They have learned how to make contact with legislators, often through personal or school ties, or by deliberately seeking out the more progressive legislators. The congressional technical working groups, in which knowledgeable academics, NGOs and POs are invited to participate, give the latter groups an opportunity to insert their principles and language into proposed legislation. 'Crossover' civil society leaders who have joined the government help assess developments in governance and work out with civil society ways of influencing the outcomes of policies and procedures towards social and political reform.

As Rocamora (2005: 128) points out, however:

> The context for advocacy in the Philippines may seem difficult, but compared to neighboring countries with authoritarian single-party rulers, maybe we should count our blessings. What makes advocacy difficult in the Philippines is not often outright repression. It is at once the permeability and resilience of elite rule. There are all kinds of room for advocacy: in Congress, in the bureaucracy, in local government. But the system has seemingly inexhaustible capacity for side-stepping, postponing, somehow preventing change.

The Emergence of NGOs and POs

NGOs in modern guise emerged with full force on the Philippine scene during the Marcos Dictatorship years from 1972 to 1986. Many drew their inspiration from Social Democratic ('Socdem') principles. Some were linked to the Radical Left National Democratic Front ('Natdems'), while others remained politically unaligned. An especially prickly thorn in Marcos's side came from the organizations focusing on human rights violations, like Task Force Detainees of the Philippines. This was in part because they maintained close contact with international human rights groups which could exert some leverage on their own governments (Silliman and Noble, 1998: 33). All vigorously opposed the Marcos dictatorship but took varying positions on how to confront also the underlying structures of society that were keeping millions of Filipinos poor and powerless.

Despite growing repression through summary detention, torture and 'salvaging' (clandestine disappearances with summary execution) of individuals or groups seen as opposing the regime, NGOs avidly organized rural and urban poor communities for self-realization and action to redress poverty and social injustice. The assassination of political opposition leader Benigno Aquino in 1983 further galvanized NGOs and public opposition to Marcos's authoritarian regime. As Silliman and Noble (1998: 17) point out,

> In contrast to a state that systematically violated human rights and failed to improve the condition of the poor, the motivating principle of Philippine civil society as it materialized in the 1970s and 1980s was the right of Filipinos to both civil liberties and an equitable distribution of the society's resources. Out of the collective actions of Philippine citizens there emerged a sense of solidarity and community.

For many NGOs, support in the 1960s and 1970s came from progressive Catholic bishops' attention to human rights, the theology of liberation, the formation of Basic Christian Communities espousing strong community organizing and the social teachings of papal encyclicals on development, justice and peace. The Church's protective umbrella, along with that of the Protestant churches, reinforced the capacity and determination of many NGO workers to resist the closing down of political spaces for democratic action. Later, the Catholic bishops, alarmed at the infiltration of NDF community organizers in their midst, and worse still, the political shift into Radical Left circles of a few priests and nuns, began to distance themselves from NGOs.

As martial law dragged on, the government took advantage of these developments by raiding Catholic premises, arresting and detaining suspected Communists. International donor flows to civil society increased correspondingly. Even the business community entered the fray in the mid-1980s, angered by the Aquino killing and alarmed at the looming economic crisis. These birthing decades established NGOs on a trajectory of increasingly stronger confrontation with government in the 'Parliament of the Streets' ,where diverse and often conflicting groups coalesced to topple the regime. Sociologist Constantino-David comments (1998: 35–6):

> There was a frenzy of activity, and coalition building was the name of the game, even among NGOs and POs that had tried to shun outright political involvement. In the midst of almost daily rallies and demonstrations, organizing work expanded and more NGOs and POs were formed. Development NGOs and networks actively participated in the protest movement, largely through mass actions. Those who were already identified with specific ideological forces and had overlapping leadership generally followed the splits and turns of the anti-dictatorship struggle [which now] took center stage.

The snap elections called by an overconfident Marcos for early 1986 spawned NGO responses ranging from voter education and clean elections campaigns, to support for Corazon Aquino's candidacy or outright election boycotts. Organized civil disobedience followed reports of massive cheating and election-related violence. The attempted coup led by Reform the Armed Forces Movement (RAM) and military and defence leaders Fidel V. Ramos and Juan Ponce-Enrile was teetering dangerously when Cardinal Jaime Sin called on people to converge on the highway between the two military camps to protect the 'rebels'.

And so began the People Power Revolution of February 1986. Also known as EDSA I, this defining event represented the culmination of painstaking, multi-sectoral civil society organizing over many years. More than a million Filipinos massed on the national highway to stop the tanks from attacking the rebel-held military camps. Groups kneeling on the concrete roadway reciting the rosary, nuns offering flowers to the tank commanders, ordinary citizens making and distributing sandwiches and water to the massed protesters – all this has become part of the extraordinary history of People Power. After four fateful days, ordinary people suffused with a sense of collective power toppled the fourteen-year dictatorship of Ferdinand Marcos in a non-violent uprising, forcing his family and close cronies out of Malacanang Palace into exile.

The democratic space opened up by President Corazon C. Aquino generated a virtual explosion of NGOs throughout the country. Bilateral donors, like CIDA (Canada), USAID, CEBEMO (the Netherlands) and others, showed their elation at the return of democracy and its NGO champions through significant funding (Racelis, 2000: 159). Perhaps it was the exciting drama of a courageous, well organized, and non-violent citizenry out on the streets and determined to oust a dictator that attracted their support for at least another decade.

The writers of the 1987 Philippine Constitution recognized the outstanding roles played by NGOs and POs in mobilizing the peaceful overthrow of a dictator. Articles II and XIII stipulate that

> The State shall encourage non-governmental, community-based, or sectoral organizations that promote the welfare of the nation.
> The State shall respect the role of independent people's organizations to enable the people to pursue and protect, within the democratic framework, their legitimate and collective interests and aspirations through peaceful and lawful means.
> The right of the people and their organizations to effective and reasonable participation at all levels of social, political and economic decision-making shall not be abridged. The State shall, by law, facilitate the establishment of adequate consultation mechanisms.

By 1995 some 3,000–5,000 registered development NGOs were employing a total of 100,000 staff. Most of them were small, with annual operating budgets averaging $80,000. The bulk of their funding came from bilateral donors and international NGOs, like the Ford Foundation, the Asia Foundation, Oxfam, CARE and Save the Children, supplemented by multilateral agencies (UN Development Programme, UNICEF, World Bank, and Asian Development Bank), government, other Philippine NGOs, and churches. Government regulations on foreign funding were flexible. Only multilateral and bilateral funding for NGOs had to go through the government, for which a simple authorization from the National Economic Development Authority sufficed (Asian Development Bank, 1999: 8).

International NGO donors could deal directly with their Philippine partners, no government clearances being required Recognizing their uneasy dependency on foreign funding, however, many NGOs supplemented their incomes through alternative modes. They generated funds from training fees, domestic donations, loans, parallel business ventures, and contracts for services in partnership with government and multilateral institutions, like the United Nations, Asian Development Bank and World Bank.

NGOs became independent entities, including those that had operated under the umbrella protection of the churches. Although many NGO leaders continued to maintain friendly relations with church social action groups and progressive bishops, the larger number of conservative bishops still smarting from 'being used' by the Radical Left, distanced themselves from NGOs. Basic Christian Communities with strong community organizing and empowerment features now became Basic Ecclesiastical Communities, limiting themselves mainly to prayer, spiritual matters and welfare support to destitute community members.

Meanwhile, NGO leaders began moving, gingerly at first, into government. Yet, as Constantino-David (1998: 36) assessed the NGO scene, 'The deep-seated strains and the lack of a coherent vision produced a tenuous unity that would eventually splinter in the post-Marcos era.' In the closing days of the Ramos administration (1992–98), political scientists Silliman and Noble (1998: 178) summarized NGO roles and contributions this way:

> First is the *vibrant public discourse*, both within NGO circles, as divergent opinions are fashioned into some kind of workable consensus, and outside them, when the NGO community must make its views heard and get them adopted by often reluctant partners. Second, NGOs are attempting to *redefine the content of politics*. Topics that would once have been deemed inappropriate for legislation – rape, other violence against women, the rights of indigenous people – have become subjects of debate and successful parliamentary legislation. Third, civil society is becoming *progressively institutionalized*. Coalitions are structured for greater permanence, while NGOs learn good management and financial practices and professionalize their staff.

Critical collaboration or cooptation? the NGO/PO scene today

Gone with the turn of the century are the heady days of NGOs capturing the high moral ground of public action. Critical assessments lament their moving away from basic principles, like accountability derived from their altruistic cast, their bias in favor of the poor and marginalized, and their championing of democracy:

> [T]he halo of saintliness around NGOs has disappeared, eroded by, among others, the persistence of fly-by-night NGOs, the failure of NGOs to deliver on promises to their various constituencies, alleged corruption, various controversies... and the political partisanship of high profile NGO personalities because of their identification with a certain administration.
>
> ... Ironically, erosion of its moral position is due to the widespread adoption ('cooptation') of the NGO concept by mainstream society, thus making NGOs the victims of their own success. Today, there is an NGO for every persuasion [reflecting]... the broad (and often, conflicting) diversity of interests found in Philippine society, from the most crooked to the most altruistic, thus making it difficult for NGOs to continue their claim of being the 'conscience of society' or 'guardians of the guardian'. (Association of Foundations, 2005: 2)

This kind of soul-searching is taking place in every nook and cranny of the archipelago where NGOs are engaged in organizing poor and marginalized people, helping transform poorly functioning local government bureaucracies and processes into more constituent-friendly and poverty-reducing institutions, or engaging in national-level advocacy around a host of issues. Successes and failures are identified in regular monitoring sessions that generate revised strategies and tactics, and renewed enthusiasm for the organization's mandate. Donor partners seeking to assess their support to an NGO often require formal evaluations, but in recent years have begun agreeing to NGOs engaging in a self-diagnostic exercise to rectify identified weaknesses and chart new courses.

Despite the growing number of positive NGO engagements with government, the former continue to adhere to the long-standing principle of critical collaboration. This implies their readiness to work with governments that are serious about people's empowerment, while maintaining the critical or critical-collaboration stance mandated by their watchdog function.

The role of NGOs in promoting empowerment has been recognized by several multilateral institutions, among them the Asian Development Bank. Together with the World Bank, it has been in the forefront of highlighting NGO contributions and promoting them among governments. In order to further that cause, however, the Asian Development Bank has emphasized the need to rethink its own internal organization and procedures.

Retooling the Asian Development Bank for partnering with NGOs

To advocate more realistically the importance of forging active partnerships with NGOs for development and poverty transformation, the Asian Development Bank commissioned a study (Asian Development Bank, 1999: 66–71). The ensuing report made numerous recommendations and emphasized the importance for Bank and NGO officials of clarifying at the outset mutual roles, interests, and expectations. Subsequent actions have seen most of these prescriptions put in place with the assistance of a Task Force on Nongovernment Organizations. In 2001 the initially low-level NGO desk was transformed into the NGO and Civil Society Center under the Regional and Sustainable Development Department with responsibilities to gain first-hand knowledge of and experience with NGOs, engage NGOs in a continuing dialogue, and improve Asian Development Bank's institutional capacity to interact proactively with NGOs. The Center forms part of the Bank's NGO Cooperation Network, with 'anchors' from the Bank's operational departments, Resident Missions, and Representative Offices. It also facilitates monitoring and evaluation of Bank projects by NGOs as a regular feature of Bank operations (Asian Development Bank, 2007a, b).

The changes that have taken place in the Asian Development Bank as regards NGO/PO efforts illustrate the efficacy of decades-long NGO advocacy. The same kind of determined push has led to reformed donor institutions. For some academic intellectuals to dismiss NGO/PO efforts, therefore, as inconsequential for social transformation because they do not appear to be making a significant dent in global hegemonic arrangements is not only inaccurate, but naive. They *are* making a dent; but other sectors also have to do their share in solidarity with active community movements. Indeed, some NGOs have suggested that if academic researchers studying NGOs were more regularly exposed to the work on the ground and had direct day-to-day experience of community processes, instead of promoting the typically critical academic stance, funding partners might be less inclined to withdraw support from NGOs today!

Disembedding: From Local to Global and Back

Three mini case studies follow, illustrating variations on d/D phenomena. I have selected them because as an academic–NGO activist researching the civil society scene, I followed or was involved in the events as they unfolded. Each case describes how NGOs and POs are transforming local efforts into events and processes affecting national and even international situations, and effecting changes in donor operations and outlooks. The transformational sequence of local to national to global to national back to local is also generating new responses to on-the-ground activities, affecting community institutions and actions as well as donor preferences. This embedding/disembedding process approximates the notion of globalization 'as the intensification of worldwide social relations which link distant localities in a way that local happenings are shaped by events occurring many miles away and vice versa' (Giddens, 1990: 64).

Changing the rules

Case 1: Community initiatives for donor-government policy reform in a community-managed slum upgrading micro-drainage project. Stakeholders: Naga City Urban Poor Federations, Inc. (NCUPFI, Naga City Government, World Bank, Japan Social Development Fund, Community Organization of the Philippines Enterprise Foundation (COPE), and Philippine Support Services Agency (PhilSSA).

Faced with the prospect of a long-awaited community infrastructure upgrading scheme in Naga City through a pending World Bank–Japan Social Development Fund grant, the Naga City Urban Poor Federation, Inc. (NCUPFI) in 2004 examined carefully the terms of reference proposed for its participation. Public–private construction partnerships between local government (LGUs) and NGO/POs were still rare on the Philippine development scene; community groups were apprehensive about engaging with the city on the project. Extensive discussion facilitated by COPE organizers convinced NCUPFI to take on the project, but on one condition: the latter would exercise major control over project planning and implementation. To accomplish this, NCUPFI designated COPE, the partner NGO involved in their struggles since 1985, to be the contracted implementing agency.

In those twenty years of community organizing, Naga City's urban poor had mastered the non-violent, demand approach to gaining victories. Their triumphs included secure land tenure on abandoned railroad tracks long appropriated as residential sites or in alternative resettlement areas. They now had electricity and potable water, along with organized leadership structures. Moreover, they had succeeded in getting local legislation passed, notably the People Empowerment Ordinance of 1995, affirming their participation rights in governance. This Ordinance also created the Naga City NGO/PO Council, which enabled them to engage systematically in policy reform.

The proposed Naga City community micro-drainage project was envisioned as forging a dynamic new relationship between the NCUPFI, the city government and the World Bank. Three poor barangays (urban neighbourhood communities) were to benefit from the rehabilitation and de-clogging of existing canals, and the construction of micro-drainage systems. The People's Organizations that made up the community-generated Federation insisted from the outset that as on-site residents, *they* were most qualified to determine the layout of the new sewerage and drainage canal network. This meant that any technical support provided by government must defer to the communities' local knowledge and preferences, and not the other way around.

With COPE as its partner implementing agency and adviser, NCUPFI worked out a technical training programme that brought in volunteer professionals eager to transfer the needed knowledge and skills to local residents. Thus, by the time the drainage project began, the community had already acquired a good grasp of the technical processes, adding greatly to their self-confidence.

In due course, both the Naga City government and the World Bank concurred with NCUPFI's position that COPE should initiate and manage the bidding process for the technical consultants. COPE subsequently chose local contractors willing to work in a participatory way that would enable the people to learn by doing. As a result, a relationship that might have foundered on the 'outside expert' syndrome became agreeably collaborative.

The engineers and other technical staff showed respect for community ideas, preferences and queries; the POs, in turn, felt comfortable working with them. When it later emerged that certain technical recommendations had to take precedence over the residents' own choices, the latter deferred gracefully. Experience had convinced them they could trust the technical staff.

The next contentious issue arose when the World Bank informed the informal settler households and COPE that the residents would be expected to pay modest user-fees for services. The NCUPFI protested that its poor constituents already lived a hand-to-mouth existence. Why should they be expected to draw from their meagre incomes to pay for infrastructure services when rich neighbourhoods seemed to receive these automatically and without user-fee requirements!

The Bank insisted, nonetheless, on its no-subsidy, fee-for-services policy. The NCUPFI then proposed an alternative scheme: the city government should pay the user-fee costs! This was justified, they insisted, because the expected rise in land values stemming from the people-generated project improvements would add to the City's coffers through increased investments, heightened land values and higher taxation rates. The people proposed their counterpart should be to pay for landfill for their individual house lots at an average payment per household of P1,500, or $30.

They also argued that the city should take on responsibility for maintenance and add P1 million to develop other urban poor areas. In return, the community agreed to share in the costs of garbage collection at a daily household charge of P1 (2 US cents).

World Bank project staff agreed and then convinced Washington to agree. Whether the arrangement will become standard for all community-driven infrastructure projects in the Philippines remains to be seen. However, because PhilSSA, the urban NGO network that channelled the funds from the World Bank to NCUPFI, is in touch with other collaborating NGO members, the precedent set in Naga City may well be applied to them. Or, what may be institutionalized is a willingness on the part of government and the World Bank to negotiate with POs presenting alternative proposals. The outcomes may turn out to be compatible not only with community capacities but also with new orientations on the part of government and the World Bank. Overall, the project's sustainability through effective community management will be affirmed.

The three barangays extol their upgraded neighbourhoods. Having invested so much time and effort in this infrastructure improvement, the residents have voluntarily moved into community maintenance. NCUPFI-city government agreements are being implemented, and the POs express confidence that if another such project comes along they can handle it.

Progressive Naga City Mayor Jesse Robredo takes pride in the upgraded sites and their effect on increasing land values and an enhanced tax base. They symbolize his conviction that participatory governance approaches are advantageous to local administrators. As for the World Bank, its representatives enjoy the satisfaction of having brought greater flexibility into their standard practices and of knowing that they have worked out practical ways of promoting participatory community-driven development.

Forming a global NGO funding system

Case 2: The Philippine-Misereor Partnership. Stakeholders: Philippine NGOs/POs, Misereor.

Misereor, the German Catholic Bishops Fund for Development, has for many decades been a major donor to NGOs and Church Social Action groups (SAs) in the Philippines. In keeping with its worldwide re-examination of donor–recipient relations in the 1990s as well as its long experience with NGOs and SAs in the Philippines, Misereor proposed to its local grantees that they explore new and more egalitarian modes of relating to one another.

Both donor and recipients recognized that because decisions on funding NGO/SA requests were made in Aachen, Philippine development priorities were in effect being determined by Misereor officials. Conscientious German programme officers were disturbed at this hierarchical arrangement and the implicit dependency it appeared to be imposing on effective and highly motivated Filipino NGO and SA workers. The proposal from Misereor also traced its roots to the long-standing and broader NGO–donor debate on equity and trust in that relationship.

There is a sizeable amount of funding to the Philippines coming from foreign donors. A 1998 study of bilateral grant assistance revealed that in the period 1986 to 1996, P500 million (US$10 million) was turned over annually to NGOs and POs. In 1989, 9.1 per cent of all bilateral grants went directly to NGOs (Songco, 2002, citing CODE–NGO, 1998). Aldaba et al. highlight some of the consequences:

> This has created both opportunities and dangers for Philippine NGOs. While the funds facilitate significant enlargement of NGO activities, they have also distorted the pace and process of NGO development. NGOs had to devote more time in building their absorptive capacities (sometimes leading to bureaucratic structures); competition over funds has affected NGO to NGO relations; larger NGO budgets have eroded the voluntary nature and 'social change' orientation of NGOs. (Aldaba et al., 1992: i)

Numerous meetings and conferences over the years have tackled various facets of this problem in an attempt to create new and more egalitarian systems. After discussing a number of options, including opening a Misereor office in Manila and a local decision-making consortium, an innovative institution, the Philippine Misereor Partnership (PMP) emerged. As of 2006 the PMP has fifteen subregional clusters, covering 276 NGO/Social Action grant recipients, now called 'partners'. A wide range of activities is under way, with the NGO/SAs being the action partners and Misereor the funding-support partner (Philippine-Misereor Partnership 2005).

The projects in 2006 featured wide-ranging activities:

- *Community organizing* – agrarian reform farmers, urban poor settlers, indigenous people, pastoral concerns;
- *Sectoral organizing* – informal workers, youth, women, migrants;
- *Capability building* – education, literacy, information, technical skills, out-of-school youth training, leadership, management, volunteer formation, organic farming, workshops;
- *Service provision* – legal/paralegal, agricultural extension, consulting, medical/dental, disability rehabilitation, special protection for women, children and youth;
- *Socio-economic activities* – livelihood, resource building, micro-finance, cooperatives, tenure security, land acquisition through community mortgage schemes, low-cost housing, participatory relocation for high-risk-zone residents;
- *Networking and linkaging* – government-NGOs–POs linkaging, network and federation building, PO to PO organizing;
- *Organizational development* – project development, proposal preparation, planning, management, monitoring, evaluation, participatory social mapping, natural resources management, solid waste management, agriculture and fisheries development, costal resources management, research and documentation, participatory action research, publication;
- *Advocacy* – policy, research, sustainable agriculture, land rights, anti-mining, environment, area development, renewable energy, sanitation, alternative health, justice and peace, peace building and peace education, good governance, rural democratization, indigenous people's rights and ancestral domain claims, gender mainstreaming.

The NGO/SA leaders in each of the fifteen geographical clusters meet half-yearly, taking turns hosting the meetings. Together they identify common concerns, share experiences and clarify priorities. Leaders feed back cluster discussions to their member groups upon returning to their home communities, as well as to a three-person secretariat in Manila. The latter promotes communication and networking among the fifteen clusters. It also organizes semi-annual National Coordinating Council (NCC) meetings, with three elected representatives of the three main island regions (Luzon, Visayas and Mindanao) serving as conveners.

Strongly emphasized at the NCC meetings is 'the primacy of the cluster'. This principle affirms the sub-regional cluster's prerogative to decide on its own local or subregional priorities. The members can also opt to extend their preferences by proposing one or two programmes that the entire Partnership might want to take on. Examples of the latter are active partnership projects on the peace process, gender mainstreaming, and anti-mining action and advocacy.

Since the Germany-based Misereor programme officer participates in the NCC, at which the final decisions at the Philippine end are taken, any problems in the proposal have already been worked out by the time s/he recommends it to the Misereor board. The sub-regional composition of the NCC also forestalls attempts by 'Colonial Manila' NGO/SAs to dominate network planning.

The Misereor programme officer combines NCC participation with semi-annual field visits to various NGO/SA locations. Attending subregional meetings, listening to and discussing cluster reports of local concerns and activities at the NCC, give her a better grasp of the issues and nuances underlying programme thrusts. The debate also offers insights into the socio-political situations that affect NGO/SA operations in specific cluster areas. This gives her a distinct advantage in Germany when she has to review partner proposals and make project recommendations to the board.

Issues brought to the NCC from the clusters for discussion and review have included extending PMP membership beyond NGOs to People's Organizations (POs); seeking stronger support for grassroots organizing from social action directors, parish priests, and bishops; and clarifying the rationale for PMP participation in political protests and electoral politics. PMP nationwide programmes opposing mining and promoting peace processes in Mindanao have strongly influenced these political stances. The 2006 NCC meeting held in Mindanao, with numerous NGO/SA partner groups, six bishops and three Misereor officials from Germany in attendance, listened to the two consultants' evaluation report on the PMP and endorsed its recommendations. These generally affirmed the viability of the partnership structure.

The significance of the long consultative process for developing locally generated priorities and egalitarian relationships lies in the building of trust, not only between the donor and NGO/SA partners, but within the NGO/SA communities themselves. Some social action workers now express a greater sense of ease working with NGOs than with those bishops or parish priests who display a limited understanding of grassroots realities. Accordingly, NGOs with their secular identity and Social Action groups with their religious underpinnings have re-established ties of common cause through the PMP. Misereor's responsiveness to going beyond project funding to underwriting networking processes and partner-wide programmes developed by the NGOs and SAs has made a significant contribution to the success of the PMP.

Misereor's understanding of Philippine and developing country priorities and concerns has been profoundly affected by the Partnership. To convey to Germans the everyday meanings of development and faith, especially in relation to poverty in developing countries and equity at the global level, it periodically invites selected NGO and SA leaders to Germany. Prospects for linking Germans with ordinary Asians, Africans and Latin Americans have been greatly enhanced.

Under discussion are ways in which Philippine NGO/SAs can help Misereor affirm the partnership principle as relevant to its programmes on other continents, and possibly for other donor agencies to emulate. The PMP may, therefore, serve as a new model not only for Misereor approaches in other countries, but also in other donor foundations. Although the final decisions on funding are still made in Aachen at the insistence of the NGO/SA partners, they are based on informed tripartite discussions. Criteria for project approval are developed by the action partners, with German programme officers participating through field visits and consultative meetings.

The PMP has thus succeeded in transforming an initially unequal donor-recipient relationship into a genuine Global Partnership. Flexibility, regular interaction, on-the-ground knowledge, and mutual respect form the basis of this impressive new relationship.

Creating an NGO-controlled Filipino funding institution

Case 3: Poverty Eradication and Alleviation Certificates – PEACe Bonds. Stakeholders: CODE-NGO, Peace and Equity Foundation, Rizal Commercial Bank Corporation, RCBC Capital, Bureau of the Treasury, Department of Finance.

By the late 1990s, the love affair between external donors and NGO/POs was weakening. With the notable exception of Japan, foreign donors, who had lavished funds on NGOs/POs to support grassroots development, equity and empowerment programMEs in the late 1980s and 1990s, had begun shifting their international grant-making to eastern Europe and Africa. They justified their shifting priorities on the basis of comparative need as the Philippines was considered a 'middle-level' developing country (Asian Development Bank, 1999: 56).

The NGO argument that the economists' statistical averages actually concealed massive poverty and growing economic disparities – and therefore called for continuing external support – increasingly fell on deaf ears. Many Philippine NGOs were forced to scale down their activities or even disband.

For some NGOs, the shift in donor orientation was a blessing in disguise because it forced them to confront their dependency on external funding. Civil society leaders were challenged to think of alternative and more independent approaches to sustaining their activities. For many, the way to go was to help POs exert their claims on local government funds. This meant helping POs gain the skills and power to pressure local governments into adopting people's priorities.

More and more POs were participating in barangay (village) planning, monitoring expenditures, uncovering corrupt practices, and holding local officials accountable for their performance. Recalcitrant officials become more aware that dissatisfied constituents might well unseat them at the next election. The stakes could be high for PO and NGO leaders as vigilante death squads targeted them, presumably activated by beleaguered politicians or threatened landowners.

Successful barangay–PO negotiations sometimes led to local governments including in their budget allocations funds for local NGOs and POs to carry out priority activities. These could include land titling, slum upgrading, or environmental protection of forests or whales and dolphins in coastal domains. Local officials were realizing more and more that development NGOs were better able to grasp the nuances of village situations and culture, and could help adapt provincial government blueprints to local realities. As residents assumed community ownership of the accompanying activities, the sustainability of government-promoted activities was reinforced (Asian Development Bank, 1999:63).

Despite progress in the POs' effective implementation of basic services, this form of civil society interaction with local government nonetheless sidetracked NGOs from pursuing the cutting-edge networking and policy advocacy they regarded as central to their existence. Clearly, they had to locate more independent sources of income if they were to reform policy and operational systems of governments and donors. Accordingly, in 2001 the Caucus of Development NGO Networks (CODE-NGO, a national network of seven national NGO networks, four regional NGO networks, which together count over 3,000 individual NGOs and co-operatives as members) seized upon the idea of tapping into funds held in private and government coffers for the purpose of supporting NGO/PO programs and projects. And so was born the promising but controversial Poverty Eradication and Alleviation Certificates, or PEACe bonds (Songco, 2002).

With the help of investment bankers interested in harnessing their expertise and resources to practise corporate social responsibility, CODE-NGO leaders worked out a new financial strategy that would generate social development funds by drawing on the capital market. To raise P1 billion (US$20 million), CODE-NGO would buy bonds from the government and sell them at a profit in the secondary market. The proceeds of the sale would be used to establish an independent foundation whose board would manage a trust fund. Only the interest would be utilized to support legitimate NGOs and POs seeking financial support for poverty-reduction projects.

Since CODE-NGO was not authorized to buy government securities, it contracted the Rizal Commercial Banking Corporation to serve as its purchasing agent for the 'zeroes', or zero coupon bonds. RCBC Capital, a partner corporate organization motivated to help reduce poverty, agreed to advance the money for RCBC to buy the bonds through market trading. In a firm underwriting agreement, RCBC Capital affirmed its intention to buy all the zeroes on behalf of CODE-NGO at a pre-agreed price. The bonds would be sold for a profit in the secondary market, with eligibilities secured through selected government agencies.

In a Bureau of Treasury auction, RCBC obtained P35 billion worth of zeroes on behalf of CODE-NGO. RCBC paid P10.168 billion as current value, and government would redeem the bonds at P35 billion in ten years. RCBC sold the bonds to RCBC Capital for P11.9 billion. RCBC reimbursed the Bureau of Treasury P10,168 billion, and remitted the difference of P1.8 billion to CODE-NGO. The latter paid the various fees and divided the net profit of P1.48 billion into two portions. One was used to set up a trust fund of P148 million for the sustainability of network development activities; the rest, P1.3 billion, was constituted as a trust fund to be managed by the newly organized Peace, Equity and Access for Community Empowerment Foundation, or Peace and Equity Foundation.

The outcry from various sectors of government and civil society erupted immediately upon announcement of the transaction. A Senate investigation was launched, with NGOs, government and private traders summoned to testify. Allegations from some groups dubbed the process a scam, or a grand conspiracy between CODE-NGO and certain government agencies. Others dubbed it a blatant and unethical example of CODE-NGO's using its influence for the transaction in certain government agencies. Criticisms and allegations rocked civil society, business and government worlds.

CODE-NGO rebutted the allegations point by point:

1. The government did not lose money in the trading transaction.The P1.8 billion gross margin was a trading gain that came from private funds in the same way that money-market traders legitimately and daily operated. No special tax exemptions were accorded the PEACe bonds. The ten-year tax exemption they received stemmed from their nature as a ten-year bond. There was no forgone tax revenue. The Bureau of Internal Revenue subsequently confirmed this.

Moreover, the zeroes issued by the Bureau of Treasury were part of the government's borrowing programme to finance its budget deficit. Although CODE-NGO did gain enormously despite its not having invested its own money, this was possible because RCBC Capital, in line with corporate social responsibility, was willing to advance the money for CODE-NGO to buy the bonds on the market.

2. The transaction was done in a transparent, above-board manner and did not break any government regulations. Fifteen banks, five of them multinational, participated in the auction of the PEACe bonds. None of these seasoned traders lodged a complaint against the results of the bidding process. Indeed, the Bankers' Association of the Philippines and the president of the Money Market Association of the Philippines publicly affirmed the fairness of the auction, as did the Management Association of the Philippines and the Bishops Businessmen's Conference.

On the charge that CODE-NGO had used its connections to pursue the deal, in particular through the brother–sister relationship of the Secretary of Finance and CODE-NGO's chair, it was pointed out that the project was conceptualized and developed even before the Secretary joined the government. Moreover, the siblings were not involved in the project upon the brother's entry into government, to avoid a conflict of interest. The cooperating government agencies attested to having made their decisions independently.

3. This legal transaction will generate substantial funding from Filipino sources for NGOs and POs to carry out social development and poverty-reduction activities. The Peace and Equity Access for Community Empowerment Foundation, or the Peace and Equity Foundation (PEF) for short, did carry out its promise. From 2002 to 2005, it approved 569 projects loans and grants for poverty alleviation and development, amounting to P674,500,000, or US $13,490,000 (Peace and Equity Foundation, 2005: 36).

Conscious of its role as a Filipino donor institution, PEF gives priority to groups in the poorest and most disadvantaged provinces. In 2005, it has provided loan support to livelihood and employment-generating projects amounting to P82.54 million. Grants totalling P100.57 million went to new projects. Project support activities of P36.38 million furnished technical assistance, including poverty mapping, research and capacity building, project development, monitoring and evaluation, and institutional support. To expand its outreach, PEF has worked with civil society networks in the priority poorest provinces to create Partnership and Access Centers to 'open windows for the poor'. Their ten projects in 2005 received grants or loans totaling P64.4 million.

The Foundation's investment income since its creation in 2002 comes to P664 million, or 50 per cent of the principal amount of the Endowment Fund of P1.318 billion. Adding cumulative reflows (loan payments, interest income), the four-year returns have reached P808.7 million, or an average of 15.3 per cent a year (Peace and Equity Foundation, 2005: 35–6).

The leadership structure is being reformulated for greater diversity. Initially, the Board of Trustees was composed of eminent personalities representing one each from the business, religious and basic sectors (market vendors and informal workers associations), and six member-representatives designated by CODE-NGO. Sitting in an *ex officio* non-voting capacity were one representative each from the government's National Anti-Poverty Commission and the Department of Finance. As the terms of office of the six trustees from CODE-NGO expire, they are being replaced by other prominent NGO leaders not from CODE-NGO, in line with the aim of making the PEF independent of its founding organizers.

The PEACe bonds and their institutional successor, the Peace and Equity Foundation, have enabled hundreds of NGOs and POs in the priority provinces to reduce their dependence on external donors. Especially noteworthy has been the creative approach compatible with standard business operations that saw money transferred from elite coffers to the needs of poor people. This institutional revolution was made possible by increasingly sophisticated NGOs joining forces with socially oriented business leaders to identify latent financial opportunities and formulate legal means of making them available to NGOs and POs. The process by which it was created represents an innovative, entirely Filipino effort to divert local funds normally monopolized by the well-to-do into the service of the poor.

Concluding Reflections

Intellectuals eager for rapid social transformation are increasingly disparaging NGO and PO efforts in developing countries because they do not seem to be bringing about significant structural change. External donors echo the argument, and increasingly exact from NGOs and POs evidence of quantifiable outputs attributable to donor funds. In making these demands, they often undermine the very strengths that NGOs exemplify. To reinforce their position, donors argue that their own citizens are demanding greater accountability for the taxes paid or contributions made to developing countries.

This brief discussion of civil society in the Philippines emphasizes how NGOs, POs, and church social action groups have tenaciously expanded the democratic boundaries of the society to effect both incremental and transformative shifts in power relations. While these activities take place in real communities with real people, they are complemented by advocacy efforts at various levels. The People Power uprising of 1986 reflected some elements of a social movement in dispensing with an authoritarian leader and restoring a democratic society. The second EDSA event of 1992 forced a corrupt and inept president, Joseph Estrada, out of the presidential palace.

NGOs and POs thus continue exercising vigilance to constrain those in power from abusing their positions and pressuring them to act more responsibly for the people's benefit. Without these resurgent demands for accountability, governing elites would have gone unchallenged and ridden roughshod over the rights and future of the poor and powerless. Because these challenges are becoming ever more demanding, civil society groups have had to go beyond their local activities to address operational and policy reform issues in government and among donors. This has understandably led to a re-examination of NGO/PO/SA relationships with donors in keeping with the demands and spirit of the times. The three case studies offer glimpses into the many initiatives under way that are reshaping partnerships between donors and NGOs/POs.

Seen from the distant vantage point of the North, multiple, small-scale community efforts in Africa, Asia and Latin America blur in the face of dominant and inequitable social systems highlighted by the media. Community efforts may appear minuscule in academic or Northern wide-angle lenses, but to the millions of poor and once-powerless people who have learned how to mobilize and pressure governments and business into sharing assets, resources and power, these organized successes are no mean achievement. For them, the struggle will continue and become increasingly sophisticated, whatever the comments of armchair social analysts.

Philippine and Asian NGOs certainly agree that community-based activities must be simultaneously woven into movements for policy change at the national and global levels. Having actually had to make it happen, they understand how slow and painstaking the process can be. The difficult and often dangerous struggle to achieve their aims calls for skill, determination and courage.

The cases described here highlight the evolution of NGO-PO interaction with government and donors. The Naga City Urban Poor Federation turned its involvement in slum upgrading activities into a platform for questioning impractical, unsustainable or inequitable City Government and World Bank procedures, succeeding in their attempts to get the Bank to change their rules! These precedents may well affect the World Bank's community-driven projects in other parts of the country as well as the world. The cases also serve as 'lessons learned' for local governments in the Philippines.

The Philippine Misereor Partnership illustrates how rectifying dependency relationships between donors and NGOs/POs/SAs can improve their interaction, reorient the donor partner's operating procedures, and promote a better understanding of development in the North. The PEACe bonds and the resulting endowed Foundation underscore how a crisis situation, in this case foreign funding declines, can set the stage for creative initiatives that bring about institutional change. In this case, an imaginative NGO network, building on existing market processes, worked out with socially oriented banking and government leaders legal ways through which complex financial structures would benefit poor people. The Asian Development Bank, for its part, has actively reorganized its internal structures and procedures for improved partnerships with NGOs and other civil society groups.

The process of social transformation, therefore, takes place simultaneously as well as incrementally, affecting many elements in society. The locus of struggle may occur now in the community, tomorrow in local government settings, the following day at the national legislature, the day after that at the Human Rights Commission in Geneva, then back to a convention of large landowners facing a farmers' land reform mobilization, controversial decision-making at the presidential palace, or a women's micro-enterprise training activity. The process of effecting change is a dynamic, iterative one.

Many other examples can be cited to affirm that effectively organized 'small d' and 'big D' links can and do bring about important reform efforts. Inevitably these involve a struggle or at the very least strong effort and creativity on the part of NGOs and civil society allies. Philippine NGOs/POs have acted and continued to resist or engage with every administration since Marcos. Had they not demanded a better deal for the poor and marginalized, often putting their own lives and well-being at risk, and had they not championed basic human rights and fought oppressive governments, the country might still be mired in the stultifying and destructive evils of authoritarian leadership.

The NGO legacy therefore lies in maintaining the openness of that political space through concentrated advocacy and by supporting people's empowerment. Because militant and committed NGOs and POs have pursued these efforts, with or without external funding, the prospects for a truly democratic and just society continue to offer hope and fulfilment to poor Filipinos struggling for lives of dignity.

References

Asian Development Bank (1999) *A Study of NGOs – Philippines*, Asian Development Bank, Manila.

Asian Development Bank (2007a) 'NGO and Civil Society Center', www.adb.org/NGOs/ngocenter.asp.

Asian Development Bank (2007b) 'Task Force on Non-government organizations', www.adb.org/Documents/Reports/NGOs/default.asp?p=coopngos

Aldaba, F., D. Arao, E. Gonzales, J. Lacambra, R. Oliverons and J. Rocamora (1992) *Resource Manual on NGO-Managed Fund Mechanisms*, Caucus of Development NGO Networks (CODE-NGO) and Transnational Institute, Quezon City.

Constantino-David, K. (1998) 'From the Present Looking Back: A History of Philippine NGOs', in G. Sidney Silliman and L. Garner Noble (eds), *Organizing for Democracy: NGOs, Civil Society and the Philippine State,* Ateneo de Manila University Press, Quezon City, pp. 26–47.

Giddens, A. (1990) *The Consequences of Modernity*, Stanford University Press, Stanford.

Mangahas, M. (2006a) 'Hunger at a New Record High 19.0 per cent', SWS Media Release, 19 December (email distribution).

Mangahas, M. (2006b) 'The SWS Quarterly Surveys on Poverty and Hunger Show the Emptiness of GNP', Survey Analysis, 20 November, Manila (email distribution).

Peace and Equity Foundation (2005) 'Report for 2005: Creating Access through Partnerships', PEF Quezon City.

Philippine Misereor Partnership (2005) 'Expertise Inventory', PMP, Manila.

Racelis, M. (2000) 'New Visions and Strong Actions: Civil Society in the Philippines', in M. Ottaway and T. Carothers (eds), *Funding Virtue: Civil Society Aid and Democracy Promotion*, Carnegie Endowment for International Peace, Washington DC, pp. 159–87.

Racelis, M., A. Desiree and M. Aguirre (2005) *Making Philippine Cities Child Friendly; Voices of Children in Poor Communities*, Institute of Philippine Culture, Ateneo de Manila University, Quezon City.

Rocamora, J. (2005) 'Impact of Civil Society Advocacy', in *Policy Advocacy: Experiences and Lessons from the Philippines*, Institute for Popular Democracy, Quezon City, pp. 127–34.

Schelzig, K. (2005) *Poverty in the Philippines; Income, Assets, and Access*, Asian Development Bank, Metro Manila.

Silliman, G.S., and L. Garner Noble (1998) 'Introduction', in G.S. Silliman and L. Garner Noble (eds), *Organizing for Democracy: NGOs, Civil Society and the Philippine State*, Ateneo de Manila University Press, Quezon City, pp. 10–11.

Social Weather Stations (2006) www.sws.org.ph.

Songco, D. (2002) 'CODE-NGO's PEACe Bonds: Financing Civil Society's Fight Against Poverty', *Philippine Daily Inquirer* (Opinion), Talk of the Town, Juan V. Sarmiento Jr., ed., 17 February, A10.

PART IV

Being Alternative

Reinventing International NGOs:
A View from the Dutch Co-financing System

Harry Derksen and Pim Verhallen

The international aid chain has been successfully integrated into the neo-liberal development paradigm. Despite lip service to 'ownership', bottom-up and rights-based approaches to poverty alleviation, policies, instruments and outcomes are almost exclusively determined outside the domain of the poor and excluded themselves. Macroeconomics are dominant, outcomes only valid if quantifiable, and structural causes of poverty and exclusion are left intact. For international ODA funded NGOs, pressure to align with the mainstream agenda is such that they and their local partners risk losing any claim to an 'alternative' development agenda.

In such a context, it is time to re-invent the system. In this chapter, we will show how our organization, ICCO (Interchurch Organization for Development Cooperation), a Dutch co-funding organization working with more than one thousand local partners in eighty countries, is trying to do just that. The chapter first gives a brief description of developments in international debates on development. We draw attention to the depoliticization of development thought and practice, as well as the introduction of neo-liberal policies of privatization and market instruments in the development architecture both in general and more specifically in the Dutch co-funding programme. We will try to identify the most important implications of these changes, for the work of Dutch international NGOs (INGOs), for the activities of their non-governmental partners overseas and for their joint ability to contribute effectively to the fight against exclusion and poverty. Lastly, we will describe how in the face of these different pressures, our own organization introducing substantial changes to its strategies and ways of working, changes that aim to ensure our possibilities for making a difference for the poor and excluded.

The Development Context of the 1980s and 1990s

Successive so-called development decades have brought about much less in terms of economic growth of poor countries (and even less in diminishing the gap between rich and poor within those countries) than had been expected. In itself, this perception was less important for policy development than the debt crisis and near collapse of the international economic system in the beginning of the 1980s. One direct consequence of the Mexican default was the strengthening of the role of the World Bank and the IMF: the 'Washington consensus' became the leading development paradigm and neoliberal policies the standard recipe. Many donor countries followed this lead, and aligned themselves with this process, which included a widespread use of standardised policies that favoured a focus on macroeconomic management, the liberalization and broadening of markets and the imposition of various conditionalities on debtor countries. Meanwhile in many debtor countries, 'structural adjustment' became a byword for social hardship and deterioration in the already grave position of the traditionally poor and excluded.

Many (but certainly not all) non-governmental development organizations in Africa, Asia and Latin America, with their roots in the politically effervescent 1960s, defined their programmes and the ideals that drove them in terms that were either alternative to, or in direct opposition to, state policies. Societal transformation, human rights and social justice were key elements in their projects. Dutch co-funding organizations, with roots also in the 1960s, favoured working relations with local NGOs that strove to identify and combat the structural causes of poverty rather than merely the symptoms of it. This self-definition made for difficult and sometimes problematic relationships with governments and the state. However, on the whole, the international donor organizations generally regarded NGOs as marginal actors in development processes. They were seen as useful in providing services and emergency aid (where states could not or would not) and as a political nuisance when denouncing human rights abuses.

The first experiments with 'structural adjustment' came with a new recognition among policymakers of the practical advantages of development-oriented NGOs. A prime consideration in the neoliberal adjustment agenda was to diminish the role of the state in favour of the market. Investment in education, health and other services was cut to the bone. However, the need for 'social safety nets' was recognized, particularly after the first symptoms of social unrest endangering political stability – for instance, in Venezuela in 1991. As it was necessary to avoid bringing the state back in, the local NGO sector was seen as a useful alternative to deliver basic social services, especially to those sectors of the population hardest hit by 'adjustment' measures. Over the years, many of the established NGO's – sometimes after heated debates on the risks of 'co-optation' – accepted the new roles assigned to them. They assumed these new roles would offer opportunities to influence social policies, but also accepted them for practical reasons, in particular the access to increasing levels of funding. Furthermore, where NGOs did not agree to assume these roles, international donors did not hesitate to establish their own NGOs, as was the case, for example, in El Salvador after the peace agreements of Esquipulas. New arrivals on the scene also included NGOs founded by civil servants who had lost their jobs in the downsizing of the state.

The international donor community assigned quite large amounts of finance to this 'sector'. Some did this directly, as in the case of the Interamerican Development Bank's very substantial programme for micro-credit channelled to local NGOs. Others donors, such as many European bilateral agencies, channelled resources indirectly through their own national non-governmental co-funding organizations.

The 1990s can be described as a high point in the involvement of development NGOs in executing (but not designing) national social policies, such as they were. Political sensitivity in relation to local NGOs had lessened: their numbers had multiplied, the sector was much more heterogeneous and many had become cautious and pragmatic in their public statements of intent. With the collapse of the Soviet Union, the disappearance of any political alternative to liberal market-oriented democracies strengthened a tendency to assume apolitical and practical social tasks. For many development NGOs (especially in Latin America and Asia) increased resources and access to new generations of well-trained professionals (who no longer looked to the 'downsized' state for employment) meant growth and professionalization. To consolidate their place in the system, these NGOs also tended to dedicate time and resources not only to strengthening their own organizations, but also to creating national – and sometimes international – networks and other structures to improve coordination, strengthen advocacy and learning abilities, and to defend their specific interests as a sector.

At the end of that decade, dominant thinking about the state changed again. The Washington consensus came under increasing attack from respectable critics such as Joseph Stiglitz – former chief economist of the World Bank. It had become clear that markets either could not or would not solve many underlying social and economic problems in developing countries and that political instability resulting from an increase in the numbers of people excluded from any gain in economic growth was a real threat in many countries. It had also become clear that markets needed certain guarantees that only a functioning state could provide. 'Good governance' became an important – if only vaguely defined – concept, but attention was also growing for the role of civil society as an autonomous actor and as a countervailing power. Participation by civil society organizations in, and contribution to, various international conferences organized by the UN (e.g. Cairo, Copenhagen and later others) further heightened this public profile.

All this said, counter-currents were also at work. The high visibility of NGOs in developing countries now in many cases turned against them. While in earlier years, critical debates had centred on their political identity and agenda, public criticism now concentrated on their management of the resources channelled through them, the lack of evidence regarding their effectiveness, and their own questionable transparency and accountability. By accepting a role of substituting state responsibilities, many NGOs had subsumed some of their original ideals and aspirations in the process of elaborating their own pragmatic responses to the changes in their societies and in the development debate. It became clear that many of them, as a consequence, faced a serious identity crisis.

We may therefore conclude that the position, tasks and responsibilities of non-governmental development organizations have changed substantially over the years. From being a marginal actor with a distinctive analysis of poverty and exclusion, mainly in opposition to the state in the 1960s and 1970s, they now represent a significant sector in terms of resources and service responsibilities. For many of them, the cost of this evolution has been high in terms of dependence and dependence-generated pragmatism, and a weakening of their relationships with their target groups. For many, this evolution is problematic and represents a challenge to define their *raison d'être* anew.

The Dutch Co-funding Programme between 1965 and 2000

Until a few years ago, the ministry in charge of Dutch development cooperation and four development organizations (Cordaid, Hivos, Icco, Novib) shared responsibility for the Dutch co-funding programme. The co-funding programme, now in existence for forty years, started out as a partnership, based on an agreement reached in 1965. This recognized that combating international poverty was a moral responsibility for state and civil society organizations alike. These four organizations were recognized as representing the main sectors of Dutch society – Cordaid was Catholic, ICCO Protestant, Hivos humanist and Novib 'secular'. This societal representation and support was understood to be a mainstay of a system that depended on public – taxpayer – support.

In the mid-1960s, the Netherlands was at last emerging from a post-war reconstruction phase in the aftermath of occupation and the destruction of the productive infrastructure that had occurred during the Second World War. In response to international debates on poverty in the first UN 'development decade' of the 1960s, nearly all political parties supported a decision to assign – initially modest – budgets to the newly created post of Minister for International Cooperation. Dutch development aid was to aim at fostering economic independence and eradicating extreme poverty. The start-up of a bilateral aid initiative was slow, but the government moved to involve a broad segment of Dutch society in the endeavour. In this vein, one of the first programmes to be launched was the co-funding programme.

In the mid-1970s the picture changed quite rapidly. The four development organizations had shown success in building partnerships with local organizations to deliver aid, especially in the fields of health and education, in a variety of flexible and effective ways. They had assumed as their target group the 'poorest of the poor' and defined interventions aimed at 'structural' poverty eradication. Their central strategy was to support local initiatives and work in partnership with local organizations. Although this approach sometimes caused political tensions, government also came to see the advantages of a non-official aid channel in the rapidly growing number of countries under authoritarian rule (making bilateral relationships politically undesirable or impossible). Funding for the programme grew and the mandate was broadened.

The framework for this cooperation was called the Programme Funding Agreement: it established a generous level of lump-sum funding over four-year periods (indexed to the country's economic growth rate), delegated responsibilities for policy- and decision-making on projects to the agencies themselves and even left them to decide on exactly how the ODA-funding allocated to the programme would be distributed among them. Next to yearly reporting, the main instrument for oversight was a system of programme evaluations, in which joint teams (from the ministry and the agencies) would study the development of the programme, its instruments and policies and the interaction between the parties. It was accepted – not always in good grace by either side – that the evaluations would also look at official government policies in their relationship to INGO policies. When introducing this new working relationship in 1980, the then Minister for Development encouraged the four main agencies to actively seek the same sharing of responsibilities for the Programme with their local partners overseas.

The rapid growth of ODA funding assigned to the INGOs can be illustrated in the case of ICCO: in 1973, total ODA assigned to ICCO was Nfl.22 million, while in 1990 this had grown to nearly Nfl.120 million. This growth also reflected public perception of the work of non-governmental organizations. Parliament and the press were largely uncritical, and the press reserved most of its attention for the bilateral programmes of the ministry.

This situation changed markedly at the end of the 1980s. A spate of very critical analyses appeared in the media, not only on the effectiveness of aid in general, but also specifically questioning the results of the NGOs' efforts. The Dutch agencies were relatively unprepared for this critical debate on their activities, accustomed as they were to being seen as dependable, committed and legitimized both by their constituencies and their local, Southern partners. The level of public debate obliged the four co-funding agencies to launch a wide-ranging independent review of their own performance. The report of this review, the *Impact Study*, presented in 1991, constituted a substantial let-down compared to the claims and ambitions that the agencies had formulated for themselves and their constituencies. The central conclusion was 'there are no complete failures nor complete successes'. The study recommended, among other things, more cost-consciousness, more research and evaluation of results and more inter-agency cooperation.

This review led to substantial changes in all four agencies, not only in their policies (which became more focused and explicit in terms of aims and outcomes) but especially within the organizations themselves. Ambitious reorganizations were launched, internal work processes were standardized, evaluation and measurement instruments developed, (which entailed defining in much more detail targets and goals), and professionalization became the catchword. To a large degree, these measures helped in regaining lost ground. The Ministry for Development Cooperation adopted a policy paper on civil society which defined it as an autonomous actor with which the state needed to interact. Cooperation between the ministry and the main INGOs was still quite intensive, especially in relation to the bilateral regional programmes, most of whose content was actually devised in cooperation with the main agencies. This level of interaction lessened substantially (without immediate consequences for the co-funding programme) when in the mid-1990s the ministry decided to decentralize most regional policy and decision-making to the Dutch embassies in the main partner countries.

The collapse of the Soviet bloc brought about substantial changes in public perceptions of development cooperation. Although (in the Netherlands) it was never very explicit, the East–West divide was an important element driving the debate on international commitment to continuing development aid. With the East–West confrontation now apparently out of the way, the international debate of the beginning of the nineties on the effectiveness of aid constituted the political springboard to review existing development policy and arrangements. A contributing factor was also the widespread perception that development aid was, on the whole, not delivering on its promises.

With neoliberal, free-market thinking dominating the political spectrum in the Netherlands, right-of-centre politicians sought to reformulate the aims of Dutch development in order to align them with the Netherlands' own political and economic interests and lobbied for more private-sector involvement. In other cases they simply proposed abolishing development aid altogether. Many other commentators also questioned the need for the level of commitment that had, from the beginning of the 1970s, constituted a political consensus bordering on dogma – namely that the country would adhere to the UN standard of making available 0.7 per cent of net national income for development aid.

Dutch government had rewarded the agencies for their efforts to implement the recommendations of the Impact Study with an increase in funding available to them (to 10 per cent of ODA, up from the previous 7 per cent). However, public debate on their role and functions did not diminish. New objections were raised, among them that the four original co-funding agencies constituted a privileged and exclusive cartel and that they represented 'special interests'. In 1999 a new government coalition decided to launch an inter-ministerial review (under the direct oversight of the prime minister's office) of the state's relationship with the co-funding agencies. This study concluded that the co-funding system needed to be opened up to more competition (with funds being allocated on the basis of results), that ODA-funded NGO programmes needed to be more aligned with official Dutch development policies, and that agencies should be obliged to coordinate wherever possible with existing bilateral programmes. It also recommended much more direct ministerial control of the co-funding programme as such.

In a parallel development, the Dutch public, traditionally quite generous in their voluntary contributions to a host of good causes, now developed a more 'do it yourself' approach to development: a wide variety of local groups no longer limited themselves to fund-raising, but also tended increasingly to insist on delivering aid directly. This trend can be seen as both part of a general loss of trust in existing institutions (visible in Dutch society at the end of the 1990s) and as a sign of continuing social commitment.

Although the then Minister for Development Cooperation, the social democrat Evelien Herfkens, was hesitant to accept all the recommendations of the inter-ministerial review immediately, she did decide to open up the co-funding programme partially by including two additional organizations in the system. She also advised the agencies that, for the new funding period starting in 2002, they would need to present much more detailed work plans as a condition for funding.

Meanwhile, ministry personnel were already preparing for a more comprehensive overhaul of the system, in line with the recommendations of the inter-ministerial review. ODA funding for the programme was to be based on the results of a tendering procedure which would be open to a wide range of (Dutch) organizations. Entry criteria were defined and a very ambitious and demanding format was prepared for presenting work plans. Systems were developed to determine the merits of proposals and measurement of outcomes – again, exclusively quantifiable – and, especially, to enable the ministry to monitor the work of the organizations receiving grants. This new system was officially launched by the new Christian Democrat minister Agnes van Aardenne. For the period starting in 2007, tenders were to be presented by mid-2006.

In 2006, our organization, together with 115 other Dutch organizations, tendered for access to government development funding. On average, each organization submitted some *two kilogrammes* of written material detailing, among others, what the results of their work would be in 2010. Of these, 58 applications were accepted for funding for a total of 11 per cent of the Dutch ODA budget (increasing tenfold the number of participants in the programme). For the fiscal year 2007, these organizations are to receive a total of €500 million (US$650 million).

The co-funding programme had started out as a partnership between state and civil society based on shared objectives and trust. Today, in the wake of a wave of social and economic changes in the country following the introduction of free-market liberalization since the 1990s, the programme can best be described as a system of governmental subcontracting of extraordinary bureaucratic complexity and high transaction costs, with accountability rules stipulating outcomes that are only acceptable if quantifiable.

What Has Happened to Us?

Distortions

Proponents of the dominant development model point to the fact that, over the last decade, many developing countries have experienced respectable economic growth. Yet, despite the substantial changes in the international development architecture, aid instruments, alignment, commitment to development goals and substantially increased research on aid effectiveness, the disheartening reality is that economic growth is rarely benefiting the poor. Recent research by the IMF's own Independent Evaluation Office for sub-Saharan Africa once again confirmed this situation (IMF/IEO, 2007). The explanation for the general ineffectiveness of measures to eradicate poverty resides at least partly in the fact that the international donor community does not acknowledge that poverty and exclusion are rooted in complex societal and political realities that official aid policies do not address. Many of these structural causes have, over the years, been well documented in the UNDP *Human Development Reports*. Examples of this include the 2005 *HDR* chapter on inequality and the 2006 report describing the problems of politics behind access to water (UNDP, 2005, 2006). Similarly, there is a wide range of studies – including research done in Northern countries (Rupasingha and Goetz, 2003) – that refer to the social and political determinants of structural poverty, and there are some hopeful signs that the neglect of these political dimensions could be changing (for example, the IMF has recently designated as its chief economist professor Simon Johnson, who at MIT has explored the political roots of poverty; *The Economist*, 2007).

Development NGOs that in the past worked to identify, understand and combat these 'structural' causes in their own societies have in many cases been effectively marginalized or have opted for mainstream programmes that provide them with institutional stability. For their Northern non-governmental donors, the increasing demands that their back-donors make on their policies and working practices have lessened their willingness to venture into disputed areas of intervention. These back donor demands are increasingly passed on to the NGOs' local partner organizations. This effectively limits the scope of their programmes to the policies of their donor.

System demands, centring on accountability and originating from back donors, absorb an ever greater portion of Southern partner resources. Especially in Africa, where in many countries substantial percentages of social service delivery is NGO-based and well-trained human resources are scarce, these demands are clearly distorting and disproportionate.

Insistence, within the system, on 'results' (and accepting by and large as results only 'what can be counted') is a powerful distorting factor, in that it leads organizations to 'safe' areas of intervention and sometimes to abandon their primary target groups where no significant material gain is to be expected. A case in point would be those organizations that, joining the apparently successful trend for micro-credit schemes (for which a vast amount of development funding is available), choose target groups with more chances of success (i.e. not the poorest segments of society).

Another distorting effect of these NGO funding policies is that they stimulate competition among agencies, generating the desire (and perhaps the need) to be the best performer in delivering quantifiable results. This leads agencies to emphasize their own public relations and 'plant the flag', maintain project-type interventions specifying concrete outcomes (and sometimes overstating them afterwards), and to steer away from multi-actor initiatives and innovations where they will be less visible and where outcomes are more uncertain – this despite recognition of the need for more cooperation to upscale successful strategies and stimulate innovation.

Paradoxes

Many of the changes described above come together to define a 'development chain' involving civil society organizations that, in size, organization, strategies and working practices, is quite different from the chain that existed at the end of the 1970s. At one look, it would seem that the chain has evolved in ways that are positive for NGOs, both North and South. If they were once considered to be marginal actors, now there is public recognition of the importance of civil society; if once deemed a political nuisance when they talked about human rights issues, now they are the object of extensive cooperation and transfers of resources. However, these changes have been accompanied by a series of paradoxes over the last twenty-five years.

Although certain basic original concepts such as 'cooperation' (not 'aid'), 'partnership' and 'participation' (by the target groups) are still common currency, the reality is that the aid chain is dominated by top-down blueprint approaches, donor micro-management of development initiatives and 'upward accountability'. Despite much use (and the proven validity) of the concept of local 'ownership' as a precondition for the relevance and sustainability of development initiatives, there is in fact ever less 'local ownership' to be found. Another and related casualty has been partnership. Indeed, in the field of international NGO cooperation, partnership was a central concept: the notion that both parties, sharing values and ideals, worked together as autonomous entities within their own societies to bring about change. While of course true equality was seldom achieved, the notion of partnership at least defined a common horizon for which to strive. Under the present rules of the game, it is clear that this is no longer the case, as ever more detailed back-donor requirements are simply transmitted to local organizations, and agencies tend to treat their local counterparts as subcontractors to implement work which the agencies have already committed themselves to implement as part of their agreements with their back donors. Donors willing to be accountable to their local partners and their target groups (on their policies and mechanisms, for example) are few and far between.

The second paradox, resulting from these trends is that, despite a general consensus existing in most democracies on the intrinsic value of an active civil society, over the past years, most governments and multilateral institutions have been doing much to bring development NGOs under control, either to pacify civil tensions and neutralize potential political opposition or to consolidate a system of outsourcing and quasi-privatization. In many developing countries, this has led governments to pass legislation on the sector, often combining access to resources from national budgets with limits on the freedom of movement of NGOs and attempts to bring them under fiscal control. (Such legislation is also sometimes blatantly designed to enable governments to skim off percentages of resource flows.) This tendency has been strengthened within many countries, using the 'war on terror' to introduce legislation limiting NGO freedom to engage in human rights issues (and sometimes without even the pretence of legislation to that end – see Alan Fowler's chapter in this volume).

In the case of the Netherlands, this trend also holds true, despite official policy recognizing the autonomous nature of civil society organizations in development and accepting that one of the central goals of the co-funding programme is 'strengthening civil society'. Government demands that NGOs align their work with official Dutch aid policy, pressure on upward account-ability and the trend to stimulate competition between non-governmental organizations in their access to ODA funding are together redefining this sector as an additional aid channel. The relationship is defined by govern-ment as one in which the Dutch government is effectively subcontracting NGOs to perform services that the government itself is unable to undertake, and to do this on terms wholly defined by the state. (In effect, the ministry recognizes this utilitarian approach to the whole chain by stating that, in its view, the co-funding agencies work 'through' their local counterparts, instead of 'with' them.)

A third paradox can be found in the market-driven introduction of competition in the system. It is widely accepted that one of the weaknesses of the NGO sector is the dispersion of scarce resources, leading to many small-scale and usually ineffective and/or unsustainable interventions. Project-type interventions, limited in time and scope, and planned and executed by individual organizations, still constitute the majority of INGO funding decisions. At the same time in the Dutch system, the number of NGOs with access to ODA funding has multiplied tenfold, and the assigna-tion system more or less actively discourages them from working together or even sharing information.

Finally, we have the problem of knowledge and learning in development practice. It is useful to point to the contradictory effects, in the present system, of the increased emphasis on accountability. Assignation of fund-ing in the Dutch system is based largely on the prediction of outcomes and results and accompanied by a formalized and demanding protocol for monitoring on these and other aspects. Two important consequences are being disregarded. First, the tension that already exists between research for accountability and research for learning (leading to evident distortions) will now be increased as short-term rewards for coming up with success-stories will be greater than for critical analyses. Second, no rational basis has been devised to understand, much less to manage the costs and benefits of this very heavy accountability burden, especially at a local level.

Summary

These trends would be acceptable if the aid chain could, under these ar-rangements, deliver on its original intentions – namely, to produce results showing a structural improvement in the position of the poor. However, studies of aid policies and practices, including those of Dutch govern-ment, demonstrate that they are not. In one recent study by the official Policy Review Unit (IOB), implementation in bilateral programmes of the so-called sector-wide approach is criticized for its exclusive attention to national sectoral policies of the receiving country and for disregarding outcomes at local level: 'Target groups have literally disappeared from view', the report concludes. The same study concludes that monitoring of development programmes is mainly for management purposes rather than for learning (IOB, 2006).

We have shown that changes in the dominant system are quickly trans-ferred to ODA-funded non-governmental organizations. If organizations such as ICCO want to maintain their original ambitions to contribute to structural change in society and in the conditions that generate poverty and exclusion, that part of the system which they still control clearly needs to be reinvented.

Reinventing the System in ICCO: Aiming for Change

Reinventing the system and making it work for ICCO and its partners essentially means reinventing ICCO itself. It necessitates that ICCO rethink its vision on the relationship with 'the South': who are our partners in the South and how are they really involved in policymaking and priority setting within ICCO? This 'reinvention' of ICCO centres around two main areas of change:

1. In 2010 ICCO will have changed from a Dutch co-financing organiza-tion working in 50 countries in the South into an international network organization.
2. Changing the *dynamics* of North–South cooperation for it to become relevant to grassroots communities, in addressing the structural causes of poverty, involving new actors and being legitimate in Southern countries and in the Netherlands.

Both areas of change require a change in present power relations.

The challenges to our policies and working practices became progres-sively clearer between 2003 and 2004. Exchanges with key partners in our network as well as with independent researchers confirmed that answers needed to be found if the credibility of our intentions was to be maintained.

A series of intensive consultations was organized in Africa, Asia and Latin America. These involved both important local partners and independent local experts. Local experiences with and expectations of international development policies were examined. Participants were presented with and invited to comment on an analysis prepared by ICCO on the European context. Certain basic elements of consensus were identified in that process. It was obvious that, to increase relevance and sustainability, decision-making on policies needed to be much more rooted in local contexts (to offset a trend towards 'one-size-fits-all' policies) and also needed to increase the involvement of (organizations of) the target groups themselves. At the same time, it was necessary to find responses to fragmentation of resources (increasingly characteristic of NGO initiatives both in the North and in the South), and the existing disincentives to collaboration that derive from competition for access to resources. There was also clear consensus on the need to adapt to a globalizing environment.

To respond to all this, it was also clear that we had to redefine our role and functions. It had become evident that working practices and instruments were largely determined by ICCO in its role as funder (while availability of monetary resources was not always the key problem it may have been in the past). At the same time, demands from our partners for other services (such as support for their lobby and advocacy efforts, for brokering new partnerships with other actors, or for increasing investment in learning and capacity-strengthening) could not always be met.

Before starting the preparations for a new programme submission to the Dutch government, a small internal working group developed a first sketch of specific answers to these challenges. In 2006, this sketch was submitted for internal debate within our organization and discussed with a group of independent international experts. In the consultations with partners and staff, the ideas for the future received rather mixed responses; conversely the international experts often concurred with the underlying analysis, though also formulated some important reservations, pointing to, among other things, the existence of vested interests in maintaining the status quo. The results of all these consultations and debates were such that the ICCO board decided to go ahead, subject to certain issues (such as the need for dialogue with Dutch government to ensure that choices to be made would not limit the organization's eligibility to the co-funding programme).

The changes we will be introducing in the system as a result of this process can be divided into two broad categories: our place in the international aid-chain and our roles and tasks in that system. We take each in turn. Some aspects of these two areas concern changes that are also under way in various forms and guises in a number of other European NGOs. Truly devolving power (instead of relocating or decentralizing) is, we feel, a far more significant and radical change than most currently being considered with international aid, and is the one that might make the most persuasive claim to being alternative. To a considerable extent, this decision to devolve power drives our whole programme of renewal.

ICCO as an International Network Organization

In 1977 and in 1979 ICCO organized two consultations (called 'reverse consortia') with partners from the South. The main question at the time was how to reverse the then dominant North–South power relation. Interesting at the time was the conclusion from Southern partners that the time was not yet ripe for such moves. Since then ICCO has 'muddled through' its policy vis-à-vis its southern partners. Key aspects of this partnership policy included: an emphasis on institutional and long-term support to provide partners a maximum of freedom within 'the system', consultations with partners on policy changes, and respecting partners' room to manoeuvre and tailor programmes to the specific context in which they work. The latter policy meant that ICCO, contrary to the trend, did not open field offices in Southern countries. It remained at a distance, working from its head office in Utrecht.

The process we started in 2005 opened up once again this discussion with partners on power-sharing and devolution. The main conviction driving this discussion is that Southern civil society has gained strength and is now in a better position to steer its own process of change in the direction it wants to take, while international donor organizations are now lagging behind in adapting their support strategies to this new context. Since 1980, ICCO has worked with three main intervention strategies: direct poverty alleviation, the strengthening of southern civil societies, and lobby and advocacy on policy. These are still valid domains in which to work, but partner organizations in the South now need to be able to share responsibility for policy choices and priority setting with organizations such as ICCO.

A second argument for change in the relations between ICCO and its Southern partners is the certainty that many Southern partners and local communities are integrating rapidly into the contemporary world of information sharing, rapid communications and networking for knowledge and new ideas. ICCO should facilitate this integration by offering its global network of over 800 Southern partners, international networks such as the World Council of Churches, ACT Development, and Aprodev, as well as its contacts with universities and international institutions such as the European Union.

At present ICCO is developing and testing a new model that is based on the establishment of about twelve regional councils in Latin America,

Africa and Asia, as well as the formation of an international council. In the regional councils, 'representatives' of important sectors of civil society are elected from the region. These representatives are well informed about the regional and local context, and are highly motivated and creative personalities with no vested interests in existing partner organizations or services provided by the system. The main functions of these regional councils – which will be supported by teams of professional staff – will be to develop new and context-specific regional policies, devise strategies, and engage new actors in the development process. Funding decisions will also be made at the level of the councils. Within the international council, representatives of regional councils as well as independent, international members are elected and have similar functions to members of the regional councils. A Dutch supervisory council ensures that there is cohesion and coherence in the system and that decision-making, priority-setting and control over financial resources are conducted in a proper way. Small and effective regional working organizations and an international working organization will implement the policies and priorities.

A major hurdle for ICCO is to achieve this change within the boundaries of present overhead costs (12.5 per cent of total programme funds) and with the active engagement of the present staff in the Netherlands. To clear this hurdle, ICCO has to resolve a paradox. A key factor for success in this process of change is the active support of the present stakeholders, among them the present staff of ICCO. Yet, the model for renewal foresees a much reduced number of staff in Utrecht than there is at present. We are therefore asking (some of the) present staff to support the process by actively seeking new opportunities outside ICCO. We now foresee a gradual process of more or less natural staff reduction. In the first few years, (Dutch) ICCO staff may play a role in some of the regional working organizations. Some others will be asked to work on new roles in the international working organization. For a significant number of present staff, however, these changes will mean that they will indeed be requested to pursue their career elsewhere.

An important question for ICCO has been whether this change fits within Dutch government criteria on the co-funding programme. ICCO has received indications from the Ministry of Foreign Affairs that this might be the case, and the ministry does indeed view the relation between Dutch organizations and their Southern counterparts as a major area that requires innovations that will allow Southern civil society organizations a larger say in the way resources should be allocated. The ministry has requested the Radboud University, one of the universities participating in the IS-Academy, to conduct comparative research on examples of such changes in relations between Northern and Southern organizations and ICCO's process of change has been chosen as one of the three or four models to be studied.

At the moment of writing it is unclear whether the recent handover to a new governing coalition will have any implications for ICCO's agenda.

Changing the Dynamic of North–South Cooperation

The 'marketization of aid', the competition for public and private funding, the need to gain a public profile and the pressure to show concrete results have together led to a situation of atomization and fragmentation, both in the North and in the South. The net result of this is a centralization of power and decision-making in the North or in Northern institutions located in the South.

In an attempt to reverse this trend, ICCO is doing several things. First of all it formed an alliance with five other Dutch organizations and agreed on one joint business plan for the coming four years. Second, ICCO is introducing a programmatic approach to funding in which Southern organizations are encouraged to co-operate and complement each other based on a shared vision and on shared strategies. Together they would work on commonly defined and tangible objectives. An example of such an endeavour is a programme involving some twelve Central American organizations aiming at the creation of a safe environment and development opportunities for young people in that region. The condition that ICCO lays down, however, is that the approach must be *inclusive*, involving partners and non-partners of ICCO, traditional development NGOs, as well as new actors such as the private sector, as well as local governments and others who have the means and influence to achieve a *real* change.

The regional councils and regional working organizations will play a major role in the creation of regional and national programmes. First of all they will select which (thematic) areas should take priority and offer the best chances for effective transformation. Second, the regional councils will have the role of ensuring collaboration and promoting value-added or synergy between programmes – for instance, the 'Youth and Violence' programme in Central America mentioned above will be strengthened if and when a job opportunities programme is related to it. A third function of the regional councils will be actively to promote and enable exchange of knowledge and information both within the region as well as with other regions. The object would be to contribute to strengthening capacities at the level of the organizations themselves, but especially at institutional level – that is, building up disposition and abilities necessary for more collaborative programmes.

For the regional councils and the programmatic approach to be successful, present power dynamics must be transformed. Over the years, Southern partner organizations have developed good working relations with ICCO (or at least with individual ICCO desk officers). For many of them, the shift in ICCO's *modus operandi* will have serious consequences. Their future funding will depend on their willingness and ability to co-operate with others, to discuss and agree with others the direction of change processes in their area of work, to work with new actors and to come up with new and creative ideas that sometimes involve risks. It will no longer be their *power* (based on their strong relation with ICCO and other donors) that is important, but their ability to *influence* other stakeholders in the process for change. This transformation from depending on power to active influencing is a profound change which among some partners is already generating insecurity and resistance. Others, however, see this transformation as an opportunity for real change.

Can the System be Reinvented?

Development aid has come under considerable pressure in recent years. Once, especially during the 1970s, the Netherlands was regarded as a pioneer in various domains of international affairs such as human rights, international law and development aid. It was one of the first countries to comply with the UN target of reserving at least 0.7 per cent of net national income for development efforts. Meanwhile some of our experts and motivated politicians – such as Tinbergen and Pronk – played key roles in the international debate on poverty. Dutch society at large was not only aware but also proud of this record. Nowadays, however, international affairs move into the political agenda only when issues of migration and asylum are at stake. Development aid is even less relevant politically.

Development aid organizations, in particular the larger or more visible of them, have a distinct credibility problem. Several scandals regarding the high salaries of directors of aid organizations and stories in the press about the lack of (tangible) results of development aid have proven sufficient to strengthen doubts about the entire sector. Meanwhile, big development institutions have had little success in reaching out to the public, in particular to young people. In short, development institutions are no longer seen as dynamic, flexible and well-equipped to address the issues at stake.

It should therefore not be surprising that in recent years both the general public and representatives of certain right-of-centre political parties have asked whether development aid is still relevant in today's world. The question as to whether the present aid budget, set at 0.7 per cent of GDP, should be maintained is raised with monotonous regularity.

Responses from the development sector to these criticisms have been largely defensive. Using studies, evaluations and audits, the sector tried to 'prove' that everything was more or less in order and that development aid institutions can in fact be trusted. Meanwhile, no real introspection is taking place, perhaps out of the (not entirely unfounded) fear that this would fuel the critics of development aid or would further erode funding support. Another serious handicap for real public debate is the absence of clear alternatives to present arrangements and policies. Indeed, one serious effort of several organizations to start a serious debate on some of these issues, such as the problems arising from the erosion of trust in the system, quickly fizzled out, as a result, among other things, of discrepancies from within the sector itself and because it was presented while the government was studying the applications for the period starting 2007. The development sector very much looks like a rabbit caught in the glare of the headlamps of an approaching car.

There is a conviction among many *individuals* active in the sector that change is necessary and indeed inevitable. Some people fear that if reform is not undertaken from within the system, sooner or later the sector will be confronted with changes forced upon it from outside. At an *institutional* level, however, it is much more difficult to discuss reform. Vested interests might be harmed. The responses to ICCO's initiative will be diverse and it is quite likely that some organizations will feel that ICCO is opening up a Pandora's box. Given the standard reactions from the right in the political spectrum there are concerns that once the box is opened, the political debate will spiral out of control. However, there are also clear indications, now that the dust raised by the recent tendering procedure begins to settle, that an open and constructive debate *could* now be opened to address the very real distortions that exist within the current aid system.

A major question is, of course, whether ICCO will be able to reinvent itself. In a way, we could compare the effort to Baron von Munchausen's attempt to hoist himself out of the swamp by his own bootstraps. We realize there are no guarantees for success, but we are confident we will be able to change ourselves. In this effort, we have the help and support of an International Advisory Group consisting of respected international and Dutch individuals who know the 'system' well. Above all we are certain that there is no way back if we want to continue our work and stay relevant. It is also time for everybody inside and outside the sector to realize that development aid is an investment in a world full of uncertainties. As in the business sector, starting a new company with new ideas is no guarantee of success. Some 30 per cent of new business initiatives do not survive the first year. Development aid can only stay relevant and successful if it starts to accept risks as the necessary investment for renewal and real innovation.

References

Bebbington, A. (2005) 'Donor–NGO Relations and Representations of Livelihood in Non-governmental Aid Chains', *World Development* 33(6): 937–50.

Dijkstal, H. (2006) 'Vertrouwen in een kwetsbare sector?' (Trust in a Vulnerable Sector?), report of the committee on public support in the Netherlands for development cooperation in relation to its effectiveness, the Dijkstal Committee, April.

GOM (1991) *Significance of the Dutch Co-funding Programme: A Review*, GOM, The Hague September.

IMF/IEO (2007) /www.imf.org/external/np/ieo/2007/ssa/eng/pdf/report.pdf (accessed March 2007).

IOB (2006) www.minbuza.nl/binaries/en-pdf/iob-evaluatie/rapporten/final-report-301.pdf

Rupasingha, A., and S. J. Goetz (2003) 'The Causes of Enduring Poverty', *Rural Development Paper* No. 22, Northeast Regional Center for Rural Development, Pennsylvania State University,www.nercrd.psu.edu/Publications/rdppapers/rdp22.pdf (accessed December 2003).

The Economist (2007) 'Sister Talk: World Bank and IMF', 3 March 2007.

UNDP (2005) *Human Development Report 2005*, Oxford University Press, New York.

UNDP (2006) *Human Development Report 2006*, Oxford University Press, New York.

12

Transforming or Conforming?
NGOs Training Health Promoters and the Dominant
Paradigm of the Development Industry in Bolivia

Katie S. Bristow

Since the end of World War II NGOs have played a central role in development assistance, with many taking a radical stance, challenging the dominant view (Eade, 2000; Hailey, 1999). In the 1980s and 1990s NGOs received substantial funding from national and international governmental organizations (IGOs). This, in part, was a consequence of reduced financial support from private sources during this period but also due to recognition by IGOs of the role that NGOs can play in achieving their agendas. It was argued that, through their ability to provide cost-effective welfare services and encourage citizenship, democracy and the creation of social capital, NGOs could play an important role in strengthening key components of what some term the New Policy Agenda (NPA) (Robinson, 1993; Edwards and Hulme, 1995). Midway through the present decade, the 'Golden Age' of international government funding for NGOs may be in decline as IGOs move to partnership agreements with a selected few (Agg, 2006). Whatever the case, IGOs continue to impose their agenda for international development, whether on NGOs with partnership agreements or on those striving for such agreements. Rather than challenge this agenda by implementing alternative approaches, most NGOs find themselves and their policies drawn in and subsumed to those of government funders (Edwards and Hulme, 1995; Edwards and Hulme, 2000; Pearce, 2000).

The reasons NGOs appear to have moved – consciously or unconsciously – towards a pro-market (neoliberal) and technology-orientated agenda of the IGOs are complex. This chapter argues that this move can be explained by four types of factor: ideological/philosophical, politico-economic, socio-cultural and pragmatic. These factors are, furthermore, interlocking, as illustrated in the following scenario. If an NGO's ideology leads it to refuse to align itself with the NPA, this could lead to a reduction of financial support (a political economic factor). The organization may then need to make a pragmatic decision to reduce the number of its staff, which in turn will affect the services it can offer. For example, cutting back on learning support in training for women health promoters who already lack education may compound the socio-cultural factors that have already put these rural/indigenous women at a disadvantage.

The chapter will argue that the mesh of factors are part of the conscious and unconscious strategies used by social groups, in this case relating to different health systems, to maintain, promote and defend their specific world-view, knowledge and practice. A theoretical framework will be used to explore how power to influence is made relative using Gramsci's (Gramsci, 1971) conscious hegemonic strategies together with Bourdieu's (Bourdieu, 1989) unconscious mechanisms of habitus and field.

The framework will be applied to two NGOs in Bolivia, 'CODÍGO' Bolivia and World Vision's PDA in Santivañez (Programa de Desarrollo del Area, Area Development Programme), and their training and management of community health promoters. The prevention and treatment of diarrhoeal diseases have been chosen as the foci or tracer issues for the study. Diarrhoeal diseases are one of the 5 main causes of death in children under five and as such they are included in WHO's and UNICEF's Integrated Management of Childhood Illnesses (IMCI) strategy. The reduction in the number of children who die from diarrhoeal disease is also an important intervention to address child mortality, MDG (Millennium Development Goal) four.

The NGOs CODÍGO and PDA have been chosen because they take different stances in their approaches to health and development issues. CODÍGO aims to challenge or transform the neoliberal development model that was dominant in Bolivia at the time of research, while PDA appeared to conform to this same model. To compare these two organizations, the chapter proceeds as follows. It opens with a brief description of the current development paradigm and analysis of different conceptual models of health and health care, in particular the biomedical, social and Andean models. This includes revealing how the biomedical model – using the IMCI strategy – has taken centre stage and supports broader global socio economic goals and therefore the current development paradigm. The next section will discuss the ways in which the current development paradigm subsumes and weakens approaches that might hinder its pro-market, technical orientation. From this platform, I discuss examples of the ways in which both CODÍGO and PDA are affected by the current approach to development, and the mesh of factors that influence this process. To elucidate the processes at work, the section also discusses the cases of two health promoters, Carolena and Felipe, who work with these organizations. The final section gives an explanation of the relative power of CODÍGO and PDA to influence the knowledge and practice of their health promoters.

The Current Development Paradigm

This chapter takes the position that the current socio-economic development model espoused by the International Development Community (IDC), in particular the World Bank and International Monetary Fund (IMF), is essentially neoliberal with an emphasis on science and technology. That is, despite acknowledgements of the value of other forms of development, in practice a pro-market Western scientific agenda dominates based on ideas of progress arising from the Enlightenment (Powell and Geoghegan, 2006; Bourdieu, 1998). A specific case in point is the relationship of biomedicine to other models of health.

Biomedical model of health

'Biomedicine' as a concept and in its practice has evolved along a similar path to other forms of Western knowledge (Burke, 2000). It is possible to use Hippocrates (460–360 BC), not as the start of medical practice, but certainly as a pivotal point in its history (Carr, 1997; Kiple, 1993). Biomedicine's evolutionary process has, then, taken it away from Ancient Greece, to the Middle Ages and the Middle East, before returning to Europe and the influence of the Renaissance and the Enlightenment periods in the eighteenth and nineteenth centuries.

The term 'medicine' means the 'art of healing' and is based on a wide range of natural sciences but especially biology (Wiseman, 2004). The prefixes 'bio', 'Western' or 'modern' are often added to 'medicine' to distinguish this form of medical practice from others. I prefer the term 'biomedicine' as it is no longer solely practised in Europe or the Western hemisphere, and Ayurvedic and Chinese medicine also have modern-day forms (Scrimshaw, 2006).

Indigenous medical models

Indigenous medicine refers to medical practice and concepts of health and illness relating to specific cultures and/or ethnic groups. Indigenous medicine is more commonly known as 'traditional medicine'; this is to contrast it with so called modern medicine (biomedicine). In fact all medical systems are indigenous, but some, such as biomedicine, Ayurvedic and Chinese medicine, are now practised beyond their original socio-cultural contexts (Scrimshaw, 2006).

Andean medicine is the indigenous medical system of the Aymara and Quechua people groups of the Andean Region in South America, of which highland Bolivia is a part. Like all aspects of Andean culture, health cannot be understood without understanding the cosmovision of which it is an integral part. Communal, symbolic ritual and reciprocal practices link individuals and families to the wider social organization of the community, nature and the gods (Allen, 1988). Human and animal disease, or problems with the productive capacity of the land, signify a break somewhere within this cyclical relationship and a world no longer in harmony (Quiroga, 1997; Carrizo, 1993).

Social model

The social model of health proposes that various layers of socio-economic factors and conditions affect or determine health. These determinants include affordable food, education, employment, environment, health care, housing, income, sanitation and clean water, and transport. In order to improve health, all these factors need to be addressed both with the individual and across different socio-economic policies (Povall, 2005; Whitehead, 1995).

Indeed this understanding of health is at the heart of the World Health Organization's (WHO) definition of health: 'a state of complete physical, mental and social well-being and not merely the absence of disease and infirmity' (PAHO, 2002; Povall, 2005). However, as in the way neoliberalism dominates the current development model, biomedicine overshadows this more holistic approach to health.

Biomedicine as central to the dominant development paradigm

It is possible to argue that there is a clear historical trajectory linking European culture, especially its knowledge and world-view, to current approaches to social and politico-economic development. Europe's colonial endeavours since at least the fifteenth century have been influential in defining the politico-economic and social structures of many nation-states worldwide. This influence includes a biomedical approach to the development of national health-care systems – systems that, it must be said, tended to be for the use of the colonializers rather than the indigenous population (Powell and Geoghegan, 2006; Cammack, 2002; Burke, 2000; Bergesen and Lunde, 1999; WHO, 2000). The next section explores this claim further by demonstrating how health-care initiatives, such as Integrated Management of Childhood Illnesses (IMCI), are also used to support a neoliberal approach to development.

To establish IMCI's link with neoliberalism it is necessary to go to the post-colonial era, the newly independent states' development of their health-care services and the Alma Ata Declaration in 1978 'Health for All by the Year 2000', through universal primary health care (PHC) (Morely et al., 1983).

The fledgling PHC systems initiated after the Alma Ata declaration in these new nation-states were allowed little opportunity to develop. This was because PHC implementation coincided with a period of oil crises, which led to a subsequent downturn in the global economy and large national debts incurred by most of these countries. From the 1980s onwards many countries were required by the World Bank and IMF to follow the pro-market structural adjustment programmes (SAP) and more latterly the Comprehensive Development Framework (CDF) and Poverty Reduction Strategy Papers (PRSP) to help address national debt. PRSPs were developed to provide at least some opportunity for national and international agencies to address the need for welfare services in the context of debt-reduction measures (Cornia et al., 1987; Marshall and Woodroffe, 2001).

An important consequence of these measures in the 1990s was the change in primary health care from the idea of 'health for all' as universal health coverage to what the WHO calls 'the "new universalism" – high quality delivery of essential care, defined mostly by the criterion of cost-effectiveness, for everyone, rather than all possible care for the whole population or only the simplest and most basic care for the poor' (WHO, 2000: 5). In other words, selective health care relating to the most cost-effective interventions for specific health issues or populations. IMCI is an example of this approach as it targets the five main causes of death in children under 5 – malaria, measles, respiratory infections, diarrhoea and malnutrition (WHO, 2004). Linked to these strategies was the endorsement by a UN Summit in September 2000 of the Millennium Development Goals (MDGs), a group of eight targets to be achieved by 2015 (World Bank, 2003; WHO, 2000). IMCI is seen as an important strategy for achieving MDG target four – reduction of child mortality by two-thirds by 2015 (World Bank, 2004).

The Health Nutrition and Population department of the World Bank directly links IMCI to PRSPs. The quotations and graphics below are taken from a PowerPoint presentation made by Dr Hans Troedsson, Director of Child and Adolescent Health and Development at the WHO. The presentation, addressing child mortality, was given at a World Bank consultation, called 'Monitoring HNP (Health Nutrition Population) Goals using the PRSP 'Framework'. Dr Troedsson describes the way the IMCI strategy can be employed to address MDGs relating to child mortality within the context of the PRSP framework.

The PRSP provides an opportunity to improve child health: (i) determinants and indicators in the PRSP can have a major effect on country priorities; and (ii) focusing on the implementation of a limited set of effective interventions will lead to achievement of the MDG for child mortality (Troedsson, 2001: slide 38).

To address child mortality, he argues, PRSPs will need to include health and other relevant policies to develop the capacity of the health system to respond appropriately. Such appropriate responses would include health interventions, such as good nutrition, clean water or oral rehydration solution, that reach the target population, children under 5. The IMCI strategy and its selected interventions are deemed the effective way forward for achieving a reduction in child mortality and therefore MDG target four.

To summarize the argument so far, the current paradigm of socio-economic development practised by the IDC is by and large based on neoliberal ideas, science and technology. It was also proposed that European cultures and scientific knowledge have had a significant influence on the evolution of this paradigm, especially in relation to Europe's colonial past. Biomedicine and interventions such as IMCI clearly have many of their roots in Europe and are principal components of the current development paradigm (Powell and Geoghegan, 2006; Cammack, 2002; Burke, 2000; Wiseman, 2004; McGrath, 2001). Using Gramsci and Bourdieu, this chapter will now address how actors within the international development community use conscious and unconscious strategies to maintain their dominance over others.

Conscious and Unconscious Strategies of Power and Influence

As discussed earlier, the model of development that the IDC seeks to promote is essentially neoliberal with an emphasis on science and technology. Gramsci argues that influence is not exerted through outright dominance but by the consent of the other groups to the dominant group's perspective.

> Indeed the attempt is always made to ensure that force will appear based on the consent of the majority, expressed by the so-called organs of public opinion – newspapers and associations – which, therefore, in certain situations, are artificially manipulated. (Gramsci, 1971: note 49)

The elite, in Gramsci's view, will also compromise and sacrifice if necessary and will attempt to maintain the equilibrium as long as it does not interfere with the overall direction of their cultural and economic project.

> [I]n other words, that the leading group should make sacrifices of an economic-corporate kind. But there is no doubt that such sacrifices and such a compromise cannot touch the essential. (Gramsci, 1971: 161)

The conscious use of consensus and compromise to gain support can be seen in the ways in which the Bank and IMF responded to strenuous criticism of the Structural Adjustment Programmes (SAPs) in the 1980s. These responses, as embodied in the subsequent compromise approaches of the Comprehensive Development Framework (CDF) and the Poverty Reduction Strategy Papers (PRSPs), supposedly offer a more human face of development (Cornia et al. 1987). Attention to social and human development issues, including health strategies such as the IMCI, are now components of the neoliberal project to improve the economies of low- to middle-income countries and thereby the global market (Troedsson, 2004).

Consensus and compromise can also be detected in the way that NGOs are arguably losing their radical edge in order to gain financial support and recognition from the main development players such as the World Bank and other multilateral and bilateral agencies (Edwards and Hulme, 1995). This phenomenon of consensus and compromise in the face of power has been termed 'subsumation' by some (Cammack, 2002; Kothari and Minogue, 2002). It is a process in which ostensibly alternative approaches to development, such as participation, gender and ethnodevelopment, are taken over and domesticated to suit the neoliberal model. In biomedicine this can be seen in the way consideration of local health beliefs and practice is stressed in policy documents but is rarely followed through in practice (Bristow, 2005).

The notion of subsumation has particular importance for NGOs that train community health workers, especially in multi-ethnic and socio-economically diverse societies like Bolivia. Instead of indigenous medical knowledge and practice being actively combined with Western biomedical elements of health-care provision, these local knowledges are either subsumed or ignored. Ultimately this leads to missed opportunities to improve health-care practice. For example, in relation to diarrhoea – one of the health problems treated through IMCI – the main concern is to prevent dehydration by giving oral fluids. In Andean medicine mothers bathe their children in herbs, giving only small amounts of fluid orally. It is not hard to imagine that if the value of both medical systems were acknowledged in practice as well as in policy, biomedically trained health workers might be able communicate the importance of increasing oral fluids alongside bathing in herbs (Bristow, 2005; Nichter, 1988).

Domestication (subsumation) is an aspect of a process that combines both conscious Gramscian hegemonic notions of power and influence with concomitant unconscious processes. These unconscious processes can best be explained by using Bourdieu's notions of habitus and field (Bourdieu, 1989, 1999). Habitus relates to the way the norms, actions and representations associated with a particular social group are embodied, produced and reproduced within individuals. Past experiences inform actions in the present, and, in turn, present actions anticipate without conscious effort their future outcome. In this way the character of the group is maintained and structures are reproduced. It is an 'embodied history, internalised as second nature and so forgotten' (Bourdieu, 1999: 111). It guides and directs individual behaviour while still giving choice, although limited to those decisions that might be consistent with the habitus of the social group.

> Agents shape their aspirations according to concrete indices of the accessible and the inaccessible, of what is and is not 'for us', a division as fundamental and as fundamentally recognized as that between the sacred and the profane. (Bourdieu, 1999: 117)

To explain how social groups, particularly dominant groups, reproduce themselves and maintain their influence, Bourdieu talks of primary and secondary habitus and of pedagogic action and authority. Primary habitus is the type into which a child is born, and learns though pedagogic action that has been authorised (pedagogic authority) by their family and class (or ethnic group) (May, 2001). Secondary habitus is developed, by pedagogic action, most notably, within schools but also through training in specialized areas such as health care.

Specialized training brings us to Bourdieu's other notion of 'field'. Field could be described as social space, a concept that is similar to physical space – divided up into regions, spaces within spaces, which are moulded by the taste and disposition of the dominant class or social group. Class itself is a field; so too are politics, education, art, health care, international development and ethnic groups, for example. These spaces, however, are 'constructed in such a way that the closer agents, groups or institutions which are situated within th[ese] space[s], the more common properties they have; and the more distant, the fewer' (Bourdieu, 1989: 16 col. 1).

Even within fields there will be those at the centre who will be more readily recognized by the pedagogic authority and identify more closely with each other. For instance, in the field of a UK national hospital, doctors and nurses will be near the centre and have much in common. Conversely, an acupuncturist may well be employed by the same hospital but have a lot less in common with both it and its doctors and nurses and therefore less influence.

Subsumation, therefore, can be described as the unconscious and conscious cultural processes that enable one social group to influence another, in particular where different social fields overlap.

Bolivia, Social Fields, Health Care and the NGO Sector

In order to understand how subsumation might be at work in training community health workers in Bolivia, a description of the various fields involved is necessary as they pertain to Bolivian society in general and the two case-study NGOs in particular. Bolivia, like many other Latin American countries, is in reality at least two nations in one, Andean Indian and Creole Hispanic, with distinct cultures – two coarse categories, with variation within each. Subsequently, the two have very different habitus and fields, including their health beliefs and practices. Andean Bolivia is an integrated social, physical and metaphysical whole that grows out of its history and pre-Incan past. Creole Bolivia, by and large, conforms to the ideas and practices of the neoliberal Western scientific stance that character-izes most of the development community. However, there are those who have always fallen between the two, the Mestizos. Some of these, through marriage, education or wealth, have been able to move into the Creole Bolivia, while a few have returned to their Andean roots. Yet many, the Cholos, or urban and semi-urbanized poor, are left living on the edge of both cultures with minimal opportunity to make their views known or to effect change.

Health promoters who are associated with CODÍGO and PDA tend to be spread along an Andean/Cholo continuum depending on their proximity to the city. Two such promoters are, Felipe who is nearer to the Cholo end and Carolena the Andean end.

Felipe and Carolena

Felipe is a voluntary health promoter with PDA but received his training from CODÍGO. He is 18 and lives with his mother, grandmother and younger brother in Kuturipa, a rural community located a good ninety-minute steep walk from the road and then a forty-minute bus journey to either Cochabamba or the subdistrict capital Santivañez. Family members describe themselves as subsistence farmers and pastoralists. Though they have electricity, they have no running water; and their land is very arid. The nearest potable water is an arduous forty-minute walk away.

Felipe left school after six years of primary education, but CODÍGO inspired him to return and he has subsequently started at a *SEMA* (second-ary school for adults), which he attends once a week. As it takes him half a day to walk there, he usually stays overnight.

Carolena was sent by another organization, INDICEP (Instituto de Investigación para Educación Popular, Research Institute for Popular Education), to be trained by CODÍGO. She is 20, unmarried and a goatherd on her parents' smallholding in Tapacari, the high valleys of Cochabamba. Their home is a two-hour hilly walk to the nearest small town (the district subsection of Waca Playa). If a member of the family wants to get to Cochabamba he or she has to wait for a Saturday or Monday to make the three-hour lorry or bus journey. During the dry season they can go by a different route through another small town, from which lorries leave every day. However, during the rainy seasons the paths to this town are treacherous.

Carolena is the eldest of nine children, with three sisters and five brothers. She and her sister Maria left school before completing the primary level, as will the two younger girls. The boys, on the other hand, are expected to complete and graduate from high school.

I have placed Carolena and Felipe at different positions on the Andean/ Cholo continuum even though both live in rural areas. Felipe's primary habitus arises out of a greater mixture of fields than Carolena, because living nearer to urban areas he and his family are influenced by both rural and urban social fields. This does not necessarily give him an advantage when it comes to being able to work effectively as a health promoter. To understand this we need to look at the organizations providing the opportunities to become promoters, CODÍGO and PDA.

CODÍGO and PDA

CODÍGO and PDA are both NGOs working in community health and involved in training health promoters; however, there are some clear differences, especially in their relationships to the current development paradigm. A brief description of each organization and in particular how each approaches community health will demonstrate how CODÍGO aims to challenge or transform the current view of development while PDA appears to be conforming with it. The description also demonstrates that, despite CODÍGO's radical edge, in practice it, like PDA, also conforms.

CODÍGO Bolivia

CODÍGO Bolivia is one of the country programmes of CODÍGO International, a church-based and health-related NGO based in the United States. The work in Cochabamba Bolivia was begun in the late 1980s by a Colombian couple, Dr Juan Carlos De Pedro and Mgr Roxana Velasquez. Initially, they had expected to be developing a community-health programme that largely followed the standard biomedical model recommended by WHO after Alma Ata. Once acquainted with the specific Bolivian context of ethnic diversity, inequity coupled with paternalism, and poverty, they concluded that a new approach was needed. In 1992, inspired by the work of the Brazilian radical educationalist Paulo Freire, they moved to Chirimoyo, a semi-urban community on the outskirts of Cochabamba. Using Freire's theories of 'conscientization' and 'praxis', CODÍGO Bolivia's approach is one that aims to transform people from passive objects of somebody else's world into active subjects contributing to their own individual and collective livelihoods (Gramsci, 1971).

In conjunction with their Frierean ethos they have also developed a very clear approach to health care that they call 'integrated health', based on the social model of health (Whitehead, 1995). Health is regarded as part of the wider socio-cultural, politico-economic context at all levels of society – local, national and international. CODÍGO describes its approach as a 'systemic ecological healthgenic' model. This concept is intended to emphasize healthy people rather than disease, and to be participatory, democratic and sustainable. Within this, they attempt to address a range of interrelated issues: basic health care and prevention, including the use of traditional and local medicines as well as Western biomedicine; income generation; organic agriculture; protection of the environment; human rights and community law (De Pedro and Velasquez, 1992).

Implicit in this concept of health is the expectation that the health promoters will have an integrated knowledge where they are confident and conversant in both their own local health knowledge and practice and in biomedicine. Through this approach CODÍGO also hopes to distance itself from Bolivia's national health service and other NGOs. At worst, according to CODÍGO, the approaches of other NGOs and the public health system are reductive, 'hospital-based pathogenic biomedical' models, focusing on the signs and symptoms of disease and not on people. Or, at best, they are 'community-based pathogenic biological' models that, while they address the social setting of health, are still biomedical and disease-focused (De Pedro and Velasquez, 1992).

CODÍGO makes a clear distinction between its understanding of the term 'integrated' and the way it is used in IMCI programmes. It means health as an integrated part of individual and communal life, while in IMCI health is regarded precisely as what it says: 'integrated management of illnesses related to children' – for example, diarrhoea and pneumonia – may be secondary problems in cases of measles. CODÍGO's health-care and training programmes do cover some of the aspects found in IMCI, such as the management of diarrhoeal diseases, but as part of their overall work. The organization has resisted getting involved with IMCI initiatives with the SEDES (local health authority) in Cochabamba. They also wrote to CODÍGO International stating their opposition to the organization's intention to obtain funding from IMCI programmes. This instance highlights another area of tension for CODÍGO Bolivia. Funding, and therefore survival, is increasingly tied to the very initiatives or approaches, such as IMCI, to which CODÍGO Bolivia is opposed.

PDA Santivañez

PDA Santivañez is involved in a range of community development projects in the subdistrict of Santivañez. It is one of six such organizations established in Cochabamba by the large international Christian NGO, World Vision. The long-term aim is that eventually the PDAs will be financially independent from World Vision, but at the time of the field research they were all fully funded by it (pers. communication, director of World Vision in Cochabamba).

The main areas of PDA's work are maternal and child health, food security and nutrition, Christian pastoral support and child sponsorship on behalf of World Vision. At one time all the PDAs in Cochabamba sent their health promoters for training with CODÍGO. In 2003 PDA Santivañez was the only one; the rest stopped after the initial training because they felt uncomfortable with CODÍGO's ecumenical stance. They prefer to work with organizations that are more clearly evangelical (pers. comm., director of PDA's work in Viloma and CODÍGO staff).

Normally, the Santivañez PDA will send people for training to CODÍGO who have been selected by their local *sindicato* (community organization). Having completed their initial training they then have to work voluntarily for the PDA, running health promotion talks with either a group of children or women once every two weeks. They are also expected to complete their CODÍGO training and attend monthly training meetings at the PDA office in Santivañez (pers. comm., PDA doctor).

My experience of the PDA in Santivañez and interviews with the director of World Vision in Cochabamba led me to believe that their approach to community development and health care followed the standard approach used within the development community more generally. For instance, they use the monthly training meetings to reinforce a very standard biomedical approach to diarrhoeal disease and nutrition. The PDA doctor is involved in the local health authority initiative to implement the IMCI programme at a community level. Finally, PDA's sponsor, World Vision, is a large, well-established, international NGO which receives funding from USAID and other bilateral and multilateral agencies (World Vision, 2005). The director in Cochabamba made a clear statement of the type of health care World Vision practises.

> Health, we say more, let's see ... clinical ... no? scientific, yes! And ... we are aware of how we might be able to talk about traditional medicine ... maybe to know *curanderos* [the Spanish name commonly used for traditional medical practitioners] also. I say maybe, because we have not yet taken, we have not fully reviewed, reflected on this. (interview with director of World Vision in Cochabamba)

To summarize, CODÍGO aims to be a NGO that transforms. This can be seen through its commitment to a Freirean ethos, its integrated approach to health rather than disease, and the way it has distanced itself from strategies such as IMCI. Alternatively, PDA appears to be an NGO that conforms. Through its financial dependence on World Vision it is directly linked to the wider international development community and a Western biomedical approach to health. It has adopted the IMCI strategy and subsumed notions of socio-culturally appropriate practices.

Theoretical Aims and Actual Practice

Having identified some of the differences between the two organizations, further distinctions need to be made between the theoretical aims of the organizations and what occurs in practice. This is particularly marked for CODÍGO, because in practice it conforms to the current development paradigm despite its claims to the contrary. This can be demonstrated in how health promoters trained by CODÍGO, instead of integrating their different forms of health knowledge, still keep them separated. Because PDA's approach is consistent with a biomedical approach, the differences between its theory and practice have different implications.

Separation of different forms of health knowledge by CODÍGO-trained health promoters

Focus group work conducted early on in my field research proved to be significant. Focus groups were carried out with some of CODÍGO's promoters taking their second-level course. The discussion involved the promoters answering the following question:

> Where or from whom have you heard information or learned about ARIs (Acute Respiratory Infections) or ADDs (Acute Diarrhoeal Diseases) before coming to CODÍGO?

I made sure that I used words that CODÍGO uses in their training manuals and that are therefore familiar to the promoters. Their reply, which I noted down in my diary, was that they had never heard of ARIs or ADDs before coming to CODÍGO. After some discussion and clarifications in Quechua (the most widely spoken Andean language), the promoters did start to talk about the traditional illnesses such as 'Sipi Chupasqa'. I was somewhat surprised by this response, as, in line with CODÍGO's stated approach, I was expecting the promoters to talk with ease and respect about their local knowledge. In fact, what I seemed to be seeing was a separation or compartmentalizing of what they knew. This was confirmed later by observing training sessions, interviews, visits to health promoters and their families, as well as by responses to the questionnaire I designed. For instance, Carolena was involved in the group research but I found out later that she frequently diagnosed and treated family members using her local knowledge.

> Her young brother had bad diarrhoea last year and they went to the *posta* [local state clinic]. He was given *suero* (ORS) but it didn't help. Instead they used local plants that everyone here knows about. Also *pepa de palta* (avocado stone). (research diary, 11 August 2003)

Felipe admitted to having very little local health knowledge but eventually acknowledged that his mother Angela had considerable knowledge, which she had learnt from her grandmother.

> *Katie* Did she learn from someone in her community or from her grandmother?
>
> *Interpreter* Yes, her grandmother. Her grandmother treated everything, including a baby or child with constipation. She put a little bit of matchstick in and they would start.
>
> *Katie* Where did her grandmother learn this information, here or did she go and train somewhere else?
>
> *Interpreter* Her grandmother has always known and she does not know from where. But she [Angela] learned from her grandmother. Her grandmother was always teaching her; she'd say, 'When I die you are going to do the treating!'(interview with Felipe's mother, Angela)

Four categories of interlocking factors

Health promoters on the Andean/Cholo continuum fall within a range that either, like Carolena, have both Andean and biomedical knowledge but do not use them together, or are more like Felipe, who has access to his mother's local knowledge but is reluctant to acknowledge its importance. In both cases the two forms of knowledge are not integrated despite the theoretical aims of the health workers' training institutions.

This is because the four types of interlocking factor – ideological/philosophical, politico-economic, socio-cultural and pragmatic – make the power of a field's pedagogic authority relative in relation to other fields that might be competing with it. Put a different way, CODÍGO's power to influence its promoters is affected by both the interlocking factors and the strength of the other fields the promoters encounter -Andean, Creole/state and other NGOs like PDA.

Philosophical/ideological

In the initial CODÍGO training course there are two modules that could be linked together to emphasize its ideological approach to integrated health: 'Process of Health and Illness' and 'Management of Common Illnesses'. The former involves the promoters' previous knowledge and the biological, socio-cultural determinants of health and illness, while the latter addresses the prevention and treatment of diseases, such as diarrhoea. Yet in practice they are given as two very separate courses, with the 'Managing Common Illnesses' module run along clear biomedical lines. This, I believe, is because an integrated approach is not consistent with some of the staff's evangelical beliefs and their previous biomedical training. The clinic doctor, who ran the 'Managing Common Illnesses', was also an evangelical lay preacher. When he left, the module was not changed.

A further example is that while PDA sends its promoters for training with CODÍGO, it has endorsed the IMCI strategy. This can only compound the unintentional biomedical emphasis of the training that the promoters, such as Felipe, receive.

Politico-economic

Many NGOs secure funding through aligning themselves with current international and national strategies, such as IMCI. CODÍGO will not do this and therefore lacks the level of financial support enjoyed by other organizations, such as PDA. CODÍGO also excludes itself from different arenas that reduce its opportunity to influence the dominant model. For instance, by not working with the Cochabamba SEDES (local health authority) on their IMCI implementation strategy it is unable to exercise any influence over this strategy.

Socio-cultural factors – Age and gender are important factors in determining whether people who have undergone training with CODÍGO are recognized as health promoters by their communities. For example, Carolena, despite her training with CODÍGO, was not chosen by her community to work as the health promoter to organize the three-monthly visits by the nurse from the local state clinic. Instead a male with no previous training was chosen and Carolena was asked to assist him. Neither was Felipe officially recognized by his community, even though he was selected by PDA for training. This was because there were two other older male promoters present in the community.

Educational approach and achievement also have socio-cultural relevance. CODÍGO interprets gender-sensitive and inclusive learning to mean mixed-ability groups and the use of Spanish to improve competency in the lingua franca. The consequences appear to be that men, better-educated women and first-language Spanish speakers dominate group work and plenary sessions that put others, especially rural women such as Carolena, at a disadvantage. This observation leads us to our final category: CODÍGO has made a pragmatic decision that it did not have the resources to give sufficient support to these women.

Pragmatic

Alongside insufficient resources to address the mixed educational and linguistic needs of the promoters, CODÍGO also has very limited capacity to provide practical experiences, assess learning and make home visits for follow-up. The consequence of this is that they cannot reinforce learning or assess what knowledge their promoters actually use in their communities.

The promoters also have to make pragmatic decisions not to attend CODÍGO training courses because of planting or harvest seasons or special occasions such as Todos Santos (All Saints Day). They may also be prevented from attending because of the frequent strikes and road blocks associated with the ongoing political and social unrest in the country or simply because the rains have made the roads impassable. During my year in Chirimoyo, five courses were cancelled because there were insufficient promoters.

The four categories of factor affecting the promoters' use of health knowledge interlock with each other. For instance, CODÍGO's ideological stance leads to the political economic consequence of reduced financial support. This in turn leads to CODÍGO making pragmatic decisions that have led to lack of support to the minimally educated non-Spanish-speaking part of the population where they work. This then compounds the socio-cultural relationships that can put rural/indigenous women at a disadvantage.

Figure 12.1   Diagrammatic representation of relationships between fields

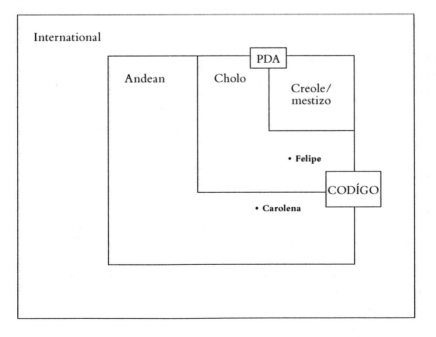

The four categories therefore work against CODÍGO being able to produce in the health promoters it trains a secondary habitus that is stronger and more enduring than both their primary habitus and that of the Creole state system. Bourdieu talks in terms of positions within fields (Bourdieu, 1989); the closer an individual is identified with a particular group, the more their personal habitus will reflect the dominant habitus of that group. Unlike CODÍGO's health promoters, Bourdieu's schooling was sufficiently long and effective that the primary habitus instilled in him by his poor rural parents was replaced by an enduring secondary habitus of the French intellectual elite (Webb et al., 2002).

Figure 12.1 is a diagrammatic representation of the relationships between the habitus and fields of the various social groups involved in the research as expressed through their different forms of health (medical) knowledge and practice. The outer box represents the international sphere from the perspective of the multinational and bilateral development agencies relating to Western biomedical knowledge and practice within the IDC. The next box represents the health (medical) knowledges and practices of Bolivia and within it separates the Andean and Creole representations (fields). The Cholos (urban poor) straddle both fields with their health knowledge and practice being a mixture of the two main forms. CODÍGO and PDA are also represented. Figure 12.1 uses different shading to represent the various fields and the extent to which an individual's or an institution's habitus is influenced by their proximity to and or overlap with another field. Carolena is positioned clearly in the Andean field marking her health knowledge and practice from this field. The Creole state health system's (Bolivia's national health system), despite being in the Bolivian box, is clearly continuous with the international biomedical field. Felipe is positioned in the indeterminate Cholo field that overlaps both the Andean and Creole. CODÍGO and PDA as institutions are positioned overlapping the other fields to represent the idea that the four categories of factors make their fields weak in much the same way as the Cholo field.

In the context of their roles as health promoters, Carolena and Felipe encounter at least three or four fields: Andean, Creole, CODÍGO and PDA. For example, Carolena's primary habitus is Andean, yet she comes into contact with both the Creole field through her assisting the male health promoter and nurse from the local clinic, and CODÍGO's field through her participation in its training courses.

CODÍGO's power to influence is relative while the promoters are doing its courses, but in the final instance it is not able to produce durable or consistent changes in the habitus of these promoters. It is affected not only by the constraints of the four interlocking types of factor but also by the conscious and unconscious cultural influences of the Andean and

Creole fields. When promoters, like Carolena, leave CODÍGO and return home, the Andean field re-exerts its more powerful influence. In these circumstances CODÍGO is not able to support its promoters to integrate Andean knowledge with biomedicine. Instead, the promoters' knowledge is separated into different realms, with different forms of knowledge being used at different times. Ultimately this leads to less efficient health care practices and demonstrates the limitations of CODÍGO's ability to challenge the dominant system.

Separation of forms of health knowledge by PDA and Creole/state-trained health workers

The processes that affect the treatment of non-biomedical knowledge by fields that conform to the current development paradigm differ from those of CODÍGO. Although the IDC, including PDA and the Creole/state health system, acknowledge that non-biomedical knowledge and practice are important, they are adapted and subsumed into a biomedical framework. The presence of the four categories of interlocking factors works to the advantage of the hegemonic processes of consensus and compromise because they help to keep both CODÍGO's field and the general Andean field relatively weak – as such they do not have any influence outside of their own immediate contexts. This has the effect of ensuring that the cultural hegemony of the IDC is maintained.

Nevertheless the power of the dominant paradigm to reproduce its habitus is also made relative due to the presence of the interlocking factors, although to a lesser extent than for CODÍGO. The Creole state-run clinic may exert a powerful influence on rural promoters like Carolena when they are in contact, such as during the three-monthly community visit. Yet the influence of the clinic is too infrequent and short for it to change her enduring Andean habitus. The field and habitus of Felipe are mixed, because he has had more contact with mestizo Creole life through his proximity to urban areas and through PDA. Unless he moves into one or other of the main Andean or Creole fields via, for example, marriage or education he is likely to remain in an indeterminate Cholo field. Neither he nor others will then be able to benefit from his mother's considerable local knowledge.

In conclusion, this chapter has argued that the power of different fields to reproduce their particular habitus, is compromised by the existence of four categories of interlocking factors, which I have outlined. This is so both for NGOs that aim to challenge the dominant biomedical approaches as well as for those who conform to it. Yet, in the final instance, these interlocking factors have the effect of strengthening the hegemonic processes of consensus and compromise that has the ultimate effect of maintaining the current dominance of neoliberal culture. This process comes at a price as it seems to limit the effectiveness of programmes like IMCI that are central to the success of the MDGs and part of the overall approach to poverty reduction strategies (PRSPs). This is because, other approaches, such as Andean beliefs and practices are subsumed, with the result that although they may be acknowledged in theory they are not in practice. Opportunities for constructive engagement between the Andean and biomedical systems that might lead to improved health care are missed.

References

Agg, C. (ed.) (2006) *Trends in Government Support for Non-Governmental Organizations – is the 'Golden Age' of the NGO Behind Us?*, U.-C.S.a.S.M. Programme, UNRISD.

Allen, C.J. (1988) *The Hold Life Has: Coca and Cultural Identity in an Andean Community*, Smithsonian Institution, Washington DC.

Bastien, J.W. (1987) *Healers of the Andes: Kallawaya Herbalist and Their Medicinal Plants*, University of Utah Press, Salt Lake City.

Bergesen, H.O., and L. Lunde (1999) *Dinosaurs or Dynamos? The United Nations and The World Bank at the Turn of the Century*, Earthscan, London.

Bourdieu, P. (1989) 'Social Space and Symbolic Power', *Sociological Theory* 7(1): 14–25.

Bourdieu, P. (1998) 'Utopia of Endless Exploitation: The Essence of Neoliberalism', *Le Monde Diplomatique*, December.

Bourdieu, P. (1999) 'Structures, Habitus, Practices', in A. Elliot (ed.), *Contemporary Social Theory*, Blackwell, Oxford.

Bourdieu, P., and J.C. Passeron (1990) *Reproduction in Education, Society and Culture*, Sage, London.

Bristow, K.S. (2005) 'Integration, Separation or Subsumation? How Community Health Workers in Bolivia use their Knowledge', Ph.D. thesis, Faculty of Education, University of Manchester.

Burke, P. (2000) *A Social History of Knowledge: From Gutenberg to Diderot*, Polity Press, Cambridge.

Cammack, P. (2002) 'Neoliberalism, the World Bank, and the New Politics of Development', in U. Kothari and M. Minogue (eds), *Development Theory and Practice*, Palgrave Macmillan, London.

Carr, I. (1997) *The Far Beginnings: A Brief History of Medicine*, www.umanitoba.ca/faculties/medicine/history/histories/briefhis.html (accessed 2 October 2004).

Carrizo, E.V. (1993) *Autopsia de La Enfermedad – La Automedicacion y El Itinerario Terapeutico en El Sistema de Salud de Vallegrande – Bolivia*, AIS, La Paz.

Cornia, G.A., R. Jolly and F. Stewart (eds) (1987), *Adjustment with a Human Face: Protecting the Vulnerable and Promoting Growth*, Clarendon Press, Oxford.

Cowen, M., and R. Shenton (1996) *Doctrines of Development*, Routledge, London.

De Pedro, J.C., and R. Velasquez (1992) *Comprehensive Health: Exploring a New Model for Health Work*, CODÍGO International, Bolivia.

Eade, D. (ed.) (2000) *Development, NGOs, and Civil Society*, Development in Practice Readers, Oxfam GB, Oxford.

Edwards, M., and D. Hulme (1995) 'NGO Performance and Accountability: Introduction and Overview', in M. Edwards and D. Hulme (eds), *Non-Governmental Organizations:*

Performance and Accountability Beyond the Magic Bullet, Earthscan and Save the Children, London.

Edwards, M., and D. Hulme (2000) 'Scaling up NGO Impact on Development: Learning from Experience', in D. Eade (ed.), *Development NGOs and Civil Society*, Oxfam GB, Oxford.

Gramsci, A. (1971) *Selections from the Prison Notebooks of Antonio Gramsci*, ed. Q. Hoare and G.N. Smith, Lawrence & Wishart, London.

Hailey, J. (1999) 'Ladybirds, Missionaries and NGOs. Voluntary Organizations and Co-operatives in 50 Years of Development: A Historical Perspective on Future Challenges', *Public Administration and Development*, 19(5): 467–86.

Kiple, K.F. (ed.) (1993) *The Cambridge World History of Human Disease*, Cambridge University Press, Cambridge.

Kothari, U., and M. Minogue (2002) 'Critical Perspectives in Development: An Introduction', in U. Kothari and M. Minogue (eds), *Development Theory and Practice*, Palgrave, London.

Marshall, A., and J. Woodroffe (2001) *Policies to Roll Back the State and Privatise? Poverty Reduction Strategy Papers Investigated*, World Development Movement, London.

May, S. (2001) *Language and Minority Rights: Ethnicity, Nationalism and the Politics of Language*, Longman, London.

McGrath, S. (2001) 'Knowledge for Development – The Case of the Department for International Development', in UKFIET, Oxford International Conference on Education and Development, Oxford.

Morely, D., J. Rohde and G. Williams (eds) (1983) *Practising Health for All*, Oxford Medical Publications, Oxford.

Nichter, M. (1988) 'From Aralu to ORS: Singhalese Perceptions of Digestion, Diarrhea, and Dehydration', *Social Science and Medicine* 27: 39–52.

PAHO (2002) *Basic Documents*, Official Document 308, 16th edition, PAHO.

Pearce, J. (2000) 'Development, NGOs, and Civil Society: The Debate and Its Future', in D. Eade (ed.), *Development, NGOs, and Civil Society*, Oxfam GB, Oxford.

Povall, S.L. (2005) 'The Merseyside Health Action Zone: A Case Study in the Implementation of an Area-based Public Health Policy', Ph.D. thesis, School of Sociology and Social Policy, University of Liverpool.

Powell, F., and M. Geoghegan (2006) 'Beyond Political Zoology: Community Development, Civil Society and Strong Democracy', *Community Development Journal*, 41(2): 128–42.

Quiroga, I.C. (1997) *Abril es Tiempo de Kharisiris – Campesinos y Medicos en Comunidades Andino-Quechuas*, ASONGS, PCI, MAP International, PROSANA, SITUMSS, Cochabamba.

Regalsky, P. (ed.) (1993) *Los Jampiris de Raqaypampa*, CENDA, Cochabamba.

Robinson, M. (1993) 'Governance, Democracy and Conditionality: NGOs and the New Policy Agenda', in A. Clayton (ed.), *Governance, Democracy and Conditionality: What Role for NGOs?*, INTRAC, Oxford.

Scrimshaw, S.C. (2006) 'Culture, Behaviour and Health', in M.H. Merson, R.E. Black, and A.J. Mills (eds), *International Public Health: Diseases, Programs, Systems and Policies*, Jones & Bartlett, London.

Troedsson, H. (2001) *Consultation on Monitoring HNP Goals Using the PRSP Framework* [cited June 2004] World Bank http://wbln0018.worldbank.org/HDNet/hddocs.nsf/c840b59b6982d2498525670c004def60/9b8389c97eafeaa885256b17005921d6/$FILE/Troedsson.ppt.

Vargas, T.E. (2001) *Sit'uwa (2001) – Purificacion y Vida Armonica en Pacha Contemporanea*, ASONGS and PROPINA, Cochabamba.

Webb, J., T. Schirato and G. Danaher (2002) *Understanding Bourdieu*, Sage, London.

Whitehead, M. (1995) 'Tackling Inequalities: A Review of Policy Initiatives', in M. Benzeval, K. Judge and M. Whitehead (eds), *Tackling Inequalities in Health: An Agenda for Action*, King's Fund, London.

WHO (2000) 'The World Health Report (2000) – Health Systems: Improving Performance', www.who.int/whr/2000/en/ (accessed 2 October 2004).

WHO (2001) 'IMCI a Joint WHO/UNICEF Initiative', www.who.int/child-adolescent-health/New_Publications/IMCI/imci.htm (accessed 4 October 2004).

Wiseman, (2004) 'Designations of Medicines', *Evidence-based Complementary and Alternative Medicine* 1(3): 327–9.

World Bank (2002) 'Child Health at a Glance', www1.worldbank.org/hnp/ (accessed 10 June 2004).

World Bank (2003) 'Development Goals', www.developmentgoals.org/ (accessed 23 September 2003).

World Vision (2005) 'World Vision', www.worldvision.org (accessed 4 February 2005).

13

Political Entrepreneurs or Development Agents: An NGO's Tale of Resistance and Acquiescence in Madhya Pradesh, India

Vasudha Chhotray

NGOs the world over have been regarded positively for their capacities both as 'political entrepreneurs' and as 'development agents', but there is growing cynicism in their abilities to combine these two roles.[1] As political entrepreneurs, NGOs have been known to act as catalysts of radical and transformative social change, through their association with grassroots struggle in various forms. As development agents, NGOs have increasingly become key partners of both governments and donor agencies in implementing development programmes. The definitive mainstreaming of NGOs within international development during the last two decades has entailed growing pressures on NGOs, many of which may have started out as small and informal cadre-based organizations, to compete for development funds, formalize their organizational structures and 'scale up' their work. All this seems to have compromised the inclination and ability of NGOs devoted to development to engage in acts that are radically transformative.

Such cynicism afflicts development in general, perceived as an activity or set of relations that is divorced of 'politics'. Here, politics is understood in terms of radical and transformative change or 'the discourse and struggle over the organization of human possibilities' (Held 1984: 1). In this chapter, I will refer to this meaning as politics with a big P to distinguish it from the entire range of politics with a small p, from arbitrary interest-seeking to organized electoral party politics, all of which regularly mediate development. While it would be hard to argue that development is devoid of 'small p' politics, it has increasingly been distanced from 'big P' politics: with the result that development has been cynically viewed as contrary to social transformation and preserving of the status quo instead. It is this cynicism that explains why NGOs are viewed as ineffective agents of alternatives in development. This is one side of the story. The other side points to the continuous attempts made by the development machinery (including states and other institutions of international development cooperation) to present development as a technocratic process that does not involve politics, a phenomenon that has been referred to as depoliticization (Ferguson, 1990; Harriss, 2001; Kamat, 2002). And yet discussions of 'depoliticization' have systematically refrained from specifying which meaning of politics is being referred to in this ostensible depoliticization project.

I would argue that it is necessary, perhaps imperative, to do so for two reasons. First of all, the depoliticization discourse is a discourse of denial for projecting development to be free of 'small p' politics even in the face of overwhelming, everyday, indeed public knowledge to the contrary. For example, which junior government official or contractor, responsible for implementing a rural development project in India, can credibly claim that locally powerful interests do not join hands with local project officials to influence project resources? Second, however, and more seriously, the de-politicization of development discourse is impoverished by its limitedness, for it shuns 'big P' politics. So when a social movement like the Narmada Bachao Andolan (NBA) launches into a prolonged protest against the construction of a major hydroelectric dam, it is regarded (by the 'pro-development' camp) to be 'anti-development'. In the same vein, some NGOs in India that might have confronted the state on contentious issues to do with bringing about social transformation have had to face difficult consequences. In this process, what is often forgotten is that development agencies – both from the government and from NGOs – regularly encounter politics, in its 'big P' and 'small p' forms.

It is this entanglement that forms the context for my story: of an NGO working among tribals in the central Indian state of Madhya Pradesh. But before I can proceed, some key points need to be made by way of setting out the context. All have to do with rejecting different types of binaries that have come to dominate development debates, none of which is particularly helpful in appreciating the potential of NGOs in development. The first is drawn between the state and civil society, with NGOs being regarded as shorthand for civil society. Donors are especially guilty of this because identifying NGOs as symbolic civil society actors presents manifold opportunities for them to set up development project funding in support of their objectives, say democratization or participatory development (Igoe, 2003). However, NGOs are 'neither synonymous' nor 'entirely congruent with civil society' and their place within the latter must be treated 'carefully', 'historically' and 'relationally' (Bebbington and Hickey, 2006). Moreover, a simple state–civil society dichotomy actually disregards the profound interrelationships between the two especially in the developing world (Kaviraj and Khilnani, 2001). Viewed from a Gramscian perspective, it becomes possible to appreciate that the state and civil society share a dialectical relationship, where the civil society can serve both to reinforce hegemony and to foster counter-hegemonic struggle (Gramsci, 1971).

The second binary that I will not use is between 'mainstream' and 'alternative' development, mainly because it is no longer clear what exactly these terms refer to (Pieterse, 1998). Besides, upon problematizing the idea of 'alternative' development, it becomes evident that NGOs are often accused of not promoting alternatives to 'big D development' or imminent and intentional development that requires clear and concrete interventions (Cowen and Shenton, 1996; Introduction, this volume). However, not enough attention is paid to the attempts by some NGOs to provide alternatives to 'little d development' or immanent development that refers to the social, economic and political processes underlying capitalist development. The third binary I will discard concerns power as a zero-sum process where the dominant act continually to oppress the subordinate and the latter are understood as victims in unidimensional terms. Anthropological research, notably by Scott (1985, 1990) and many others subsequently, has revealed the complicated interface between domination and resistance that characterizes all social interactions (see Masaki, 2004).

And through the course of this chapter, I will reject yet another binary – that drawn between the roles of NGOs as political entrepreneurs and as development agents – for it seriously limits consideration of their potential. NGOs are uniquely positioned in the interface between governments at different levels (both elected representatives and bureaucrats), local communities and foreign donors. Using case study evidence, I will argue that NGOs that seek to be effective in meeting their development objectives need not, indeed cannot, be *either* political entrepreneurs *or* development agents. I will show how, over an entire decade, one central Indian NGO has been able to combine development work regarded as legitimate by the state with practices resisting state action in development in general. In the process, it will demonstrate how and why the 'depoliticization' of development is not always a successful state project with predictable consequences. The chapter will reveal that the NGO's seemingly dual stance was itself unreal, as resistance and acquiescence were interwoven with one another in subtle ways. It will focus on key factors – of composition, location, legislation, organizational interrelationships and politics – all of which contributed to this NGO's local power and effectiveness. It will conclude with general implications concerning the nature of, and also limits to, NGO power. My evidence here derives from qualitative research undertaken during a two-month stay with the NGO in 2000, involving interviews with a broad range of stakeholders and local documentary sources. Proxy names are used to protect anonymity.

The Making of an NGO

The proliferation and composition of the 'NGO universe' in India has been competently described elsewhere (Sen, 1999; Kamat, 2002). By and large, NGO activity in development and relief work has been received favourably by the state, and indeed explicitly encouraged. But, simultaneously, NGOs that have adopted a politically confrontational stand against state policies, institutions or actors have typically been disassociated from the state's development agenda, and occasionally repressed. The Seventh Plan document of the Government of India even defined NGOs as 'politically neutral development organizations that would help the government in its rural development programmes' (cited in Sen, 1999: 342).

The organization that forms the subject of my study started its association with Bagli *tehsil* (block) in Dewas district in south-west Madhya Pradesh in 1992. Dewas is a dryland district and contains striking regional disparities between its plateau (*ghaat-upar*) and valley (*ghaat-neeche*) portions as divided by the Narmada river. Non-tribal upper castes in the relatively fertile and irrigated plateau portions dominate the district's politics and political economy. The valley areas, however, have been marked by decades of resource degradation and political marginalization (Shah et al 1998). Large tribal pockets comprising the Bhil and Bhilala tribes are interspersed with an exploitative non-tribal majority. The roots of this enduring conflict lie in the post-independence settlement process, when the Forest Department took over administration of forest areas, thus dispossessing tribals of their lands. While most tribals in Bagli's 100–village belt were compensated with small plots, these lands are largely dry and of poor quality. Poor tribals practise a combination of rainfed agriculture, wage labour and an annual routine of tortuous migration to the plateau areas during the long, dry summer.

The choice of Bagli as an area of work by our NGO was a considered one. None of the organization's eight founding members had resided or worked in this *tehsil*, or anywhere in Dewas district, prior to their arrival in 1992. They were a group of friends who had met at the Jawaharlal Nehru University in Delhi, known for its left-oriented political thinking. All group members are from 'high castes', most come from middle-class families and a few from more affluent backgrounds with important political connections. They are educated and English-speaking, while conversant in Hindi, the main regional language. Nearly all had fulltime academic careers before they decided to start work that allowed them to engage more directly in pursuit of their beliefs. The social backgrounds of group members would prove to be consequential in the course of their interactions with the local people of Bagli, as with government functionaries at senior levels.

The group sought to work in Bagli because it represented long periods of political and economic marginalization, which had in turn produced official disinterest in the region and, simultaneously, the marked absence of popular mobilization. Group members wanted to build a 'peoples' organization' that would engage in grassroots work and advocacy. The formation, thus, of a 'critical mass within policy making, so that marginalized tribal areas would get the benefit of increased state intervention and public investment' was central to the stated discourse of the group, and of the organization it eventually formed. It specifically wanted to promote local natural resource management, which it believed would offer a lasting solution to chronic resource poverty. Its overarching aim would be to increase local awareness of the laws of the state and constitutionally prescribed rights. In terms of ideology, the group professed an explicit belief in development, and, equally importantly, in the state as the principal guarantor of rights. This belief was certainly in 'big D' development, in concrete interventions, but importantly also in 'little d' development, given its understanding and recognition of underlying or immanent processes of development (see Introduction). Theirs was an ideology of 'positive engagement', with the state, its policies, institutions and actors – one prominent member denounced anti-state activism as easier than 'serious development work'. Not entirely aware of what was to follow, the group registered itself as an NGO, and set up a makeshift office in Bagli town, using the personal savings of its members. The NGO was called Samaj Pragati Sahyog (in Hindi, 'Support for Social Progress'), henceforth referred to as SPS.

Acquaintance with Neelpura Village:
Setting Up Home Base

Local curiosity about the newly formed SPS only increased when group members attempted to acquaint themselves with Bagli and the *ghaat-neeche* (valley) villages. Group members recounted how local officials and politicians based in Bagli, a small market town, were distinctly unfriendly. According to the group, they were most perplexed because SPS, unlike other NGOs in the district, was not there to implement any particular development project. The lack of a clearly spelt out role also aroused incomprehension on the part of villagers during SPS's initial forays, on motorcycles, into the *ghaat-neeche* village belt. Soon enough, group members decided to concentrate their attention on one small village, conveniently located close to the main road, and comprising almost entirely of the Bhilala and Korku tribes, a village called Neelpura. This decision may have been motivated by convenience at the time, but quickly became vital to the identity of SPS in the region, and initially, to its very survival. The socio–economic characteristics of Neelpura closely matched SPS's idea of a 'base village'. It is almost uniformly poor, with most tribals owning lands between 1 and 3 acres in size and dry. A handful of farmers own more than 6 acres and only three out of the hundred-odd households in the village are presently landless. This relatively egalitarian pattern of land ownership follows from government distribution of similar land plots to the new migrants, nearly a century ago. Neelpura is also relatively homogenous socially, since caste-based social polarization is conspicuously missing in this predominantly tribal village.

SPS's quest for local contacts within Neelpura to facilitate initial dialogues soon revealed the nature of power relationships in this seemingly unstrati-fied village. Mahbub Khan, a Muslim landowner with more than 30 acres of land, was economically dominant, his social clout evident in his near exclusive engagement of hired labour and cultivation of a second irrigated crop. Politically, however, Mahbub remained reclusive, and a Bhilala family that had long performed functions of tax collection and dispute resolution assumed the title of *Patel* or village headman. The Patels were respected within the village, and the family's patriarch traditionally acted as the sarpanch of the village panchayat, which in turn was practically defunct (panchayats are three-tier locally elected bodies at the district, block and village levels.). Shortly before the 73rd constitutional amendment (granting constitutional recognition to panchayats), Neelpura was unfortunately paired with its large non-tribal neighbour Bhimpura. Lakhan Singh, a landless though politically connected individual from Neelpura, became sarpanch. Singh was friendly with other sarpanches in *ghaat-neeche* and with politicians at the Bagli *tehsil* office.

Of all three 'power-holders' Singh was most hospitable to SPS group members, perceiving them to be potential allies in the village's develop-ment prospects. This was logical given how SPS members repeatedly asked villagers to tell them of their problems. In doing so, they created expecta-tions of solutions, and soon enough the NGO slid into its intended role of 'developer'. It earned greater familiarity in Neelpura, whose residents began referring to it as *sanstha* (Hindi for 'organization'). As the scarcity of water was the key problem, SPS offered to dig wells on people's private lands, and build water-conservation structures like earthen bunds and field ponds. SPS soon received funds from the Government of India under different central government schemes for the purpose. Although initially sceptical of SPS's offers of 'free wells' (due to bitter memories of a loan scheme in the 1970s that had led to government 'harassment' for repayment), most people in the village soon agreed to have their old wells deepened or new wells dug.

These development activities by SPS constituted an important moment in its relationship with the people of Neelpura. Working on the individual lands of people in this small village allowed SPS to come into close contact with their families. It was not long before group members were engaged in personal acts of help to villagers. By 1995, SPS had come a long way. It had a base village from where to begin its task of building a 'people's organization', and it was acquiring a clear role for itself in relation to development work in the area. As evident in its well-digging initiative, SPS also had no qualms about extending a highly 'individualized' approach to development through beneficiary creation. And, as the following events will illustrate, it did not view this approach as necessarily antithetical to the formation of collective solidarities, as has been suggested by some authors (Kamat, 2002).

A Troubled Period: Confrontation, Resistance and Development

During its implementation of the well-digging and water-conservation projects in Neelpura, SPS stumbled upon two types of exploitative practices in the region. These revealed the nexus of domination by anti-tribal forces in the *ghaat-neeche* area. It detected that the overall wage structure, especially for public works, in this tribal belt was not in keeping with the equal minimum wage laws of the country enacted in 1948. Both large farmers and panchayat sarpanches (acting through contractors), who engaged labourers for the execution of construction works, perpetuated this injustice. SPS also discovered that land records of poor tribals throughout the *ghaat-neeche* had not been updated in accordance with the Madhya Pradesh Land Revenue Code of 1950, and essential information, such as correct rates for land transactions, was being kept out of their bounds by the local revenue bureaucracy. This included both the village *patwari* as well as the subdistrict magistrate of the revenue division, who stood to gain monetarily from such malpractices. Emboldened by the absence of challenge, these junior state officials had also acquired near autocratic status locally.

Despite its infancy in the area and the nature of the backlash any protest would invite, SPS chose to confront the perpetrators of such exploitation. First of all, it insisted on paying equal minimum wages to all labourers hired on its development projects, an unprecedented act that upset old wage relations in the area. At one stroke, SPS had made enemies of large farmers, sarpanches and contractors in *ghaat-neeche*. Although some sarpanches like

Lakhan Singh in Neelpura were tribal, this was predominantly an anti-tribal coalition. A minor though not insignificant detail is the alienation that SPS suffered in its own little base, as it had angered its principal ally, Singh, and also Khan, the richest landowner. Even as these developments brought SPS into public scrutiny beyond *ghaat-neeche*, it went further and contacted the District Collector with a proposal to organize a 'land records camp' in order to rectify the appalling records situation. The most senior official of the district lent her support to SPS, and in January 2005 such a camp was organized in Neelpura village. It was a huge success, with more than 13,000 tribals travelling far to attend, and the district collectorate backed it with two additional camps.

The turn of events described here constituted a vital moment in the evolution of this NGO. It marked the beginning of antagonistic relationships with junior officials (like the subdivisional magistrate), whose vested interests suffered following SPS's intervention, but more favourable relationships with senior district- and state-level officials, who had no such interests at stake. Moreover, SPS communicated easily with elite and influential members of the Indian Administrative Service, aided by the social mobility that an 'English' education and privileged upbringing can bring in India. While these constituted important explanations for events, the most important was SPS's successful emphasis on the idea of the state as the guarantor of rights, and therefore of the need to uphold legislation that no civil servant could possibly disregard in public.

This episode reiterated SPS's engagement with immanent development processes and its willingness to challenge the exclusionary forms of political rule that commonly characterize state functioning. But, interestingly, it had done so without deviating from the legitimate framework of state laws and exposed the intricate politics of exploitation that impeded the development of the *ghaat-neeche* region (both within the *ghaat-neeche* and the *ghaat-upar* regions through the subordination of the tribal population). This conveyed how regular development work mandated by the state rested on critical political issues like the disregard of law (that codifies important rights) and abuse of authority. And yet, following the contradictory nature of the state, there are simultaneously existing laws like the Charitable Trusts Act of 1950 which apply to voluntary organizations, and state that

> The achievement of a political purpose, in the sense of arousing in the people the desire, and instilling into them an imperative need to demand changes in the structures of the administration and the mechanism by which they are governed … is not a charitable purpose as being one 'for the advancement of any other object of general public utility within section 9(4) of the Act'. (cited in Kamat 2002: 56)

This clearly illustrates the use of law by the state to act as an instrument of depoliticization (of 'big P' politics), and, but for the fact that SPS had discovered malpractices in relation to *existing* law, it too may have been in trouble with its funding agencies, notably CAPART (Council for Promotion of Rural Arts and Technology). Equally important was its location in *ghaat-neeche*, the site of subordinate politics within the district, as opposed to *ghaat-upar*, where SPS may have found it a lot harder to campaign for change. Greater political stakes embedded in the long history of non-tribal and upper-caste domination would have meant lesser space for tolerance of opposition, a point conceded by both SPS and district government officials whom I met.

However, even in *ghaat-neeche* SPS experienced considerable resistance. A powerful sarpanch from a village neighbouring to Neelpura took umbrage at the fact that SPS had initiated the deepening of the main tank there, on a show of written support by other members of the panchayat and ordinary residents, but without his 'permission'. He galvanised thirty other discontented sarpanches and with the help of the local Congress MLA (Member of Legislative Assembly), took a delegation to the Chief Minister (of the ruling Congress party at the time) to complain that the NGO was 'corrupt … bypassed panchayats and misappropriated their money' and should be 'removed'. This reaction was interesting and a testimony to pro-panchayat decentralization initiatives under way in Madhya Pradesh, which had greatly bolstered the confidence of sarpanches. These allegations lacked credibility and SPS reacted by pursuing a vigorous policy of image building as a transparent organization that worked in the popular interest. The local press further dramatized these unprecedented developments. The situation was ultimately resolved through the appointment of an 'inquiry committee' headed by the district-level panchayat (a clever ploy by the state bureaucracy to assuage angry sarpanches). The committee, however, acquitted SPS of the charges and publicly commended it for its 'good work'.

SPS gained tremendously from public approval by the highest elected authority in the district. Its local opponents realized that 'the luxury of direct confrontation' against SPS was one that they could no longer afford (Scott, 1990), although private confrontations between individual sarpanches and members of SPS ensued on a number of occasions. From being an 'outsider' to the region, SPS was clearly an ascendant power due to its successful strategy of development, legality and positive engagement with the state, particularly through dialogue with panchayat raj institutions. At a time when the ruling Congress leadership in Madhya Pradesh was emphatic on decentralization to panchayats, SPS seemed to have stumbled upon the right language for creating necessary local institutional space.

Formal Agent of the State: Doing Development Daily

Recognition from the state government came soon, and in the summer of 1995 SPS was invited by the Dewas district administration to become a Project Implementing Agency (PIA) for watershed development projects (under the central Ministry of Rural Development's programme) in the *ghaat-neeche* villages. SPS's selection as a PIA for a state-funded and managed development programme was particularly significant for two reasons. First, it showed that the NGO's resistance to certain types of state practices did not preclude its appointment as a formal agent of a premier state development programme. It showed that there were no definite boundaries between NGOs that implement development projects using government money and those that resist state practices. Second, it brought about the extension of the state's watershed development intervention to the impoverished and politically subordinate *ghaat-neeche* area in the very first year of the programme, even as the district administration experienced pressures for allocating watershed projects to electorally important villages in the *ghaat-upar* area.

The selection of *ghaat-neeche* villages, and of SPS as PIA, highlights the presence of a distinct political process that translated popular mobilization by an NGO into greater involvement with the state's development agenda. In this respect, moreover, SPS's confrontationist trajectory exposed the limitations of the state's depoliticization discourse by revealing the intricate connections between development and politics with a small p (of vested-interest-seeking). But, more importantly, its pro-active role as an agency of politics with a capital P, whereby it overturned unfair wage relations and updated land records, actually paved the way for a more substantial role in state-led development. Depoliticization clearly was not a 'successful' state project with predictable consequences, although the lack of success proved to be in the state's own interest. The marked improvement in condition of a large number of people in the *ghaat-neeche* as a result of SPS-led initiatives could only have restored their faith in a state, otherwise known to them mainly through its horrific acts of exploitation and abuse of authority.

As the PIA of Neelpura watershed project, SPS was in a vastly different position from other PIAs, as the village and its intrapersonal dynamics were extremely familiar to it. It did not need to 'facilitate' the creation of a watershed committee through a 'consensual' process in a public gathering, as other PIAs were advised to do by the national watershed guidelines of 1994. On the other hand, it chose to have a clear say in committee formation on the grounds that it was responsible for creating an 'effective cadre of leaders' that would be able to take 'contentious decisions'. The committee was formed and two prominent members of the Patel family, by now very friendly with SPS, became its chairman and secretary. Both Lakhan

Singh and Mahbub Khan stayed away from these new developments. The style of committee formation set the tone for a flexible and non-procedural interpretation of project management, and SPS did not bother with regular committee meetings, recording minutes and so on, claiming that decision-making worked best in the 'natural' rhythm of village life. In its daily administration of the watershed project, SPS tried to create a political culture of 'genuine devolution' and 'demystification' of technical project management by training local committee members in a range of skills.

This discourse, however, had an unflattering underbelly. By the time the project was under way, there was a small constituency (predictably including Khan and Singh) within Neelpura that thought SPS had deliberately adopted a divisive policy in the village in order to build a support base for itself. The widespread perception was that SPS was there to stay. The physical embodiment of this came in 1998, when SPS received a large grant from CAPART to establish a 'field station' about one kilometre away from Neelpura. SPS's growing physical presence no doubt had an increasing impact on the formation of local consciousness and the mobilization of local identities. There were growing allegiances for and against the NGO: so while members of the watershed committee in Neelpura formed its core support, others outside the village resented it bitterly. A good example was the sarpanch of the Bhimpura–Neelpura panchayat, a rich non-tribal landlord from Bhimpura, who was among those accusing SPS of trying to influence the outcome of the 2000 panchayat election by propping up favoured candidates (mostly using unsubstantiated claims). SPS adopted a relatively non-confrontationist stand here, quite distinct from its reactions in the earlier phase. Its strategy gradually gave way to a more sanguine discourse of 'partnership' with the panchayats, so that individual opponents like the new Bhimpura sarpanch could appear to stand isolated in their bickering. In a manner strangely similar to the influential institutions of international development cooperation, SPS's new and positive message of partnership reeked of a rosy confidence that only secure power holders can afford.

Common Property Resource Agreement: Using Law to Effect Local Rights within a Project Framework

One case of explicit intervention by SPS in its capacity as PIA of Neelpura watershed project merits special mention, for it reveals a remarkable act of political entrepreneurship to facilitate the material and symbolic overturning of local power relations within the legitimate project framework. This involved rectifying a highly inequitable arrangement of access to the only common water source in the village. SPS was well aware that the use of this *naala* (stream) had been improperly appropriated by a small group of upstream farmers, Mahbub Khan in particular, who drew waters continuously through *naardas* (underground channels) and, daringly, even from the surface itself through the use of through electric pump sets and diesel engines. With several farmers siphoning off waters upstream, those downstream had practically no access to running water or the opportunity to recharge their wells. Village livestock were the worst affected, since the *naala* ran dry after the rainy season.

Watershed project works included treatment of the *naala*'s catchment, but SPS realized that under the existing arrangement a rich upstream minority would corner the likely benefits. It resolved not to go ahead with project activities until the arrangement had been overturned. It is clear that SPS was attempting to intervene in a highly contentious area, which other project agencies may have disregarded, but one which had actually been specified within its role as a PIA. The guiding Ministry of Rural Development's policy framework emphasizes common property resources. So, interpreting the powers accorded to it within this policy to the fullest, SPS went ahead and mobilized popular opinion in the village to formulate a collective agreement to regulate the use of *naala* waters. In consequence, 139 farmers from Neelpura and adjacent villages signed a written resolution, which in translation from Hindi reads as follows:

> It is decided by consent [*sarvasammati*] that nobody will ever draw water from the naala using a *naarda*. Those farmers who have wells will also not draw water from the *naala* using pumps. Those farmers who do not have wells have agreed to draw water from the *naala* on a limited basis according to rules. After the water in the *naala* stops flowing, nobody will draw water from it, irrespective of whether they have wells or not. This water will be kept for cattle only. *All villagers* agree to this resolution [stress added].

Mahbub Khan protested vehemently, but under the weight of collective opinion and the NGO's vigilant stand had to block the underground channels with cement, along with the other farmers. Those who had water in their wells or lands on which wells could be dug had to remove pumps from the *naala*. SPS even constructed additional wells wherever necessary, free of any contributions from the farmers. The *naala* agreement was a matter of tremendous pride for SPS, and it mediated every detail of it. In the initial days after the agreement, enthused villagers set up a system of rotation to monitor the *naala* against possible violators at night. SPS claims that the agreement benefited everyone, although those with lands upstream were at a greater advantage than the rest.

Mahbub Khan went to court over the agreement, claiming 'easementary rights' over the *naala*, under the Indian Easementary Act of 1882. The Act's principal clause allows a single user or group of users exclusive or predominant use over a village resource, on the basis of 'long use or prescription', on the grounds that this use has been peaceable, open and uninterrupted for at least thirty years, as an easement and over a resource that is not owned by anyone in particular. SPS fought back, claiming that none of these grounds was valid. It offered convincing reasons – the *naala* was actually owned by the government, which in 1993 had issued an order prohibiting villagers to refrain from its use, and Mahbub himself had claimed right of use for the last seventeen years only. Mahbub was reprimanded for going to court with 'unclean hands' and his appeal for 'easementary right' was struck down. This had the effect of upholding the *naala* agreement and effectively altered the local field of power. Mahbub Khan was dealt a clear blow, symbolic and material, and SPS once again established itself as a proactive agency of change.

Scaling Up Development and Scaling Up Politics

SPS has energetically scaled up its development work, and, from a couple of villages in Bagli *tehsil* in the mid-1990s, it now implements a range of development projects in forty villages spread over three *tehsils* in Dewas and adjoining Khargone district, with further plans for expansion. Its staff strength exceeds one hundred and it has constructed new and impressive offices in Bagli. The main focus of its projects continues to be related to watershed development and drought proofing, and the funding agencies include the state government, CAPART (an old supporter of SPS) and, more recently, the American India Foundation. It has also developed an 'Agricultural Programme' spread over forty-five villages, and an initiative for micro-finance through women's self-help groups is rapidly growing.

In all these projects, SPS is emphatic on transparency and has initiated regular public meetings or *Jan-Sunvaayis* (literally translated from Hindi as 'hearing of the people'). A typical *Jan Sunvaayi* involves a large public gathering in the village, attended by grassroots workers of SPS and frequently its founding members. They apprise the public of the project's progress and financial status and answer questions from the audience. SPS hopes that this exercise will promote a culture of accountability among local bodies in the region. This method of accountability is in tune with the idea of 'social audit' in the panchayat gram sabha promoted by the state.

In addition, SPS has adopted a much more proactive strategy to contribute to the 'real' empowerment of panchayat institutions. It seeks to create a 'cadre of local leaders from amongst those who are committed to village development, but who are also from the poorer sections (tribals and women), to carry forward the panchayat process with systematic training'. These activities go beyond the scope of 'regular' development project work and are visionary in a political sense. SPS views itself as an agent of decentralized development and intends to network with other grassroots organizations and orient them to conduct training exercises for panchayats in their regions. Its work in this area has found abundant favour with the state government.

And yet SPS has not (so far) shied away from issues that are politically contentious. It has continued to oppose the politics of state oppression of tribals, by allying itself with forces that have arisen to resist it. Bagli *tehsil*, with its forested areas, has been the site of exploitation of the tribal population by the Forest Department and, more recently, their collective mobilization against it through organizations called the Adivasi Morcha Sangathan and Adivasi Shakti Sangathan. The nadir of such exploitation came in March 2001, when the district administration authorized police firings upon tribals in a number of villages in Bagli, ostensibly to evict them from forest land which they had illegally occupied. The act was condemned widely in the popular press. According to the 'Friends of the River Narmada', a volunteer-based solidarity network, this attack was unjustified and fuelled by state animosity against the growing strength and local political influence of the tribal *sangathans*. SPS played an active part in investigating the firings, compiling a detailed report of the atrocities and supporting many tribal families that had been affected.

Unlike the earlier period in its history, when confrontation with established stakeholders was risky and support from certain quarters of the state administration untested, SPS was able to take a firm stand on critical issues without worrying about its own position. Over the decade, it had built up a popular following in the *ghaat-neeche* villages, exposed the vested interests of local opponents and marginalized them, built firm connections with the district- and state-level administrations, and embedded itself firmly in state-funded development activity. Thus, even as it championed politically thorny issues like tribal exploitation, it denounced radical politics that were delinked from positive engagement with the state and its development agenda. Its view of 'big P' politics was at no time detached from the state. Given that a large number of panchayats in the *ghaat-neeche* area are vying to collaborate with SPS for development work, it would appear that the NGO has successfully created a discourse that 'good economics can make excellent politics'.

Hegemony or Counter Hegemony

The narrative so far has described how counter-hegemonic initiatives against various forms of domination – which reflect the existing underlying characteristics of development – have underlined SPS's strategy time and again since its arrival in the *ghaat-neeche* part of Bagli *tehsil* more than a decade ago. Through its struggle against exploitative wage practices, outdated land registrations and unfair appropriation of essential common property, SPS concretely overturned the fortunes of a dominant minority, and shattered even the 'public transcript' of their hegemony (Scott, 1990). In each case, the concerned actors suffered not just material loss but also public shaming and a sharp curtailment in their previous authority.

Simultaneously, however, SPS has rapidly gained in terms of local standing and prestige, with a visible rise in material capacity. It is acutely aware of its new position and projects itself as the 'only agency, either governmental or non-governmental, that is talking about development'. This seeming appropriation of a legitimate mandate is not surprising; it closely follows from the NGO's iteration of positive ideas of the state, as a guarantor of rights (during its early confrontations) and, subsequently, as a doer of development. While SPS may have resisted state structures or actors or processes, it never discredited the idea of the state as such, and has painstakingly moulded both its organizational practice and its discourse to complement this state idea. This has made it all the more difficult for local stakeholders to oppose SPS, which stands tall in its demonstrated conviction in all the 'good things' that the state might embody, and drastically changed the politics of the 1990s. Even the Congress MLA, which once facilitated a sarpanch-led petition to the Chief Minister for the ousting of the NGO, is seeking its support to bolster its constituency.

But what are the implications of the sort of power that this NGO is beginning to wield? I would argue that the latest phase in SPS's life history has witnessed the emergence of a new hegemonic position in *ghaat-neeche*, backed by a winning discourse, a popular base, connections with influential state officials, and a clearly charted yet expanding agenda with active fund flows. While SPS has up to now used its position to speak out in favour of subordinate interests, it will be interesting to observe the kinds of issues it takes up in the future without compromising its own critical leverage. It would be equally important to understand the kinds of subject-positions that SPS is fostering as a hegemonic power in the area, amongst its supporters, employees as well as patrons.

Conclusion: The Nature and Limits of NGO Power

In my attempt to understand SPS's trajectory in the Narmada valley, the profound links it has carved and sustained between political entrepreneurship and development agency have been made clear throughout. It was aware of these links to begin with, as evident in its guiding objective to direct the state's development resources to marginalized areas, and it has persevered so as not to separate them in its continuing practice, striving to create a new type of politics in its development work with the state. Its own transformation from new, even subordinate, actor to dominant player in *ghaat-neeche* development and politics is an inescapable part of the story. So how are we to understand and appraise this NGO's praxis?

Recent discussions of grassroots activity are increasingly recognizing the blurred boundaries between resistance and acquiescence, struggle and compromise, activism and development, all binaries that have typically distinguished radical social movements from NGOs. In her discussion of examples of 'powerful' NGOs in the developing world, Michael (2004) identifies two key commonalities: their interest in linking activities with 'mainstream' economic systems and their engagement with political activity. The founder of one Indian NGO, SEWA, sums up the story I have narrated in this chapter in her succinct remark that NGOs ought to pursue 'the twin strategies of struggle and development' (Michael 2004: 40). Yet it is admittedly not easy for NGOs to do this. Kamat remarks on the difficulty of maintaining a balance between 'a struggle based organization supported largely through popular participation and nominally paid tribal cadre on the one hand, and a development organization flush with funds managed by a professional paid staff on the other' (2002: 77). In SPS's case, much of this transformation has been remarkably nuanced, mostly because it started out as an organization with a philosophy of positive engagement with the state, invoking confrontation and cooperation in alternate measure. At the same time, one wonders if the more radical elements of its strategy would not be blotted out by the constraints of a new-found hegemony with its own dynamics of subordination. My account offers some insight into perceptions of this NGO's strategies to wield local power and popularity, especially among those piqued by it.

And yet the nature of SPS's praxis perhaps offers a way forward to numerous NGOs seeking to forge transformative change without rendering themselves unsustainable. Indeed, SPS's experience reveals how engaging with both 'small d' and 'big D' development is integral to the articulation of transformative or 'big P' politics. Here, it is precisely the synergies between state and civil society, mainstream and alternative development, and dominance and resistance that matter, not their separation as is mistakenly believed. The chapter also reiterates the fallacy of depoliticization – and affirms the fundamentally political nature of development – since it is quite clear how 'small p' politics pervades development (evident through the actions of appropriation by local officials in Bagli), but also that 'big P' politics can accompany development. While senior officials were more likely to preserve a technocratic façade to development, they were also formally bound to the idea of the state as a guarantor of rights. It was precisely this disjuncture that allowed SPS to obtain its support to orchestrate transformative development politics.

While SPS's experience cannot possibly be a blueprint for non-governmental action, it offers some general lessons about the power of NGOs. Many of these reiterate key points made by Michael (2004) in her theorization of NGO power: the need for NGOs to 'capture' or 'protect' space, be based within 'communities', set their own 'agendas', prevent conflict, and acquire synergetic relationships with the state. Here, I present four aspects to delineate the power available to NGOs as observed in this case study.

First, NGOs have the power to effect concrete changes in local power relations, as SPS did by overturning wage relations, transforming common property access and challenging an exploitative anti-tribal coalition. This may also mean that their power can sometimes be exclusionary. Second, their power is often text-oriented. SPS relied on a correct reading of the laws and official guidelines of the Indian state to fuel its radical initiatives. NGOs do not have constitutional power and face a greater need to justify their actions within existing notions of legality. Undoubtedly, many NGOs campaign to go beyond this, for a drastic change in state laws and policies. Third, it is performance-oriented and increasingly enacted in settings like the *jan-sunvaayi*. SPS, especially in its early days, repeatedly chose to create public events out of confrontations and chased a 'good reputation' in the local press. Quite in contrast, a district collector can simply order the closure of a road; she need not resort to a public debate on the matter. There is little consensus or legal validation of what power NGOs should have. Finally, as key episodes in this chapter – for example, the land records camp, the opportunity to work on the watershed project, and panchayat-related activities – illustrate, NGO power greatly depends on its ability to elicit government support. It is necessary to take this argument one step further. SPS's actions reveal a continuous interface not only with government officials but with key actors within 'political society', including political representatives, activists and local courts. NGOs cannot afford to limit their interactions to government officials alone; the impetus for transformation comes from their messy entanglements and struggles with political actors that impact upon the very fabric of development and society. Indeed, it is the synthesis of their roles as political entrepreneurs and development agents that holds the key to their power.

Note

1. I gratefully acknowledge the Economic and Social Research Council (ESRC) for awarding me a Postdoctoral Fellowship (PTA number PTA-026-27-0360) 2004–2005, during which time this chapter was written. I also thank David Mosse, Subir Sinha and the editors of this book for their incisive comments. I am indebted to members of Samaj Pragati Sahyog for their warm hospitality and support with this research. All views expressed in this chapter are mine.

References

Bebbington, A., and S. Hickey (2006) 'NGOs and Civil Society', in D.A. Clark (ed.), *Elgar Companion to Development Studies*, Edward Elgar, Cheltenham, pp. 420–22.

Cowen, M., and Shenton, R. (1996) *Doctrines of Development*, Routledge, London.

Ferguson, J. (1990) *The Anti-Politics Machine: 'Development', Depoliticisation and Bureaucratic Power in Lesotho*, Cambridge University Press, Cambridge.

Gramsci, A. (1971) *Selections from the Prison Notebooks*, ed. Q. Hoare and G.N. Smith, International Publishers, New York.

Harriss, J. (2001) *Depoliticising Development: The World Bank and Social Capital*, Leftword, New Delhi.

Held, D. (1984) 'Central Perspectives on the State', in G. McLennan, D. Held and S. Hall (eds), *The Idea of the Modern State*, Open University Press, Milton Keynes, pp. 29–79.

Igoe, J. (2003) 'Scaling up Civil Society: Donor Money, NGOs and Pastoralist Land Rights Movement in Tanzania', *Development and Change* 34(5): 863–85.

Kamat, S. (2002) *Development Hegemony: NGOs and the State in India*, Oxford University Press, New Delhi.

Kaviraj, S. ,and S. Khilnani (eds) (2001) *Civil Society: History and Possibilities*, Cambridge University Press, Cambridge.

Masaki, K. (2004) 'The "Transformative" Unfolding of "Tyrannical" Participation', in S. Hickey and G. Mohan (eds), *Participation: From Tyranny to Transformation*, Zed Books, London, pp. 125–39.

Michael, S. (2004) *Undermining Development: The Absence of Power among Local NGOs in Africa*, James Currey, Oxford, and Indiana University Press, Bloomington.

Pieterse, J. (1998) 'My Paradigm or Yours? Alternative Development, Post-Development, Reflexive Development', *Development and Change* 29(2): 343–73.

Scott, J.C. (1985) *Weapons of the Weak: Everyday Forms of Peasant Resistance*, Yale University Press, New Haven CT.

Scott, J.C. (1990) *Domination and the Arts of Resistance: Hidden Transcripts*, Yale University Press, New Haven CT.

Sen, S. (1999) 'Some Aspects of State–NGO Relationships in India in the Post-Independence Era', *Development and Change* 30: 327–55.

Shah, M., D. Banerji, P.S. Vijayshankar and P. Ambasta (1998) *India's Drylands: Tribal Societies and Development through Environmental Regeneration*, Oxford University Press, New Delhi.

Tideman, E.M. (1998) *Watershed Management: Guidelines for Indian Conditions*, Omega Scientific Publishers, New Delhi.

14

Is This Really the End of the Road
for Gender Mainstreaming? Getting to Grips with
Gender and Institutional Change

Nicholas Piálek

The Death of Gender Mainstreaming?

According to a growing consensus among development academics and practitioners, we are witnessing the death of gender mainstreaming in development (Moser, 2005; Mukhopadhyay, 2004; Oxfam GB, 2005). Not ten years after the crystallization of gender mainstreaming at the 1995 Beijing Platform for Action (PfA), it is being spurned not only by those it was supposed to change but by many who sweated and toiled to breathe life into the process. In failing to create substantial change in the practice of organizations and institutions both locally and globally, gender mainstreaming has at best been labelled as ineffective and at worst as another barrier to promoting social justice on gender, the very antithesis of its original conception.

Feminists are taking stock and are trying to move on. Academics and practitioners alike have started to wander away from the ambitions of gender mainstreaming as well as the explicit focus on 'Gender and Development' (GAD) with its prioritizing of the category of 'gender' over and above the category of 'women' in development. They suggest that the process has (inadvertently or not) resulted in the depoliticization of the feminist project (Mukhopadhyay, 2004; Porter and Sweetman, 2005; Standing, 2004; Subrahmanian, 2004). Gender mainstreaming has reduced feminist action in development to a technocratic approach devoid of any political content, making it something 'diluted, denatured, depoliticised, included everywhere as an afterthought' (Cornwall et al., 2004: 1). It has led to the overuse of 'gender', resulting in "the widespread tendency in academic, policy and activist contexts to ignore women and their needs while naming, and purportedly mainstreaming, gender" (Eveline and Bacchi, 2005: 496).

Gender mainstreaming has become a process that draws attention away from tackling women's subordination rather than highlighting it. Such analyses have led to the suggestion that we should move beyond gender mainstreaming – feminists involved in development should not be diverted by the myth of institutional transformation but instead should focus on supporting grassroots feminists and go back to empowerment projects focused on 'women' (Porter and Sweetman, 2005: 5).

Such perspectives suggest that gender mainstreaming has gone the same way as so many other apparently 'alternative' approaches that have become co-opted within the mainstream of international development work. However, this chapter suggests that a more sanguine approach is required, and that this critique itself should be subject to closer appraisal. Gender mainstreaming (and those implementing and analysing it) should not lose sight of the fact that such a process is fundamentally political. Gender mainstreaming is a form of feminist politics and policy (Walby, 2005: 463) that challenges dominant modes of thinking and practice in organizations working in development. As a consequence, the question that becomes most pertinent to ask is not, 'is this the end of gender mainstreaming?', but instead, 'how are gender policies and strategies consistently silenced across a range of organizational and institutional contexts? It was with this question in mind that I conducted a three-year research project into gender mainstreaming in development organizations, and in particular Oxfam GB.

Oxfam GB (hereafter referred to as Oxfam) formally adopted a gender policy on 16 May, 1993. Prior to this formal recognition of GAD as a core aspect of development interventions, Oxfam had created a Gender and Development Unit (GADU) in 1984 to raise awareness of gender issues among staff and in the organization's activities. In one form or another, driven by feminists and gender advocates in the organization, Oxfam has over two decades of commitment to GAD approaches, with gender mainstreaming being a central concern within the organization for over a decade. As a consequence, levels of understanding and technical capacity to implement GAD approaches in development projects and programmes is good throughout the organization (Dawson, 2005: 82). However, by Oxfam's own admission, gender mainstreaming has failed to achieve as much as it should have in promoting gender within the organization's work.

Between September 2001 and May 2002 Oxfam undertook an internal review of progress in gender mainstreaming, which produced eight evaluations: institutional arrangements assessment, women's human rights evaluation, gender evaluation of the Cut the Cost Campaign, mainstreaming gender in advocacy work on Poverty Reduction Strategy Papers (PRSPs), gender and participation in Senegal, gender in humanitarian response, annual impact report analysis, and Links evaluation (Oxfam GB, 2002). Within these reviews, Oxfam recognizes that gender is still an irregularly applied perspective in all areas of the organization. For example, the overall assessment of the reviews draws attention to a range of problems: 'gender policy is not fully enforced', the 'SCO framework does not consistently integrate a strong and explicit commitment to gender equality' and 'Oxfam does not employ sufficient staff with the necessary gender expertise to deliver high quality programmes'.

Translating Oxfam's progressive gender policy into solid practice has proven difficult and continues to be the subject of much internal research and debate (e.g. Oxfam GB, 1996; Oxfam GB, 2002; Oxfam GB, 2006; Smith, 1995; Smyth, 2005). The difficulties seem all the more perplexing given that resistance to gender mainstreaming is not significantly present within the organization. Most staff recognize the importance of gender transformative goals, not just for their instrumental value in creating broader and more sustainable solutions to poverty, but for the intrinsic value in them. This makes Oxfam a particularly interesting case study for understanding the significant challenges that face gender mainstreaming within NGOs.

Understanding Gender Mainstreaming in Oxfam GB

Gender mainstreaming faces what many bureaucrats call the problem of policy evaporation. For example, most development organizations have policies on gender as well as detailed strategies on how to include gender approaches in their work (Moser and Moser, 2005). Yet, when it comes to assessing an organization's practice, even the best recognize that gender is usually poorly incorporated into projects and programmes, if at all (Khan, 2003: 5; Kusakabe, 2005: 1). This transition from gender-rich policy to gender-poor practice is frequently cited as an example of policy evaporation, which in turn has become the focus of much academic and in-house institutional research (e.g. Derbyshire, 2002; International Labour Organization, 2002; Khan, 2003; Mukhopadhyay, 2004). This literature reveals two approaches to analysing gender mainstreaming. The first is the 'technical approach'. This approach highlights direct problems in transferring policy into practice. In seeking answers and solutions, it asks questions along the lines of 'what knowledge is lacking among staff?' or 'how much/little money is allocated to gender work?' The second is the 'political approach'. This approach focuses on more fundamental issues associated with policy evaporation. It asks questions such as, 'in what ways are staff perceived to lack knowledge and why?' and 'why is gender work seen as something separate to budget for?' The technical approach is important as it provides specific and direct advice for institutions trying to create change and is by far the most popular form of gender mainstreaming analysis. However, its level of analysis can be simplistic, whereas the political approach draws our attention to the more deep-seated problems that underlie the silencing of gender mainstreaming across institutional contexts.

In developing this political approach for analysing how GAD approaches evaporate at the policy–practice interface, and given the apparently positive environment that Oxfam offered for gender mainstreaming, I was keen to start my research at a point where no conflict over implementing GAD approaches was visible but where policy evaporation still occurred. Drawing on Lukes's (2005: 28–9) notion of potential conflict, I labelled these points as sites of 'non-conflict' (also see Piálek, 2007). This involved developing a multi-sited ethnography, which was carried out in three phases. The first phase was conducted from June to September in 2003 when I was based in Oxfam's South American (SAM) Regional Office in Lima, Peru, working with the Regional Gender Advisor. This experience was invaluable for understanding how gender was constructed, understood, analysed and incorporated into the work of staff in the organization. The second phase was conducted from May to December in 2005 when I was based in the Oxfam head office in Oxford, UK, supporting the Lead Gender Advisor (in the Policy Team). This work enabled me to survey the array of approaches Oxfam is using – and hopes to use – to overcome the problem of gender policy evaporation in the organization. The third phase of the research was conducted from January to November 2006; it was based on my involvement in a number of key meetings, planning sessions and workshops on gender issues. Such meetings brought staff together from across the regions and allowed me to assess the similarity of experience of gender mainstreaming with the South American region.

What's Happened to Gender Mainstreaming at Oxfam?

It seems from this research that the wholesale incorporation of GAD into the organization has resulted in a situation whereby creating real change around gender has become increasingly difficult. GAD approaches have become both mainstreamed and marginalized in Oxfam: 'mainstreamed' in the sense that they have directed a process of institutional change and have, in many ways, radically altered the organizational make-up in line with GAD beliefs about development; 'marginalized' in the sense that they are almost entirely excluded from the majority of Oxfam's actual programme and project work. Mainstreaming, subverted through sites of 'non-conflict' embedded within organizational structure and discourse, has created an organizational reality whereby gender is both appreciated as a crucial aspect of development work and, at the same time, not seen as a personal responsibility among individual staff.

For instance, 'Gender Equity' in Oxfam is one of the nine strategic goals of the organization – the GAD approach can therefore be seen to have been directly incorporated into the most formal institutional structure in Oxfam – the Strategic Change Objective (SCO) framework. Incorporating GAD into this framework serves to place gender at the core of institutional policymaking and programming. Nevertheless, the benefits of this to creating positive transformation in practice have been questionable. In creating SCO 5.1, 'gender equity', gender issues are set up as a distinct aspect of Oxfam's development work. They become pigeonholed into some projects and programmes while at the same time being ignored or forgotten about within others. SCO 5.1 develops an appreciation of GAD among staff, but its very existence also propagates the idea that gender equity is something to be planned for and achieved within specific gender projects.

To overcome this problem, part of SCO 5.1's remit is to 'mainstream gender within other SCOs'. However, the interference of SCO 5.1 in other SCOs calls into question the validity of the SCO framework. The framework is designed to categorize and separate development work to make the organization more effective at tackling poverty and the use of resources more efficient. The framework does not operate to define and then merge development issues. As a consequence, rather than the validity of the SCO framework being called into question, and the ensuing confusion that this would cause, the logic of the system prevails – 'gender equity' is an issue that must be dealt with by SCO 5.1 programmes and projects and not other SCOs. In this form, then, gender mainstreaming becomes an aberration of the system to be skirted over. The impact of this upon staff is clear. Not only does this ambiguity provide a legitimate reason not to develop a GAD approach within SCO 1–4 projects and programmes, but it actually creates an environment that encourages gender issues to be ignored by staff in order to maintain consistency in organizational practice. This situation makes it increasingly difficult for those concerned with promoting gender equity in the organization to encourage staff to deliver on the gender policy – responsibility among staff cannot be promoted or developed if the underlying structure in which GAD is embedded acts to remove anything to be formally responsible for.

Oxfam did not initiate the process of mainstreaming with the intention of marginalizing gender in the organization. Yet this is the situation in which it now finds itself. This raises a number of wider questions and issues. Is the marginalization of a GAD approach in organizations an inherent danger in the mainstreaming process? Is the removal of individual responsibility an inevitable consequence of institutional change? Despite an organization's commitment to raising the level of gender awareness among its staff, can it actually make its staff act on this knowledge? Does gender mainstreaming fundamentally require replacing all staff with 'gender experts' or 'feminists' to achieve its goal and would this be a productive or desirable solution? And, perhaps most crucially, does my analysis of gender mainstreaming in Oxfam give support to those who believe that the process of gendered institutional change should be put to rest as a well-intentioned but failed attempt at achieving social justice and creating an alternative type of organization?

I wish to broach some of these questions in this chapter. However, to explore some of the fundamental concerns around gender mainstreaming, there is first a need to take an analytical step backwards and pose a much more rudimentary question: what has my examination of gender mainstreaming in Oxfam highlighted about the nature of institutional change in development organizations?

Understanding Institutional Change: Master Plans or Misconceptions?

Moser and Moser argue that 'an organizational culture which is male-biased, in terms of attitudes, recruitment, working conditions, and structures and procedures, discriminates against female staff and clients' (Moser and Moser, 2005: 16). As a consequence, institutional change, along the lines suggested by gender mainstreaming, is a process embedded within a patriarchal system – the organization (and society more generally) – and it is therefore inevitable that the interests of women will be marginalized. Change is constrained by a system that places the 'feminine' as secondary. But how far can this type of analysis of GAD, organizations and the process of institutional change take us?

Patriarchy is no doubt an important concept for understanding resistance to processes of change around GAD. However, I felt that such an analysis did not easily fit with the lived experience of gender mainstreaming in Oxfam. I found it hard to characterize Oxfam as an organization with a culture that is male-biased and essentially patriarchal. Rather, there is good evidence that it has nurtured and developed gender mainstreaming from the very beginning. To blame the failure of change upon an embedded patriarchal culture seems too simplistic as well as obscures the complexity of institutional change in the organization. Foucault has drawn attention to the idea that power is at its most persuasive and pervasive when it can no longer be 'substantially identified with an individual who possesses or exercises it …; it becomes a machinery that no one owns. … It's a machine in which everyone is caught, those who exercise power just as much as those over whom it is exercised' (Foucault, 1980: 156). To blame the failure of gender mainstreaming upon a patriarchal system ignores the complex ways in which power operates in organizations.

Ferguson's analysis of development apparatus in Lesotho highlights this point well. He states that

> it is tempting to see in the discourse and interventions of such parties the logic that defines the train of events. Such a view, however, inevitably misrepresents the complexities of the involvement of intentionality with events. Intentions, even of powerful actors or interests, are only the visible part of a much larger mechanism through which structures are actually produced, reproduced and transformed. Plans are explicit, and easily seen and understood; conspiracies are only slightly less so. But any intentional deployment only takes effect through a convoluted route involving unacknowledged structures and unpredictable outcomes. (Ferguson, 1994: 276)

'Plans are explicit, and easily seen and understood; conspiracies are only slightly less so.' To question the relevance of patriarchy as an answer to the failure of gender mainstreaming in Oxfam is not to deny the idea of or belief in the masculine 'conspiracy' but to acknowledge that 'master plans' do not provide true accounts of reality. They merely place a façade of intentionality on reality after the fact. The failure of institutional change, in this instance, cannot and must not be seen as the result of intentional subversion by 'controlling minds'. Instead, the answers must be seen within the more mundane aspects of change. If an outcome – the failure of insti-tutional change to support GAD approaches to development – is not the product of intentionality, then the fundamental process of change must in some serious way be conceptually and practicably lacking. It is this 'lacking' that will be explored in this section.

'Values' and 'values': organizations and their staff

Gender mainstreaming is a process of radical institutional change. It is a process that must challenge the status quo in organizations, both in what they do and in how they do it. As such, it is a political concept that im-plicitly accepts that there is a dominant approach or idea to be altered. It is about changing what is considered important and creating the desire to act on this. Gender mainstreaming is essentially a process of value change. However, value change as a concept within organizations is not a simple one to understand or achieve. What are values? Can organizations hold values? Can there be more than one set of values within organizations? Making and understanding these distinctions are crucial. By ignoring them, a radical process of change can easily become deradicalized, technicalized and managerialized. Gender mainstreaming in Oxfam is a case in point.

For many, Oxfam can be seen to have transformed its values with a certain amount of success. Policies, reviews, performance management guidelines, organizational objectives, strategic frameworks, toolkits, concept notes and the wealth of other material and structures within Oxfam that can be seen to express the values of an organization have adopted GAD language and concepts. Perhaps most importantly of all, the adoption of a Gender Policy in 1993 is a clear and unequivocal statement of gendered organizational values:

> Oxfam believes in the essential dignity of people and their capacity to overcome the problems or pressures which can crush or exploit them. Oxfam's principles apply across the gender divide – to allow women as well as men their essential dignity, and to work with women and men in its emergency and relief programmes in overcoming the pressures which exploit them. To achieve this, gender relations need to be transformed. (Oxfam GB, 1993)

In a break from the past, where organizational values could be considered sexist or at the very least unconcerned with women or gender, the gender policy redefines Oxfam. Oxfam is an organization that values GAD approaches both for what they can achieve in creating a lasting solution to poverty and because they tackle an unacceptable and unjust form of inequality. However, to expect this process to lead to substantive changes among staff practices suggests a model of institutional change whereby 'an organization can have values and that these values should be fully shared by the employees; the way to undertake strategy, then, is to have a strong vision for the organization ... and to find ways of airing this vision so that employees can commit to it' (Mowles, forthcoming: 1). However, this model for change has not unfolded around gender in Oxfam. Despite expressions of affirmation of the gender policy among staff, their sense of personal responsibility or motivation for implementing GAD approaches frequently stay at the level of rhetoric.

One of the ways to understand this problem in Oxfam is to distinguish between the organization's Gender Policy or the Aim 5 Strategic Framework, which are organizational 'Values', and the 'values' held more generally within organizations. 'Values' are not the same as 'values'; confusing the two prevents an understanding of how change occurs in organizations. Organizational 'Values' should more accurately be defined as norms. They are 'obligatory and constraining and provide moral criteria for assessing what ought to be done' (Mowles, forthcoming). On the other hand, 'values' held by individuals within organizations are 'compelling (in a voluntary sense) and uplifting at the same time, as they are freely chosen' (Mowles, forthcoming). Within this approach, individuals cannot be seen as components of organizations – miniature expressions of the whole – but instead must be perceived as autonomous agents within that whole. Their free choice distinguishes them from the framework they are embedded in. Their 'values' cannot be set by the organization; they are the very thing that distinguishes the individual from the organization. Importantly, such values may be harder to shift, given that they are often both innately personal and extremely resistant to changes, especially large ones. This has three implications: first, successful institutional change requires a corresponding shift in both norms and values; second, shifts in norms within organizations cannot be assumed to change automatically an individual's values; and third, substantially changing an individual's values is a more negotiated and drawn-out process.

Ignoring 'values' and submerging conflict

The establishment of GADU and the development of a gender policy in Oxfam are good examples of the problems that emerge when this difference is not recognized. At first this conflict will be visible, as two employees of Oxfam noted at the time. Bridget Walker noticed that an initial reaction to GADU by some colleagues was to refer to it openly as 'feminist thought-police', and to deride its role (Walker, 1999: 101), whereas Dianna Melrose was taken aback in a meeting of trustees and management when she was asked, 'why gender?' after using the whole meeting to argue for practice to be brought in line with the 1993 Gender Policy (Melrose, 1999: 110). Visible conflict, such as this, is in many ways a good thing, offering a clear target that can be reacted against. While conflict is visible, dialogue can occur and the need to tackle values is clear.

However, more serious problems occur when value change continues to be ignored in favour of reinforcing norms – once visible conflict becomes submerged and hidden. An individual will ultimately find it easier to agree and work within organizational norms than to contradict and fight them. Yet conformity to norms does not necessarily mean value change. An individual's values can essentially remain unchanged. They may accept the organizational norm as important within the context of the institution, but a personal belief in this norm as an important principle in their life may not exist. Oxfam's approach to institutional change has shown this repeatedly. The approach has tended to focus solely upon differing aspects of norm change and ignore the more difficult process of value change. For example, the Oxfam Gender Policy is a clear organizational norm and rightly so. The policy has also been complemented by a number of differing forms of norm change to increase its basis as an important and overarching 'moral' framework in the organization, such as gender objectives within the performance management system, gender indicators and targets within monitoring and evaluation procedures, and the development of a 'Gender Equity' strategic framework.

Work on value change is less clear, however. Gender training is a key part of the induction process for new staff, as well as a part of the ongoing development of staff in Oxfam. Yet can it seriously be contended that a one-, two- or three-day course on gender creates value change? Value change is a long-term process, involving dialogue and negotiation, not a 'quick fix' session on policy, gender analysis frameworks and monitoring and evaluation techniques. Such courses can only really be seen as mechanisms for disseminating organizational norms, rather than a serious attempt to develop values among staff. Furthermore, other more explicit attempts at value change among staff have also failed to do little more than reinforce norms. The Gender Action Research project in Oxfam is a good example of how a strategy that could have potentially developed staff values on gender through practitioner-led research merely became a distorted form of norm change. For instance, the organization's need to generate 'good practice stories' (in an attempt to produce a new 'tool' for mainstreaming) overrode any real concern for personal development among practitioners. As a consequence, by the end of the set-up phase the 'action research' aspect (designed to stimulate consciousness-raising among staff) was scrapped in favour of helping project staff develop an elaborate gender monitoring and evaluation system. Any loose attempt to promote value change among staff through the process of 'research' was further undermined when it was agreed that project staff could partner a local research institutions to do the work. As a consequence, the project merely became a mechanism for reinforcing norms on gender.

How, then, has my analysis of gender mainstreaming in Oxfam developed an understanding of institutional change around gender? Effective change in organizations requires changes to both norms and values. The processes associated with each tend to be quite different. Norms are the 'moral' criteria or boundaries by which individuals within organizations must abide. Values, on the other hand, are the 'freely' chosen beliefs of individuals that motivate their actions. As a consequence, strategies to create change are essentially different, depending on whether they are tackling norms or values. Norm change is a managerial process of technical change, involving changing policies and human resources strategies, disseminating rules and regulations, altering language and terms used in the organization, and the like. The process may be contentious, and even construed as political, but it is still essentially technical and managerial (non-political) – the organization has no 'personal' relationship to its norms, it has no particular preference or bond with them, norms can be changed (but not necessarily accepted) rapidly and easily. This is not the case with values. Individuals are intrinsically attached to their values, as the individual is, in a sense, a sum of the values it holds. Value change is therefore intensely personal and intensely political. It is rarely, if ever, technical and managerial. However, if institutional change goes against or is not supported by commonly held values, then norm change alone is not sufficient. The more radical the nature of change, the more focused the process must be on values. If norms become the focus at the expense of values, then the process of change will become subverted, as conflict, far from disappearing, becomes submerged within the institution. It is with this more nuanced understanding of institutional change that it will be possible to produce a clearer picture of how gender mainstreaming has consistently failed across organizational contexts.

Gender Mainstreaming:
Some Critical Reflections on Ideas and Activists

How did 'doing gender' become something different to 'doing feminism'? (Cornwall, Harrison et al., 2004)

In seeking to explain both the failure and the success of alternative development approaches in retaining their radical and political character, there has been a belated recognition of the critical role that ideas and activists play here. A similar realization emerges here, whereby questions are being raised about how the 'gender and development' project has become increasingly detached from both the wider feminist project that it emerged from and from feminists themselves. For example, Smyth (1999: 17) highlights that, with few exceptions, 'most of the literature generated by Northern development agencies on gender and on women shares one characteristic: the absence of the term feminism'. This absence of any reference to feminism within NGOs that claim to be mainstreaming gender is a worrying point given the fact that GAD is an approach developed out of the ideas of feminism and the critiques of development by feminists (Rathgeber, 1990). Smyth states that

> we write and talk about gender-sensitive policies and strategies, of gender work and gendered activities or approaches, and even of engendering or genderizing (!) this or that aspect of our work. But on feminism, feminist policies and strategies, or on feminists, there is a resounding silence. (Smyth, 1999: 17)

Oxfam has been no exception to this trend. It has readily adopted GAD concepts, ideas and frameworks. However, it is hard to find any direct reference to specific feminist ideas or even reference to the more general ideas contained within feminist literature. For instance, one particular member of staff I interviewed stated that he was attracted to Oxfam because it was concerned with gender issues but also because it was not 'one of those feminist organizations'. Having valued the importance of a GAD approach in the organization, he paradoxically goes on to disassociate it from the ideas and beliefs of feminists. Is such a dislocation between GAD and wider feminist literature and ideas a healthy basis for a development organization attempting to mainstream gender?

The concern for achieving social justice, particularly for women, is what primarily binds together even the most divergent feminist thinkers. To this end, it is possible to say that feminism is 'essentially activism against gendered inequality and injustice' (Porter, 1999: 4). From this common ground, feminists often take radically differing viewpoints and approaches to how gender inequality and injustice can best be perceived and overcome. The feminist literature and practice surrounding the issue of women/gender in the development process, such as WID, WAD and GAD, is a case in point (Rathgeber, 1990). However, despite this diversity, there are critical ideas that bind advocates of feminism together into a coherent approach. Perhaps most importantly among these are those I will term epistemological issues. Establishing how we know what we know is a key aspect of the feminist approach, and a constant theme here is that of 'positionality'. For instance, Haraway states that 'feminist objectivity means quite simply *situated knowledges*' (Haraway, 1997: 57) – the belief that it is possible to see only partial truths about the world as knowledge is dependent upon the viewers own position in the world. This understanding about the nature of knowledge is a common assumption among feminist academics. As a consequence, the concept of 'positionality' forms a central theme throughout feminist literature, research and activity (Grosz, 1986; Haraway, 1997; McDowell, 1997; Stacey, 1997). For instance, feminists aim to recognize that they are not detached impartial observers of the world, but are deeply embedded within the social structures and cultural frameworks they are trying to understand.

Recognizing 'positionality' does not prevent feminists from making inferences about or acting in the world; rather, it requires feminists to qualify inferences or reflect on actions with a certain degree of introspection. McDowell and Sharp raise this issue in their review and discussion of research methods literature in geography (McDowell and Sharp, 1997). Such a perspective requires the researcher to ask him- or herself who they are, what are their assumptions, what is their position in society, how do these factors influence the people around them, and so on. Critically locating yourself within your own research or activity is a key aspect of feminist thinking and stems directly from an epistemological assumption of 'partial truth'. In turn, the ideas and beliefs formed by feminists are very much a product of this process and cannot be fully understood, appreciated or acted upon in isolation from this perspective. Ignoring the introspective process of feminist understanding is detrimental to embracing successfully ideas and practices stemming from feminist thought.

Attempting to promote a GAD approach in an organization, therefore has implications that go far beyond the specifics of development work in itself. To understand how an organization's work can create change among men and women and alter current gender relations in a community, the organization must first reflect upon itself and understand its own embedded power dynamics. Kabeer highlights that

> [Organizations] are relations of power. Very few institutions are egalitarian: they allocate decision-making power in a hierarchical way and they give authority to some people over other people. They give command over resources and command over people, and determine structures of power within institutions. (Macdonald, 1994: 31)

Nicholson (1994) takes this perspective further and suggests that if organizations fail to examine themselves in a critical fashion, they tend to make do with inherited institutional structures and routines, rather than develop more appropriate new ones to meet the organization's changing needs and objectives – an interesting point given my own analysis of Oxfam. Staff within organizations must recognize that they are not neutral actors in the development process, but are located in 'rules, resources, practices and hierarchies of command' that place gender in a relationship of inequality through silences on gender issues more often than through direct discrimination (Kabeer, 1994: 87). Gender mainstreaming that fully embraces its feminist underpinnings must go beyond trying to change practice and attempt to look critically at and change the organization and the individuals therein. Mainstreaming is political and challenging because it fundamentally deals with challenging one's own personal values and relations of power. It is a process that values change for its intrinsic rather than its instrumental value. However, without embracing these feminist roots, the political element to mainstreaming is lost. Institutional change is no longer valued in itself and is only willingly accepted for its potential instrumental possibilities. Gender mainstreaming becomes synonymous with 'GAD', and the politics of change is externalized onto the communities with which an organization works. Oxfam provides a clear example of this problem.

The case of Oxfam: avoiding feminism, losing change

In failing to acknowledge gender mainstreaming's roots in feminist thinking – and therefore the fundamental ideas and beliefs upon which the concept rests – Oxfam staff have overlooked the most important aspect of the institutional change process. Up to the present day, gender mainstreaming in the organization is peppered with the understanding that external change, change in the 'real world', is of primary concern. Mainstreaming, or any issues for that matter, must primarily focus upon what it can achieve in the projects and programmes of Oxfam. A departmental meeting set up to discuss a review of an 'Oxfam International Identity' was a good example of this. During this meeting a number of staff members raised the need for more than just a 'paper identity'. They suggested that there was a need actually to cultivate shared identity and beliefs among staff, as this would be a key mechanism for getting policies, such as gender, implemented. When these comments were aired, they were met with responses (from the manager running the meeting) in the order of 'too much to do to deal with direct organizational change' and 'we don't want to open that box', expressing a clear belief that external needs should and will be prioritized over and above internal change.

Although understandable given the stated mission of the organization, this prioritization of 'real world' change has tended to denigrate the need to tackle internal issues, such as working with staff to develop a sense of common purpose or identity on gender. At the Oxfam Global Gender Meeting in March 2006, the scorn for internal matters was openly expressed. Following a brainstorming session, three key members within Oxfam's management were upset that the vision of what a gender-mainstreamed organization would look like was too inward looking, one going as far to suggest that 'always thinking about ourselves is pathetic ..., we need to look at what we can change in the world' (Oxfam GB, 2006). This outlook on gender mainstreaming reflects a wider devaluation of the need for internal reflection and changes to the organization. Even Oxfam's own definition of gender mainstreaming highlights the organization's continual focus on the external. Three of its four objectives look at changes in the communities in which Oxfam works, while only the fourth and final objective refers directly to Oxfam and only then to say that it should make strategy consistent with the other three (externally focused) objectives. Gender mainstreaming is not seen as a process primarily focused upon changing the organization and staff per se, but as a process that promotes GAD approaches in the organization's projects and programmes – the 'real world'. The difference is subtle but nonetheless crucial.

Putting feminism back into gender mainstreaming

What are the implications for putting feminism back into the process of gender mainstreaming? For some, embedding a gender perspective into the heart of an organization is not enough; organizations need to be 'reconceptualised and restructured' (Rao and Stuart, 1997: 10). Such an idea fits well with Haraway's conception of feminist accountability (based on ideas of positionality). She suggests that there should be a certain degree of 'resonance' between researcher and the researched (Haraway, 1997). GAD approaches intend to transform society, within the context of development projects, by essentially nurturing values of equality among people. However, this process of value change needs to apply equally to both elements in the process: the development participant and the development agent. An organization that fails to recognize and challenge the influence and power of unequal relations, whether they be gendered or not, within its own structure and discourse is woefully unprepared for recognizing and transforming gender relations in society at large.

Rather than going 'beyond' gender mainstreaming, as many feel is necessary, the process needs to be reinvigorated and become a process that is more inclusive of and more explicit with broader feminist ideas and beliefs. Gender mainstreaming at present is all too reminiscent of the 'add women and stir' approach of WID. Organizations are frequently found taking what could be termed an 'add gender and stir' approach, leaving GAD approaches sandwiched among inappropriate organizational structures and discourses, with the inevitable consequences that follow. With this in mind, Goetz suggests that instead of the term 'mainstreaming', there should be a movement towards the term 'institutionalization'. She stresses that

> in the politics of institutionalizing gendered perspectives on development policy, different experiences of policy according to gender are taken to represent a challenge, not of political interest revolving around the question of *inclusion*, but rather of involving divergent meanings of social and economic change. In this sense, efforts to 'integrate' women into development policy are not necessarily transformative, so the concept of 'institutionalizing' women's interests in policy processes is used here to indicate a more transformative process. Sometimes the term mainstreaming is used to indicate this process, but the term 'institutionalizing' will be preferred here because it puts the accent on institutional change. (Goetz, 1998: 17)

Such a shift in terminology more accurately reflects the requirements demanded of an organization that wishes to adopt a GAD approach in its work. Institutionalizing gender implies a process that above all else both seeks and requires the organization to remodel itself around the needs of the GAD framework. Adopting a GAD perspective becomes not just an objective to be achieved in an organization's work, but a guideline for how relationships and structures should be cultivated and developed within an organization. Any organization that is attempting to transform gender relations in society must necessarily start with understanding and transforming structures and discourses of power that discriminate against gender and on the basis of gender within itself. The importance of the internal 'community' of an organization must be recognized and reasserted within the mainstreaming process if gender policies in development organizations have any chance of being put into practice.

However, recognizing the internal focus of gender mainstreaming is just the first step. Creating a shift in terminology to account for this may be appropriate, but it is far from enough. In fact, shifting terminology in this way without fully accounting for what is actually necessary to create an organization that implements GAD approaches may do more harm than good. A shift in terminology that refocuses attention on the internal – that puts the accent on 'institutional change' – but fails to examine what the actual process of institutional change involves continues to make the same definitional mistakes as those who have defined gender mainstreaming. The process of institutional change – and the consequent need to recognize explicitly the differences between norms and values in the change process – is key to gender mainstreaming. It is the actual process of change that needs to take centre stage.

Making Institutional Change
Central to Gender Mainstreaming

Only when organizations, and those implementing change in organizations, fully acknowledge the feminist roots of gender mainstreaming and recognize that the process of change is primarily concerned with the 'self' – the internal dynamics of organizations and not the external impact of the organization – will the accent on 'gender mainstreaming' shift. No longer will the principal focus of 'gender mainstreaming' be on 'gender' (or rather GAD approaches) per se, but on the process of organizational change – 'mainstreaming'. In recognizing this, the puzzle of institutional transformation will demand greater attention and the differing pieces of that puzzle will have to be placed at the fore of this process. In my discussion of institutional change, I noted that the process, to be successful, requires an understanding of three elements: the nature of change, the organizational context (its norms), and the individuals within the organization (their values). Thus far, gender mainstreaming in development organizations has not seriously examined and acted upon these elements. Gender mainstreaming has not been recognized for what it is – a process of radical political change within an organization – and the implications of this for both developing the norms and values in organizations have been neither appropriately distinguished nor seriously examined.

The example of gender mainstreaming in Oxfam is a case in point. Values and norms have not been recognized as separate issues requiring separate approaches in the organization. As a consequence, gender mainstreaming has failed because the process of change has failed to challenge directly and develop the values of individuals in the organization. This failure to tackle value change has become less clear as the continual focus upon norms within the organization has submerged previously visible conflict within the underlying organizational culture – its structure and discourse. A situation now exists where acceptance of GAD approaches is widespread, yet acceptance of responsibility for implementing GAD approaches is elusive.

The fundamentally political nature of gender mainstreaming's needs to be acknowledged, and the distinction between the technical process of norm change and the political process of value change needs to be made and acted upon in the organization. As Tiessen highlights, gender mainstreaming is both a technical and a political process (Tiessen, 2004: 690). Both elements need to be recognized and placed within the context of the organization. Gender mainstreaming must come to represent and promote a new maxim for feminists in development organizations. In the words of a friend who has worked for many years in development organizations on gender equality, 'as it came to be that *the personal is political*, it must now be recognized that *the professional is political*'. It is now the task of those promoting gender mainstreaming to establish this.

References

Cornwall, A., E. Harrison and A. Whitehead (2004) 'Introduction: Repositioning Feminisms in Development', *IDS Bulletin: Repositioning Feminisms in Development* 35(4): 1–10.

Dawson, E. (2005) 'Strategic Gender Mainstreaming in Oxfam GB', *Gender and Development: Mainstreaming – A Critical Review* 13(2): 80–89.

Derbyshire, H. (2002) 'Gender Manual: A Practical Guide for Development Policy Makers and Practitioners', Social Development Division, DFID, London.

Eveline, J. and C. Bacchi (2005) 'What Are We Mainstreaming When We Mainstream Gender?' *International Feminist Journal of Politics* 7(4): 496–512.

Ferguson, J. (1994) *The Anti-Politics Machine: 'Development', Depoliticization, and Bureaucratic Power in Lesotho*, University of Minnesota Press, Minneapolis.

Foucault, M. (1980) '*The Eye of Power*', Michael Foucault: Power/Knowledge: Selected Interviews and Other Writings, 1972–1977 ed. G. Colin, G. Fraisse et al., Harvester, Brighton.

Goetz, A.M. (1998) 'Mainstreaming Gender Equity into National Development Planning', in C. Miller and S. Razavi (eds), *Missionaries and Mandarins: Feminist Engagement with Development Institutions*, UNRISD, London.

Grosz, E. (1986) 'What is Feminist Theory?', in C. Pateman and E. Grosz (eds), *Feminist Challenges: Social and Political Theory*, Allen & Unwin, Sydney.

Haraway, D. (1997) 'Situated Knowledge: The Science Question in Feminism and the Partial Perspective', in L. McDowell and J. P. Sharp (eds), *Space, Gender, Knowledge: Feminist Readings*, Arnold, London.

International Labour Organization (2002) *The ILO Gender Audit*, ILO, Geneva.

Kabeer, N. (1994) 'Gender Aware Policy and Planning: A Social Relations Perspective', in M. Macdonald (ed.), *Gender Planning in Development Agencies: Meeting the Challenge*, Oxfam GB, Oxford.

Khan, Z. (2003) *Closing the Gap: Putting EU and UK Gender Policy into Practice – South Africa, Nicaragua, and Bangladesh*, One World Action, London.

Kusakabe, K. (2005) 'Gender Mainstreaming in Government Offices in Thailand, Cambodia, and Laos: Perspectives from Below', *Gender and Development: Mainstreaming – A Critical Review* 13(2): 46–56.

Lukes, S. (2005) *Power: A Radical View*, Palgrave Macmillan, London.

Macdonald, M. (1994) *Gender Planning in Development Agencies: Meeting the Challenge*, Oxfam GB, Oxford.

McDowell, L. (1997) 'Doing Gender: Feminism, Feminists, and Research Methods in Human Geography', in L. McDowell and J. P. Sharp (eds), *Space, Gender, Knowledge: Feminist Readings*, Arnold, London.

McDowell, L., and J.P. Sharp (eds) (1997) *Space, Gender, Knowledge: Feminist Readings*, Arnold, London.

Melrose, D. (1999) 'Two Steps Forward, One Step Back: Experiences of Senior Management', in F. Porter, I. A. Smyth and C. Sweetman (eds), *Gender Works: Oxfam Experience in Policy and Practice*, Oxfam, Oxford.

Moser, C. (2005) 'Has Gender Mainstreaming Failed?' *International Feminist Journal of Politics* 7(4): 576–90.

Moser, C. and A. Moser (2005) 'Gender Mainstreaming Since Beijing: A Review of Success and Limitations in International Institutions', *Gender and Development* 13(2): 11–22.

Mowles, C. (forthcoming) 'Values in Organizations: Negotiating Non-Negotiables', *Development in Practice* 17.

Mukhopadhyay, M. (2004) 'Mainstreaming Gender or 'Streaming' Gender Away: Feminists Marooned in the Development Business', *IDS Bulletin: Repositioning Feminisms in Development* 35(4): 95–103.

Nicholson, T. (1994) 'Institution Building: Examining the Fit between Bureaucracies and Indigenous Systems', in S. Wright (ed.), *Anthropology of Organizations*, Routledge, London.

Oxfam GB (1993) *Gender and Development: Oxfam's Policy for its Programme*, Oxfam GB, Oxford.

Oxfam GB (1996) *Learning about Gender and Change: Report on the Gender Policy Implementation Workshop*, Oxfam GB, Oxford.

Oxfam GB (2002) *Executive Summaries of the Gender Review Evaluations*, Oxfam GB, Oxford.

Oxfam GB (2005) *Beyond Gender Mainstreaming: Understanding Mechanisms for Improved Impact on Gender Equality and Women's Empowerment*, Oxfam GB, Oxford.

Oxfam GB (2006) *Aim 5 Gender Equity Global Meeting Notes*, Oxfam GB, Oxford.

Piálek, N. (2007) 'Gender Mainstreaming in Development Organizations: The Perils of Organizational Change', in N. Payne (ed.), *Building Feminist Movements and Experience: Lessons from Diverse Experiences*, Zed Books, London.

Porter, M. (1999) 'Caught in the Web? Feminists Doing Development', in M. Porter and E.R. Judd (eds), *Feminists Doing Development: A Practical Critique*, Zed Books, London.

Porter, F., and C. Sweetman (2005) 'Editorial 2', *Gender and Development* 13(2): 2–10.

Rao, A. and R. Stuart (1997) 'Rethinking Organizations: A Feminist Perspective', *Gender and Development*, 5(1): 10–16.

Rathgeber, E. (1990) 'WID, WAD, GAD: Trends in Research and Practice', *Journal of Developing Areas* 24 (July): 489–502.

Razavi, S., and C. Miller (1995) 'Gender Mainstreaming: A Study of Efforts by the UNDP, the World Bank and the ILO to Institutionalize Gender Issues', *UNRISD Occasional Paper* 4.

Smith, S. (1995) 'People, Programme and Policy from a Gender Perspective', Oxfam GB, Oxford.

Smyth, I. A. (1999) 'NGOs in a Post-Feminist Era', in M. Porter and E.R. Judd (eds) *Feminists Doing Development: A Practical Critique*, Zed Books, London.

Smyth, I. (2005) 'Report on the Gender Action Plan Review', Oxfam GB, Oxford

Stacey, J. (1997) 'Can There be a Feminist Ethnography?', in L. McDowell and J.P. Sharp, *Space, Gender, Knowledge: Feminist Readings*, Arnold, London.

Standing, H. (2004) 'Gender, Myth and Fable: The Perils of Mainstreaming in Sector Bureaucracies', *IDS Bulletin: Repositioning Feminisms in Development* 35(4): 82–8.

Subrahmanian, R. (2004) 'Making Sense of Gender in Shifting Institutional Contexts: Some Reflections on Gender Mainstreaming', *IDS Bulletin: Repositioning Feminisms in Development* 35(4): 89–94.

Tiessen, R. (2004) 'Re-inventing the Gendered Organization: Staff Attitudes Towards Women and Gender Mainstreaming in NGO's in Malawi', *Gender, Work and Organization* 11(6): 689–708.

Walby, S. (2005) 'Introduction: Comparative Gender Mainstreaming in a Global Era', *International Feminist Journal of Politics* 7(4): 453–70.

Walker, B. (1999) 'Changing the Rules: Implementing a Gender Policy through Organizational Procedures', in F. Porter, I.A. Smyth and C. Sweetman, *Gender Works: Oxfam Experience in Policy and Practice*, Oxfam GB, Oxford.

15

The Ambivalent Cosmopolitanism
of International NGOs

Helen Yanacopulos and Matt Baillie Smith

NGOs, therefore, can unequivocally be viewed as genuine cosmopolitan actors. Their establishment of an agenda and political community that transcends the state or local community, their 'transnational competence', particularly their transnational analytical skills, and their moral legitimacy are pivotal features in demonstrating their cosmopolitan character. This places NGOs in a position to act as legitimate advocates for humanity and wider concerns. (Carey, 2003)

In the global neoliberal age, an increasing number of tasks, missions and capacities are being ascribed to development NGOs.[1] Not least of these is their association with cosmopolitanism. The simultaneous search for future roles for NGOs alongside attempts to identify the foundations, values and structures of a cosmopolitan politics may seem to offer a political and strategic marriage of convenience. The link between NGOs and cosmopolitanism also seems intuitively sensible. The notion of a 'citizen of the world' would seem to fit rather well with the image of the globetrotting humanitarian worker, addressing need regardless of ethnicity, gender and nationality, and perhaps personal safety. Supporters of development NGOs would seem to be moving beyond national affiliation and transcending difference in response to distant suffering. Through their demands on states, corporations and global institutions such as the World Bank, NGOs are surely part of the development of a cosmopolitan democracy. Through their stated commitment to human rights and the alleviation of poverty, surely NGOs are developing the kinds of universal values on which cosmopolitanism rests.

In this chapter we argue that the relationship between cosmopolitanism and NGOs demands greater caution and serious interrogation. This is not to deny the broad thrust of the connections we have just identified, but to highlight that the relationship is contested and, in some senses, rather more ambivalent than intuition would allow for. We do not necessarily seek to undermine a connection between NGOs and a cosmopolitan politics. But a more systematic exploration of the relationships between development NGOs and cosmopolitan politics can help us understand the capacity of NGOs to offer serious development alternatives, most notably in the form of a transnational politics of justice based on the values of solidarity.

This chapter is motivated by conceptual, strategic and normative agendas. We start as authors strongly committed to supporting the future development and practice of NGOs. Our involvement in research on NGOs is informed not only by intellectual interests, but by our experiences as staff of NGOs and through our collaborative work alongside NGOs. As a result, our interest is both conceptual and applied. We hope not only to contribute to the conceptualization of NGOs but to inform debates outside and within NGOs about their future roles and the strategic choices organizations may have to make. We also hope to contribute to debates around the meaning of cosmopolitanism, and at the same time to ground discussion of cosmopolitanism in the complex practices of NGOs. We believe this is particularly important in the light of a growing disjuncture in debates around NGOs and global politics. International development NGOs are facing growing scrutiny of their legitimacy, authority and effectiveness, and yet are also being ascribed increasingly important roles in the reshaping of global politics and society. This not only reflects strategic contradictions and dilemmas, but also hints at the separation of some of the voices speaking on the future of NGOs and the development of cosmopolitan politics. Since much of the research on NGOs is conducted in order to respond to NGO needs, there is a strong emphasis on 'practice' rather than 'grand theory'. On the other hand, much of the writing on cosmopolitanism is rooted in social and political theory which is articulated in highly abstract and sometimes inaccessible language. This chapter represents an initial attempt to start to bridge this gap by identifying key points of contact between NGOs and cosmopolitanism.

The first section offers an outline of the key aspects of cosmopolitanism on which the chapter is focused. Whilst we do not offer a definitive overview, we do aim to map some of the levels and dimensions of cosmopolitanism in order to provide a foundation for the exploration of the points of contact between NGOs and cosmopolitanism. We explore these in section two, outlining the potentially diverse ways in which NGOs and cosmopolitanism can be linked. In section three we explore the connections in more detail and more critically through the prism of two areas of NGO practice: development education and advocacy. We conclude by offering some suggestions about the significance of further research in this area.

Ideas of Cosmopolitanism

Recent years have seen a growing interest in a broad set of ideas under the heading 'cosmopolitanism'. But, despite the confident assertion that 'cosmopolitanism is back' (Harvey cited in Vertovec and Cohen, 2002a: 1), what exactly has returned is less clear:

> For some contemporary writers on the topic, cosmopolitanism refers to a vision of global democracy and world citizenship; for others it points to the possibilities for shaping new transnational frameworks for making links between social movements. Yet others invoke cosmopolitanism to advocate a non-communitarian, post-identity politics of overlapping interests and heterogenous or hybrid publics in order to challenge conventional notions of belonging, identity and citizenship. And still others use cosmopolitanism descriptively to address certain socio-cultural processes of individual behaviours, values or dispositions manifesting a capacity to engage multiplicity.

Whilst cosmopolitanism has increasingly entered debates over the last fifteen years, it is not a new concept and can be traced back at least to the political philosopher Immanuel Kant. This return has not been uncontested, and serious debates are ongoing within sociology and international relations concerning basic precepts that underpin cosmopolitanism. Although these debates have significance for thinking and acting around development, for reasons of space we focus here on identifying the key features of cosmopolitanism that offer analytical and normative purchase in relation to development NGOs.

The return of cosmopolitanism has been reflected in growing debates around its desirability and feasibility, the forms it takes, and the consciousnesses, legal frameworks, institutions and dispositions and commitments that it might demand. It also crosses the normative and analytical domains, at one level being seen as an opportunity to map alternative modes of social, political and cultural organization, whilst at the same time being deployed to capture existing practices. Vertovec and Cohen disaggregate the diversity outlined by Harvey, outlining six ways in which cosmopolitanism can be 'viewed or invoked as a) a sociocultural condition; b) a kind of philosophy or world-view; c) a political project towards building transnational institutions; d) a political project for recognising multiple identities; e) an attitudinal or dispositional orientation; and/or f) a mode of practice or competence'(2002a: 18–22).

As such, cosmopolitan thinking is a rich area and we find that there are diverse views as to what cosmopolitanism is; there is not one unified theory of cosmopolitanism and it is not, in Fine's terms, 'a body of fixed ideas' (2006: 242). The breadth of cosmopolitan theorizing provides a range of contact points with NGOs and the search for development alternatives.

A conceptualization of contemporary socio-cultural conditions which challenges traditional conceptions of cultural borders and acknowledges and even celebrates the importance of multiple and overlapping identities presents a markedly changed context to the one into which international development NGOs emerged in the middle of the last century. Whilst 'cosmopolitan' may have been an epithet applied to the staff and experts of the development industry since that time, cosmopolitan theorizing which recognizes the skills, competences and knowledge that make up an 'ordinary cosmopolitanism' (Lamont and Aksartova, 2002: 1) present a challenge to this. This presents a challenge to some of the assumptions around subjectivity, authority and knowledge that have underpinned international development NGOs' work, highlighting the skills, knowledge and agency of the poor, and in doing so, suggesting alternative ways of understanding and promoting development. As organizations increasingly working across national borders and addressing transnational issues – such as development – NGOs could be seen as the expression of a key cosmopolitan norm. In seeking to communicate global ideas and persuade individuals to respond to the welfare of the 'distant other', development NGOs could be seen as promoting a post-national cosmopolitan agenda which challenges difference and which seeks to change dominant attitudes and dispositions. Underlying these connections is a contestable notion of NGOs as values-based organizations seeking 'alternatives' which better address poverty and injustice.

Many cosmopolitan theorists have already made the connection between cosmopolitanism and development (e.g. O'Neill, 1986), and are now increasingly exploring the strong connections between the ways NGOs are represented and understood, and the development and construction of cosmopolitan theory itself. For one,

> Even the ideas of cosmopolitan democracy and humanitarian activism ... reflect an awareness of the world that is made possible by the proliferation of NGOs working to solve environmental and humanitarian problems, and by the growth of media attention to these problems. These are important – indeed vital – concerns. (Calhoun, 2002: 91)

This is not without its difficulties. As Calhoun goes on to suggest, 'Nonetheless, the concerns, the media and the NGOs need to be grasped reflexively as the basis for an intellectual perspective' (2002: 91), and the links between NGOs and cosmopolitanism cannot be assumed. However, there has been surprisingly little effort to conceptualize development NGOs in terms of a cosmopolitan framework. This is somewhat surprising. If, as Lu (2000: 265) argues, cosmopolitanism is fundamentally concerned with humanity, justice and tolerance, then at an immediate and superficial level we can begin to see connections between NGOs and cosmopolitanism.

Indeed, it could be argued that NGOs' public commitments to universal rights, to global and post-national representing and advocating, and to aiding and engaging with distant strangers, suggest a thoroughly cosmopolitan position.

Our use of these elements of cosmopolitan theorizing does not mean they are not problematic. There are a wide range of critiques of cosmopolitanism and we will reflect on some of these as we explore NGOs' connections to cosmopolitanism, suggesting not only an ambivalent cosmopolitanism on the part of NGOs, but also that in expressing some elements of cosmopolitanism NGOs are reproducing their weaknesses and problems. Prior to this, however, it is important to note some key difficulties with cosmopolitanism.

Thomas Pogge (2003: 169) outlines three elements that are essential in the universalism which cosmopolitans embrace. Individualism: the unit of analysis is the human being rather than a group, community or country. Universality: where concern is focused on every human being equally. Generality: this special status has a global force – people are ultimate units of concern for everyone, not only for their own compatriots. However, Van der Veer (2002: 166) has a different view of cosmopolitan universalism: 'Cosmopolitanism is the Western engagement with the rest of the world and that engagement is a colonial one, which simultaneously transcends the national boundaries and is tied to them.' Critics of cosmopolitanism's colonialism argue that, far from being from nowhere and expressing universal values, cosmopolitanism is very definitely from the West. If this is the case, then some would say that these interventions can be characterized as 'colonial' in their imposing of external value systems as part of a process of domination and appropriation. Cosmopolitanism then has roots in modernity and colonialism and engages with the 'other' in order to shape it in the image of the 'self' (Van der Veer, 2002: 168).

This would appear to contrast strongly with conceptions of cosmopolitan democracy which argue for a fuller recognition of voice and demand greater accountability. Cosmopolitan democracy, as we discuss later, is based on the assumption that certain objectives, such as control of force and respect for human rights, will be obtained only through the extension and development of democracy (Archibugi, 2003: 7). However, it can be argued that such a democracy will be highly uneven, since its constitution cannot be abstracted from existing global inequalities of power. Some critics have criticized cosmopolitan democracy as a means of creating a world government, and, although this has been countered, there remain significant difficulties around the framing and definition of legitimacy in the absence of a nation-state framework.

The development and possibility of 'thinking and feeling beyond the nation' is also not without significant problems. At the heart of normative ideas of cosmopolitanism is a view of all people in the world counting equally – one human does not count any more than another, regardless of their nationality or geographical locale. Therefore, some would argue a cosmopolitan would have the same obligation to their next-door neighbour as they would to someone living in a distant place who they have never met. This connection to the 'distant stranger' is a defining characteristic of cosmopolitan ideals. However, as the response to Nussbaum's paper (2002) on patriotism shows, the meanings and implications of this are highly contested (Cohen, 2002), with critics questioning both the feasibility and the political desirability of any undermining of parochial identities (Appiah, 2002; Barber, 2002):

> It is because humans live best on a smaller scale that we should defend not just the state, but the country, the town the street, the business, the craft, the profession, and the family, as communities, as circles among the many circles that are narrower than the human horizon, that are appropriate spheres of moral concern. (Appiah, 2002: 29)

Here, we have sought to outline some of the key issues in cosmopolitan theory. In particular, we have focused on the normative elements of cosmopolitanism, the commitment to multiple affiliations, the emphasis on universals and on the relationships with the 'distant stranger'. Whilst there are significant critiques and difficulties with elements of cosmopolitan theorizing, we start from the perspective that they express broad values to which we subscribe and that we identify as offering normative and analytical purchase in understanding NGOs' roles in engendering development alternatives. The critiques outlined here urge caution against elitism, ethnocentrism and a lack of attention to political economy, but do not in themselves undermine attempts to realize the goals and values that underline the elements of cosmopolitanism we identify here as most significant for conceptualizing NGOs. What they do highlight is the importance of the processes through which cosmopolitan values, systems and commitments are defined and grounded. Given this, in the next section we explore some of the connections between these elements of cosmopolitanism and the work of international NGOs, and argue that, despite the apparent resonance between NGOs and cosmopolitan norms, NGOs' cosmopolitanism is currently somewhat ambivalent.

NGOs and Cosmopolitanism

The combination of diverse forms and practices of NGOs and complex and diverse theories of cosmopolitanism presents significant challenges for this chapter. We cannot hope to speak of the practices of all NGOs, but focus

instead on large international development NGOs because of their geopolitical and cultural significance, as well as their association with practices that
are frequently defined as cosmopolitan. These organizations are increasingly
identified as crucial players in international development, humanitarianism
and democratization. They are also powerful players in diverse national
settings, have the capacity to attract global media attention, maintain a bold
image as fighters for the poor and maintain capacity to engender emotional
and, increasingly, political engagement from diverse publics. Moreover, the
links between cosmopolitanism and the practices of development NGOs
can be made in myriad ways. The focus here on development alternatives
leads us to emphasize the normative political senses in which cosmopolitanism can be deployed. In particular, we identify four commitments within
cosmopolitan political theorizing that offer an analytical frame for consider-
ing the ways in which NGOs are or can contribute to the formation of
development alternatives: the commitment to and promotion of a form
of cosmopolitan democracy; the promotion of political authority beyond
the nation-state; the recognition and promotion of universal values; the
development and expression of 'thinking and feeling beyond the nation'.
This does not mean that NGOs would necessarily recognize their practice
as fostering these cosmopolitan norms, but we see significant elements of
NGO practice as resonating in different ways and at different levels with
these norms. This provides a more specific way of exploring the complex,
contradictory and, we argue, ambivalent relationship between NGOs
and cosmopolitan theories. Finally, we draw particularly on our ongoing
research on the ways NGOs present a 'public face of development' (Smith
and Yanacopulos, 2004; Yanacopulos, 2004; Smith, 2004b) and the ways
these NGOs engage with publics. Not only is this aspect of their practice
under-researched, but it is central to the ways NGOs engender engagement
in transnational politics, inform global consciousness and construct notions
of difference and universality, providing important conceptual connections
between notions of cosmopolitanism and development NGOs.

Whilst we need to be cautious about the global political roles sometimes
ascribed to NGOs, not least in terms of their purported capacity to supplant
aspects of the state, it is nonetheless the case that NGOs have become significant global players whose agendas, interests and actions are not primarily
defined by the nation state. Lupel (2003: 28) suggests that

> an emerging global civil society populated with a diversity of movements and
> institutions based in a variety of communities with transnational interests con-
> tinues to be an integral part of the project of transcending an international order
> constituted by the narrow competition of national state interests.

Of course, the establishment of this basis is not without problems. Alleged
differences between the UK and US Save the Children Funds over state-

ments from the former about the conflict in Iraq – denied by SCF UK – demonstrate that NGOs are not immune from national boundaries and orientations (Maguire, 2003; Save the Children Fund UK, 2003). Indeed, whilst maintaining a transnational profile and identity, the recent emphasis on devolution within the large NGOs, and the development of national members of wider NGO families, hint at difficulties with maintaining a post-national organizational form. However, their wider roles within transnational governance (Yanacopulos, 2005), the recognition of their 'expertise' and their interventions across national borders demonstrate that NGOs do exercise some form of authority beyond the nation-state, the legitimacy of which is often framed by a claimed connection to cosmopolitan democracy.

NGOs' roles in shaping a global democracy are seen by some to signify their cosmopolitanism (Carey, 2003; Linklater, 2002). David Held, a key cosmopolitan democracy theorist, outlines the need for democracy on several layers, from the local to the international level, such that 'Today, if people are to be free and equal in the determination of the conditions which shape their lives, there must be an array of fora, from the city to global associations, in which they can hold decision-makers to account' (2003: 387). Given that 'people will have to have access to, and membership in, diverse political communities' (2003: 387), individuals are then defined as global citizens, and citizen participation at different levels acts as a means to globalize democracy and as a means of democratizing globalization. As such, the work of NGOs in seeking to open participatory spaces from the transnational through to the local level can be closely aligned with this particular cosmopolitan project.

When set in opposition to the 'top-down' nature of state governance and in terms of their early support of participatory methodologies, NGOs have often been seen as enhancing or deepening democracy. As alluded to at the start of this chapter, NGOs are often associated with ideas and ideals of world and global citizenship. Whilst acknowledging the problems of an obligation rather than a rights-based approach, due to the lack of political community and common culture, Linklater (2002: 265) suggests that

> Cosmopolitan citizenship is an important weapon in the critique of exclusionary forms of political community and in the development of global harm conventions which reject the assumption that the welfare of co-nationals matters more than the welfare of other members of the human race. Judged by these criteria, many non-governmental organizations can be regarded as the latter-day custodians of the ideal of world citizenship.

This connection could be in terms of the extension of global citizenship rights to NGOs – among others – as part of cosmopolitan democratic structures (Calhoun, 2002: 94). It could be argued that the 'formation of transnational bonds among humankind through the construct of NGOs establishes a new transnational political community' (Carey, 2003). In other words, NGOs are producing a form of global citizenship in which the foundational social relationships are defined beyond the nation-state. However, this is problematic on two levels. First, the concept of citizenship demands the existence of a recognizable political community, and there is little evidence to suggest significant numbers of people are re-imagining themselves as global citizens. Second, in his discussion of NGOs' relationships with their Northern supporters, Desforges suggests that the need for organizations to reproduce themselves financially means that the global citizenship they offer is 'highly circumscribed' (2004: 566). However, it is worth noting that Desforges does not extend his focus to the development education element of NGOs' activity, the remit of which is more explicitly centred on global citizenship, as discussed below.

A second way in which NGOs are aligned with cosmopolitan democracy is through their role as 'key players in the development of a worldwide public sphere' (Linklater, 2002: 265), which begins to address what we have just identified as an apparent absence of such a political space for 'global citizens' to engage in. By their very existence, and as part of an emergent global civil society, NGOs are contributing to the formation of political spaces which go beyond the nation-state. This is significant for Carey (2003) for two reasons:

> regardless of a specific commitment to spreading and promoting adherence to democratic values, NGOs are also indirectly responsible for propounding democratic ideals by virtue of the process of giving voice to ordinary citizens of the world, thus facilitating the construction of a more cosmopolitan and democratic world order.

Here, the formation of a global public sphere also provides a forum in which to 'ascertain the validity of cosmopolitan norms through discourse and argumentation, ultimately leading to the building of consensus' (Carey, 2003). If NGOs are playing such a key role, then this shaping and opening up of new political spaces in which to articulate alternatives is surely a crucial political role. However, and aside from the continued dominance of nation-states as the pre-eminent political space, writers such as Anderson and Rieff (2004) have highlighted a lack of democratic legitimacy and authority of NGOs in terms of who they can they claim to speak for and on what basis their views are representative. In some senses the difficulties faced by NGOs in this context point to the wider conceptual and practical difficulties of global civil society; celebratory accounts of its democratizing capacity and political importance often skirt over the history of the concept and what this suggests for its capacity to effect change (Colas, 2002). Nonetheless, we would argue that by virtue of taking political and moral debates beyond the confines of the nation-state, NGOs are in some respects supporting the development of a cosmopolitan order underpinned by global values.

The issue of universal values provides a third dimension of cosmopolitanism which connects with NGOs. At the centre of this is the view that NGOs are committed to humanity as a whole, perhaps best exemplified in Kofi Annan's characterization of them as the 'conscience of the world' and Chandhoke's (2002: 41) view that NGOs set a 'moral frame' for the international community. One could argue that NGOs are based on principles and values which are also central to conceptions of cosmopolitanism: humanity, justice and tolerance. One element of this global moral frame is a challenge to distance, seen in NGOs' facilitation of assistance to the distant needy. This intersects with debates around affiliation and patriotism, exemplified in Nussbaum's treatise on education and the responses to it (Cohen, 2002) and centred on the challenging of the local as taking precedence. NGOs would certainly seem to be in line with the idea of 'thinking and feeling beyond the nation', although it is less clear how and when they connect with Nussbaum's view that 'only by seeing oneself in the eyes of the other can one recognize what is deep and shared rather than local and unnecessary' (Fine and Cohen, 2002: 155). Perhaps more significant is the critique of the ways NGOs – and the development industry more generally – has proclaimed universal values which are in effect firmly rooted in the particular Western liberal traditions and histories from which NGOs have emerged. This then reproduces Van der Veer's (2002) notion of a colonial cosmopolitanism in which the desire to empathize and understand the 'other' is part of a system of controlling and managing the 'other'.

A second problem with this proclamation of universal values allied to an engagement with the distant 'other' has been the way it has largely been realized in terms of charity towards the 'other' as opposed to justice (Yanacopulos, 2007). There has been a lively debate within the cosmopolitan tradition concerning the relative merits of charity vis-à-vis justice-based approaches, often centred around a much publicized debate between Kuper (2002) and Singer (2002). For Singer, the surplus income of individuals in rich countries should be sent to those in poor countries through international aid organizations such as Oxfam and UNICEF, thus placing charity-based finance at the centre of his cosmopolitan project. Against this, other cosmopolitans argue that charity commodifies cosmopolitanism – by giving money, individuals can feel better about themselves. In arguing against the 'myopic communitarian or realist', Lu suggests that charity results from the mistaken conception of distant injustice as 'misfortune' (Lu, 2000: 262). For such critics, moving towards a cosmopolitanism founded on justice cannot be derived from an impulse to give to the poor, but rather from changing the terms of engagement. Kuper (2002: 120) supports Edwards (this volume) in arguing that

> there remains the deep disjunct between the perspective of a system of global justice and the sedimented power structures of the current global order. Part of what a clearly articulated theory reveals is that some individuals' giving away income may do little to remedy this schism. While charity may produce improvements, it may at worst cause harm, or at least the relevant resources might be better used in another way.

This section has sought to outline some of the connections between NGOs and cosmopolitanism in relation to: the promotion of cosmopolitan democracy; the promotion of political authority beyond the nation-state; the recognition and promotion of universal values; the development and expression of 'thinking and feeling beyond the nation'. In so doing we have been careful to highlight the contradictions and weaknesses in cosmopolitan theorizing which NGOs may reproduce, and ways in which NGOs' commitment to some of the political values and goals of cosmopolitanism are somewhat ambivalent. However, and although there are some significant challenges for NGOs to negotiate here, we have suggested that it is through some adherence to elements of cosmopolitan politics that NGOs are in a position to offer development alternatives. The next section considers this ambivalence in more detail through an analysis of two key areas of NGO practice: development education and advocacy.

Cosmopolitanism in Practice

Our purpose in this section is to investigate the connection between a number of different functions of development NGOs and cosmopolitan politics. Development NGOs are a diverse grouping with complicated organizational structures and strategies, and whilst it is simpler to speak of Development NGOs as a homogenized grouping and of individual NGOs as homogenized organizations, this is simply not the case in practice. Some of these complexities have been previously outlined (Smith and Yanacopulos, 2004) but in using two examples, development education (DE) and advocacy, we hope to briefly illustrate how these functions, found in larger international NGOs, tap into different forms of cosmopolitanism. We argue that these different practices reflect what we term an 'ambivalent cosmopolitanism'. In other words, the degree to which NGOs' exemplify a cosmopolitan politics is, in reality, far from clear-cut not only at the broad conceptual level but also in relation to specific practices.

Development education

Most international development NGOs undertake DE. Like advocacy, DE is orientated towards the wider contexts and causes of inequality. However, it has not traditionally emphasized singular messages but rather, in the UK at least, has focused on developing peoples' capacity for critical reflection about the world they live in and empowering them to act in response to this. In this sense, DE is about both content and process. Although under-researched, DE is closely linked to wider NGO debates in terms of values and approaches, and projected future political mobilization roles for NGOs (Edwards, 1999: 194). Moreover, critical debates within DE (Humble and Smith, 2007: 26) reflect those focused on in this volume. Bourn suggests that DE is 'rooted in two distinct but interlinked theories: development theory and Freirean liberation education' (Bourn, 2004: 4), whilst Huckle suggests the need for a stronger link to critical theory and Marxism (Huckle, 2004: 29). Such competing perspectives on the political role of DE hold different views of the mainstreaming of DE in the UK in the last ten to fifteen years (e.g. the arrival of a national curriculum in England and Wales) and the arrival in 1997 of government funding for DE via the Department for International Development, with some arguing that DE has been co-opted, and its radical roots compromised (Huckle, 2004: 30). However, within NGOs there are also ongoing debates and negotiation not only about promoting DE in formal settings, but in forging productive relationships with the other aspects of NGO work, such as campaigning, advocacy and fundraising (Smith, 2004a).

Whilst conceptualization of DE remains contested, it is possible to identify ways in which this area of NGO practice intersects with different levels of cosmopolitan thought. We can also see ways in which these connections indicate degrees of ambivalence. If we follow the definition of DE offered by the UK Development Education Association (DEA), which includes exploring 'the links between people living in the "developed" countries of the North with those of the "developing" South' and working 'towards achieving a more just and a more sustainable world' (DEA, n.d.), we can see that DE is explicitly concerned with 'thinking and feeling beyond the nation'; it reflects Nussbaum's assertion that 'through cosmopolitan education, we learn more about ourselves' (Nussbaum, 2002: 11). Emphasis is placed on commonality as well as difference, and on acting on the basis of rights and responsibilities that are defined in global or human rather than national terms. That DE practice is increasingly framed in terms of global citizenship underscores the degree to which DE resonates with cosmopolitanism's emphasis on forms of political action and authority beyond the nation.

DE's connection to cosmopolitan political formations and cosmopolitan democracy can also be seen in its emphasis on linking the local and global, and on its emphasis on empowerment. In the UK, NGO DE teams often work in partnership with small local organizations, such as Development Education Centres, and there is considerable emphasis on pedagogies and resources that establish the foundation of learning and engagement in the learners' local experiences. In this regard, we could argue that DE has links to Calhoun's call for a greater emphasis on the local grounding of cosmopolitanism, and on engagement with the foundations of solidarity at local and global level (Calhoun, 2001, 2002).

However, whilst a critical engagement with difference may support NGOs' wider emphasis on motivating people to respond to the plight of the 'distant other' by engendering feelings of solidarity, it may also undermine NGOs' capacity to generate funds and transfer resources to that 'distant other'. Emphasizing common ground does not fit easily with NGOs' realization of care for the 'distant other' through fundraising, and DE has traditionally challenged representations of the South that produce emotional and, hence, financial responses. This means that a contradictory cosmopolitanism is produced by international NGOs, who, on the one hand, are encouraging solidarity and feelings of commonality in motivating people to 'think and feel beyond the nation', but who, at the same time, need to emphasize difference in ways which undermine notions of solidarity in order to generate funds through a more charitable impulse. This tension perhaps reflects both the selective and the instrumental deployment of cosmopolitan norms by NGOs, as well as the difficulty, in cosmopolitan thought, of recognizing diverse voices and authorities alongside the promotion of universal values and commitments.

Advocacy

To advocate means to promote the causes of others, and involves an inherently political set of actions. Keck and Sikkink (1998: 8) describe NGO advocacy networks as 'plead[ing] the causes of others or defend[ing] a cause or proposition.... [Advocacy groups] are organized to promote causes, principled ideas, and norms.' In line with the challenge of promoting development alternatives, Jordan and Van Tuijl (2000) have defined advocacy as action that attempts to rectify unequal power relations and rectify power imbalances. The advocacy aspect of NGO work thus addresses the causes of unequal development, rather than just alleviating its symptoms (although most development organizations engaging in advocacy are also working in some form of poverty alleviation). However, Jordan and Van Tuijl also challenge the oft-made distinction between NGOs as either 'operational' or 'advocacy' NGOs, noting that all acts which create space for the weak and powerless are political acts. Advocacy is increasingly fundamental to the work of development NGOs, particularly in the form of 'advocacy coalitions'

or 'transnational advocacy networks' that target local and national governments, as well as international organizations. These exemplify Pogge's (2003)
key elements of a cosmopolitan project in cutting across state boundaries
and focusing on issues affecting individuals. However, tensions have arisen
both between development NGOs and within individual organizations
– tensions around the legitimacy of advocating on behalf of others, tapping
into sentiments of a colonial cosmopolitanism.

Two of the largest international advocacy campaigns during the last
decade have been the Jubilee 2000 debt cancellation campaign and the
Make Poverty History (MPH) campaign. Specifically, the MPH campaign
is useful in highlighting a cosmopolitan ambivalence. At one level, the
campaign emphasizes the capacity of civil society to exert political power
beyond the nation-state, targeting the G8 when it met in Scotland in
2005. It also made it impossible, through the media and political pressure,
to ignore the 'other'. By explicitly rejecting fundraising and emphasizing
the need for justice, the campaign went some way to challenging distance
and the idea that the poor are poor due to 'misfortune' (Lu, 2000: 262).
On the other hand, it has been suggested that many supporters understand
little of the campaign objectives (Baggini, 2005), with additional criticism
of the associated wearing of a white band as a fashion statement rather
than a political one. Also, the level of southern engagement in the 'global'
campaign was limited. We could see this as an uneasy mix between democratic and banal cosmopolitanism. It would seem to underline Calhoun's
argument that NGOs rely on categorical identification – 'cultural framings
of similarity among people' (Calhoun, 2001: 25) – to engender solidarity.
Calhoun argues that within international civil society, few of these identities are linked to 'strong organizations of either power or community at a
transnational level', meaning that international civil society 'offers a weak
counterweight to a systemic integration and power' (Calhoun, 2001: 29). On
the other hand, we could also see MPH more dynamically as exemplifying
Tomlinson's (2002: 253) argument that the cultural openness engendered by
a global consumer culture needs to be built and shaped 'in the direction
of consensually emergent global solidarities'.

Conclusion

Cosmopolitanism requires the confronting of profound and complex challenges. It is about finding ethical ways to negotiate the universal and the
particular, local and global, nearby and distant. This requires the development of capacities for deciding between multiple affiliations and identities in
which the local and familiar may not take precedence. It also requires the
establishment of the means for democratic voice which goes beyond national

political systems. NGOs, meanwhile, work in contradictory ways, expressing a range of values, working across and within different national boundaries, expressing varying commitments to diverse forms of democracy.

Our discussion of NGOs' potential cosmopolitanism through the prisms of development education and advocacy highlights the ambivalence within and also between the different functions of the organizations. For example, there are contrasts between DE and advocacy in relation to the forms of democracy that are practised. In one recent instance, the DE team sought to empower participants to identify what they saw as priorities for campaigns, while the campaigns team were keen to focus on strategic priorities identified by a policy team (Baillie Smith, forthcoming). We could argue that each is working to different conceptions or aspects of cosmopolitan democracy, with one prioritizing the local, and the other the global.

A number of authors (Calhoun, 2002; Linklater, 2002; Tomlinson, 2002) emphasize the need for dialogue as the basis for establishing cosmopolitan values that have relevance to people's daily lives, and that will avoid what Calhoun (2002: 31) refers to as an 'attenuated' cosmopolitanism which is not grounded in 'mutual commitment and responsibility'. As Fine and Cohen (2002: 160) put it: 'The problem with Kant's metaphysics of justice is that it instructs people and rulers in what they must do, without involving them in the process of deciding what must or must not be done.' However, what we find is that democratic dialogue does not necessarily fit easily with NGO commitments to targets around income generation or focusing political pressure in relation to particular political opportunities (see Baillie Smith, forthcoming). In addition, NGOs lack a clear constituency with whom to engage in dialogue: 'NGOs at the global level can be very large organizations highly removed from any basic social or political community' (Lupel, 2003: 27). As a result, their policies are a 'product of specialized professionals and not public deliberation' (27); Desforges quotes an NGO employee commenting that their supporters do not want to be involved in decisions around the organization's work 'because they trust the organizations' competence in delivering improvement in people's lives' (Desforges, 2004: 562).

The lack of support for a democratic or deliberative approach indicates a degree of ambivalence in relation to what could be seen as a foundational element of cosmopolitanism – the democratic establishment of universal values. It also undermines NGOs' capacity to counter criticisms of elitism. If cosmopolitanism remains in the realm of 'abstract universal obligations at the expense of concrete particular loyalties and affiliations' (Lu, 2000: 249), then it is only likely to exist among 'persons whom fortune has relieved from the immediate struggle for existence and from pressing social responsibility and who can afford to indulge their fads and enthusiasms' (Boehm cited in Lu, 2000: 250).

This points to a fundamental dilemma for both NGOs and cosmopolitanism relating to the balance between expressing and supporting universal values and providing space for their identification and development. On a functional level, NGOs are faced with very practical tensions, one of which is funding. Even the most aspirationally cosmopolitan NGO will have to obtain funding for its operations, and this can present different challenges in how the NGO engages with the varied needs and interests of its different constituencies. NGO attempts to articulate alternatives is strongly circumscribed by being embedded within a neoliberal aid system and by needing to draw support from constituencies in the North whose lives are defined by highly commodified forms of consumption.

The purpose of this chapter has been to explore the relationship between cosmopolitanism and development NGOs and, more specifically, the ambivalent relationships that NGOs have in engaging their publics and the different forms of cosmopolitanism that they tap into. It is important to understand these ambivalent relationships, particularly if we are to look at their changing nature and at the realization of forms of cosmopolitan politics. The practical importance of this research is that, in investigating NGOs engagement with their constituents, we are looking not only at the future alternatives NGOs can offer, but at the future of NGOs themselves.

Whilst we have demonstrated that there is a strong degree of ambivalence in NGOs' cosmopolitanism, we have also shown that the different elements of NGOs' work strongly resonate with different cosmopolitan ideals as they unsettle other aspects. There are contradictions within and between the different areas of work, adding to the complexity. However, functional separation of these different elements within the organizations means that organizations are able to avoid resolving tensions around the universal and the particular, the local and the distant, and the democratic and the top-down. This not only diminishes NGOs' cosmopolitan credentials, but is likely to become a problem in the context of growing collaboration and networking within and across organizations. More worryingly for cosmopolitans of various shades, it denies their multiple projects a significant source of support.

Note

1. This chapter was authored equally by Matt Baillie Smith and Helen Yanacopulos. For the sake of equity, we alternate the name order in our joint publications.

References

Anderson, K. and D. Rieff (2004) 'Global Civil Society: A Sceptical View', in H. Anheier et al. (eds), *Global Civil Society Yearbook 2004*, Sage, London, pp. 26–40.

Appiah, K. (2002) 'Cosmopolitan Patriots', in J. Cohen (ed.), *For Love of Country?*, Beacon Press, Boston MA, pp. 21–9.

Archibugi, D. (ed.) (2003) *Debating Cosmopolitics*, Verso, London.

Baggini, J. (2005) 'Marching on Empty', *Guardian*, 3 June.

Baillie Smith, M. (forthcoming) 'International NGOs and Northern Constituencies: Development Education, Dialogue and Democracy', *Journal of Global Ethics*.

Barber (2002) 'Constitutional Faith', in J. Cohen (ed.), *For Love of Country?*, Beacon Press, Boston MA, pp. 30–37.

Bourn, D. (2003) 'Towards a Theory of Development Education', *Journal of Development Education* 10(1): 3–6.

Calhoun, C. (2001) 'The Necessity and Limits of Cosmopolitanism: Local Democracy in a Global Context', paper presented to the UNESCRO/ISSC conference 'Identity and Difference in the Global Era', Candido Mendes University, Rio de Janeiro, 20–23 May, www.ssrc.org/programs/calhoun/publications/limitsofcosmo3.doc (accessed 15 May 2005).

Calhoun, C. (2002) 'The Class Consciousness of Frequent Travellers: Towards a Critique of Actually Existing Cosmopolitanism', in S. Vertovec and R. Cohen (eds), *Conceiving Cosmopolitanism*, Oxford University Press, Oxford, pp. 86–109.

Carey, D. (2003) 'The Cosmopolitan Epoch: Configuring a Just World Order', *The Culture Mandala* 6(1), www.international-relations.com/wbcm6–1/WbCosmopolitanNew.htm (accessed 10 May 2005).

Chandhoke, N. (2002) 'The Limits of Global Civil Society', in *Global Civil Society 2002*, Centre for the Study of Global Governance, www.lse.ac.uk/Depts/global/Yearbook/outline2002.htm (accessed 15 June 2005).

Cohen, J. (ed.) (2002) *For Love of Country*, Beacon Press, Boston MA.

Colas, A. (2002) *International Civil Society*, Polity, Cambridge

DEA (n.d.) www.dea.org.uk/dea/deved.html, (accessed 15 June 2005).

Desforges, L. (2004) 'The Formation of Global Citizenship: International Non-governmental Organizations in Britain', *Political Geography* 23: 549–69.

Edwards, M. (1999) *Future Positive*, Earthscan, London.

Fine, R. (2006) 'Cosmopolitanism: A Social Science Research Agenda', in G. Delanty (ed.), *Handbook of Contemporary European Social Theory*, Routledge, London, pp. 242–53.

Fine, R., and R. Cohen (2002) 'Four Cosmopolitan Moments', in S. Vertovec and R. Cohen (eds), *Conceiving Cosmopolitanism*, Oxford University Press, Oxford, pp. 137–62.

Fowler, A. (1997) *Striking a Balance*, Earthscan, London.

Held, D. (2003) 'Democratic Accountability and Political Effectiveness from a Cosmopolitan Perspective', in D. Archibugi (ed.) *Debating Cosmopolitics*, Verso, London, pp. 184–202.

Huckle, J. (2004) 'Further towards a Theory of Development Education', *Journal of Development Education* 11(1): 29–30.

Humble, D., and M. Smith (2007) 'What Counts as Development Research?' in M. Smith (ed.), *Negotiating Boundaries and Borders. Qualitative Methodology and Development Research*, Elsevier, Oxford, pp. 13–34.

Jordan, L., and P. van Tuijl (2000) 'Political Responsibility and Transnational NGO Advocacy', *World Development* 28(12): 2051–65.

Keck, M., and K. Sikkink (1998) *Activists beyond Borders*, Cornell University Press, Ithaca NY.

Kuper, A. (2002) 'More Than Charity: Cosmopolitan Alternatives to the "Singer Solution"', Ethics & International Affairs 16(2): 107–20.

Lamont, M., and S. Aksartova, (2002) 'Ordinary Cosmopolitanisms: Strategies for Bridging Racial Boundaries among Working-class Men', Theory, Culture & Society 19(4): 1–25.

Linklater, A. (2002) 'Cosmopolitan Harm Conventions', in S. Vertovec and R. Cohen (eds), Conceiving Cosmopolitanism, Oxford University Press, Oxford, pp. 254–67.

Lu, C. (2000) 'The One and Many Faces of Cosmopolitanism', Journal of Political Philosophy 8(5): 244–67.

Lupel, A. (2003) 'Democratic Politics and Global Governance: Three Models', draft paper prepared for the Work in Progress Seminar Series, Department of Political Science, New School, New York, www.newschool.edu/gf/polsci/seminar/Lupel_11-20-03.pdf (accessed 10 May 2005).

Maguire K. (2003) 'How British Charity Was Silenced on Iraq', www.guardian.co.uk/Iraq/Story/0,,1095116,00.html (accessed 20 February 2007).

Nussbaum, M. (2002) 'Patriotism and Cosmopolitanism', in J. Cohen (ed.), For Love of Country?, Beacon Press, Boston MA, pp. 3–17.

O'Neill, O. (1986) Faces of Hunger: An Essay on Poverty, Justice and Development, Allen & Unwin, London.

Pogge, T. (2003) 'The Influence of the Global Order on the Prospects for Genuine Democracy in the Developing Countries', in Archibugi, D. (ed.) Debating Cosmopolitics, Verso, London, pp. 117–40.

Save the Children Fund UK (2003) 'Save the Children UK Not Silenced on Iraq', www.globalpolicy.org/ngos/fund/2003/1128nosilence.htm (accessed 20 February 2007).

Singer, P. (2002) 'Poverty, Facts, and Political Philosophies. Response to "More than Charity"', Ethics and International Affairs 16(2): 121–4.

Smith, M. (2004a) 'Mediating the World: Development, Education and Global Citizenship', Globalisation Societies and Education 2(1): 67–82.

Smith, M. (2004b) 'Contradiction and Change: NGOs, Schools and the Public Faces of Development', Journal of International Development, 16: 741 – 749.

Smith, M., and H. Yanacopulos (2004) 'The Public Faces of Development: An Introduction', Journal of International Development 16: 657–64.

Tomlinson, J. (2002) 'Interests and Identities in Cosmopolitan Politics', in S. Vertovec and R. Cohen (eds), Conceiving Cosmopolitanism, Oxford University Press, Oxford, pp. 240–53.

van der Veer, P. (2002) 'Colonial Cosmopolitanism', in S. Vertovec and R. Cohen (eds), Conceiving Cosmopolitanism, Oxford University Press, Oxford, pp. 165–79.

Vertovec, S., and R. Cohen, (2002a) 'Introduction: Conceiving Cosmopolitanism', in S. Vertovec and R. Cohen (eds), Conceiving Cosmopolitanism, Oxford University Press, Oxford, pp. 1–22.

Vertovec, S., and R. Cohen (eds) (2002b) Conceiving Cosmopolitanism, Oxford University Press, Oxford.

Yanacopulos, H. (2004) 'The Public Face of Debt', Journal of International Development 16: 717–27.

Yanacopulos, H. (2005) 'Patterns of Governance: the Rise of Transnational Coalitions of NGOs', Global Society Journal of Interdisciplinary International Relations 19(3): 247–66.

Yanacopulos, H. (2007) 'Cutting the Diamond: Networking Economic Justice', paper presented at the Institute for International, Comparative, and Area Studies (IICAS), University of California, San Diego, 25–27 January.

16

Development as Reform and Counter-reform:
Paths Travelled by Slum/Shack Dwellers International

Joel Bolnick

Context

There is now a general consensus that the two major challenges facing humanity in the twenty-first century are climate change and the urbanization of poverty. Both present very real threats to modernity, this remarkable epoch in which humanity has entered into a Faust-like pact in which it has traded its future for the sensational magic triggered by the unleashing of the energy that has been stored for billions of years in the earth's carbon deposits. The attendant growth of the human population and the rampant consumerism of a grossly unequal and exploitative global socio–economic order have created conditions for a very grim tomorrow.

But it is not the magnitude of these problems that is the most disturbing feature. It is clearly recognized that humanity has the resources, technology, knowledge and instruments of regulation to reverse global warming and to eradicate landlessness and homelessness in our cities and our towns. Why, then, would nobody of sane mind bet their worldly possessions on a resolution of either?

The slightly shorter odds would probably be on sorting out the problems relating to climate change. This is because it is only a matter of time before the elites of the global order will no longer be able to shield themselves from the consequences of their environmentally destructive consumer habits. As soon as the elites recognize that they themselves are at risk they will apply resources, technology, knowledge and instruments of regulation to address the problem. When it comes to fighting global warming, we are becoming aware of the fact that we are all at risk and that all of us have the capacity to be positive actors in the struggle against its spiralling effects.

The situation is distinct for the case of poverty and its consequences, which only directly affects the poor and the homeless in ways that either threaten or dramatically impede their lives. When the poor threaten to impose themselves on the rich, through illegal migration most recently, then there are increased efforts to 'barricade' the doors of the wealthy nations and/or communities. However, in spite of rising levels of criminality and the occasional health risk in our cities, the rich and the powerful are by the very nature of their material privilege almost completely screened from the misery of the poor. Indeed, on the one hand, they are increasingly secluded within gated communities whilst, on the other, there are continuing attempts to beautify city centres and ensure that middle-class interests dominate in public spaces (Bromley, 2000). The problem in building the bases for poverty eradication is that we are not all subjectively affected by poverty. What is worse, those who *are* subjectively affected, and therefore have the material motivation and the will to address the enormous challenge, do not have control over the resources, technologies, knowledge and instruments of regulation required to eradicate it.

All along the development continuum the tools for transformation are in the hands of individuals, social classes and groupings who use them badly precisely because as a collective critical mass they are inured from the consequences of their ineffectiveness. This contribution discusses one attempt to build a new alliance between social movements and NGOs to address recognized failures in poverty-reduction strategies. This process has, in a period of twenty years, grown from a single initiative to a transnational network with fifteen affiliates and a number of relationships with other interested organizations. This network seeks to establish new, more creative and more effective partnerships between the urban poor and professionals that facilitate a process by which the poor take control of poverty-reduction efforts.

A History of Development in Five Paragraphs

Different methodologies for the disbursement of foreign aid have evolved over time, and today more dated systems operate side by side with more recent strategies. Whilst traditional bilateral aid arrangements continue, official development assistance agencies have introduced increased numbers of decentralized aid programmes to support NGOs, civil societies and local government. These programmes have engaged NGOs in both North and South to develop and extend their own poverty-reduction programmes. In part, this diversification has resulted from ever-increasing attempts to find new and more effective poverty-reduction strategies. Whilst aid agencies continue to invest in food relief and in large-scale infrastructure projects, they have also been interested in exploring new approaches related to governance and the participation of a variety of groups in policymaking. In the last decade, there have been efforts to make aid more effective with the introduction of specific targets, now embedded within the Millennium Development Goals. These include specific targets related to better living conditions in urban areas with improved access to basic services and the improvement in the lives of 100 million slum dwellers. These goals and the related processes supported by the official development assistance agencies have sought to draw diverse agencies into the projects and programmes associated with development.

Diversification has also taken place among social movements. 'Old' social movements of trade unions and labour have been joined by movements that focus on feminism, environmental issues, animal rights and a wide diversity of other citizen interests (Mayo, 2005; Tarrow, 1998). A crucial difference is that these social movements have emerged in many different contexts, rather than out of a narrowly based context (as most bilateral aid strategies appear to have been dominated by the so-called "Washington Consensus") (Maxwell, 2005). Sometimes there have been direct transfers of knowledge and experience over time and distance; but often these movements have emerged while having little contact with one another, strategizing to advance their interests within their own localities. More recently, social movements have tended to evolve convergently, pushed to the realization of a particular orientation by structural realities that now have some global uniformity and international impact.

This chapter discusses the experiences of Shack/Slum Dwellers International (SDI), a transnational movement of homeless and landless people's federations. Try as it might SDI can never escape the fact that it has these two trajectories as its ancestry, the movement experiences of its affiliates and the aid industry as its benefactor. This coalescence is de facto proof both of the failure of the radical projects of the social movements and of the emergence of the hegemony of foreign aid as the major vehicle for social and economic transformation in the South. Movements have failed to identify and articulate an autonomous alternative to mainstream development, and development assistance, regardless of its often compromised intent, has emerged as a source of financial support for the continued search for new and more equitable forms of development. Paradoxically, the very countries that are engaged in increased global trade, and who (generally) host the multinational companies that are a powerful engine in the economic dynamics of globalization, provide the investment finance for alternatives to current development trajectories.

Of course the SDI model is not the only institution that has evolved,

in one form or another, from that period in history – post World War II
– in which the age of Western social movements (arguably in decline since
the 1920s) was eclipsed by the age of Bretton Woods and donor aid. The
aid-dependent methodologies of poverty eradication have diversified so
significantly over the years that it is easy to consider them as completely
unrelated. In spite of their current range of overlaps, their shared ancestry
and their resemblances are often disguised. The older more traditional
institutional forms such as the provision of donor aid for large infrastructure
projects (usually tied to country of origin expertise and technologies) remain
dominant in terms of their share of aid funds.

In respect of social development, it is possible to reconstruct a foreign aid
'family tree' which traces the way in which official aid to governments has
cross-pollinated with church aid to create welfare-driven initiatives. If the
exploration were extended it would be possible to trace the lineage through
to an important current sub-branch: donor funds for NGOs. Whilst this may
account for a small percentage of official development aid in financial terms,
it has led to the flowering of civil society initiatives, and effectively drawn
professional activists, academics and practitioners into a huge new industry
– the commodification of poverty eradication (Smillie, 1995). Donor-driven
NGO programmes have become a highly diversified institutional subgroup
within official aid programmes. This group includes superficially different
initiatives such as those that are driven by struggles for rights, those that
are focused on research, those that focus on social services such as health,
and those that focus on micro-credit. However, these initiatives share a
common institutional structure as they receive and manage aid finance on
behalf of intended beneficiaries. All these institutional arrangements share a
common objective, although it is normally obscured by many institutionally
specific agendas that often have nothing to do with this objective. The
objective, of course, is improving the lives and livelihoods of the billions
of poor people on this earth.

What is Shack Dwellers International?

Before going on to look at the structures and experiences of SDI, it is necessary to pose and answer the question: what is Shack Dwellers International,
or, rather, who is Shack Dwellers International? As Jane Weru, director of
Pamoja Trust (NGO affiliate in Kenya) has said:

> The people in Shack Dwellers International, in the leadership of the Federations
> and in the support organizations, are mainly people who are discontent. They
> are discontent with the current status quo. They are discontent or are very
> unhappy about evictions. They are people who feel very strongly that it is wrong

for communities, whole families to live on the streets of Bombay or to live on the garbage dumps of Manila. They feel strong enough to do something about these things. But their discontent runs even deeper. They have looked around them, at the poverty eradication strategies of state institutions, private sector institutions, multi-laterals and other donors. They have looked at the NGOs and the social movements from which they have come and they are unhappy with most of what they see. (SDI, 2006)

As before, this discontent has become a catalyst for change. In this case it has driven the formation and expansion of SDI, an alliance of people's organizations and NGOs seeking new and different ways to eradicate homelessness, landlessness and poverty. SDI brings together and capacitates homeless and landless people's federations and their support NGOs. These people's federations are engaged in many community-driven initiatives to upgrade 'slums' and squatter settlements, improving tenure security and offering residents new development opportunities, developing new housing that low-income households can afford, and installing infrastructure and services (including water, sanitation and drainage). All these federations learn from and support each other. The federations have a membership of savings schemes, locally based groups that draw together residents (mainly women) in low-income neighbourhoods to share their resources and strategize to address their collective needs. The initiatives undertaken by these savings schemes demonstrate how shelter can be improved for low-income groups, and how city redevelopment can avoid evictions and minimize relocations. The strategies (shared across the network) build on existing defensive efforts by grassroots organizations to secure tenure, and add to these existing efforts by measures designed to strengthen local organizational capacity and improve relations between the urban poor and government agencies.

The network was launched in 1996, building on existing relationships between federations in Cambodia, India, Namibia, Nepal, South Africa, Thailand and Zimbabwe. It now includes fifteen federation affiliates with emerging processes of grassroots savings groups in ten further countries.

By any measure SDI has achieved success with its new methodology and been more effective, in many ways, than other civil-society-based initiatives that seek to achieve the same objectives. The network has mobilized over 2 million women slum dwellers in twenty-four countries in the South. This is not an arbitrary figure of residents with a superficial engagement in this process. SDI members are savers, who interact on a daily basis around savings and loans. Records of these transactions and related levels of participation are maintained by most affiliates. Over 250,000 families have secured formal tenure with services, and about half of these have also been able to improve their housing through their own savings and a range of loan and subsidy finance. Many more families have been assisted as groups

Box 16.1   SDI influence in city and national policies to address urban poverty

In Namibia, the government has been supporting the loan fund of the Federation for over five years with annual contributions. At a housing policy conference in November 2006 (the first housing policy review since independence in 1991), invited Federation speakers were represented in each session with numerous contributions from local government officials in the floor of the meeting supporting a people's centre shelter development approach. The land and housing policy in Windhoek draws on Federation experiences and lobbying with support for incremental community development. Most recently (November 2006), the Namibian Federation has an agreement from national government to conduct a government-supported enumeration of all shack settlements in the country.

In South Africa, the Federation has long negotiated with city and national politicians. The housing minister (also chair of the African Ministerial Conference on Housing and Urban Development) hosted a Slum Summit in June 2006, granting the president of SDI a similar status to that of the housing ministers. At this meeting she pledged her government to work closely with the Federation through the allocation of 6,000 housing subsidies to Federation self-build groups (Sisulu, 2006). Late in 2006, the SA Federation and uTshani received an award from the national ministry for the best savings initiative. SDI was given a matching award for one of four institutions to have provided the most effective support to the ministry during the previous nine months.

In Zimbabwe, the Federation has had a difficult relationship due to the state's eviction campaign against the urban poor (Operation Murambatsvina); nevertheless the minister recently signed an agreement to allocate 5,000 plots to the Federation in recognition of their continuing investment at a time when the state is struggling to deliver the housing committed through Operation Garikai/Hlanlani Kuhle ('We promise things will be better').

In Kenya, the savings schemes and support NGO, Pamoja Trust, secured state support for an upgrading process in Huruma, a low-income settlement in Nairobi. This has ensured tenure for 2,000 families although has been even more notable as an example of how landlords and tenants are able to share land (Weru, 2004). Significant capacity in terms of enumerations and settlement profiling has resulted in the Kenyan Federation conducting a full enumeration of all 80,000 slum dwellers in the city of Kisumu – with the full official backing of the local authorities. This is preparation for an upgrading process within the city.

In Malawi, the Minister of Housing has pledged support for the loan fund of the Federation following the construction of almost 1,000 houses in the last two years (Manda et al., forthcoming). City authorities have allocated plots for hundreds of homeless families in Blantyre, Lilongwe and Mzuzu. Two directors and one deputy minister accompanied the Federation on an exposure visit to India, Thailand and South Africa in August 2006.

In Brazil, the Federation and support NGO are working in the area around Sao Paolo. In the two large industrial cities in the greater Sao Paulo area – Osasco and Vila Real – the support NGO Interacao has worked with private sector partners and the municipalities to regularize land tenure, prepare engineering reports, plan sanitation and explore funding possibilities for housing. Although this initiative has been active for only three years, over 7,000 families have secured legal land tenure.

The Homeless People's Federation in the Philippines launched the community-led slum upgrading process. Their pilot project involving the relocation of 10,000 families was begun in Iloilo City in 2006.

In Mumbai (India), Ethekwini (South Africa), Accra (Ghana), Iloilo (Philippines), Osasco and São Paulo (Brazil) and Kampala (Uganda) local affiliates have signed formal Memoranda of Understanding with Local Governments as a result of widespread recognition of SDI achievements.

Sources: Mitlin and Muller, 2004; Sisulu, 2006; Weru, 2004; Manda, forthcoming.

have negotiated alternatives to eviction and/or secured other services. In Mumbai and Pune (India) alone, SDI affiliates have provided sanitation to hundreds of thousands of slum dwellers. Through its grassroots organizing capacity and demonstrated delivery, SDI has had a major impact on urban policy in many cities (see Box 16.1).

Discontent with the status quo has propelled SDI to evolve new social technologies with which to fight against landlessness, homelessness and poverty. However, SDI remains historically linked and, what is more, materially dependent on aid agencies, to the institutional arrangements and methodologies that have failed to achieve significant poverty reduction, or at best continue to deliver only enough to hold out promise of significant change to keep a given developmental food chain alive (see, for example, Sahn and Stifel, 2003, for a discussion of progress towards the MDGs). Many local activities take place within SDI affiliates and these are not supported by development assistance. However, once the scope of activities extends beyond the neighbourhood and city, then resources are required. These resources are, overwhelmingly, drawn from official development assistance, international NGOs and, in some countries, national government grants and subsidies.

It is too soon either to herald SDI as a new path that will lead to a decisive impact on poverty and landlessness, or to dismiss it as another dead end. However, there is enough accumulated evidence to suggest that the Federation model that is championed by SDI may represent a developmental watershed; that it is a pointer towards a future configuration that may one day have the effect of tipping power relations in the development world in favour of the urban poor.

NGO Support Professionals for the Urban Poor: Arsenic in the Jam?

When professionals in the land and shelter sector organizations relate to collectives or to community organizations (rather than individual households), they tend to do so in one of five ways:

1. They operate from a welfare base, as deliverers of entitlements or needs.
2. They locate themselves as technical experts, delivering specific services such as training, construction management or information.
3. They position themselves as champions of tenure security and housing rights, normally enabling affected communities to challenge the state or large private institutions through the media or the courts.
4. They act as intermediary financial institutions, providing access to development capital.
5. They conduct research and generate documentation for lobbying, training or general intellectual curiosity.

These distinct types of professional engagement with the landless and homeless poor have several characteristics in common, in particular the emphasis on community participation and the role of the NGO as intermediaries.

Ever since the 1970s there has been a steady emphasis on people's participation. At face value this is little more than an assertion of the obvious. It is difficult to see how human needs such as land, housing, water and sanitation for the urban poor are to be met without their participation – whether it be a demand that rights be respected or collective self-help. Participation, of course, comes in different shapes and forms (Cooke and Kothari, 2001). For some NGOs, community participation means that the role of the NGO is to train community collectives to participate in the institutional arrangements, policy frameworks and projects of others – especially government. For others, community participation means enabling communities to participate in processes that are designed by professionals. The most progressive espousals of people's participation get articulated as 'partnerships'. This implies that the playing fields have been levelled and that all stakeholders – from the World Bank to community organizations – have the same capacity to ensure their self-interest through bargaining power and the cutting of deals. These important differentiations notwithstanding, there is hardly an NGO in existence — in the North or the South — that does not espouse participation as a platform of its programmes.

The problem, of course, is that the playing fields are never level. As described in Mitlin (2001: 383), communities (when asked) have expressed their reservations about working with NGOs whose agendas may not coincide with their own and that dominate project and financial decision-making. The lack of a level playing field can be traced to the second characteristic of almost all NGOs that — as indicated above — warrants a specific focus.

Whatever methodology these different institutions espouse, they all ensure that they are the intermediaries between Northern donor agencies, financial institutions or government departments that administer funds, on the one hand, and the collectives of households for whom these resources are intended, on the other (Hulme and Edwards, 1997). This is the second critical characteristic of almost all NGO relationships with social movements of the urban poor. The rationalizations are myriad, and some have foundation. However, what needs to be recognized is that it is not possible to talk of real people's participation or equal partnership when the decision to keep power and resources within the hands of professionals and out of the hands of the communities is one of the preconditions of the engagement.

SDI: An Evolutionary Watershed?

This brings the discussion back to SDI. If the SDI model is to be accorded the status of a watershed point in the struggle against urban poverty, then it is in part because SDI has sought constantly to tackle this conundrum head-on. The affiliates do so because, from the outset, SDI has been driven by the rationalities and interests of organizations *of the urban poor* to work with professionals. This is fundamentally different from many other alliances between NGOs and grassroots organizations where the motivation for the partnership derives from the interests *of the professionals*. The SDI partnership with professionals can be called a partnership of *conscious choice*.

The words 'from the outset' are used deliberately. During the 1970s, the National Slum Dwellers Federation (NSDF) in India, led by Arputham Jockin, tried and failed to work with NGOs. Persistent attempts at domination by the NGOs, coupled with strategic strangulation of resources, led NSDF to decide to break ties with all NGOs and to go it alone. A decade of non-collaboration brought its own litany of problems. Donors refused to fund the social movement directly. Government required technical data, and the Federation's organic, grassroots means of mobilization and communication failed to translate into a formal context. There were also the perennial problems of internal accountability and the need for more rigorous financial management. These factors led the Federation to try again in 1986, and over the years it has evolved a strong relationship with an NGO called SPARC, the Society for the Promotion of Area Research Centres (Patel and Mitlin, 2004; D'Cruz and Mitlin, 2007). This partnership between NGO and independent Federation is the template that has been adapted and replicated in fourteen other countries. Jockin has described this partnership as follows:

> [I]t is hard for the poor. They have many demands. The NGOs and the Social Movement – they take care of each other. Look out for each other. Make sure the money is spent in the right way. Make sure Government is willing to dialogue with us. I say SPARC is our washing machine, our *dobi*. It takes the community process and makes it clean.

Jockin identifies two related functions. First, the NGO helps to establish and monitor systems that minimize the risk that individual leaders will abuse their positions of trust. The National Slum Dwellers Federation learnt through its own earlier experiences that it can be very difficult for membership organizations to manage money. If community leaders abuse their positions of trust, then the movement cannot accomplish what is needed, loses credibility and reputation in the external world and may face damaging internal disputes. What is more, donor agencies and financial institutions simply refuse to enter into direct financial relationships with very poor, generally illiterate slum dwellers – either individually or as collectives. NGOs reduce these internally and externally perceived risks, and help to establish systems of financial accountability that ensure that money is monitored and all groups held to account for the funds that they receive.

The second reason is that the NGO helps make the processes of the savings schemes and the Federation acceptable to the external world. The external world is often critical of the poor, and positively anti-poor, not taking them seriously. Hence support NGOs often find themselves working with the Federation to ensure their emerging solutions for pro–poor urban development are acceptable to the world of decision-makers. The role of the NGO is to make things presentable and persuasive to an external world that is dominated by professional ways of doing things. The sequence is often that the people's activities, lobbying, meetings and demonstrated construction activities attract political interest. NGO staff then work more closely with the officials and technical experts, articulating the people's plans in the context of broader city policies, plans and programmes.

It is astonishing to note that the two primary reasons why the federations have decided to build relationships with professionals are the two

critical characteristics of NGOs that reinforce the structural contradictions that tend to make aid-based development so ineffectual. First the
federations draw the NGOs into a partnership in order to maximize
their own participation, and second they call on them to regulate and
manage their resources. Having struggled to secure their autonomy as
subjects in command of their own struggles, they are forced to relinquish
this important space and turn professionals into their own gatekeepers.
Where federations are strong or where they emerge independently from
the NGO, these are professionals of their choice. Within SDI, this has
happened only in India and Kenya. Even in these exceptional situations
this arrangement depends enormously on *trust* and is completely vulnerable to co-optation by SDI's partner NGOs and by their economic
masters, the donor agencies in the North. The federations have to trust
that the NGOs do not use the power vested in them by the federations
themselves to dominate the partnership and control the process. This is
in a context in which international development is putting increasing
pressure on the NGO sector to deliver specific outcomes regardless of
the underlying relationships and (in some cases) far-reaching objectives
(Bebbington, 2005).

Why have Federation leaders agreed to participate in this alliance and
commit themselves to such a relationship in return for resources? Is this
a case of consciousness evolving faster than, and therefore independently
from, historical or material conditions? Or is it only a handful of Federation
leaders and grassroots activists in the slums who belong to the SDI network,
be they from Colombo or from Accra, who have consciously grasped the
notion of their uniqueness as a class? Is it because it is only a handful of
key leaders who are ready to assume the responsibilities that go hand in
hand with this awareness that this new development, the conscious choice
of slum dweller organizations to form partnerships with professionals, has
evolved?

A major responsibility of conscious and organized slum dwellers is
to challenge, albeit pragmatically, the way in which resources in their
cities are distributed, but it is clear that it has to begin with managing
that challenge themselves in terms of their own resources. Alliances and
partnerships are important, and alliances with disaffected professionals in
society make total sense. At this historical moment, then, it would appear
that the Federation's leadership have the awareness that it is their right and
their duty to be in a position to respond as they see fit to the conditions
that exploit and marginalize them. In order to be effective, they have to
find partners in the NGO sector to whom they entrust their most critical
instruments for change.

Possibilities and Constraints
Born from a Conscious Partnership with NGOs

What are the main characteristics of this partnership between NGOs and Federations – this partnership that may represent a watershed in the struggle against homelessness and landlessness, because it is a partnership that has been solicited consciously by the slum dwellers themselves?

Alliances with professionals are in place in the fifteen countries where the Federation has achieved citywide scale. These alliances are determined by the existence of citywide or nationwide Federations of the Urban Poor, whose members are predominantly women shack/slum dwellers saving together. These federations range in size from hundreds of thousands of households in India to a few hundred in Tanzania. They forge alliances with small professional support organizations. Where the federations are able to secure land, install services and construct houses, the NGOs have set up urban poor development funds to scale up savings and secure development capital.

Federations cede control to their NGO partners or agree to share with them the responsibilities associated with seven specific functions. They task the staff responsible for their revolving funds with (1) the management of urban poor development funds; and (2) technical assistance for housing projects. They transfer all or part of the following responsibilities to their professional support NGOs: (3) fund-raiser and fund manager; (4) internal governance; (5) lobbying and brokering deals; (6) facilitation of learning through horizontal exchange programmes; and (7) research and documentation.

These alliances have certainly been effective. In almost every outcome they outperform or at the very least match other civil society initiatives in the land and shelter sector. In fact the 15,000 to 30,000 housing units that they are annually constructing worldwide just about places them in a league of their own among NGOs and social movements. (Although it is sobering to remember that while SDI built over 30,000 houses in nine countries in 2006, those same countries experienced a growth in homelessness that was at least twenty times greater.) There is also no doubt that the structure of the alliance, the close partnerships with independent NGOs, contributes significantly to these outputs. These NGOs help to negotiate for both international and state funds, manage the demands of professionals and other state officials, and disseminate the experiences realized. The significance of the NGOs' presence is demonstrated by the slow progress made in Uganda when the local groups were dependent on the local authority for professional support.

However, these are not necessary and sufficient conditions to hail the SDI model as an evolutionary breakthrough. After all, major transformations do not occur overnight. There is never a dramatic volte-face. But there are often seminal moments, perhaps even moments of value-laden progress. Such a moment occurred when a social movement in India made a conscious choice to seek out a professional partner and to negotiate the terms of engagement from a position of autonomy and relative strength. In this case (as introduced above), the National Slum Dwellers Federation, frustrated by their attempts to secure funding when they worked on their own, built an alliance with SPARC and an emerging network of women's collectives (Mahila Milan). Part of the relationship is a shared understanding that the collective experience and perspective of the urban poor is central; as a result the specific roles within the relationships are in permanent transition. As the federations and savings schemes grow stronger and local capacity is developed, there is a constant shifting down of tasks. All fourteen other SDI affiliates in fourteen different countries have inherited this element of value-laden progress. It is embedded in their relationships with their NGOs and it is increasingly regulated by SDI itself, as a proactive network. (However, it remains vulnerable to NGOs themselves, donor agencies, governments and even to community leaders who exploit the principle of grassroots autonomy for purposes of narrow self-interest.)

Also embedded in the relationship are the contradictions that emerged from that negotiated agreement: the control of resources by the NGO and therefore the ever-present possibility that the NGO, either of its own voli-tion or as a result of pressure from back donors (i.e. those who finance the Northern NGO activities), will overwhelm the federation process. It is important to remember that this contradiction is fundamental to aid-driven development as a whole. SDI is pushing the boundaries of acceptance of the aid industry, and to date it has been able to go as far as the solution worked out by SPARC and NSDF and no further: namely collaboration between NGO and network of CBOs, around CBO priorities but secured only through trust and interpersonal relationships. Every time the federations try to push for greater economic independence and the autonomous management of funds by the poor, the conditions of the aid industry shut them down.

So comprehensive is the neutralization of such a radical autonomous project that the status quo is seldom openly challenged by the federations. On the rare occasions that this challenge manifests itself as a form of collective consciousness (not as the self-interest of leaders) it is the NGOs that fall back on the discourse of the aid industry (and the global economy as a whole) to shut the federation agenda down or to retard its move to autonomy.

These tensions are illustrated by the experience in South Africa where the Federation experienced deep problems in 2003/4 which were partly related to weak financial practices and from intractable leadership disputes. How did the South African NGO respond to the crisis that paralysed the Federation during those years? First, it failed to acknowledge that the Federation was the senior partner in the alliance and that the NGO had let the Federation down. It had not honoured its part of the agreement, which was to assume management of the finances, and governance, capacity building and dialogue with external agencies, especially the state. Instead it responded by analysing the problem as a lack of financial control, and hence by introducing new management systems. Then it felt obliged by the regulatory environment and its own professional predilections to declare the problems intractable. Instead of admitting its failure and resigning from its support role, it decided to close itself down, in the process shutting off the Federation's access to donor and government funds. The challenges were more complex than a short reflection can demonstrate, and one of the arguments that the NGO presented was that it was not able to hand control back to the Federation since the leadership was deeply divided. This rationalization sidesteps the fact that uTshani Fund, the Federation's revolving fund, was there to be offered the responsibility, as was its international umbrella body, SDI, whose secretariat is based in South Africa. The immediate consequence was to exacerbate tensions within the Federation leading, along with the other factors, to several years of inactivity and bitter dispute. In spite of these setbacks the Federation has been able to regain a strong presence in many informal settlements in the country with the capacity to resolve its govern-ance disputes, and address its financial problems. Working in conjunction with a new NGO partner on a similar basis to the other SDI affiliates, it has once again become a significant actor on the South African land and housing scene. A dramatic turnaround in 2005/6 resulted in an allocation of 6,000 housing subsidies and demonstrates conclusively that the Federation never lost its capacity to reconfigure itself, to rally tens of thousands of poor, landless women into its collectives and to draw Government into serious partnerships.

The purpose of this example is not to critique the role of one particular NGO partner in the SDI stable as much as it is to demonstrate how the constraints inherent in the current structural form of the alliances in SDI can place the federations at considerable risk. The particular South African experience is an extreme example, but the contradiction and the risk are present in all SDI formations at present. They are not of the NGOs' making. They are the doing of the aid industry as a whole, transmitted through NGOs when they accept donor funds. On the macro-level they are the doings of a development paradigm that is defined by the global economy and its dominant and all-pervasive ideology; an ideology that astonishingly asserts that the very economic system that has lumpen-proletarianized as much as 40 per cent of most Southern cities is also the instrument for their growth and development.

The First Signs of an Important Mutational Leap

It is clear that the conscious solicitation of professional partners by slum dwellers themselves may represent an evolutionary benchmark in its own right. Material conditions have already developed in South Africa to propel the South African alliance (and perhaps, in time, other SDI affiliates) to another level. This level is not necessarily progressive – indeed, it may lead to a developmental cul-de-sac. But it is clearly a response to a locally generated crisis that sheds light on one of the underlying tensions in the structure of the alliance. This structural tension, in turn, can be traced back to SDI's pedigree as part of the international aid industry. The experiences which led to the shutting down of the support NGO in South Africa seem to have propelled systematic, progressive changes in a reformed South African affiliate, leading it towards a new alignment in which NGO accountability to its partnership with people's movements is rooted in a new financial relationship. Should this new alignment prove socially and economically sustainable and then be replicated in the SDI network as a whole, it will be recognized with hindsight as an important mutational leap that will enable SDI to couple its pragmatic engagement with formal institutions with a deeper grassroots autonomy.

When the South African NGO closed down in early 2005 it terminated contracts with donor agencies and returned all available funds. Fortunately the Federation's capital funds were not affected, since they were secured in a separate entity – the Federation's urban poor fund called uTshani Fund. (uTshani Fund had to ward off a hostile takeover attempt by a self-styled leadership. The Federation's own internal governance structures managed to turn this around and protect the capital fund. Another demonstration of the potential dysfunctionality of the relationship between NGO and social movement in the SDI network was that the South African Federation not only had to beat off the onslaught of a leadership interested only in self-gain, but found its then-NGO partner interfering in its internal governance structures to strengthen the position of this leadership that had detached itself completely from its base.) The Federation found itself – at its most vulnerable moment – without any funds to continue its programmes, to run its offices and to maintain its networks. Propelled by necessity and with support from its slum dweller partners in other countries, the Federation began to reconfigure itself. Active members created an overall facilitation structure that they have called Federation of the Urban Poor (or FEDUP – the key actors in the network explain that the name reflects their anger at their erstwhile colleagues who hijacked their name and conspired with formal professionals to hijack their capital fund.). They have reconstructed the Federation model into a learning initiative with a core of over 200 leaders, who have the capacity to enable and empower local groups to set their own priorities and drive their own development, acting in partnership with other stakeholders operating on a settlement-wide and citywide basis. This has enabled them to form alliances with other social movements such as Poor People's Movement, Coalition of the Urban Poor and over ninety independent residents' committees, thereby swelling its network to over 700 informal settlements countrywide. The Federation groups have returned to the basic building blocks of SDI, savings schemes, experimenting with new ways in which this strategy can address basic needs in communities and build an autonomous movement.

Most importantly, though, from the perspective of this chapter, the South African Federation chose to set up a Trust to serve as a conduit for all its funds – to be used to drive its learning, advocacy and governance, and to pay for its office and operating costs. When and where the Federation feels the need for professional support, it will now be in a position to enter into contracts with any one of a number of possible NGOs through its Trust. The NGOs are likely to perform the same functions as they do in other SDI affiliates where the older structure is still in place. The critical difference is that the Federation is in a position to cancel or decide not to renew these contracts should the NGO fail to meet the terms and conditions brokered at the outset.

Not only will this give the Federation leverage over the NGO that it has lacked to date, but, perhaps more significantly, it promises to generate a new dynamic around decision-making, the setting of priorities and accountability – within the social movement and between the social movement and its NGO partners. If the Federation and the NGOs that it contracts are able to widen and diversify their funding sources, this new instrument may lead to a situation in which the primary relationship in the continuum of partnerships is no longer between the NGO and the donors, with community participation in the process defined by this external relationship. Instead there is more chance that the Federation's relationship with NGOs will become primary, with donor and government participation being defined by this internal relationship. The implications for the other relations within the continuum are not yet clear.

Conclusion

The concept of Slum Dwellers Federations is rooted in the realization by very poor and marginalized men and women living on the margins of our cities of the need to rally together and to operate as collectives in order to rid themselves of the dependency and exclusion that binds them to perpetual poverty. SDI is therefore a global manifestation of a new realization that by seeking to run away from themselves and give their problems to professionals and politicians, the urban poor are condemning themselves to continued marginalization, regardless of the number of houses that get built for them or the number of plots that are given to them.

SDI, through its local affiliates, seeks to infuse homeless people with pride in themselves, in their efforts, capacities, value systems and their outlook on life. To date the SDI affiliates have been obliged to hand over key aspects of their programmes to trusted professional partners in order to advance this project. As a general rule this arrangement has worked well, but embedded within it are profound contradictions. As the South African experience demonstrates, it leaves the slum dwellers vulnerable and dependent on external actors for the continuation of their programmes. It is only when the vulnerability is exposed that the federations will be propelled to explore alternatives, even though there is an under-current of restlessness in regard to power relations between federations and NGOs in all mature affiliates.

Recent institutional shifts in South Africa, may, therefore, be providing the SDI network as a whole with an image of its own future. Ironically it has been the near terminal implosion of the South African alliance in 2005 and the subsequent strategies of reconfiguration that may, over time, provide SDI with its next developmental watershed and assist the global network to scale up its impact on urban poverty and the development of inclusive and sustainable cities.

References

Bebbington, A. (2005) 'Donor–NGO Relations and Representations of Livelihood in Non-governmental Aid Chains', *World Development* 33(6): 937–50.

Bromley, R. (2000) 'Street Vending and Public Policy: A Global Review', *International Journal of Sociology and Public Policy* 20(1/2): 1–28.

Cooke B., and U. Kothari (eds) (2001) *Participation: The New Tyranny?*, Zed Books, London.

D'Cruz, C., and D. Mitlin (2007) 'Shack/Slum Dwellers International: One Experience of the Contribution of Membership Organizations to Pro-poor Urban Development', in R. Kanbur, M. Chen, R. Jhabvala and C. Richards (eds), *Membership Based Organizations of the Poor,* Routledge, London.

Haddad, L., M.T. Ruel and J.L. Garrett (1999) *Are Urban Poverty and Under-nutrition Growing? Some Newly Assembled Evidence*, Food Consumption and Nutrition Division, International Food Policy Research Institute, Washington DC.

Hulme, D., and M. Edwards (eds) (1997) *Too Close for Comfort? NGOs, States and Donors*, Macmillan, London, and St Martins Press, New York.

Manda, M.A.Z. (forthcoming) 'Mchenga-Urban Poor Housing Fund in Malawi', *Environment and Urbanization* 19(1).

Maxwell, S. (2005) 'The Washington Consensus is Dead: Long life the meta-narrative', *Working Paper* 243, Overseas Development Institute , London.

Mayo, M. (2005) *Global Citizens: Social Movements and the Challenge of Globalization*, Zed Books, London.

Mitlin, D., and A. Muller (2004) 'Windhoek, Namibia – Towards Progressive Urban Land Policies in Southern Africa', *International Development Policy Review* 26(2): 167–16.

Patel, S., and D. Mitlin (2004) 'Grassroots-driven Development: The Alliance of SPARC, the National Slum Dwellers Federation and Mahila Milan', in D. Mitlin and D. Satterthwaite (eds), *Empowering Squatter Citizen*, Earthscan, London, pp. 216–44.

Sahn, D.E., and D.C. Stifel (2003) 'Progress toward the Millennium Development Goals in Africa', *World Development* 31(1): 23–52.

Satterthwaite, D. (2003) 'The Millennium Development Goals and Urban Poverty Reduction: Great Expectations and Nonsense Statistics', *Environment and Urbanization* 15(2): 181–90.

SDI (2006) 'The Rituals and Practices of Slum/Shack Dwellers International', SDI, Cape Town.

Sisulu, L. (2006) 'Partnerships between Government and Slum/shack Dwellers' Federations', *Environment and Urbanization* 18(2): 401–5.

Smillie, I. (1995) *The Alms Bazaar: Altruism under Fire – Non-Profit Organizations and International Development*, IT Publications, London.

Tarrow, S. (1998) *Power in Movement: Social Movements and Contentious Politics*, Cambridge University Press, Cambridge.

Weru, J. (2004) 'Community Federations and City Upgrading: The Work of Pamoja Trust and Muungano in Kenya', *Environment and Urbanization* 16(1): 47–62.

PART V

Taking Stock and Thinking Forward

Reflections on NGOs and Development: The Elephant, the Dinosaur, Several Tigers but No Owl

David Hulme

One of the pleasures of being an ageing academic is to see the work that one has done in the past revisited by younger colleagues.[1] Whether they build on your work, or point to its fundamental weaknesses, this is much better than it simply disappearing. One of the downsides of this pleasure is the realization that the concepts and ideas that one used earlier have both evolved and multiplied and, perhaps, become even more amorphous. In this short chapter I make no attempt to explore such theoretical advances. This task has already been admirably and concisely achieved in the introductory chapter to this volume. Another downside is that the empirical research base on which to test ideas has expanded so much that I am unable to master the rich resource it provides. The chapters in this volume, the larger number of papers at the 2005 Conference and the wider literature are only drawn on to a very limited degree in this chapter. In effect I am 'shooting from the hip' – though given the lowly standing of cowboy metaphors since George W. Bush came to office, I need to be careful about such an analogy.

One of the valuable points made in the Introduction and in other chapters in this volume is to recognize the fluidity of analytical boundaries and to avoid taking analytical bifurcations too strictly (Chhotray, this volume). Defining NGOs and precisely separating them from social movements may be less important than exploring the relationships between entities that seem to have NGO or social-movement characteristics. Rather than judging whether an NGO has contributed to development (the broad set of processes underlying capitalist development) or to Development (the subset of consciously identified interventions aimed at the 'third world') it may be more useful to look at the relationship between an NGO's actions on its 'little d' and 'big D' impacts. I shall strive for clarity in this chapter but recognize that ambiguity is an inevitable component of interpreting the role of NGOs in developmental processes.

I should also point out here that I have 'changed my spots' over the years. My recent work has focused much more on poverty, and especially the poorest (CPRC, 2004; Hulme and Shepherd, 2003), than it did in the 1990s and my concerns about NGOs undermining processes of public sector reform and state formation have reduced. For example, the concerns I had about BRAC substituting for the state in Bangladesh have evaporated. BRAC provides services that ideally I think the state should provide (primary education and basic health services) as well as services the private sector should provide (cash transmission and ISP services). However, I do not believe it is 'crowding out' the state or the market: there is plenty of unmet demand for such services if the public and/or private sectors in Bangladesh get their acts together. And the ideas, systems and staff of BRAC are resources on which the state and private sector can draw in the future. The question asked at the 1991 conference related to how NGOs can progress from their small islands of success to having an impact on the systemic pressures that cause and reinforce poverty, has been answered, at least in part (Edwards and Hulme, 1992: 7).

While there is little evidence that NGOs have made a profound difference, I take heart in some of the developments that have occurred since the early 1990s (see also Edwards, this volume). In 1992 BOND (British Overseas NGOs for Development) was a vague idea floating around the first Manchester conference. Today it is a functioning organization that, as part of its remit, helps small and medium-sized UK NGOs engage in lobbying and advocacy work and have a better grasp of the wider environment they are engaging. It may provide them with advice about applying for EU grants to deliver services, but it also helps to explain to them why the EU is such a weak donor.

Also, I take heart in the fact that economists, and particularly economists that are neoliberal or inclined in that direction, wish to devote time and energy to criticizing NGO advocacy. Deepak Lal (2004) devoted an entire chapter of a recent book to the NGO scourge, and Paul Collier has proposed setting up an annual award for the NGO that advocates the 'worst policies' for African countries (i.e. policies that challenge economic liberalization and/or an export orientation). If NGOs have registered with heavyweight economists of the right and centre-right they must be doing something worthwhile. Back in 1992 virtually all (maybe 'all') serious development economists could ignore NGOs, as NGOs were merely 'social development'.

NGOs, Neoliberalism and Development Alternatives

While many of the chapters in this volume explicitly or implicitly indicate that over the last fifteen years NGOs have failed in relation to their promoting an alternative to the neoliberalism that seized control of Development in theory, policy and practice in the 1980s, I have a slightly different view. I believe that by the late 1990s full-blooded neoliberalism was vanquished as the global public policy prescription for all developing and transitional countries. Around that time policy shifted to a hybrid position (Bazan et al., this volume) or a post-Washington Consensus (Fine, 2001) or a Third Way (Giddens, 1998). No longer were the crude prescriptions of whole-hearted neoliberalism — minimalize the state, transfer as many roles as possible to the private sector as quickly as possible, go for export-oriented growth whatever the consequences — dominant in discourse or practice. The hybrid was not a concise counter-narrative or a clear alternative to neoliberalism but a broad church that moderated the neoliberal fundamentalism of Development, and gradually impacted on development. It confirmed that economic growth was necessary to improve the lives of the poor, non-poor and rich; it believed that globalization was positive for human well-being in aggregate, but that it needed managing to offset its negative consequences; it recognized a significant developmental role for the state as well as the private sector; and it affirmed that human rights and participation were desirable, although it avoided pushing this issue when it encountered significant opposition (as with China).

This hybrid was highly plastic — while many key actors could agree in their discourse that a hybrid model was most appropriate, the prescriptions varied widely. On the right, the emphasis remained on the primacy of the private sector and growth; poverty was recognized as a concern (but not inequality); education and health were important (but in instrumental terms as raising human capital and productivity); environmental problems could be managed through technological advances; and social policy was acceptable but from a residualist perspective. Those to the left of centre highlighted human rights and/or human development as the starting point. While they agreed that growth was essential and that the private sector had a major role, they sought to reduce inequality as well as poverty; viewed access to education and health services as a right; believed that moderating consumption was an essential component of environmental policy; and saw a major role for publicly financed social policy. At the extremes, outside of the hybrid consensus, were powerful actors in the USA and the IMF on one side, and anti-globalists and eco-warriors on the other.

What role did NGOs, and particularly development NGOs, play in this shift? I say 'shift' because this hybrid has in practice yielded a moderated neoliberal strategy for development and not a clear alternative. It is hard to judge, but the answer probably has to be 'relatively little'. Other factors and actors were much more important. To a very high degree, full-blooded neoliberalism undermined itself by its outcomes, most obviously in the former Soviet Union. The short, sharp shock that neoliberals predicted as the states of the FSU 'took the medicine' yielded a chronic, comprehensive collapse in economic growth, material living standards, life expectancy, educational quality and security. Self-evidently the pure neoliberal model did not work. Alongside this, rich-country practitioners such as the UK decided to move to a hybrid model and abandon neoliberalism. The intellectual inputs that supported the shift focused on human rights (and their reaffirmation in Vienna in 1993) and the conversion of Sen's concepts of endowments, entitlements and capabilities into the more comprehensible idea of human development. UN agencies played important roles in this (UNDP with the *Human Development Report* and UNICEF with its reactivation of UN global summits and conferences), as did social movements, especially the women's and environmental movements. Many NGOs provided support for these more powerful actors – propagating UN messages and occasionally playing more significant roles (for example, the International Coalition on Women's Health, and many others, in advancing the agenda for reproductive and sexual health).

If one were to take a more critical look – as much at academics researching NGOs as at NGOs themselves – then two key omissions in the 1980s and 1990s need highlighting. The first was the neglect of analysing and challenging those who would gain control of both discourse and practice in development. NGOs focused on publicizing and mitigating the consequences of neoliberalism in the developing world and launched attacks on the World Bank and IMF and sometimes the G7 and the USA. However, development NGOs failed to stand back and look at some key players in the underlying processes – as did researchers on NGOs (*mea culpa*). In the UK, development NGOs criticized what Margaret Thatcher was doing with British aid, and international development policy more broadly, but failed to examine the way in which neoliberal think-tanks, and particularly the Institute of Economic Affairs (IEA), had shaped and were shaping conservative thinking. International development was only a minor issue for the IEA – it was focused on development and not Development – but the ideas and prescriptions of this small cabal swept away the ideas and criticisms of the UK's development NGOs. They could carp and criticize, but could not provide a concise and coherent narrative of an alternative.

This was not just a UK phenomenon: the omission spread across to the USA (the G1 as John Clark has accurately described it in the early twenty-first century) where think-tanks that were not mentioned at the Manchester and Birmingham conferences of the 1990s – the American

Enterprise Institute, Hudson Institute, Cato Institute, Heritage Foundation and others – had made significant contributions to ensuring that the G1 was, at best, ambivalent to the goals of poverty reduction or social development in developing countries. Even after 9/11, US political parties and public opinion were so well conditioned that there was no serious thought given to a 'soft power' (Nye, 2004) strategy to strengthen US security – such as taking a leadership role in global poverty reduction or the MDGs to counter the continual global rise in anti-Americanism.

This takes me to the second omission – the failure of developmental NGOs outside of the USA, but also probably in the USA, to fully examine the ways in which American civil society and media understand and relate to the problems of poorer people and the developing world. The task of shaping development discourse, policy and practice in developing countries was not matched by understanding and seeking to re-shape the way that US citizens and the US media deal with these issues. At a general level, NGOs outside the USA (and probably within the USA) might be able to criticize US government and civil society policies and positions, but they failed to move beyond criticism to try and work out how, as a long-term project, they might contribute to reshaping US public attitudes about poverty and social problems in the developing world. More concretely, when US environmental NGOs were able to seize policy agendas and block off World Bank investments that might foster growth and poverty reduction (Mallaby, 2004), development NGOs could gasp at the influence of such minorities but could not mount an effective challenge to the eco-imperialism promoted by such groups.

These omissions generate very difficult questions. How might a domestic constituency be built up in the USA to support the forms of 'moral vision' for international development that have evolved in Scandinavia, the Netherlands and, most recently, the UK? What can be done to make the US media less negative about the struggles of poor people and poor countries and more honest about the US role in such problems? Even, what can be done to reduce the isolation of the US population and help them engage more in a global civil society? Developmental NGOs can only be a component part of tackling these big questions, but surely this must be a significant part of the future task? ... which takes me to looking into the crystal ball, to the future.

The Elephant, the Dinosaur, Several Tigers but No Owl

So, what can we learn from the condensed and highly oversimplified account I have provided? Building on Mike Edward's 'elephant in the room', I shall provide an expanded menagerie of issues that I think are staring NGOs in the face. First, I have to confirm the elephant. NGOs have been slow to take up the innovative approaches to accountability and strengthened legitimacy that were discussed in earlier conferences and in Edwards and Hulme (1995) and Hulme and Edwards (1997), or to change their relationships and escape the aid chain. The renewed availability of aid, the recent rise of mega-philanthropy and, in some cases, more effective marketing and fundraising, have allowed many NGOs to drift on ameliorating social conditions in many poor countries but avoiding genuinely strategic thinking (see Chapter 1).

But there is also a dinosaur in the room — the USA. With the wisdom of hindsight it is clear that a component of all NGO strategic analyses in the future should pose the question, 'can we do anything to help reshape US public opinion, the content of the US media and (even) the nature of the US media?' The answer will often be 'no' but for some NGOs there may be new strategies for experimentation. Could Comic Relief assist its UK comics to meet up with US comics? Not to get them to ask the US public for money, but to encourage them to seek out air-time (on private and public television and radio) to get a message across to US citizens about the need to engage with Development and development. Could the Christian NGOs in Europe, and their many church-based groups, link or 'twin' with Christian NGOs and church groups in the USA to foster a less isolationist, conservative viewpoint? Could Latin American NGOs find ways of mobilizing the USA's vast Latino population to challenge the conservative orthodoxy and moral vision in US public attitudes, and convert that into pressures on US congressmen? Surely there must be some possible means of trying to integrate more US citizens into an emerging global civil society.

And then there are the 'tigers in the room'. I use this to refer to the emerging economic superpowers of China, India, Russia and Brazil (or the BRICs, as bankers call them). In the future they will be big players in the world economy, with Chinese and/or Indian GNP likely to overtake US GDP mid-century, and by choice or default will take on roles in both Development and development. China is already beginning to play a major role in Africa and Central Asia from what political scientists would describe as a 'realist' position — strict national self-interest. India is moving into Development with the establishment in 2007 of the Indian International Development Cooperation Agency (IIDCA). It also seems to be adopting a 'realist' stance, with 99 per cent of Indian aid going to South Asian neighbours and being tied, but there may be the possibility of refocusing this. In the long term one might imagine the creation of a domestic constituency in India for a more progressive engagement with 'little d' development (Hulme, 2007). Russia appears to be solidly 'realist', given its stance to both rich and poor nations. As for Brazil, I must confess my ignorance, while noting that political trends in Latin America appear to have a distinct autonomy from the rest of the world with their shift to the left and talk of 'socialism'. Any serious development NGO should be revising its strategy to ask what it could do to help contribute to at least one of the BRICs seeking to be not merely an economic superpower but also a social superpower.

Last, but not necessarily least, is the owl – the missing faunal component of my menagerie of future opportunities for development alternatives. I use the owl as a metaphor for wisdom, and by that I refer to what has been missing from the contemporary environment in which NGOs operate. More precisely I am referring to a theoretical body of knowledge that can be stripped down into a persuasive policy narrative. The neoliberal hegemony of the 1980s and (at least) early 1990s was partially founded on its capacity to claim deep intellectual roots (Hayek and Friedman) to colonize the discipline of economics, and perhaps other social sciences, with rational-choice frameworks and to produce a simple policy narrative that could be repeated by the cognoscenti and the less erudite – 'private good, public bad'! The theoretical alternative of socialism and associated policy narratives waned from the late 1970s onwards with the ascendancy of neoliberal thought. It was further marginalized in the late 1980s with the collapse of the Soviet Union – argued by those on the right to be the concluding, empirical proof that socialism could never work – and the 'success' of globalization in the 1990s through economic growth and poverty reduction (if you select the 'right' datasets and turn a blind eye to Africa and the former Soviet Union).

The main theoretical alternative that has risen is Nobel prize-winning Amartya Sen's capabilities theory, and the associated policy narrative of human development. This has helped to shift Development and, to a much smaller degree, development from full-blooded neoliberalism. However, it has not created the intellectual apparatus sufficient to launch a 'development alternative' that could vanquish, rather than simply challenge, neoliberally oriented analyses and narratives. While Sen is feted in Europe, Asia and elsewhere, his theory has made only limited progress in the USA outside of its north-eastern homeland. In the absence of a global, alternative intellectual and ideological 'breakthrough' to match neoliberalism in the late 1970s and early 1980s, NGOs will have to continue their struggle with tools at hand – human rights, capabilities and human development. Other 'new' concepts, most obviously social capital in the 1990s, will need to be treated with caution as they are double-edged swords that might help or hinder the search for the intellectual high ground of a development alternative.

Conclusion

To summarize – over the last fifteen to twenty years a clearly demarcated 'development alternative' to neoliberalism has not emerged. This is not necessarily a failure of progressive NGOs, however, but a broader failure of the global, intellectual community opposed to neoliberalism to develop a theoretical body of knowledge and an associated policy narrative that could vanquish neoliberalism. Capabilities, human development and human rights have mounted a challenge that have, however, shifted discourse and subsequently policy and practice to a more 'hybrid' theoretical basis. The lessons that I take from this potted history, and the papers in this volume are fourfold:

1. Following Mike Edward's introduction, NGOs must be encouraged to move out of the 'comfort zone' provided by expanded foreign aid flows, to think about the relationships they forge – 'the elephant in the room'.
2. NGOs in both South and North need to strategize about how they might contribute to reshaping US public opinion and the media so that 'the dinosaur in the room' might become less socially isolated and narrowly self-interested. This might be individually, as coalitions of NGOs or, more effectively, as networks of NGOs, social movements and perhaps even faiths.
3. NGOs need to think long term about the emerging economic super-powers of China, India, Russia and Brazil. Can they help promote the evolution of domestic constituencies in these 'tigers' that have entered the room that will engage in a progressive fashion with Development and global development?
4. Finally, we await the creation of a theoretical body of knowledge that can underpin a full-blooded development alternative. We might gain ideas about how this might be fostered by reading the accounts of those who claim to have strategized for the ascendancy of neoliberalism (Blundell, 2007). Alternatively, a different path that is less elitist, less Eurocentric, and not financed by profits from battery hens may be required.

Whatever, progressive NGOs need to struggle on, resist the temptation to strategize only about Development and aid, and listen for the owl to start hooting.

Note

1. Many thanks to Sam Hickey, Diana Mitlin and Tony Bebbington for encouraging me, and supporting me, in the writing of this chapter. Thanks to Karen Moore for advice and research assistance.

References

Blundell, J. (2007) *Waging the War of Ideas* (3rd edn), Institute of Economic Affairs, London.

CPRC (2004) *The Chronic Poverty Report 2004–05,* Institute for Development Policy and Management/Chronic Poverty Research Centre, Manchester, www.chronicpoverty. org/resources/cprc_report_2004–2005_contents.html.

Edwards, M., and D. Hulme (eds) (1992) *Making a Difference: NGOs and Development in a Changing World,* Earthscan, London.

Edwards, M., and D. Hulme (eds) (1995) *NGOs: Performance and Accountability: Beyond the Magic Bullet,* Earthscan, London.

Fine, B. (2001) *Social Capital versus Social Theory: Political Economy and Social Science at the Turn of the Millennium,* Routledge, London.

Giddens, A. (1998) *The Third Way: The Renewal of Social Democracy,* Polity, Cambridge.

Greig, A., D. Hulme and M. Turner (2007) *Challenging Global Inequality: Development Theory and Practice in the 21st Century,* Palgrave Macmillan, London.

Hulme, D. (2007) 'Imagining Inclusive Globalisation: India's Role in Tackling Global Poverty', Exim Bank of India Annual Commencement Lecture, 20 April, Exim Bank, Mumbai.

Hulme, D., and A. Shepherd (2003) Conceptualizing Chronic Poverty, *World Development* 31(3), 403–23.

Hulme, D., and M. Edwards (eds) (1997) *Too Close for Comfort: NGOs, the State and Donors,* St Martins Press, London.

Lal, D. (2004) *In Praise of Empires: Globalization and Order,* Palgrave Macmillan, London.

Mallaby, S. (2004) *The World's Banker: A Story of Failed States, Financial Crises, and the Wealth and Poverty of Nations,* Penguin, New York.

Nye Jr., J. S. (2004) *Soft Power: The Means to Success in World Politics,* Public Affairs, New York.

Contributors

Matt Baillie Smith is a Senior Lecturer in Sociology at Northumbria University and previously worked for a Development Education NGO. His research interests are NGOs, global civil society and development, and recently development education, public engagement in development, and cosmopolitan theory. His recent publications include *Negotiating Boundaries and Borders: Qualitative Methodology and Development Research* (ed., 2007, Elsevier) and a forthcoming book on public engagement in development (Palgrave MacMillan, with H. Yanacopulos).

Anthony Bebbington is Professor of Nature, Society and Development at the University of Manchester, an ESRC Professorial Fellow, and research affiliate of CEPES (Peru). His work addresses the relationships among civil society, livelihoods and development, with focus on social movements and NGOs in Latin America and more recently development conflicts and extractive industries. Recent books include *The Search for Empowerment: Social Capital as Idea and Practice at the World Bank* (2006, Kumarian, with others), and *Development Success: Statecraft in the South* (2007, Palgrave Macmillan, with W. McCourt).

Joel **Bolnick** is Director of the Urban Resource Centre in Cape Town, South Africa. He is also one of four coordinators of Slum Dwellers International. He has been working closely with Slum Dweller collectives in Africa and Asia for seventeen years.

Katie Bristow is lecturer in International Health at the Liverpool School of Tropical Medicine. Since 1980 she has trained NGO trainers in HIV/AIDS awareness in Romania and East Africa. She also established a learning sharing network with community health NGOs in Latin America. Her current research interests relate to increasing health care provision at community level by strengthening working relationships between formal and informal health-care providers.

Vasudha Chhotray is Lecturer in Development Studies at the University of East Anglia. She was an ESRC Postdoctoral Fellow and has recently worked on a forthcoming book *Governance Theory: A Cross-Disciplinary Approach* (Palgrave, with G. Stoker). She is currently developing collaborate research on the role of legal reform in promoting equitable water rights and also on governance in aid policy.

Julius Court is a governance adviser at the UK Department for International Development. At the time of writing this chapter, he was a Research Fellow at the Overseas Development Institute. He has worked and published on issues of governance and civil society, including: *Making Sense of Governance* (Lynne Rienner, 2004) and *Policy Engagement: How Civil Society Can Be More Effective* (ODI, 2006).

Nelson Cuéllar, an economist, has been a researcher at the Fundación PRISMA since 1993. His research interests include rural livelihoods, compensation for ecosystem services, water resources management and the environment. His work in PRISMA has been carried out in association with other organizations such as IICA, WWF, IISD, UNEP and FAO. Previously he worked at the Regional Program of Research and the Confederation of Cooperatives Associations in El Salvador.

Evelina Dagnino is Full Professor of Political Science at the University of Campinas, Brazil. She has been Visiting Professor at the Universities of Yale and Göteborg. She has published several books and articles on the relations between culture and politics, social movements, civil society and participation, democracy and citizenship. She served on the Scientific Committee of the Brazilian Association of Non-Governmental Organizations and is an associate of Instituto Pólis.

Harry Derksen is policy director at ICCO and responsible for research and strategic development. With extensive experience in African countries, he worked as ICCO's desk officer for South Africa in the anti-apartheid movement and then in the Middle East (1993–2001, with special focus on Israel and occupied Palestine). From 2001 onwards he has developed ICCO's policy on the interrelation of human rights and development.

Michael Edwards is the Director of the Governance and Civil Society Program at the Ford Foundation in New York. Prior to joining the Foundation in 1999 he was the World Bank's Senior Advisor on Civil Society, and before that spent fifteen years as a senior manager in international relief and development NGOs, including periods with Oxfam UK and Save the Children–UK. His recent publications include *Civil Society* (2004, Polity Press).

Alan Fowler is an adviser, analyst and author on development issues. His publications focus on civil society and on the aid system. He is a co-founder of the International NGO Training and Research Centre, past president of the International Society for Third Sector Research, director of CIVICUS, and honorary professor at the Centre for Civil Society, University of KwaZulu-Natal.

Cynthia del Carmen Bazán Godoy is a biologist specializing in the Management and Conservation of Tropical Natural Resources at the Universidad Autónoma de Yucatán (UADY) where she teaches Biology and Ecology. She is member of the Asociación Civil Preenlaces and works in community development projects in UADY's Protropico department.

Ileana Gomez, a sociologist, is senior researcher and a member of PRISMA, El Salvador. She has worked on issues concerning human rights, social participation, social movements, rural livelihoods, rural territorial management, environment and urban sociology. She worked in the Salvadoran Ministry of the Environment and Natural Resources and has taught at the Universidad de El Salvador and the Universidad Centroamericana José Simeón Cañas.

Catarina Illsley Granich is a member of the Group for Environmental Studies AC, GEA in Mexico, where she was the General Coordinator (2001–05). An ethnobiologist by training, she has been actively involved for the last ten years in the Programme for Peasant Management of Natural Resources in the State of Guerrero, a collaborative programme for regional development between GEA and the peasant organization Sanzekan Tinemi.

Irene Guijt is an independent advisor, trainer and researcher focusing on learning processes and systems in rural development and natural resource management. She has worked with organizations including RIMISP, IUCN, IFAD, ActionAid International, and Dutch NGOs on pro-poor development issues. Her publications include *Participatory Learning and Action: A Trainer's Guide* (with others) and *The Myth of Community: Gender Issues in Participatory Development* (ed. with M. Shah).

Samuel Hickey lectures on international development at the University of Manchester and coordinates research into the politics of exclusion within the CPRC. His research focuses on the politics of development and poverty reduction, issues of citizenship and participation, and the role of civil society and NGOs in development. Recent publications include *From Tyranny to Transformation: Exploring New Approaches to Participation* (2004, Zed Books, ed. with G. Mohan) and papers in World Development and Development and Change.

David Hulme is Leverhulme Research Professor and Professor of Development Studies at the University of Manchester. He is Associate Director of the BWPI and the CPRC (University of Manchester) and also Associate Director of the ESRC Global Poverty Research Group. His recent publications include *The State of the Poorest in Bangladesh Report 2005/2006* (BIDS with B. Sen) and *The Challenge of Global Inequality* (2006, Palgrave, with others).

Diana Mitlin is an economist and social development specialist and works both at IIED and IDPM (University of Manchester). Her major focus is urban poverty reduction, in particular secure tenure, basic services and housing. Her work has explored the contribution of civil society to addressing issues related to poverty and inequality. For the last ten years she has worked with Shack/Slum Dwellers International. Recent publications include *Empowering Squatter Citizen* (2004, Earthscan, with D. Satterthwaite) and *Confronting the Crisis in Urban Poverty* (2006, ITDG, with others).

Iliana Monterroso, a biologist, with an MA in Ecological Economics, works as researcher for the Environment, Population and Rural Development programme in the Latin American Faculty of Social Sciences. She also collaborates as researcher at the Environmental Science Technology Institute in the Autonomous University of Barcelona. Her research includes community forestry, socioeconomic evaluation of biodiversity risks and environmental conflicts.

Joaline Pardo Nuñez, a biologist, has worked in NGOs for nearly ten years on sustainable agriculture, local systems for food security and environmental policy analysis. Her research work includes etnobotanical approaches for edible greens within indigenous communities and participative research on the impact of social programmes in rural communities. She was a member of the Forum for Sustainable Development.

Nicholas Piálek received his PhD from the University of Oxford in 2006. His research examines the process of institutional change around radical development movements and theories. More specifically, he investigates the contemporary process of gender mainstreaming within development organizations.

Amy Pollard is a Ph.D. candidate at the University of Cambridge. Her research interests include the anthropology of development, bridging research and policy, knowledge and power. With focus on Indonesia, her work explores relationships between international aid donor agencies, and their relations with the government. From 2002 she worked in RAPID at the Overseas Development Institute. She has undertaken consultancies in the UK with DFID and in Indonesia.

Mary Racelis is a social anthropologist and research scientist at the Institute of Philippine Culture, Ateneo de Manila University. She is actively engaged in activities with Philippine NGOs as well as Asian NGO networks. In 2004–05 she served as a member of the United Nations Secretary General's Panel on UN–Civil Society Relations ('the Cardoso Panel').

José Luis Rocha is a researcher and member of the editorial board of academic journals at the Universidad Centroamericana. He coordinated the Social and Economic Policies team in Nitlapán. His research topics include youth gangs in Managua, local governments, natural disasters mitigation, coffee crisis, and migration. Currently he coordinates the 'Regional Migration Analysis and Policies in Central America' research project for the Jesuit Service for Migrants in Central America.

Alan Thomas is a visiting professor at the Centre for Development Studies, Swansea and at the Open University. He researches and writes on meanings of poverty and development, learning and knowledge sharing, cooperative development, and the role of NGOs in environmental policy and development governance, globally and in Southern Africa. He is a member of the expert panel for the Welsh Assembly Government's 'Wales for Africa' programme.

Pedro Torres, an educator and agricultural scientist, is with the Red de Desarrollo Sostenible–Honduras. His work is in micro-credit, micro businesses, coordination of technical assistance, migration and remittances, and information technology for development. He has participated in collaborative projects on organic agriculture, solar energy, milk producers and local economic development with national and international research centres.

Pim Verhallen is adviser to the board of directors of ICCO. He worked in Bolivia as the director of a rural training institute. Between 1979 and 1982 he worked for the Dutch Refugee Association, in charge of the social assistance programme for political refugees. In 1982 he began at ICCO's evaluation desk, and then was head of the Andean programme. In 1992, he became head of ICCO's Latin America Department.

Helen Yanacopulos is a Senior Lecturer in International Politics and Development at the Open Universtiy. Her work examines transnational political networks of NGOs and different forms of governance, and more recently 'public engagement in development' looking at the ways development is constructed in the 'North' and the implications this has for development research, policy and practice. She is co-authoring a forthcoming book on this topic (Palgrave, with M.B. Smith).

Index

Aardenne, Agnes van, 228
accountability, 43, 100, 139–40, 193, 231, 342; 'upward', 230; 'downward', 47, 141; feminist, 292; increased demands for, 86; mechanisms, 42; NGO financial, 325, 327; personal, 49; pressure for 'measurable', 105
ACORD (NOVIB-Uganda), 163, 165
ACT Development, 234
Action Aid, 47; ALNAP system, 42; Johannesburg HQ, 9–10
Addis Ababa Muslim Women's Council, 136
Adivasi Morcha Sangathan organization, 274
Adivasi Shakti Sangathan organization, 274
advocacy role, 21, 29, 39, 170; campaigns, 43, 83; coalitions, 310; political, 82
Afghanistan, 115–16; official aid, 84
Africa: Dutch development aid, 81; HIV-AIDS crisis, 80
agrarian reform, 199
aid: bilateral, 4, 317; boundaries of the acceptable, 191; decentralized programmes, 317; dynamics, 329; effectiveness concept, 101; foreign sources, 44; funding, 10; industry, 5, 330; international donor policies, 50, 71; 'marketization', 236; neoliberal system, 313; political economy of, 18, 23; poverty agenda, 3–4; pressure on, 191, 237; public debate need, 238; security agenda budgets, 18; top-down chain, 230
Al-Quaeda, 112, 116
Albada, F., 208
Alma Ata Declaration 1978, 243–4, 249
ALOP (Asociación Latinoameicana de Organizaciones), 8, 72
'alternative(s) development', 4, 5, 7, 12, 263, 289; co-opted, 280
Alves, M., 142
AMARC, Brazil, 144
American Enterprise Institute, 126, 341; NGO Watch, 42

American Foundation, CTM compliance, 121
American Free Trade Agreement, networks against, 74
American India Foundation, 273
Andean (Aymara and Quechua) medicine, 242–3, 246
Anderson, K., 306
Andolina, R., 190
Anna, Kofi, 44, 307
Annis, Sheldon, 92
anthropological research, 263
Aprodev, 234
Aquino, Benigno, assassination, 200–1
Aquino, Corazon, 201–2
Argentina, 65, 73–5, 139; peso crisis, 71
Arko-Cobbah, A., 135
'armed social work', 115
Asia Foundation, 202
Asian Coalition for Housing Rights, 14
Asian Development Bank, 26, 202, 205, 217; NGO Cooperation Network, 204
Asian financial crisis 1998, 198
Australian Aid, 117

Bangladesh Country Assistance Plan, 101
Bangladesh Rural Advancement Committee (BRAC), 92, 101, 138; northern world offices, 8
Bankers' Association of the Philippines, 214
Basic Ecclesiastical Communities, Philippines, 203
Bayat, A., 143
Bazán, Cynthia, 25
Bebbington, Anthony, 95
Beijing Platform for Action, 279
Benn, Hilary, 100–1
Biekart, Kees, 19, 21, 154–5
'biomedicine, 242–5, 256–7
Birmingham UK, Third International NGO Conference, 42–3, 45, 50, 96–7

Bishops Businessmen's Conference, Philippines, 214

Blair, Harry, 96–7, 100

Bolivia, 65, 72, 74–6, 83, 140, 189; Catholic Church, 140–1; Cholos, 248, 256; community health workers, 247; Creole state health system, 256; health-care NGOs, 28; neoliberal development model, 241; think-tank sector, 143

Bolnick, Joel, 5, 30, 32

BOND (British Overseas NGOs for Development), 338

Booth, D., 103, 143

Bourdieu, P., 245, 256; habitus and field notions, 246–7, 257

Bourn, D., 309

Brazil, 30, 32, 71–2, 75–7, 85, 145, 179, 342–4; 1988 Constitution, 55, 58, 66; democratization process, 62; experiments, 21; neoliberal period, 56; north eastern region, 74; participatory project, 20, 57; São Paulo, Strategic Regional Plans, 141; SDI, 322

Bread for the World, 76, 80

Breadline Africa, North World offices, 8

Brinkerhoff, D., 139

Bristow, Katie, 27–8

Brock, K., 137

Burma, 102

Bush, George W., 50, 337

Butterfly Peace Garden (BPG) (Sri Lanka–HIVOS), 164

CALDH (Guatemala–HIVOS), 162

Calhoun, C., 301, 310–12

Cambodia, 320

Cameroon, 99

Canada–NGO compacts, 42

Cancún trade summit, 47, 85

capacity-building, 88; hierarchy issues, 143

Cardoso, Fernando H., 60

CARE, 202; Bangladesh, 101

Carey, D., 306

Carothers, T., 140

Catholic Church: Bolivia, 140–1; Philippines, 200–1

Cato Institute, 341

Caucus of Development NGO Networks (CODE-NGO), Philippines, 212–15

CCFD, aid agency, 82

CEBEMO (Holland), see Cordaid

Central America, 176; development issues, 25; research funding, 185; universities, 192

Chambers, Robert, 29, 91

Chandhoke, N., 307

Chao, Elaine, 50

Chapman, J., 105

charity, 68, 91, 307

Chhotray, Vasudha, 5, 27–8, 34

children: Children's parliament initiative, 165; illnesses, 241; mortality causes, 244; rights notion, 106, 199; war-affected, 164

Chile, 72–5, 77, 88, 179, 189; Concertación, 179

China, 31, 342, 344

Cholos, Bolivian urban poor, 248, 257–8

Christian Aid, 80, 82, 86

CIDA (Canada), 202

CIFCA, aid agency, 83

citizenship, 20, 61, 64–5, 76, 165; building processes, 154; global, 305–6, 309; neoliberal redefinition, 62–3, 67–8; notions of, 56

CIVICUS (civil, society watch programme), 119

civil society, 91; associationalist concept, 177, 182, 184–5; concept of, 133; contestation, 13; 'crossover' leaders, 199; Gramscian notion, 7; neoliberal appropriation, 59–61; 'participation', 55, 155, 164, 168–71; post-Marxist/post-structuralist concept, 6; -state relationship, 262–3, 276

civil society organizations (CSOs), 90, 95, 98, 104, 133; direct action, 143; donor influence, 140; education role, 135; international development role, 134; legitimacy, 149; mediating role, 138; service provision, 142; terminology shaping, 136

Clark, John, 103, 340

clientilism, 144

climate change, 316

Coalition of the Urban Poor, South Africa, 331

CODÍGO, Bolivia, 28, 241–2, 248–54, 257; training difficulties faced, 255–6

coercive redistribution, 90

Cohen, J., 300, 312

Cold War period, 5, 112

Collier, Paul, 338

Collor de Mello, Fernando 56

Colombia, 24, 71–2, 74–7, 83, 153, 159, 161, 164, 166, 168; Conciudadania CSO, 166; intra-family violence, 167

Comic Relief, 342

Community Organization of the Philippines Enterprise Foundation (COPE), 205–7

Company of Jesús, 181

Comprehensive Development Framework (CDF), 244, 246

conflict resolution, 77

confrontations, public events, 277

CONIC (HIVOS-Guatemala), 164

Constantino-David, K., 201, 203

consumer culture, global, 311

'Copenhagen target', 78

Cordaid (CEBEMO), 80–2, 153, 158, 166, 202, 224

Corporate Social Responsibility, 46

'cosmopolitanism'/cosmopolitan politics, 29–30, 298–303; 'ambiguous', 308; 'attenuated', 312; colonialist, 307, 311; theorizing, 302, 304

cost-consciousness, 226

Costa Rica, 74, 88

Council of the Coumunidade Solidária, Brazil, 60

'counter-public', 190

country priorities, European private aid agencies, 72

Court, Julius, 24, 136

Cowen, M., 5

CPS (Centre for Policy Studies, UK), 99, 103

Cranko, P., 104

credit provision, 214; micro-credit projects, 39,

76, 223, 229; savings schemes, 320
CTMs (counter-terror measures), 19, 22, 45, 49, 114, 116–18, 231
Cuba, 72–3; -EU relations, 74

Dagnino, Evelina. 19–21, 30–2, 34, 178, 193
dams, 262
Danchurchaid, 75–6, 80
Darfur, 116
Dart, R., 136
De Pedro, Juan Carlos, 249
death squads, Philippines, 212
debt: crisis 1980s, 222, 244; relief campaigns, 85, 164; see also Jubilee 2000
decentralization, 162; pro-panchayat India, 269
decision-making processes, 156; state power, 61
decolonization period, 5
democracy: democratization dynamics, 14, 158; global, 305; theory, 44; uneven, 302
demography, Philippines, 197
Denmark, NGOs, 75, 120
depoliticization, fallacy of, 276
Dersken, H., 32
Desforges, L., 306, 312
development: agency credibility problem, 237; 'alternative' see 'alternative'; 'as-leverage', 98; counter-discourse, 191; depoliticization, 221; discourse democratization, 13; education, 29, 309, 312; empowerment model, 95; for security, 126; governance, 104; Marxian interpretations, 12; neoliberal approach, 243; poverty reduction synonymity, 185; state-centric agendas, 111; sustainable, 194; unequal, 310; urban pro-poor, 325
DFID (Department for International Development, UK), 21–2, 90, 93; aid effectiveness concept, 101; budget, 95; country offices, 99; Global Health Initiatives, 102;; 'good governance model', 104; Public Service Agreement, 97; White Paper 2006, 98, 100, 103, 195–7
DfS agenda, Westphalian principle, 124
Diakonia, 74, 76, 79, 81–2, 86
diarrhoea, 250–1
Diocese of Fort Portal (CORDAID-Uganda), 164
disaster management, participatory, 199
Dominican Republic, 74
donors: 'donor fatigue', 84; larger programme bias, 82
drought proofing, 273

economic growth, pro-poor, 164
Ecuador, 65, 72–3, 189
EDSA, Philippines, 216
Edwards, Mike, 3, 14, 17–19, 24, 31, 34, 91, 193, 308, 341–2, 344
El Salvador, 12, 71–2, 74–5, 77–8, 88, 182; Esquipulas peace agreement, 223; PRISMA, 183
elite(s), 141, 245; elitism, 303, 312; French intellectual, 256; global, 316; governing accountability, 216; national, 30; Philippine political, 197

'embodied history', 247
entrepreneurial foundations, Brazil, 67
Escobar, A., 7
Ethiopia, women's rights, 136
EU (European Union), grants, 338
European NGOs: Africa HIV priority, 80; aid politicization, 83; 'joint advocacy initiatives', 79; priority trends, 75–6, 78, 87; strategic alliances, 85–6
evaluation, processes, 144
evidence, research produced, 23, 137; credibility, 150; nature of, 138; operational relevance, 148; power of rigorous, 140; role of, 133; sharing, 144; technical, 143; use of, 141, 147

'failed states'/'fragile states', 22, 102, 124
'fair trade', advocacy, 76
Federation of the Urban Poor, South Africa, 327, 330
federations, 30
Feinstein Center, 116
feminism: depoliticized, 279, 289; social justice, 290
Ferguson, J., 285
Fine, R., 300, 312
FLASCO (Latin American Faculty for Social Sciences), 181; Guatemala, 180, 183, 186, 191–2; student training, 189
FMLN, El Salvador, 182
Fonte, John, 50
Ford Foundation, 202
Foro Chiapas, 182, 186, 189–90; Forum for Sustainable Development, 181
Foucault, Michel, 284; self-care concept, 127
foundations, 11
Foweraker, J., 142
Fowler, Alan, 17, 19, 22, 39, 93, 231
Fox, J., 145
Freire, Paulo: 'conscientiazation', 91, 249–50; liberation education, 309
'Friends of the River Narmada', 274
funding, 17; charitable impulse, 310; conditionality, 87; diversification, 88; NGO compromises, 246; Philippines shifts, 211–12; research NGOs pressure, 187

G8, targeting of, 311
G7, 340
Gandhi, Mahatma, concepts of, 91
Gatwood, M., 32
Gaventa, J., 125
GEA (Grupo de Estudios Ambientales, Mexico), 180, 182–3, 186, 189, 191–2
Geldof, Bob, 45
gender, 27, 29, 157; 'experts', 284; inequalities, 166–7, 290; focal issue, 77; terminology overuse, 279
gender mainstreaming, 280, 284, 291–2, 293–4; implementation, 295; 'policy evaporation', 281–2; subverted, 282–3; training, 288
Germany, NGOs, 81
Ghana, 99
'gift relationship', 91
globalization, debate, 46

Global Accountability Project, London, 42
Global Civil Society', 49
Global Communism, end of, 15
globalization, 196; debate, 46; democratic deficit of institutions, 43; impact, 71; neoliberal basis, 104, 112
Global War on Terror (GWOT), 17, 22, 114
Goldsmith, A., 139
'good practice stories', 288
governance: focus on, 100; 'good', 140, 223; issues, 85; local, 76
Grameen Foundation, Northern world offices, 8
Gramsci, Antonio, 58, 177, 241, 245
Guatemala, 24, 72, 74–5, 77, 83, 153, 159, 161, 164, 166, 168, 189; indigenous people organizations, 76; Peace Accords 1996, 160
Guijt, Irene, 5, 23–4, 34
Guinea, 153, 159–62, 164–5, 170; gender issues, 167

Habermas, J.177
Hadith, 139
Haiti, 72
Hamas, 120
Hansen, A., 123
Haraway, D., 290, 292
Harvard University, 45
Harvey, D., 300
health: alternative approaches, 28; care, 27; primary, 78; promoters training, 246, 255; 'integrated', 250; social model, 243
hegemony: contestations, 74; counter-discourses, 25; ideas, 33
Held, David, 305
Herfkens, Evelien, 227
Heritage Foundation, 341
Hippocrates, 242
Hirschman, A., 96
HIV/AIDS, 163; education, 167; support for orphans, 165
Hivos (Humanist Institute for Cooperation with Developing Countries), 74, 76, 80, 81, 82, 84, 153, 158, 224; Sri Lanka, 166
Holland, 341; aid agencies, 83, 95; aid policies, 33, 81, 231; co-financing agencies/projects, 24–5, 153–5, 170–2, 222, 224, 226; development sector, 157; Minister for International Cooperation, 225; Ministry of Foreign Affairs, 235; neoliberal dominance, 227; ODA budget, 228; Tanzania Embassy, 102
Honduras, 72, 75, 78, 185; European NGOs, 74; indigenous people organizations, 76; press, 191
Howell, J., 104
Huckle, J., 309
Hudson Institute, 50, 341
Hulme, David, 14, 18–19, 30, 38, 139, 193, 342
Human Rights Commission, Geneva, 217
Human Rights Observatory, 162
Humanitarian Accountability Project, 42
humanitarian relief, 78, 96, 104
Hurricane Mitch 1998, impact, 74, 78, 80; relief operation, 86–7
Hutanuwatr, P., 136

IBIS, Denmark, 74–6, 80, 82
ICCO (Interchurch Organization for Development Cooperation), Holland, 28–9, 33, 76, 80, 83–4, 158, 221, 224, 233, 236–8; 'reverse consortia', 234; ODA funding, 225; reinvention need, 232; staff reduction, 235
identity, concepts of, 14
II.II.II., NGO, 79–80, 82
IMCI (Integrated Management of Childhood Illnesses), 241, 243–4, 246, 250, 254
IMF (International Monetary Fund), 85, 222, 229, 242, 244–5, 339–40; Independent Evaluation Office for sub-Saharan Africa, 228
'impact', donor rationale, 93, 96, 103, 107
India, 31, 320, 326–7, 344; CAPART (Council for Promotion of Rural Arts), 269, 271, 273; Charitable Trusts Act 1950, 268; Congress Party, 275; CSO financial controls, 119; Easementary Act 1882, 272; International Development Cooperation Agency, 342; 'land records camp', 277; Ministry of Rural Development, 272; Mumbai, 322; National Slum Dwellers Federation, 324–5; 'NGO universe', 264
INDICEP (Instituto de Investigación para Educacion, Bolivia), 248
indigenous peoples: local assemblies, 190; medicine, 242
Indonesia, 99, 138
inequality, 123, 309; as technical issue, 67; gender, 166, 290; Latin America, 74
Inermen, 76
informal settlers, eviction resistance, 199
informal university', Latin America, 176
infrastructure: large scale projects, 318–19
Institute for Agriculture and Trade Policy, 47
Institute of Development Studies, 155
Institutionality: corrupt, 159; memory, 146
Interamerican Development Bank, 223
International Budget Project (IBP), 145
International Campaign to Ban Landmines, 9
International Coalition on Women's Health, 340
International Development Targets (IDTs), 94–5
International Finance Facilities, 45
international financial transfers, surveillance, 118
International NGO Training and Research Centre (Intrac), 120
Internet, the, 144
Interpal NGO, terrorist designated, 120
Iraq, 22, 50, 99, 115–16, 305; official aid, 84; war in, 46
IS-Academy, 235
Ivory Coast, 116

Jamaica, 74
Japan Social Development Fund, 205
Jawaharlal Nehru University, Delhi, 264
Jesuit community, 9
Jockin, Arputham, 324–5
Johnson, Simon, 106, 229
Joint Plantation Development Committees, Sri Lanka, 163
Jordan, L., 310
Jubilee 2000 campaign, 98, 100, 107, 137, 140, 311

Kabeer, N., 291
Kamat, S., 276
Kant, Immanuel, 300, 312
Keck, M., 310
Kenya, 326; animal care, 144; Nairobi Peace Initiative, 138; Pamoja Trust, 321
Keppke, R., 141
Khan, Mahbub, 266, 268, 271–3
Knowledge: problem-solving, 184; destabilizing forms, 189
Korten, David, 91–2
Krafchik, W., 146
Kuper, A., 307–8

LABE (Uganda-NOVIB), 163
Lal, Deepak, 112, 338
'land records camp', India, 268
Landless Movement, Brazil (MST), 60
Lasswell, H., 134
Latin America, 343; advocacy campaigns, 83; citizenship struggles, 65; democratization process, 62; FLASCO, see FLASCO; Northern aid withdrawal, 71
Lawson, A., 103
legitimacy, 182, 184
Lehmann, David, 176
Lesotho, 285
Lewer, N., 143
Lewis, D., 11, 140
liberation theology, 200
Lima, Oxfam Regional Office, 282
Linklater, A., 305
Links evaluation, Oxfam, 281
local government, NGO pressures on, 212
Lu, C., 301, 307
Lula (Luis Ignacio da Silva), 179

Macdonald, T., 146
Madreelva (Guatemala-HIVOS), 170
Madrid, train bombing, 117
Maglio, I., 141
Mahila Milan collective, Indfia, 328
Make Poverty History campaign, 30, 43, 100, 107, 311
Malawi, SDI, 321
Malena, C., 140
Management Association of the Philippines, 214
Management Councils, Brazil, 56
Manchester International NGO conferences, 3; first 1992, 38–9, 51; 1994, 184
MANGO, 42
Manusher Jonno, Bangladesh, 99, 102
Marcos, Ferdinand, 197, 200–2
market, the, fetish of, 66
Marshall, T.H., 68
Marxism, 309; post-, 178
Massachusetts Institute of Technology, 229
McDowell, L., 290
McGee, R., 137
media, global, 304
Melrose, Dianna, 287
Mesitzos, Bolivia], 248
Metro Manila, Philippines, 197–8
Mexico, 65, 72, 176; activists, 145; Chiapas region, 74, 77; debt default, 222; development issues, 25; public policy debate, 191; research funding, 185; universities, 192
Michael, S., 276–7
Middle East, CSOs, 143
migration: illegal, 317; politics of, 21, 237
Millennium Challenge Accounts, 45
Millennium Development Goals (MDGs), 22, 45, 79, 94–5, 97, 100–2, 175, 199, 241, 244, 318, 322, 341
Mindanao, 209; Autonomous Region of Muslim Mindanao (ARMM), 198; peace processes, 210
minimum wages, 34; struggles for, 267
Misereor (German Catholic Bishops Fund for Development), 76, 79, 208; Philippine Partnership (PMP), 209–11, 217
Mitlin, D., 324
MMK (HIVOS-supported), 164
Mohammed, B., 136
Money Market Association of the Philippines, 214
monitoring, 'participative', 145–6' quantifiable results demand, 229
Moser, A., 284
Moser, C., 284
Mujeres Maya Kaq'la (HIVOS-Guatemala), 167
Mukasa, G., 170

NAFSO (Sri Lanka-HIVOS), 162
Naga City, Philippines, 197, 206–8; Urban Poor Federation, 205, 216
Namibia, 320; SDI Federation, 321
Narmada Bachao Andolan movement (NBA), 262
nation state(s), 304; authority, 308; depoliticization discourse, 270; developmental role, 339; dominance of, 306; 'failure', 122; idea of, 275; potential role, 6; reduction of role, 68; rights guarantor, 265, 268 ; services provision, 338
National Association of Rubbish Recyclers (Colombia-NOVIB), 163
National Council of Churches of Kenya, 11
National Farmers and Livestock Producers Union, Nicaragua, 189
National Slum Dwellers Federation, India, 328
natural resources, local management, 265
Naylor, R., 138
neoliberalism, 3, 13, 57, 59, 61, 339–40; civil society concept, 6; development alternative, 344; orthodoxy crisis, 71; 'participation' definition, 20
Nepal, 320
'New Policy Agenda', 39, 92, 240–1
NGOs (non-governmental organizations): accountability, 16, 18, 325, 327; alternativism, 127; as corporate entities, 6; 'boom', 13; competence, 60; compromised, 261; counter-terrorism measures compliance, 116–18; 'democratization', 10; democratization agents, 92; depoliticization, 246, 262; devolution within, 305; donor dominance, 21, 230, 306, 319; employee checks, 119; empowerment

role, 204; European, 72, 75, 120, 342; failure non-admission, 329; federation model, 320, 323; franchising global brands, 47; fundraising, 45; geopolitical complicity, 115; government subcontractors, 231; impact indicators, 28; imperatives, 19, 48, 113–14; internal change failures, 46; international development, 299, 301, 303; neoconservative hostility, 50; neoliberal use of, 8, 222–3; Northern, see Northern; official finance dependency, 18, 21, 94, 112; 'onion-skin' strategy, 39; personal accountability, 49; poverty-reduction ideology, 124; power dynamics, 291; private resources, 93; pro-market shift, 240; professionalization, 223; professional partners, 324, 326–7, 330–1; research, 175–7; resources access competition, 233; self-censorship, 118–21; Southern footholds in the North, 7; Southern regional councils, 236; terminology, 15; transnational networks, 9; transparency, 224; value-based ideas, 91

NGO Monitor, Jerusalem, 42
Nicaragua, 72, 74–5, 77–8, 185
Nicholson, T., 291
Nigeria, 99
9/11 attacks, impact of, 50–1
Nitlapán, Nicaragua, 180, 182–3, 186, 188–9
Noble, L. Garner, 200, 203
North–South cooperation, dynamics, 232
Northern NGOs: as bilateral agencies, 17; contradictions, 12; private donations, 94; Southern dependence on, 26
Novib, 76, 78, 80, 158, 224; Uganda, 166
Nussbaum, M., 303, 307, 309

Oasis (HIVOS-Guatemala), 163
OECD, (Organization of Economic Cooperation and Development)112; official aid, 93–4
official aid, access to, 93–4
ONE World, 144
organization; norms, 287–8; 'internal 'community' of, 293
Orissa civil society fund, 99
Ottaway, M., 140
Oxfam, 33, 47, 79, 86, 202, 289, 307; -Belgium, 76, 81–2, 84; GB, 29, 80, 82–3; Gender Action Research Project, 288; gender mainstreaming/policy, 27, 280, 282, 284, 287, 291, 294; Global Gender Meeting, 2006, 292; institutional change failure, 285; International, 76; NOVIB, 153; organizational 'values', 286; output-related criteria, 78; Strategic Change Objective, 283

Pakistan, land rights, 120
Pamoja Trust, Kenya, 319, 321
Panama, 74
panchayats, India, 266; 'real' empowerment, 273
Paraguay, 72
parish development committees, 165
'Parliament of the Streets', Philippines, 201
participative poverty assessments (PPAs), 137

participation: budgeting, 20, 60, 65, 76; civil society, see civil society; democracy, 30, 34; individualistic perspective, 61; political, 75; rural appraisal, 91; unequal, 324; urban poor, 323
Partido dos Trabalhadores (Workers Party – PT), 65
Pastrana, Andrès, 163
patriarchy, 284
Paul, Samuel, 96
PDA, Bolivia (World Vision), 242, 248–9, 252–3, 257; evangelical beliefs, 254; Santivanéz, 250
Peace and Equity foundation, Philippines, 213–15
PEACE bonds, 213–14, 217
peace building, 77
Pearce, J., 104, 159
peasantry: economy, dynamics of, 183; Latin American Associations, 84
'people-centred development', 91
People Power revolution, Philippines 1986, 201, 216
Peru, 65, 71–2, 74–7, 189; environmental struggles, 120
'perverse confluence'/'convergence', 58–9, 69, 178, 193
Pettifor, A., 137
PHC systems, 244
philanthropy, 11, 67; defined, 59
Philippines, 12, 25; Constitution 1987, 202; funding shifts, 211–12; Homeless People's Federation, 322; NGOs, 26, 197; poverty rates, 198
PhilSSA (Philippine Support Services Agency), 205, 207
Piálek, Nicholas, 29, 33
PICA, 83
Plan Netherlands, 153, 158, 162, 164, 166
Pogge, Thomas, 302, 311
Polanyi, Karl, 91
policy processes, 137–8, 147, 149; CSOs, 135–6; evaluation, 148; 'narratives', 136, 343; participative formulation, 139
'political entrepreneurs', 261, 271
Pollard, Amy, 24
Ponce-Enrile, Juan, 201
Poor People's Movement, South Africa, 331
Poorest Areas Civil Society (PACS) programme, UK, 99
popular collective movements, urban, 64
Population Services International, 103
Porto Alegre, Brazil, 65; independent radio station, 145
'positionaility', 290, 293
post-conflict reconstruction, 114–15
post-structuralism, 178
poverty, 165; agenda, 15; aid-dependent methodologies, 319; as technical issue, 67, 124; narrow goals, 192; political roots, 229; reduction ideology, 16, 20, 25, 194, 317; 'structural eradication', 225; urbanized, 316, 324
Poverty Eradication and Alleviation Certificates, 211–12
Poverty Reduction Strategy Papers (PRSPs),

15, 45, 75, 83, 85, 95–6, 102, 124, 137, 140, 244, 246, 258, 280
power: cube framework, 155–6, 168–9; de facto dynamics, 159; hegemonic notions, 246; inequitable relations, 157
'praxis', 249
PREDO, CORDAID-Sri Lanka, 162
'primacy of the cluster', 210
PRISMA (Programa Salvadoreño de Investigación sobre Desarollo y Medio Ambiente), 180–3, 186, 189
privatism, 68
Process of Articulation and Dialogue(PAD), Brazil, 83
professionals, volunteer, 206
Programme Funding Agreement, Holland, 225
Pronk, J., 237
proscribed individuals, lists of, 117
Protestant churches, Philippines, 201
PROTROPICO, 186, 192; student training, 189
public shaming, 275
public-private partnerships, 46
Pune, India, 322

Qu'ran, 136, 139

Racelis, Mary, 24–5, 34
Radboud University, 235
Radical Left National Democratic Front, Philippines, 200
Ramos, Fidel V., 201, 203
Rasbach, J., 136
reciprocity, 21, 90–1, 95, 105, 107
Reform the Armed Forces Movement, Philippines, 201
relative deprivation, 123
religion, rise of, 47
representation, issue of, 60, 125, 138, 169
research: excluded groups, 24; funding, 185; negotiating power, 188;; NGO contract lengths, 187; non-profit, 175, 177; -policy linkage 176, 179–80; quality of, 184, 188; resource pressures, 192–3
Rieff, D., 306
rights, 62–3; -based approach, 21, 154; basic social services, 339; children, 106, 199; culture of, 68; education work, 157, 160; notion of, 64; state as guarantor, 265, 268; to equality, 65
Rizal Commercial Banking Corporation (RCBC), 213
Robinson, M., 142
Robredo, Jesse, 208
Rocamora, Joel, 197, 200
'Roll-Back Malaria' partnership, 102
rural development projects, support loss, 77
Rushford Report, USA, 42
Russia, 342, 344
Rwanda, 'Ubdbeme' initiative, 137

Sachs, Jeffrey, 45
Samaj Pragati Sahyog (SMS), Madhya Pradesh NGO, 27, 265–9, 275; as Project Implementing Agency, 270, 272; counter-hegemonic initiatives, 274; public meetings,

273; transformation, 276
Save the Children, 202
Scandinavia, 341
Schumacher, E.F., 91
Scott, J.G., 263
sector-wide approaches (SWAps), 95
securitization, aid system, 111, 114
security agenda, 3–4, 15, 17; compliance, 22; pressures of, 19
Sen, Amartya, capabilities theory, 340, 343
Senegal, Oxfam, 280
service delivery, 164–6, 222; empowerment approach, 170; 'gap-filling', 92; NGOs, 22
SEWA, 276
Shack/Slum Dwellers International (SDI), 9, 30, 32, 318–19, 324, 327–8, 331; discontent catalyst, 320; federation model, 323; leadership, 326; professional partners, 332; South Africa, 329
Sharp, J.P., 290
Shenton, R., 5
Short, Clare, 97–8
Sidel, Mark, 126
Sikkink, K., 310
Similelli, L., 142
Sin, Jaime, 201
sindicato cidadão(citizen trade union, 64
Singer, P., 307
Singh, Lakhan, 266, 268, 271
'Small is Beautiful', 12, 91
SMARTNET, 102
Smith, Matt, 29
SNV, 76
social authoritarianism, 63–4
social classification, hierarchic, 63
social movements, 32, 59, 84, 123, 337; counter-hegemonic, 178, 276; demand-led, 144; diversification, 318; NGO partners, 331
Social Weather stations, Philippines, 198
Society for the Promotion of Area Research Centres, 325, 328
solidarity(ies), 91; collective, 267; neoliberal version, 67
South Africa, 12, 99, 104, 320; libraries, 135; NGO contract work, 16; SDI, 329–30, 332
South-South cooperation, 84
Southern Africa Trust, 99
Southern NGO partners: regional councils, 236; resources, 229
Sri Lanka, 24, 153, 159, 161, 166–7, 170; women's movements, 23
staff retention, research NGOs, 188
Stiglitz, Joseph, 223
Stillman, G.S., 200, 203
Stone, Diane, 179
structural adjustment policies, 13, 95, 222, 245
subsumation , NGOs, 246–7
Sudan, official aid, 84
Summers, Larry, 45–6
'sustainability', dynamic loss, 77
Swiss Agency for Development and Cooperation, 99

Tandon, R., 103
Tanzania, 99, 102, 327

Task Force on Nongovernment Organizations, Philippines, 204
Task Forece Detainees of the Philippines, 200
TDDA (CORDAID-Sri Lanka), 163
technical project management, 'demystification', 271
Telles, V. da S., 63
terminology, limits to shifting, 294
Terre des Hommes, 158
Thailand, 320
Thatcher, Margaret, 340
The Network for Sustainable Development (RDSD), 181, 186, 190
think-tanks, 142–3, 184, 186, 340–1; conservative, 175; funding, 177; neoliberal, 31
'third sector', 59, 68; philanthropic projects, 63
Thomas, Alan, 19, 21–2, 106
Thompson, S., 136
Tiessen, R., 295
Tinbergen, J., 237
Titmuss, Richard, 91
Tomlinson, J., 311
trade and debt issues, 21, 79
Trade Union movement, 84
transparency, promotion of, 145
tribal peoples (Bhilala and Korku), Madhya Pradesh, 27, 262, 264, 266; forces against, 267; resistance, 274
Trocaire, 75–6, 78, 82, 84, 86
Troedsson, Hans, 244
trust, 326
Tusnami, Asia, 45

UDN (Uganda-CORDAID and HIVOS), 163

Uganda, 24, 153, 159, 160–2, 164–5, 168, 170, 327; Domestic relations Bill, 166; UDN (Uganda-CORDAID and HIVOS), 163; women's movements, 23, 167, women's organizations, 167
UK (United Kingdom), 309, 341; Charity Commission, 120–1; Development Education Centres, 310; Development Education Association, 309; DFID, see DFID; Institute of Economic Affairs, 340; National Audit Office, 97; New Labour government, 179; NGOs official support, 42, 94; Save the Children Fund, 304–5; Somali diaspora, 120
UN (United Nations), 114, 340; aid budget target, 227, 237; Development Programme, 86, 202, 229;; 'first 'development decade, 225; millenium agendas, 87; Resolution 1371, 116; UNESCO, 181; UNICEF, 202, 307
uneven development, 5
universalism, 304; individualist version, 302
Universidad Autónomia de Yucatán,181
Universidad CentroAmericana, Mangaua, 181
universities, 192; constraints on, 177; of Hull, 38
UNIWELO (Sri Lanka-CORDAID), 163
Uruguay, 65, 73–5
USA (United States of America), 120, 339–40; Army Peacekeeping and Stability Operations, 115; CODÍGO International, 249–50; counter-terrorism measures, 22; developing countries policy, 31; development NGOs, 95; Financial Action Task Force, 118; hegemony, 49, 112, 126; neoconservatives, 50; opinion shaping failure, 341–4; Save the Children Fund, 304; USAID, 117, 202, 251
USSR (United Soviet Socialist Republics)/ Soviet bloc, collapse, 111–12, 223, 226, 343
Utrecht, ICCO HQ, 234
uTshani Fund, South Africa, 330

values: Buddhist, 136; individual, 287; organizational changing, 285–6; universal, 307, 313
Van der Linde, A., 138
Van der Veer, P., 302, 307
Van Tuijl, P., 310
Vela, G., 159
Velasquez, Roxana, 249
Venezuela, 73, 222
Verhallen, Pim, 28, 32
Vertovec, S., 300
violence: against women, 166; civil society participation impact, 156, 159; criminal, 71; intra-family, 167; social change achievement, 157
'Voice' model, 96, 98, 100–3, 106–7; donor rationale, 93
voice, recognition of, 302

Walker, Bridget, 287
Wallace, T., 105
'war on terror', 19, 45, 49, 231
Washington Consensus, 223; post-, 179, 339
watershed projects, 270, 271, 273
Weru, Jane, 319
White, G., 142
women: empowerment, 105; health promoters training, 241; rights, 167; violence against, 167
Wooldridge, D., 104
World Bank, 26, 85–7, 122, 179, 185, 202, 204–8, 216, 222–3, 242, 245, 298, 323, 340–1; debate parameters, 140; 'good governance' model, 103–4; Health Nutrition and Population department, 244; Mexican activist critique, 145; World Development report 2006, 123
World Council of Churches, 234
World Health Organization (WHO), 243, 249; 'new universalism', 244
World Social Forum, 85
World Trade Organization (WTO), 15, 76, 140; Cancún summit, 85; Seattle summit 1999, 86
World Vision, see PDA

Yanacopolous, Helen, 29
Young, E., 144

Zadek, S., 32
Zapatismo, Chiapas, 182
Zimbabwe, 102, 320; SDI, 321